PROFESSIONS AND POLITICS
IN CRISIS

PROFESSIONS AND POLITICS
IN CRISIS

Mark L. Jones

Professor of Law
Mercer University School of Law

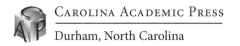

CAROLINA ACADEMIC PRESS

Durham, North Carolina

Names: Jones, Mark L., author.
Title: Professions and politics in crisis / by Mark L. Jones.
Description: Durham, North Carolina : Carolina Academic Press, LLC, [2021]
Identifiers: LCCN 2021007039 | ISBN 9781531021979 (paperback) | ISBN
   9781531021986 (ebook)
Subjects: LCSH: Law—Philosophy. | Practice of law—Philosophy. |
   Lawyers—Philosophy. | Law and ethics. | Sociological jurisprudence. |
   MacIntyre, Alasdair C.—Influence.
Classification: LCC K247.6 .J66 2021 | DDC 340/.1—dc23
LC record available at https://lccn.loc.gov/2021007039

Carolina Academic Press
700 Kent Street
Durham, North Carolina 27701
(919) 489-7486
www.cap-press.com

For Margaret
With my deepest love and appreciation

CONTENTS

PREFACE

In yet another example of the debasement of our political and cultural conversation in the Republic, the word "crisis" is used rather promiscuously nowadays, which of course risks diluting its impact. But for the reasons discussed in Chapter 1, it does not seem an exaggeration to assert that for many years now, beginning well before the Covid-19 pandemic, several of the professions in the United States, including the medical and legal professions, have been experiencing a crisis of well-being, distress, and dysfunction. And the same is true of our politics. In the case of the professions, the crisis is evident to members of the professions themselves and many others too, and in the case of our politics it must surely be evident to all who are paying even minimal attention. It is a basic contention of this book that the root of these crises, as well as the appropriate response to them, centers around our sense of meaning and purpose (or lack thereof) — our sense of meaning and purpose as professionals and our sense of meaning and purpose as citizens. And although the book is intended primarily to respond to our predicament in the United States, much of the discussion is equally relevant for the inhabitants of many other, perhaps most, and perhaps even all, liberal democracies.

Both in diagnosing the root of these crises and in prescribing an effective response to them, the book draws centrally upon the critical thought of Alasdair MacIntyre, arguably the most famous or notorious (depending on your point of view) moral philosopher of our times. MacIntyre is well known for his account of practices and the virtues, and for his provocative critique of liberal democracy, its capitalist, large-scale free market economy, and related hyper-individualism in the conditions of late Modernity.

Indeed, MacIntyre's work has inspired the creation of an international organization dedicated to the study and development of his thought and has
generated a voluminous secondary literature. A central contention of the
book, then, is that the crises in the professions and in politics can best be
addressed by encouraging professionals and citizens to pursue a flourishing life of meaning and purpose in communities of excellence and virtue
in response to a calling. Because it is my own profession and the one,
therefore, with which I am most familiar and whose well-being is of most
immediate and direct concern to me, the book uses the legal profession
as an illustrative case study. Moreover, the political vision animating the
project is the ultimate transformation of the liberal democratic state into a
"republic of virtue," not through coercive means, but organically through
example, invitation, and rational argument. And here too, I see a virtuous
legal profession as having a special role to play.

The book is intended to be of interest both to those already familiar
and to those not yet familiar with MacIntyre's corpus. Not only does it integrate relevant aspects of that corpus, including MacIntyre's most recent
work, into a clear, comprehensible, and original synthesis. It also significantly expands and supplements MacIntyre's theoretical approach, rooted in Thomistic Aristotelianism, and applies the result in novel, perhaps
surprising ways. After elaborating the foundational theoretical framework
and approach in Chapters 2–6, the book addresses practical implications
for the legal profession in Chapter 7 and then practical implications for
political conversation in Chapter 8. The book concludes with a Postscript
on the Covid-19 pandemic, because the pandemic starkly reveals the
shortcomings of our current culture and politics and the need for an alternative approach such as the one the book advocates.

Although written in more of a scholarly style rather than a popular
one, the book is sufficiently accessible to be of interest to those segments
of a lay audience with a taste for reading more scholarly works. Within
academic and practice communities, the book is intended for at least three
groups of readers: (a) moral philosophers, ethicists, and theologians, (b)
political philosophers and political scientists, and (c) lawyers, judges, law
professors, and law students, as well as members and aspiring members of
other professions and occupations. In addition to the introductory Chapter 1, everyone should read Chapters 2–6 to acquire a good understanding
of the foundational theoretical framework and approach. Ideally, every-

one should also read Chapters 7 and 8 to acquire a more complete and well-rounded understanding of this framework and approach, and to see the practical implications for professional practice and political conversation. However, some in the first group who are less interested in these practical implications may want to omit Chapters 7 and 8, some in the second group who are less interested in professional practice may want to read Chapter 8 but omit Chapter 7 except for the final section, and some in the third group who are less interested in politics, may want to read Chapter 7 but omit Chapter 8. The book could be used in law school courses such as jurisprudence, professional responsibility, or the legal profession, in analogous courses in other professional schools, and in college and university courses in philosophy, ethics, politics, or leadership.

I submitted the final manuscript to Carolina Academic Press in early December 2020 and have not attempted to update the text to take account of developments which have occurred, or additional sources which have been published or come to my attention, since that time. As far as subsequent developments are concerned, I am unaware of any that would significantly alter the judgments expressed in the book. Regarding sources, I became aware only recently of Michael Sandel's latest book, on the common good, which was published in the fall of 2020. This is clearly relevant to the discussion of Sandel's views on the common good and on justice in Chapter 6, and readers are therefore urged to consult it too.[1] Similarly, James Boyd White's book *Keep Law Alive*, discussed in Chapter 7, has generated at least one collection of excellent commentaries, published online shortly after submission, and these are also commended to the reader.[2] This said, there is one source in Chapter 5 bearing a publication date of 2021, but this is a source for which I had pre-publication access to the text.

With respect to more technical matters, I have used what can best be termed a modified Bluebook style for footnote citations. For example, although the footnotes in each chapter are a self-contained unit and sources are always fully cited the first time they appear in a chapter even when cited earlier in the book, for subsequent citations to the source in the same

---

1. *See* Michael J. Sandel, The Tyranny of Merit: What's Become of the Common Good? (2020)

2. *See Book Symposium, Keep Law Alive*, Law, Culture & Human (December 2020), https://journals.sagepub.com/page/lch/collections/book-symposium.

chapter I have opted in favor of the signal "op. cit." instead of an intermi-
nable number of "*supra* note ___." I did this for stylistic reasons and, given
the extensive (some might say excessive) footnoting, also to help make the
writing and editing process less cumbersome and error prone as the text
evolved. Although this does make it somewhat more difficult for the reader to locate the full citation, I seek the reader's indulgence on this point. On
the other hand, to help the reader navigate the discussion in the text, the
footnotes do contain cross-references to relevant discussion found elsewhere in a chapter or in other chapters. As a general matter, quotations in
the main text and footnotes omit internal citations in the original. And as
in this Preface, for stylistic reasons, in referring to chapters the text uses
Arabic numerals but chapter numbers at the beginning of each chapter
(and therefore also in the Table of Contents) are spelled out.

June 29, 2021
Macon, Georgia

ACKNOWLEDGMENTS

I am grateful to Mercer Law School and Dean Cathy Cox for supporting this book project with the grant of a partial sabbatical in spring semester 2019 and a partial research stipend in the summer of 2019. In addition to Cathy, I owe great debts of gratitude, both professional and personal, to many other people without whom this project would not have been conceived or successfully prosecuted. First and foremost, of course, is Alasdair MacIntyre himself. Whether or not you agree with what he has to say to us, no-one can come away from an encounter with MacIntyre's thought without being profoundly changed. He is indeed a transformative figure.

MacIntyre is closely followed by my friend and colleague Jack Sammons, now Professor Emeritus at Mercer University. To use a MacIntyrean idiom, Jack has been a major co-author of my life story in many, different ways. Here I mention just some of them. To begin with, it is no exaggeration to say that during his many decades at Mercer Law School, Jack was the primary intellectual engine driving faculty development, exploring numerous paths to see what each might have to offer for our understanding of law and legal practice, and taking his Mercer colleagues along for the ride in multiple workshops and individual conversations. To give just a few examples among many, Jack first introduced us to MacIntyre's seminal *After Virtue* in a workshop shortly after it was published in 1981, organized several workshops on various topics led by the renowned philosopher Robert Audi, and most recently, introduced us to Heidegger and phenomenology. Jack was also a major intellectual engine driving development of my Mercer Commons "Professionalism and Vocation Across the Professions" collaborative university project from 2005–2009, which is discussed in Chapter 1, and a 2011 Mercer Law Review Symposium on

"Citizenship and Civility in a Divided Democracy," which played a significant part in developing the political dimension of this book project. It should be no surprise, then, that the immediate occasion for writing the original manuscript that has evolved into this book, and from which a law review article was generated in 2015, was a Mercer Law Review Symposium in 2014 celebrating and honoring Jack's scholarship. In addition to this general intellectual stimulation, and as I have often told him, I am immensely grateful to Jack for being such a wonderful mentor to me — one who, in the spirit of true friendship, has not only advised and encouraged me over the years but who also has not been afraid to tell me what I needed to hear, even if it was not always what I wanted to hear.

Similarly, in a true labor of love, Jack generously read through the draft manuscript for the book so carefully and so thoroughly, and gave me so many insightful and challenging comments, that it took me several weeks to work through them all and respond appropriately in the text. And the book is much better for it. To mention just two examples that are noteworthy for their impact on the book's structure, it was Jack who prompted me to integrate explicit discussion of Heideggerian phenomenology in several chapters and discussion of Jim White's *Keep Law Alive* in Chapter 7. In short, after MacIntyre, Jack Sammons is the scholar whose work I draw upon the most in the main text, his invaluable comments on the draft manuscript are acknowledged in numerous footnotes, and his influence is generally so pervasive throughout the book that he should really be regarded as its *de facto* co-author.

Two other friends and Mercer colleagues, and important co-authors of my life story, also generously read the draft manuscript and provided very helpful comments — Gary Simson at the Law School, who is also our former Dean (a true scholar-dean, as I like to say), and Paul Lewis at the College of Liberal Arts, who is a co-director of the "Mercer University Phronesis Project for the Exploration of Character, Professional Formation, and Practical Wisdom," which incorporated the Professionalism and Vocation project mentioned above under a broader umbrella in 2009, and which is also discussed in Chapter 1. Their contributions too are acknowledged at various points in the footnotes. I am additionally grateful to Paul for introducing me to the respective work of Mark Mitchell and Jeffrey Stout, to which I refer at several points in the book, and to Gary for advising me in crafting the book proposal for the book and then recommending it to Carolina Academic Press.

Carolina Academic Press was indeed my first choice among publishers, not only because I was familiar with the excellence of their work but also because Gary, Jack, and other colleagues who had published with them had told me how enjoyable it was to work with such a professional and pleasant group of people — something I have now been able to confirm in my own experience. And in this respect two members of the Press team deserve special mention — Managing Editor Ryland Bowman, whose understanding and flexibility in extending various deadlines I have greatly appreciated, and Book Designer Kathleen Soriano Taylor, whose patience and attention to detail in making my anxious edits to the various sets of page proofs I have also greatly appreciated. I am also grateful to the Press for respecting my text, and for letting me keep *all* the footnotes!

Chapter 1 mentions several other friends and colleagues who have helped write my life story in relevant respects — Peter Brown, John Dunaway, Daisy Floyd, Tim Floyd, Pat Longan, and Kelly Reffitt — and I am grateful to all of them as well, but here I should mention someone who is in a special category of her own — my dear wife Margaret, to whom this book is dedicated. Not only is she among those who, by the power of their example, have taught me much about how to pursue a flourishing life of meaning and purpose in communities of excellence and virtue in response to a calling. Beyond this, again by the power of her example, she has shown me what it means to bear adversity in life with grace — far more than I would have exhibited in like circumstances — and she now helps others bear their own adversity as a psychotherapist practicing palliative care at our Medical Center. She has also patiently borne the distraction involved in writing this book, and she continues to tolerate my many idiosyncrasies with understanding, irritating though they must be sometimes. She is my cherished soulmate and helpmate, and the most important co-author of my life, who has gifted me with her love and a lovely family in her two daughters Catherine and Laura, granddaughter Cameron, and our son Nicholas. And she too is a true friend, who will tell me what I need to hear, even if it is not always what I want to hear. In these and so many other ways, then, I owe Margaret far more than I can ever say. It is only fitting, therefore, that the final, and most important, words should belong to her.

PROFESSIONS AND POLITICS
IN CRISIS

ONE

PROFESSIONS AND POLITICS IN CRISIS

A MacIntyrean Response

When I started working on the manuscript for this book in 2014, I intended it to be about achieving excellence and human flourishing in and through our work. I intended it, then, to be about what kind of story we will tell, about what kind of identity we will form, in and through those activities that occupy a major part — perhaps for many of us *the* major part — of our waking lives. In writing it I intended most immediately and directly to address members and aspiring members of the legal profession. However, I hoped that members and aspiring members of other professions and occupations would also find the book to be of value and would see how the explorations it undertakes can be readily adapted to their own field of work. At one level, this is still my intent and my hope. But more recently the project has taken on a special urgency because of the challenging times in which we live. At another, more troubled level, then, the book represents a response to the crisis of well-being, distress, and dysfunction that has afflicted the legal profession and other professions in recent years. At this more troubled level, too, it also represents a response to a crisis of well-being, distress, and dysfunction that has also afflicted our Republic — a crisis thrown into sharp relief by the Covid-19 pandemic we are currently experiencing as I revise the manuscript in the latter half of 2020. Before discussing these crises in greater detail, I want to say a few words about how this book relates to some other recent books discussing a scholar whose work has significantly influenced my thinking on these matters, and about how the book fits into my own life story.

3

In writing the book I have been influenced by the thinking of several scholars. Foremost among them is the moral philosopher Alasdair Mac-Intyre, who is well-known for his account of practices and virtues, and for his provocative critique of liberal democracy and its capitalist, large-scale free market economy under the conditions of late Modernity — so well known, indeed, that his work has inspired the creation of an international organization, The International Society for MacIntyrean Enquiry, and has generated a voluminous secondary literature.[1] The present book now adds to this literature by integrating relevant aspects of MacIntyre's corpus, including MacIntyre's most recent work, into a clear, comprehensible, and original synthesis, by significantly expanding and supplementing Mac-Intyre's theoretical approach, and by applying the result in novel, perhaps surprising ways, to address the crises in the professions and politics.

This emphasis upon MacIntyre, then, is something I have in common with others who have written about the philosophy and ethics of practice, on the one hand, and about political philosophy and liberal democracy, on the other. Geoff Moore's splendid book *Virtue at Work: Ethics for Individuals, Managers, and Organizations*, published in 2017, is a notable recent work in the first camp.[2] I discovered Moore's work shortly after returning to the above-mentioned manuscript — from which a law review symposium article was already generated in 2015 — in order to edit, expand, and update it for the present book.[3] However, in addressing practices (including professional practices) and the achievement of excellence and human flourishing through practices, Moore draws principally upon MacIntyre's famous seminal work *After Virtue: A Study in Moral Theory*,[4] whereas I draw extensively upon Macintyre's subsequent corpus as well, including his most recent book, *Ethics in the Conflicts of Modernity: An Essay on Desire, Practical Reasoning, and Narrative*, published at the end of 2016.[5]

1. For the website of the Society, explaining its work and listing its publications, bibliographies, and conferences, see https://www.macintyreanenquiry.org/mission.

2. GEOFF MOORE, VIRTUE AT WORK: ETHICS FOR INDIVIDUALS, MANAGERS, AND ORGANIZATIONS (2017).

3. For the law review article, see Mark L. Jones, *Fisherman Jack: Living in "Juropolis"* — *The Fishing Village of the Law*, 66 MERCER L. REV. 485 (2015).

4. ALASDAIR MACINTYRE, AFTER VIRTUE: A STUDY IN MORAL THEORY (3d. ed., 2007) (1981).

5. ALASDAIR MACINTYRE, ETHICS IN THE CONFLICTS OF MODERNITY: AN ESSAY ON DESIRE, PRACTICAL REASONING, AND NARRATIVE (2016). Although I am not familiar with

Mark Mitchell's thought-provoking book *The Limits of Liberalism: Tradition, Individualism, and the Crisis of Freedom*, published at the end of 2018, is a notable recent work in the second camp.[6] I discovered Mitchell's work only after completing the original manuscript for the present book in January 2020. Unlike Moore, Mitchell does draw extensively upon MacIntyre's corpus subsequent to *After Virtue* (up to, but not including, *Conflicts of Modernity*), as well as upon the work of Michael Oakeshott and Michael Polanyi. However, the central organizing principle in Mitchell's highly theoretical treatment is the "epistemic necessity" of tradition "as an unavoidable feature of the knowing process, a basic and necessary condition for rationality," and the "epistemological incoherence" of liberalism, with its conception of the autonomous individual — a self "who is unconstrained, unattached, and absolutely free" — in purporting to deny this necessity.[7] Mitchell's prescription for what he sees as "a cancer at the heart of the liberal cosmopolitan dream" is a "humane localism" that observes the principle of subsidiarity, avoids both "liberal cosmopolitanism," on the one hand, and "aggressive tribalism or identity politics," on the other, and achieves "tradition-constituted liberty" and human flourishing through a proper respect for one's own inherited traditions as well as those inhabited by others.[8]

---

the entire corpus of MacIntyre's work, which is vast, I am familiar with enough of it to say what needs to be said. In addition to *After Virtue* and *Conflicts of Modernity*, then, I will also draw especially upon the following of MacIntyre's works: ALASDAIR MACINTYRE, WHOSE JUSTICE? WHICH RATIONALITY? (1988); ALASDAIR MACINTYRE, THREE RIVAL VERSIONS OF MORAL ENQUIRY: ENCYCLOPAEDIA, GENEAOLOGY, AND TRADITION (1990); ALASDAIR MACINTYRE, DEPENDENT RATIONAL ANIMALS: WHY HUMAN BEINGS NEED THE VIRTUES (1999); THE MACINYTRE READER (Kelvin Knight, ed., 1998). And in addition to Geoff Moore's book, op. cit., I will also draw significantly upon the following two commentaries on MacIntyre: Kelvin Knight, *Introduction*, in THE MACINYTRE READER, *supra*, at 1–27; Ted Clayton, *Political Philosophy of Alasdair MacIntyre*, Internet Encyclopedia of Philosophy IEP, https://iep.utm.edu/p-macint/.

6. MARK T. MITCHELL, THE LIMITS OF LIBERALISM: TRADITION, INDIVIDUALISM, AND THE CRISIS OF FREEDOM (2019). For some very useful summaries and analyses of Mitchell's book, see *Reflections on The Limits of Liberalism*, XLVI TRADITION AND DISCOVERY 4–22 (February 2020): Will R. Jordan, *Land of the Lost*, *id*. at 4–9; Matthew D. Sandwisch, *Recovering Tradition*, *id*. at 10–13; Colin Cordner, *Tradition and Recollection*, *id*. at 14–17; Mark T. Mitchell, *Response*, *id*. at 18–22.

7. MITCHELL, LIMITS OF LIBERALISM, op. cit., at 2–3, 20–23; Mitchell, *Response*, op. cit., at 18–19.

8. MITCHELL, LIMITS OF LIBERALISM, op. cit., at 23–24, 219–20, 260–68.

By contrast, while I also address the concept of tradition, my central organizing principle is the existential necessity of virtue as an unavoidable feature of the process for achieving excellence and human flourishing in those spaces within liberal democracy that are hospitable to it (and indeed hospitable to respect for tradition). I am not convinced, therefore, that liberalism and liberal democracy are *necessarily* incompatible with the notions of tradition and virtue, and I remain hopeful that these notions can be successfully accommodated within the liberal democratic framework. And while I advance positions not inconsistent with the nature and goals of humane localism, I am concerned with the practical project of finding a path within liberal democracy that can lead to this and other desirable outcomes.[9] It seems, moreover, that I am not alone in regarding liberalism and liberal democracy as in principle compatible with the notions of tradition and virtue.[10] Indeed, Mitchell himself has more recently suggested that what really matters is the substantive reality rather than the label attached to it.[11] On this view, we can challenge such a substantive reality without necessarily having to dismiss liberalism or liberal democracy *per se.*

Given that the present book is still about composing the stories of our lives, especially in and through our work, I should also say something at the outset about the relevant parts of my own life story. Looking back on my career in the legal academy, I now see it as comprising three main stages of successively expanding focus. I began my career in law teaching four decades ago in 1980 — at Mercer University School of Law where I

---

9. In addition to "humane localism," some of the other outcomes Mitchell himself envisages as desirable relate to domestic relations, politics, and concern for future generations, the natural world, and our cultural patrimony. MITCHELL, LIMITS OF LIBERALISM, op. cit., at 258–60.

10. *See, e.g.,* Sandwisch, *Recovering Tradition,* op. cit., at 12 (observing that all traditions suffer from incoherencies that propel them toward greater coherency and wondering whether the liberal tradition "[c]ould … have made a proper place for tradition"); Cordner, *Tradition and Recollection,* op. cit., at 17 (suggesting that Mitchell's "working definition of liberalism" as disdaining tradition, being obsessed with freedom, and promoting a cosmopolitan liberal state "is merely an hypothesis [that] would fail tests of verification or validation"). For a book length treatment of the theme, see JEFFREY STOUT, DEMOCRACY AND TRADITION (2004) (arguing that modern democracy is a tradition of social practices that values excellence and virtue as well as rights); *see further infra* notes 47–52 and accompanying text.

11. *See* Mitchell, *Response,* op. cit., at 18–19 (proposing that we provisionally suspend using the term "liberalism" and seek instead to define "certain salient features of the modern mind").

have happily remained. My overriding passion and purpose (to the extent I thought about life purpose at all at that early stage in my career) focused on the grand liberal project of achieving peace and prosperity through the activity of international institutions promoting economic integration among nation states. Such a focus was entirely consistent with a biography that included being raised by an English father and a German mother who married just after the end of the Second World War; one year's postgraduate study in Germany; two years' work as a legal consultant practicing European Community Law in Brussels; admission to the Bar of England and Wales, followed by pupillage at the Bar in the same area; and pursuit of an LL.M. degree at the University of Michigan, with the specific goal of studying under the renowned European Community Law scholar Eric Stein and the equally renowned international trade law scholar John Jackson.

Although also teaching more mainstream subjects, for the first half of my career in the legal academy my teaching, scholarship, and professional activities remained centrally focused on the European Community (or European Union into which it later transformed) and the General Agreement on Tariffs and Trade (GATT) (or the World Trade Organization (WTO) into which it later transformed). Along the way, I also began teaching in the areas of Comparative Law and U.S. Immigration Law as natural fits and, in the latter case, also as the result of direct personal experience in making the progression from nonimmigrant student to lawful permanent resident to naturalized U.S. citizen.

Although I no longer teach or am active within professional organizations in the areas of European Union Law or international trade law, I do still teach in the areas of Comparative Law and U.S. Immigration Law. Moreover, I still believe in the grand liberal project of achieving peace and prosperity through the activity of international institutions promoting economic integration among nation states. This said, I have also long considered that a certain reductionist and naïve view of human nature and an excess of ideological zeal in pursuing the integrationist vision (and related visions such as that of American neo-conservatism), combined with an undue concern with maximizing corporate profits at the expense of other important interests, have caused the relevant elites to choose unwise means in pursuit of a worthy end. In short, the elites got ahead of themselves and, more consequentially, they got ahead of ordinary people. The rise of reactionary "Trumpian populism" in the United States and analogous movements elsewhere in the Western world should be no great surprise. I will have more to say about this subject later in this chapter.

The second stage in my career, and first expansion of focus, occurred in the late 1980s and the 1990s, beginning with the fall of the Berlin Wall and the much vaunted "collapse of communism." These momentous events invited a reflective, humanistic turn to explore the deeper historical, jurisprudential, and comparative roots that distinguished communist from liberal democratic societies within "the West" and that distinguish the West from "the Rest." A few years of exploration in seminar teaching led to eventual development of a course entitled "Fundamental Perspectives on Law" that sought to integrate the study of legal history, jurisprudence, and comparative law within a narrative framework from ancient times until the present. I taught this course until 2012, only discontinuing it after Mercer Law School eliminated the requirement that all law students must take at least one Perspectives block course.

My third career stage, and second expansion of focus, also began in the 1990s, with the teaching of a seminar entitled "The Jurisprudence of Legal Practice and Legal Education," and continues to evolve in very fruitful ways. As the title of the seminar suggests, it originated with my growing interest in jurisprudence discussed above. However, the particular book that I used as my central seminar text (after it had serendipitously come to my attention) viewed legal practice and legal education through the lens of the classical professional ideal of the lawyer-statesman, emphasizing the twin virtues of practical wisdom and civic mindedness.[12] And this perspective invited a further reflective turn, this time to explore questions of lawyer professionalism and vocation (questions that I have gradually come to see as being at the heart of a lawyer's professional identity), and thus to explore matters of the soul as well as the mind.

This new turn toward professionalism and vocation soon resulted in a long-term scholarly project I termed "Fundamental Dimensions of Law and Legal Education." This project combines all three focuses to make the case for a "liberal legal education." Specifically I argue that a basic exposure to the historical, jurisprudential, and comparative dimensions of law, as well as a basic exposure to the transnational dimensions of law, should be

---

12. ANTHONY T. KRONMAN, THE LOST LAWYER: FAILING IDEALS OF THE LEGAL PROFESSION (1993).

part of every law student's legal education because such exposure will help them develop important qualities of professionalism and a robust sense of vocation. The project has so far resulted in three published law review articles and envisages the eventual publication of several more articles and one, possibly two, books.[13] It is itself the work of a lifetime and will likely occupy me well into retirement.

No doubt my inward reflective turn toward issues of professionalism and vocation (and thus toward the heart of professional identity) in the late 1990s and early 2000s was encouraged and reinforced by the experience of getting married and becoming a parent, by the subsequent loss of my own parents within a few years, and by my longstanding Roman Catholic faith. But several wonderful Mercer colleagues have also been especially influential in encouraging and reinforcing this inward turn:

- Jack Sammons, who planted the MacIntyrean seeds among his Law School colleagues already in the early 1980s, who continued to water them (although it would be many years before they would finally germinate in my own mind and soul), and who has steadfastly continued to be an inspiring exemplar and mentor for me;
- Pat Longan, who joined the Law School faculty in 2000 and then developed an award winning and pioneering course, The Legal Profession, devoted to exploring issues of lawyer professionalism and vocation, which he graciously let me audit the second time he taught it, in spring 2005;
- John Dunaway (then Director of the Mercer Commons), who invited me to become a Mercer Commons Fellow in fall 2004, and Peter Brown (then in charge of the University Quality Enhancement Plan (QEP)), both of whom supported and encouraged me in pursuing an ambitious Commons project that I called "Professionalism and Vocation Across the Professions." In this project Pat,

13. For the three law review articles thus far, see Mark L. Jones, *Fundamental Dimensions of Law and Legal Education: : A Theoretical Framework,* 26 OKL. CIT. UNIV. L. REV. 547 (2001); Mark L. Jones, *Fundamental Dimensions of Law and Legal Education: An Historical Framework — A History of U.S. Legal Education Phase I: From the Founding of the Republic Until the 1860s,* 39 J. MARSHALL L. REV. 1041 (2006); Mark L. Jones, *Fundamental Dimensions of Law and Legal Education: Perspectives on Curriculum Reform, Mercer Law School's Woodruff Curriculum, and ... "Perspectives,"* 63 MERCER L. REV. 975 (2012).

Jack, newly arrived Dean Daisy Floyd, and Tim Floyd, Director of Experiential Education, at the Law School, together with John, Peter, and scores of other colleagues from across the University, undertook an interdisciplinary and cross-professional exploration of issues related to professionalism and vocation in several Symposia and Workshops in 2005, 2006, and 2008, resulting in a gradually developing focus on the centrality of practical wisdom;

- Paul Lewis and Kelly Reffitt, whom I joined in forming the "Phronesis Project for the Exploration of Character, Practical Wisdom, and Professional Formation" in 2009, which incorporated the earlier "Professionalism and Vocation Across the Professions" project, organized another Workshop in 2009 and Symposium in 2010, and published a book memorializing the results of both projects in 2013.[14]

Working with these colleagues — most of whom, especially Jack Sammons, make an appearance in the pages of this book — involved a more direct focus on the kind of professional character and professional identity we seek to cultivate in our students. By pursuing such a teleology we help them become the kind of people who can live meaningful, purposeful, and fulfilling lives as members of their chosen profession. In other words, we enable them to live a "happy" life in the Aristotelian sense of a "flourishing" life.[15] This point is well illustrated by Pat Longan's course on The Legal Profession at Mercer. We build on the foundation provided by this course throughout the curriculum but especially and perhaps most advertently

---

14. TOWARD HUMAN FLOURISHING: CHARACTER, PRACTICAL WISDOM, AND PROFESSIONAL FORMATION (Mark L. Jones, Paul A. Lewis, & Kelly E. Reffitt, eds., 2013). For a description of the history and nature of the Professionalism and Vocation Across the Professions Project, see Mark Jones, *Appendix A: Building Bridges and Discovering Commonality: The Story of Mercer University's Professionalism and Vocation Across the Professions Project*, id. at 217–26. For a discussion of the history and nature of the Phronesis Project, see Paul Lewis, *Appendix B: Moral Development Across Disciplines, Schools, and Life Span: The Phronesis Project, id.* at 227–32.

15. *See* ARISTOTLE, THE ETHICS OF ARISTOTLE: THE NICOMACHEAN ETHICS 63–64, 66–67, 73–76 (J.A.K. Thomson trans., rev. Hugh Tredennick 1976) (the good, the *telos* or "final end," of human beings is "happiness" in the sense of doing well or living well, in other words flourishing, and this consists in "an activity of [the rational] soul in accordance with virtue").

in our Externship program, which was established in 2006 under the direction of Tim Floyd and in which I have been privileged to teach since 2013.[16] It is no exaggeration to say that enabling our students to flourish by helping them develop their professional character and form their professional identity in these courses has been at the core of the Mercer Law School curriculum for many years now.[17]

This more direct focus on cultivating our students' professional character and professional identity by developing their qualities of professionalism and sense of vocation and in this way to help them find meaning, purpose, and fulfilment has resulted in a second strand of scholarship. In addition to the 2013 book mentioned above,[18] so far this strand has also

---

16. For accounts of The Legal Profession course and the Externship Program (formerly Public Interest Practicum but renamed Externship in 2013), see Patrick E. Longan, *Teaching Professionalism*, 60 MERCER L. REV. 659 (2009) (describing the Legal Profession course as it had evolved through 2009); Timothy Floyd, *Moral Vision, Moral Courage, and the Formation of the Lawyer's Professional Identity*, 28 MISS. C. L. REV. 339 (2009) (describing the Legal Profession course and the Public Interest Program as they had evolved through 2009); Patrick Longan & Timothy Floyd, *Mercer Law School's Focus on Professionalism*, 2 BLOOMBERG L. REP. — STUDENT ED., no. 1, at 13 (Jan. 31, 2011) (describing both courses as they had evolved through 2011); Patrick Emery Longan, *Further Reflections on Teaching Professionalism: A Thank You Note to Jack Sammons*, 66 MERCER L. REV. 513 (2015) (describing The Legal Profession course as it had evolved through 2015); Mark L. Jones, *Developing Virtue and Practical Wisdom in the Legal Profession and Beyond*, 68 MERCER L. REV. 833, 859–68 (2017) (describing The Legal Profession course and the Externship Program as they had evolved through 2017); Timothy W. Floyd & Kendall L. Kerew, *Marking the Path from Law Student to Lawyer: Using Field Placement Courses to Facilitate the Deliberate Exploration of Professional Identity and Purpose*, 68 MERCER L. REV. 767, 774, 776–87, 807–22 (2017) (describing the Externship Program as it had evolved through 2017); *see also First Year Course on Professionalism and Professional Identity*, MERCER LAW SCHOOL, http://law.mercer.edu/academics/centers/clep/education.cfm (current description of The Legal Profession course on Law School website).

17. *See* Longan & Floyd, *Focus on Professionalism*, op. cit., at 12 (observing that at Mercer "[w]e have explicitly placed character development and the formation of professional identity at the core of our curriculum"). For an in-depth exploration of professional identity, see *Educational Interventions to Cultivate Professional Identity in Law Students: A Symposium of the Mercer Law Review*, 68 MERCER L. REV. 579, 579–875 (2017) (exploring various aspects of professional identity formation in general, and the process of professional identity formation in several different professional fields, including law, medicine, the ministry, and the military, in particular).

18. TOWARD HUMAN FLOURISHING, op. cit.

produced two law review articles.[19] The present book fits into this strand. One objective of the book, then, is ethical. It is to enhance lawyers' and law students' prospects for living a meaningful, purposeful, and fulfilling life — a flourishing life — through the work to which we have been called, and in this way to enhance our prospects for achieving the professional well-being, and avoiding the lawyer and law student distress and dysfunction, that rightly receive so much attention nowadays.[20]

The Report of the National Task Force on Lawyer Well-Being, released in August 2017, explains the nature and extent of the well-being crisis currently afflicting the legal profession, and articulates a comprehensive set of "recommendations for minimizing lawyer dysfunction, boosting well-being, and reinforcing the importance of well-being to competence and excellence in practicing law."[21] Responding to the Task Force Report at its 2018 Midyear Meeting, the ABA House of Delegates adopted Resolution 105, which supported "the goal of reducing mental health and substance use disorders and improving the well-being of lawyers, judges, and law students" and endorsed the Task Force's recommendations.[22] The Task Force Report describes the high rates of substance use disorders and mental health problems among practicing lawyers:

---

19. Mark L. Jones, *Fisherman Jack: Living in "Juropolis" — The Fishing Village of the Law*, 66 MERCER L. REV. 485 (2015); Mark L. Jones, *Developing Virtue and Practical Wisdom in the Legal Profession and Beyond*, 68 MERCER L. REV. 833 (2017).

20. For a good introduction to the subject of lawyer well-being and lawyer distress and dysfunction and an overview of the initiatives undertaken by the American Bar Association (ABA) at the national level to address the situation, see Bob Carlson, *It's time to promote our health: ABA mobilizes on multiple fronts to address well-being in the legal profession*, ABA JOURNAL (December 1, 2018), http://www.abajournal.com/magazine/article/its_time_to_promote_our_health.

21. *See The Path to Lawyer Well-Being: Practical Recommendations for Positive Change*, The Report of the National Task Force on Lawyer Well-Being (ABA, August 2017), https://www.americanbar.org/content/dam/aba/images/abanews/ThePathToLawyerWellBeing ReportRevFINAL.pdf (articulating recommendations for all stakeholders as well as for specific stakeholders, including judges, regulators, legal employers, law schools, bar associations, lawyers professional liability carriers, and lawyers assistance programs). For the quoted language, see *id* at 11.

22. American Bar Association, *Resolution 105 and Report to the House of Delegates* (February 2018), https://www.americanbar.org/content/dam/aba/images/abanews/2018 -AM-Resolutions/105.pdf.

In 2016, the American Bar Association (ABA) Commission on Law-yer Assistance Programs and Hazelden Betty Ford Foundation pub-lished their study of nearly 13,000 currently-practicing lawyers [the "Study"]. It found that between 21 and 36 percent qualify as problem drinkers, and that approximately 28 percent, 19 percent, and 23 per-cent are struggling with some level of depression, anxiety, and stress, respectively. The parade of difficulties also includes suicide, social alienation, work addiction, sleep deprivation, job dissatisfaction, a "diversity crisis," complaints of work-life conflict, incivility, a nar-rowing of values so that profit predominates, and negative public perception. Notably, the Study found that younger lawyers in the first ten years of practice and those working in private firms experi-ence the highest rates of problem drinking and depression.[23]

The Report explains that a substantial percentage of law students already experience symptoms of distress and dysfunction in law school:

> Additionally, 15 law schools and over 3,300 law students participated in the Survey of Law Student Well-Being, the results of which were released in 2016. It found that 17 percent experienced some level of depression, 14 percent experienced severe anxiety, 23 percent had mild or moderate anxiety, and six percent reported serious suicidal thoughts in the past year. As to alcohol use, 43 percent reported binge drinking at least once in the prior two weeks and nearly one-quarter (22 percent) reported binge-drinking two or more times during that period. One-quarter fell into the category of being at risk for alcoholism for which further screening was recommended.[24]

And importantly, the Task Force Report cautions that even those practic-ing lawyers and law students not exhibiting such symptoms of distress and dysfunction are not necessarily experiencing well-being:

---

23. ABA, Task Force Report, op. cit., at 7. *See also* ABA, *Resolution 105 Report*, op. cit., at 2 (providing some additional details, including regarding suicidal thoughts and attempted suicides).

24. ABA, Task Force Report, op. cit., at 7. *See also* ABA, *Resolution 105 Report*, op. cit., at 1 (providing additional details, including regarding the incidence of law students' unau-thorized prescription drug use as well as marijuana and cocaine use).

The results from both surveys signal an elevated risk in the legal community for mental health and substance use disorders tightly intertwined with an alcohol-based social culture. The analysis of the problem cannot end there, however. The studies reflect that the majority of lawyers and law students do not have a mental health or substance use disorder. But that does not mean that they're thriving. Many lawyers experience a "profound ambivalence" about their work, and different sectors of the profession vary in their levels of satisfaction and well-being.[25]

Reflecting a multidimensional understanding, the Task Force defines lawyer well-being as "a continuous process whereby lawyers seek to thrive in each of the following areas: emotional health, occupational pursuits, creative or intellectual endeavors, sense of spirituality or greater purpose in life, physical health, and social connections with others." The Task Force emphasizes that "[l]awyer well-being is part of a lawyer's ethical duty of competence." It includes "lawyers' ability to make healthy, positive work/life choices to assure not only a quality of life within their families and communities, but also to help them make responsible decisions for their clients" and it also includes "maintaining their own long-term well-being." Lawyer well-being, then, "is not defined solely by the absence of illness; it includes a positive state of wellness."[26]

The Report urges leaders of the legal profession to take action to address the well-being crisis because "lawyer well-being contributes to organizational success[,] ... influences ethics and professionalism[,][and] ... from a humanitarian perspective, promoting well-being is the right thing to do."[27] The Report acknowledges that the legal profession is "struggling," suffers from an alarming "level of toxicity," and is "at a crossroads." But it recognizes that "[c]hange will require a wide-eyed and candid assessment of our members' state of being, accompanied by courageous commitment to re-envisioning what it means to live the life of a lawyer."[28] Significantly, in its Conclusion the Report states:

---

25. ABA, Task Force Report, op. cit., at 7.
26. *Id.* at 9–10.
27. *Id.* at 8–9.
28. *Id.* at 1.

To preserve the public's trust and maintain our status as a self-regulating profession, we must truly become "our brothers' and sisters' keepers," through a strong commitment to caring for the well-being of one another, as well as ourselves.... Regardless of your position in the legal profession, please consider ways in which you can make a difference in the essential task of bringing about a culture change in how we, as lawyers, regard our own well-being and that of one another.[29]

It is my belief that although Alasdair MacIntyre might look somewhat askance at, or at least quibble with, the positive psychology premises and tenets that seem to drive the lawyer well-being movement, his account of human flourishing through the pursuit of excellence in practices and exercise of the virtues has much to offer us as we seek to address the crisis of well-being, distress, and dysfunction in the legal profession in the United States.[30]

---

29. *Id.* at 47. For one very important response, see ANNE M. BRAFFORD, ABA WELL-BEING TOOLKIT FOR LAWYERS AND LEGAL EMPLOYERS, https://www.americanbar.org/content/dam/aba/administrative/lawyer_assistance/ls_colap_well-being_toolkit_for_lawyers_legal_employers.authcheckdam.pdf. (August 2018). For an additional very useful resource on the subject of lawyer well-being, see NANCY LEVIT & DOUGLAS O. LINDER, THE HAPPY LAWYER: MAKING A GOOD LIFE IN THE LAW (2010), especially at 1–17 (evaluating an older set of conflicting data on lawyer satisfaction and distinguishing among different cohorts of lawyers and types of practice), 18–48 (discussing three different meanings of the term "happiness" — as pleasure, as satisfaction, and as thriving (or flourishing) — as well as the neurobiology of happiness; explaining that 40% of happiness as "satisfaction" is within individual control, 50% being determined by genetics and only 10% by circumstances, including financial circumstances; and identifying the six components of a "thriving person" (or human flourishing), one of which, the prerequisite of security, is less subject to individual control than the other five, which are autonomy, authenticity, relatedness, competence, and self-esteem), 49–77 (reviewing various factors that contribute to lawyer unhappiness and lawyer happiness), 78–111 (examining several strategies for an individual lawyer to enhance his or her happiness), 208–42 (elaborating on these strategies). *See also* the Law.com series "Minds Over Matters: An Examination of Mental Health in the Legal Profession" [launched May 2019].

30. *See* MACINTYRE, CONFLICTS OF MODERNITY, op. cit., at 193–96 (describing the "dominant conception of happiness" in liberal democratic society as "a state of only positive feelings ... a state of freedom from unsatisfied desires[,] ... grave apprehensions and fears" and associating Martin Seligman and the Positive Psychology movement with this conception), 196–202 (offering a Neo-Aristotelian critique of the dominant conception, distinguishing between satisfying a desire and having "good reason" or "sufficiently good reason" to satisfy a desire, and explaining that one can be "happy" in the Neo-Aristotelian

But not only in the United States, for the legal profession elsewhere is also in crisis.[31] And not only the legal profession, but the medical profession and other professions too.[32] It is my hope, then, that the present book may make a contribution to "re-envisioning what it means to live the life of a lawyer [or other professional]" and to "caring for the well-being of one another, as well as ourselves."[33] As the discussion proceeds, the reader will discover that it in effect addresses not only this re-envisioning and this mutual and self-caring, but each of the dimensions in the Task Force definition of well-being.

It is also my hope that in seeking to contribute in this way, the book will complement and support the work of others working on these issues. For example, my colleagues Pat Longan, Daisy Floyd, and Tim Floyd have

---

conception even with some justifiable grief, regret, and fear). For further discussion of Mac-Intyre's views on this point, see Chapter 2, notes 95–96 and accompanying text (contrasting the dominant *subjective* conception of happiness with the *objective* Neo-Aristotelian conception). *But see* Kristján Kristjánsson, Flourishing As the Aim of Education: A Neo-Aristotelian View 6–7 (2020) (contrasting the more objective positive psychology model of the later Seligman with Seligman's earlier, more subjective psychological model). *See also* Oliver Burkeman, *The truth about anxiety — without it we wouldn't have hope*, The Guardian (February 2, 2019) (distinguishing between good and bad forms of anxiety).

31. For a discussion of the situation in the United Kingdom, for example, see Richard Collier, *How do we tackle the legal profession's mental health problem?*, Legal Cheek (April 19, 2019), https://www.legalcheek.com/2019/04/how-do-we-tackle-the-legal-professions-mental-health-problem/.

32. For discussion of the situation in the U.S. medical profession, see, e.g., Thomas P. Reith, *Burnout in United States Healthcare Professionals; A Narrative Review*, 10 Cureus (December 4, 2018), https://www.ncbi.nlm.nih.gov/pmc/articles/PMC6367114/ (focusing on physicians and nurses); Michelle D. Lall, et. al., *Assessment of Physician Well-Being Part One: Burnout and Other Negative States*, 20 West J. Emerg. Med. 278–90 (March 2019), https://www.ncbi.nlm.nih.gov/pmc/articles/PMC6404708/; Michelle D. Lall, et. al., *Assessment of Physician Well-Being Part Two: Beyond Burnout*, 20 West J. Emerg. Med. 291–304 (March 2019), https://www.ncbi.nlm.nih.gov/pmc/articles/PMC6404719/ (focusing on physicians). For discussion of the situation in the United Kingdom, see, e.g., Decca Aitkenhead, *Panic, chronic anxiety and burnout: doctors at breaking point*, The Guardian (March 10, 2018), https://www.theguardian.com/society/2018/mar/10/panic-chronic-anxiety-burnout-doctors-breaking-point (focusing on physicians). For a good sense of the forces threatening the well-being of several different professions, see William F. May, Beleaguered Rulers: The Public Obligation of the Professional (2001) (discussing physicians, lawyers, engineers, corporate executives, politicians, reporters, journalists and other media experts, ministers, and academics). For a quick sense of these forces, see *id.* at 4–5. I am indebted to Paul Lewis for reminding me of May's treatment in this context. Lewis Email (February 28, 2020) [on file with author].

33. *Supra* notes 28–29 and accompanying text.

recently published their book *The Formation of Professional Identity: The Path from Student to Lawyer*, generated by their experiences in teaching the Legal Profession course at Mercer.[34] In it they show how law students can become lawyers who live a life of meaning, purpose, fulfilment, and well-being by cultivating a professional identity that incorporates the six virtues of the professional lawyer — competence, fidelity to the client, fidelity to the law, public spiritedness, civility, and practical wisdom — and that appropriately integrates their personal values as well.[35] The MacIntyrean account given here provides a philosophical framework and foundation that seems very compatible with their own account (which I will cite frequently in this book), although I hasten to add that this does not mean they would necessarily agree with every detail. Moreover, as already suggested above, this philosophical framework and foundation applies to other professions and occupations as well. By the same token, the methodology used in the *Formation of Professional Identity* book — describing, for each virtue of the professional lawyer, the central elements of the virtue, the impediments to cultivating and exhibiting it, and strategies for overcoming these impediments, with discussion questions and hypothetical

---

34. PATRICK EMERY LONGAN, DAISY HURST FLOYD, AND TIMOTHY W. FLOYD, THE FORMATION OF PROFESSIONAL IDENTITY: THE PATH FROM STUDENT TO LAWYER (2020).

35. *See id.* at 1–5 (giving the authors' reasons for focusing on the concept of professional identity, defining "identity" as "a deep sense of self in a particular role," and a lawyer's professional identity as "a deep sense of yourself *as a lawyer*"), 5–8 (identifying and briefly describing the six professional virtues, distilled from the American Bar Association (ABA) Model Rules of Professional Conduct as well as various professional codes and creeds, that should become component parts of a lawyer's professional identity, and addressing the relationship between professional identity and personal identity), 8–9 (drawing on the insights of moral psychology, specifically the Four Component Model of Morality (FCM), to identify "four distinct but interactive components to moral action" — moral sensitivity, moral reasoning, moral motivation, and moral implementation — that are needed "to possess and deploy" the six professional virtues), 13–14 (discussing the Report of the ABA National Task Force on Lawyer Well-Being and the statistics on lawyer and law student distress and dysfunction), 14–22 (explaining how insights from positive psychology and moral philosophy, in particular virtue ethics, and specifically MacIntyre's account of a practice, demonstrate how lawyer well-being is promoted by cultivating a professional identity that incorporates the six professional virtues). The remainder of their book addresses each of the six professional virtues in greater depth.

problems providing further illumination and illustration — also seems readily adaptable beyond the legal profession.[36]

In addition to this ethical objective focused on flourishing and well-being in the legal profession and in other professions, the book has a second, more political objective because we have been witnessing not only a crisis of well-being, distress, and dysfunction in the professions, but a crisis of well-being, distress, and dysfunction in our Republic as well. The symptoms are evident to all — hyper-partisanship, political gridlock, deepening economic, cultural, and racial divisions, an identity politics of fear, suspicion, and outrage, social media tribalism, poisonous incivility and dishonesty, and so on. It is generally accepted that political, social, and technological forces have divided us into social and political tribes — frequently, it seems, even invading and poisoning relationships among family members and erstwhile friends. Related, much of our political conversation at all levels and on all sides has become lamentably degraded, and is conducted in trivial and superficial terms, tending toward mutual demonization, that are more suited to the school playground than mature discourse among adults engaged in republican self-governance. In contrast to the situation in the professions, however, and despite some hopeful signs of a desire to build bridges across our divisions — at the present time there appears to be little consensus on how best to address the crisis in the Republic.[37] But unless we address it, how can we hope to solve a litany of problems such as the following?

> We live in perilous times ... Many, if not all, of the following problems are now occurring in the United States, Europe, and in many other countries throughout the world: environmental degradation, increasing violence and terrorism, widening extremes of wealth and poverty, racial and ethnic animosity, malnutrition and hunger, gen-

---

36. Moreover, each chapter of the book ends with a very useful list of references and suggested readings. For the chapters addressing each virtue of the professional lawyer in depth, see *id.* at 25–41 (competence), 43–57 (fidelity to the client), 59–72 (fidelity to the law), 73–85 (public spiritedness), 87–101 (civility), 103–118 (practical wisdom).

37. For two illuminating attempts to understand and grapple with some of these issues, see Jonathan Haidt, *The Ten Causes of America's Political Dysfunction*, THE RIGHTEOUS MIND (NOVEMBER 2014), https://righteousmind.com/the-causes-of-political-dysfunction/; EZRA KLEIN, WHY WE'RE POLARIZED (2020).

der inequality, rising mental health problems, escalating addictions, skyrocketing medical care costs, massive government budget deficits, ballooning consumer debt and bankruptcies, unemployment and underemployment, disintegrating families, alienated youth, abandoned elders, moral and ethical degeneration, political and business corruption, energy depletion, and socioeconomic injustices of all kinds.

In the past century, corporate advertisers have painted a picture of "the good life" that is based on the acquisition of material wealth and possessions. The functioning of the U.S. economy is based on the multiplication and instant gratification of wants and desires as evidenced by government officials who tell Americans to go out and spend in order to help the economy. Sadly, in spite of material prosperity, "the good life," with its promise of happiness and fulfillment, has eluded many Americans.[38]

These words were written in 2006, even before the 2007–08 Financial Crisis and consequent Great Recession, but not much seems to have changed, except that, after recovering from the recession, we can now add all the woes and setbacks associated with the current Covid-19 pandemic. To adapt the words of the Task Force on Lawyer Well-Being, our Republic

---

38. John Fitzgerald Medina, Faith, Physics, and Psychology: Rethinking Society and the Human Spirit 1–2 (2006). Defining "worldview" as "the set of values, beliefs, ideas, and assumptions through which one perceives reality," Medina sources these problems in the destructive influence of "the predominant Western worldview"—the secular, mechanistic, and materialistic "Cartesian-Newtonian worldview"—and prescribes as the solution a combination of (a) the self-actualization movement founded by Abraham Maslow (which emphasizes "'the possibilities for spiritual growth, value growth, [and] moral development in human beings'"), (b) the holistic movement famously exemplified by physicist Fritjof Capra and now extended well beyond physics (which supports "a new, comprehensive, holistic worldview that promotes unity of science and religion and fosters the integration of mind, body, and spirit," and which "'strives to develop our latent capacity for cooperation and community'"), and (c) the Bahá'í Faith (which stresses "the oneness of humankind—the spiritual unification of humanity into one global family and the emergence of a divinely inspired global civilization"). Id. at 6–15 [quoting from Abraham Maslow as cited in Future Visions: The Unpublished Papers of Abraham Maslow 115 (Ed Hoffman, ed., 1996) and Ron Miller, New Directions in Education 2 (1991)]. The present book is not necessarily inconsistent with Medina's grand vision, but it is less ambitious and more narrowly focused, although ambitious enough.

also is "struggling," suffers from an alarming "level of toxicity," and is "at a crossroads." And similarly, "[c]hange will require a wide-eyed and candid assessment of our [Republic's] state of being, accompanied by courageous commitment to re-envisioning what it means to live the life of a [citizen]" and to "caring for the well-being of one another, as well as ourselves."[39] How, then, do we "take our country back" from the forces that have divided us? How do we overcome our mutual alienation and find our way back to one another, re-enabling meaningful political conversation to occur? These questions are likely to remain urgent even if the 2020 general election produces a change of Administration.

At the moment at least, I still optimistically subscribe to Francis Fukuyama's notorious "end of history" thesis that liberal democracy is the best and final form of human government — at least when this thesis is properly understood (and judging from the nature of some of the critiques or even flippant dismissals of Fukuyama's thesis, this is not invariably, or perhaps even usually, the case).[40] Although MacIntyre himself may well not share my optimistic commitment to liberal democracy, I also consider that among the possible range of ideological positions within the liberal democratic framework, we should strive to cultivate the liberal democratic state as a "republic of virtue" as it were. And here I am more confident of MacIntyre's agreement, although doubtless he would consider it unrealistic to hope for such a transformation of the modern liberal democratic state, however desirable it might be.

In principle, then, I agree with scholars such as Lawrence Solum who belong to the "virtue jurisprudence" school of thought and who contend that "the fundamental purpose of law is to promote the flourishing of individual humans and their communities by creating the conditions that promote and sustain the development and exercise of human excellence or virtue."[41] And I give considerable credence to John Milbank and Adrian

---

39. *See supra* notes 28–29 and accompanying text.

40. For Fukuyama's "end of history" thesis, see generally FRANCIS FUKUYAMA, THE END OF HISTORY AND THE LAST MAN (1992); Mark L. Jones, *Beyond Punks in Empty Chairs: An Imaginary Conversation with Clint Eastwood's Dirty Harry — Toward Peace Through Spiritual Justice*, 11 U. MASS L. REV. 312, 318–43 (2016).

41. Lawrence B. Solum, *Virtue Jurisprudence: Towards An Aretaic Theory of Law*, in ARISTOTLE AND THE PHILOSOPHY OF LAW: THEORY, PRACTICE, AND JUSTICE 1 (Liesbeth Huppes-Cluysenaer & Nuno M.N.S. Coelho, eds., 2013) (discussing the "proper aim, goal,

Pabst's ambitious and sophisticated recent articulation of a comprehensive "politics of virtue" addressing the economy, politics, culture, and international relations.[42] This said, my own strategy for cultivating the liberal democratic state as a "republic of virtue" is not focused on the sort of direct legislative efforts described above. Even as I would applaud and support such efforts, regrettably I do share MacIntyre's deep skepticism about the potential for the necessary virtuous activity by legislators in the current conditions prevailing in liberal democratic societies. As we will see, MacIntyre's critique emphasizes especially the deleterious influence of various kinds of exclusionary elites.[43] Indeed, the contemporary rise of "Trumpian populism" in the United States and of analogous movements elsewhere in Western liberal democracies can arguably be understood, at least partly, as a reaction to this disease of the modern body politic. There is serious

---

or *telos* of legislation" in his summary of the central tenets of the school relating to legislation and adjudication). For useful surveys of the tenets of the school of virtue jurisprudence, see *id.* at 1–31; Colin Farrelly & Lawrence B. Solum, *An Introduction to Aretaic Theories of Law, in* VIRTUE JURISPRUDENCE 1–23 (Colin Farrelly and Lawrence B. Solum, eds., 2008); Amalia Amaya & Ho Hock Lai, *Of Law, Virtue, and Jurisprudence, in* LAW, VIRTUE, AND JUSTICE 1–25 (Amalia Amaya and Ho Hock Lai, eds., 2013); Lawrence B. Solum, *Law and Virtue, in* THE ROUTLEDGE COMPANION TO VIRTUE ETHICS 491–514 (Lorraine Besser-Jones & Michael Slote, eds., 2015). Solum further addresses the goal of legislation specifically in *Virtue Jurisprudence,* op. cit., at 9–12; *Law and Virtue,* op. cit., at 508–13.

42. JOHN MILBANK & ADRIAN PABST, THE POLITICS OF VIRTUE: POST-LIBERALISM AND THE HUMAN FUTURE (2016). The authors explain that each part of their book "combines a critique of liberalism with post-liberal alternatives." *Id.* at 8. Although in some respects they seem to be advocating an alternative to liberal democracy, I read their prescriptions as compatible with liberal democracy, or at least its framework. As Francis Fukuyama describes it, this framework ensures individual freedom and popular sovereignty through the combination of three main elements: (a) Political liberalism, which is "a rule of law that recognizes certain individual rights or freedoms from government control"; (b) Democracy, which is "the right held universally by all citizens to have a share of political power, that is, the right of all citizens to vote and participate in politics," and which "can be thought of as yet another liberal right"; and (c) Economic liberalism, which is "the recognition of the right of free economic activity and economic exchange based on private property and markets" and which also goes by the name of "capitalism" or "free-market economics," although "there are many possible interpretations of this rather broad definition of economic liberalism, ranging from the United States of Ronald Reagan and the Britain of Margaret Thatcher to the social democracies of Scandinavia and the relatively statist regimes in Mexico and India." FUKUYAMA, op. cit., at 42–44.

43. *See* Chapter 6, notes 7–8, 53, 59–60 and accompanying text.

question, however, whether this reaction offers any reasonable prospect of cultivating a "republic of virtue."

My own preferred strategy for cultivating a "republic of virtue," then, places more faith in an indirect process in which excellence and virtue are nurtured within the professions and other occupations and spread outward into the rest of society, thereby leading to a gradual virtuous leavening of society. In due course, this leavening may also result in legislation aimed at the promotion of excellence and virtue. This indirect strategy appears to be consistent with MacIntyre's most recent articulation of his own project as "provid[ing] us with the resources for constructing a contemporary politics and ethics, one that enables and requires us to act against modernity from within modernity."[44] Moreover, the notion that ethical progress might also lead to political progress is resonant with recent efforts such as those of David Brooks, who considers that living a life of virtuous commitment and relational interdependence is not only the key to finding meaning and purpose, but also the path to repairing our torn social fabric.[45] Even if skepticism about the current potential for more direct legislative efforts proves to be misplaced, such an indirect strategy provides a necessary and effective complement to, and reinforcement of, any such efforts that may be feasible under current conditions. In any event, here too it is my hope that the present book may make a contribution to "re-envisioning what it means to live the life of a [citizen]" and to "caring for the well-being of one another, as well as ourselves."[46]

Once again, it is also my hope that in seeking to contribute in this way, the book will complement and support the work of others working on these issues. We have already mentioned the examples of Solum, Milbank and Pabst, and Brooks, noting that Brooks' approach is resonant with my own indirect strategy. The philosopher and theologian Jeffrey Stout also emphasizes the role of such an indirect strategy. Thus, Stout explicates

---

44. MacIntyre, Conflicts of Modernity, op. cit., at xi.

45. David Brooks, The Second Mountain: The Quest for a Moral Life (2019). Brooks emphasizes four central commitments (to a vocation, to a spouse and family, to a philosophy or faith, and to a community), considers that character formation and virtue are "a byproduct of giving yourself away" rather than an individual task or achievement, and calls for a "cultural paradigm … shift from the mindset of hyper-individualism to the relational mindset of the second mountain." *Id.* at xvii–xx.

46. *See supra* note 39 and accompanying text.

and advocates "a pragmatic version of deliberative democracy," founded upon a tradition of social practices that aim at excellence and cultivate virtue, including the discursive practice of exchanging ethical reasons (both secular and religious) with one another in democratic conversation.[47] And he stresses that the "discursive practices of ethical deliberation and political debate" — and thus the prospects for citizenship and "concerted democratic action" at both the local and national levels — depend upon our participation in the many other types of social practices, "including crafts, arts, sciences, and sports" that aim at excellence and cultivate virtue and upon "the modes of identity-formation, self-transcendence, and reason-exchange they sustain."[48]

Once again, the MacIntyrean account given here provides a philosophical framework and foundation that seems very compatible with Stout's own account, although also again I hasten to add that this does not mean he would necessarily agree with every detail. Moreover, Stout explicitly

---

47. *See generally* STOUT, DEMOCRACY AND TRADITION, op. cit. For the quoted language, see *id.* at 297 n11 [emphasis removed] ("A better way of characterizing my position in relation to contemporary political theory would be to classify it as a pragmatic version of *deliberative democracy*"). The relevant notions recur throughout Stout's book. For some examples, see *id.* at 151–52, 184–85, 203–04, 291 (tradition of social practices), 29, 151–52, 261–67, 273–74, 282–83, 292–93 (aiming at excellence and cultivating virtue), 6, 10–11, 178–79, 184–85, 195, 209, 270–73, 293, 296–97, 299, 303–05 (discursive practice of exchanging ethical reasons, including religious reasons, with one another in democratic conversation). For Stout's identification of some particular democratic virtues, see *id.* at 9 (piety, hope, love or generosity), 30, 38 (gratitude as "the better part of piety"), 42 (justice, friendship, generosity, hope as "the virtues most directly linked to the prospects of democracy"), 58–59 (hope, courage, practical wisdom, generosity, and sympathy as "ingredients" of justice), 60 (courage and justice as "cardinal virtues of democratic intellectuals"), 85 (civility, open-mindedness, will for justice, temperance regarding offense, practical wisdom, courage, tact, poise, humility in seeking forgiveness from the wronged, as virtues needed for "discursive exchange and political decision-making"), 263 (beginnings of temperance cultivated in the practice of child-rearing), 293 (courage and self-trust among the "set of interlocking virtues" making up "[t]he democratic ideal of individuality"); *see also id.* at 207 (discussing various virtues of "the common people" identified by Walt Whitman). *See also* JEFFREY STOUT, BLESSED ARE THE ORGANIZED: GRASSROOTS DEMOCRACY IN AMERICA (2010) (explicating and evaluating social practices exhibited in grassroots democracy). The social practices involved in "the actual political practice of ordinary people," when organizing and demanding accountability from the powerful, include "one-on-one conversations, small-group meetings, critical reflection, and organized action." *Id.* at xiii, xvi.

48. STOUT, DEMOCRACY AND TRADITION, op. cit., at 292–93.

distances himself from the critique and rejection of liberalism and liberal democracy he understands MacIntyre to be articulating in works prior to *Conflicts of Modernity*.[49] On the other hand, Stout expresses his own serious concerns regarding the health of contemporary liberal democracy — specifically, concerns about how various anti-democratic forces, including the influence of oligarchical elites, threaten democratic practices and ideals, about the democratic deficiencies that result, and about our ability to withstand such forces and redress such deficiencies.[50] Consequently, to recur to a distinction we made earlier when discussing Mark Mitchell's work,[51] Stout's disagreement with MacIntyre may be more of a disagreement over labels than substantive realities. On this understanding, although Stout and MacIntyre largely agree in opposing certain tendencies in contemporary liberal society, they disagree on how some of these tendencies should be labeled and on whether they are essential, or only contingent, features of liberalism and liberal democracy. In a revealing passage, Stout argues that adopting a capacious view of "the liberal project" as seeking to accommodate "the facts of pluralism" rather than as "an antitraditionalist quest"

---

49. For Stout's discussion of MacIntyre, see *id.* at 118–39. This discussion is in Part Two of his book, titled "Religious Voices in a Secular Society," in which Stout distances himself from MacIntyre and other critics of secular liberalism such as Stanley Hauerwas and John Milbank. He refers to all three as "the new traditionalists." *Id.* at 11.

50. For Stout's articulation of these various concerns, see *id.* at 9, 22–24, 47, 224, 281, 289, 291–94, 297, 305 (discussing anti-democratic forces, including oligarchical elites, and resulting democratic deficiencies), 12, 23–24, 58–59, 60, 292–94, 297, 300, 302–03, 305–06 (discussing prospects for withstanding these forces and redressing these deficiencies). Stout's attitude is perhaps best understood as hope combined with stoicism combatting something close to despair. *See id.* at 58–60 (in effect acknowledging all three stances). *See also* STOUT, BLESSED ARE THE ORGANIZED, op. cit., at xiii–xix, 278–90 (expressing similar concerns and adopting a similar attitude but offering the concrete examples of grassroots democracy discussed in the book as an inspiration for ordinary people to organize their various communities in an effort to "take back the country from the plutocrats, militarists, and culture warriors now dominating our politics"). For an illuminating recent treatment tracing the history of democracy, including its inner tensions, problems, and paradoxes, from ancient times to the present, see JAMES MILLER: CAN DEMOCRACY WORK?: A SHORT HISTORY OF A RADICAL IDEA, FROM ANCIENT ATHENS TO OUR WORLD (2018).

51. *See supra* note 11 and accompanying text.

[A]llows us to view the quest for a standpoint above all tradition and the attempt to abstract entirely from consideration of the common good as two, but only two, possible representations of the liberal project. We are free to declare them completely discredited without abandoning that project in the least. Notice that one can, on this view, remain a liberal while abhorring virtually everything Mac-Intyre identifies with liberalism …, including not least of all "the liberal self" and "the liberal system of evaluation."[52]

MacIntyre has arrived at the mature Thomistic Aristotelian philosophy he currently espouses in an intellectual odyssey spanning several different

---

52. STOUT, DEMOCRACY AND TRADITION, op. cit., at 129–30. This said, instead of re-ferring to concepts such as "*the* liberal project," or employing terms such as "liberalism" or "liberal," Stout expresses a preference for "balanced and detailed commentary on [the] various features [of liberal society] and prudent counsel on how one or other of them should be changed." *Id.* at 130. In the quoted passage Stout is referring to MacIntyre's account of liberalism in MACINTYRE, WHOSE JUSTICE?, op. cit., at 335–48. For MacIntyre's introduc-tion of the "the liberal self" and "the liberal system of evaluation" in this account, see *id.* at 337–38. For an illuminating recent historical treatment tracing the evolution of the terms "liberal" and "liberalism" and its antecedents since ancient times, see HELENA ROSENBLATT, THE LOST HISTORY OF LIBERALISM: FROM ANCIENT ROME TO THE TWENTY-FIRST CENTURY (2018). Rosenblatt claims that although liberalism had "a dark side [in] the elitism, sexism, racism, and imperialism of many liberals":

> At heart, most liberals were moralists. Their liberalism had nothing to do with the atomistic individualism we hear of today. They never spoke about rights without stressing duties. Most liberals believed that people had rights *because* they had duties, and most were deeply interested in questions of social justice. They always rejected the idea that a viable community could be constructed on the basis of self-interestedness alone. Ad infinitum they warned of the dangers of selfishness. Liberals ceaselessly advocated generosity, moral pro-bity, and civic values. This, of course, should not be taken to mean that they always practiced what they preached or lived up to their values….[T]he idea that liberalism is an Anglo-American tradition concerned primarily with the protection of individual rights and interests is … the product of the wars of the twentieth century and especially the fear of totalitarianism during the Cold War. For centuries before this, being liberal meant … being a giving and civic-minded citizen; it meant understanding one's connectedness to other citizens and acting in ways conducive to the common good.

Id. at 4–5.

works and several decades.[53] A third objective of the book, then, is to introduce readers unfamiliar with MacIntyre to MacIntyre's corpus, to highlight its relevance and value for our times, and to do so in a manner that more clearly identifies, integrates, and synthesizes the central elements in the evolution of MacIntyre's thinking than perhaps MacIntyre himself does. In making this latter suggestion, I do not intend to be critical of MacIntyre or to claim any kind of editorial superiority, let alone philosophical superiority (the very thought is laughable). I am merely reflecting something that MacIntyre has himself conceded. Thus, in *Conflicts of Modernity*, which represents the latest expression and culmination of his mature thought, MacIntyre states that although some of the theses and arguments in that book "repeat, revise, correct, or replace" theses and arguments in earlier books and articles, with very limited exceptions he decided against including any references to these earlier works.[54]

Chapter 2 considers MacIntyre's account of how we can best compose the stories of our lives, achieve our individual good in community, and fulfill our life purpose through the pursuit of human flourishing, and relates this account to accounts given by others of how we discern a calling or vocation. Chapter 3 then examines MacIntyre's account of a practice and its evolving tradition, and shows how excellence in seeking to attain the common goods of the practices to which we are called is central to our flourishing. And Chapters 4 and 5 build on these two preceding chapters and additional elements in MacIntyre's thought to explore the relationship between practices and practitioner communities, on the one hand, and the greater common good and flourishing of the broader community, on the other. Inspired by MacIntyre's short and partial account of fishing crews and a fishing village in a 1994 essay,[55] the exploration in these two chapters is facilitated by constructing life in an ideal *polis*, in the form of an imagined fishing village called *Piscopolis*, and by viewing the inhabitants' Thomistic Aristotelian way of life, politico-ethical commitments, and communitarian

---

53. The main relevant works are identified *supra* notes 4–5.

54. MacIntyre, Conflicts of Modernity, op. cit., at xii (noting that he also decided against supplying cross-references on the several occasions when he repeats the same point in different contexts in the text).

55. Alasdair MacIntyre, *A Partial Response to My Critics, in* After MacIntyre: Critical Perspectives on the Work of Alasdair MacIntyre 284–86 (John Horton & Susan Mendus, eds., 1994).

ethos through the eyes of a fishing crew member called Drew. In all four chapters we also see the central role of MacIntyre's "unitary core concept of the virtues" in the Western moral tradition of the virtues.[56]

Chapter 6 continues an exploration, already begun in Chapters 4 and 5, of the differences between Drew's situation in *Piscopolis* and that of a fishing crew member called Cash, who is much more subject to the corrupting influences of the liberal democratic state and its capitalist, large-scale market economy. Specifically, Chapter 6 contrasts the political, economic, and moral environment of *Piscopolis*, which nurtures its communitarian *ethos*, with MacIntyre's account of the dominant political, economic, and moral environment of the modern liberal democratic state and advanced capitalism, which threatens to erode or replace this *ethos* with its very different individualist *ethos* — an *ethos* that exists in paradoxical tension with the social and political tribalism that currently afflicts us. Chapter 6 also considers the extent to which MacIntyre believes it is still possible in several significant respects to pursue and protect a *Piscopolis*-like way of life informed by Thomistic Aristotelianism, and to possess the same sorts of politico-ethical commitments as Drew possesses, in various local contexts in this dominant environment. And it raises the additional question — one which MacIntyre himself seems not yet to have explicitly addressed — of whether the self-regulated professions can be viewed as professional *poleis*, analogous to an ideal local *polis* community like *Piscopolis*, within which it is also possible to pursue and protect such a way of life and possess such commitments, even though these professional *poleis* are not local, and indeed may be very large, even national in scale.

Chapter 7 then combines and integrates this general Thomistic Aristotelian *Piscopolis* ideal with two specific professional ideals to argue that, despite the many challenges legal professionals face in the dominant political, economic, and moral environment of the liberal democratic state and its capitalist market economy, we can answer this latter question affirmatively for the professional *polis* of the law, which we call *Juropolis*, and thereby help address the crisis of well-being, distress, and dysfunction that has been afflicting the legal profession and perhaps also even protect the

---

56. *See* MacIntyre, After Virtue, op. cit., at 186 (stating his goal of articulating and defending "a unitary core concept of the virtues" in the Western moral tradition of the virtues).

Republic and democracy itself. And Chapter 8 asks whether, and how, members of the legal profession who inhabit *Juropolis*, and who together with like-minded others constitute an inchoate "republic of virtue" within the liberal democratic state, should seek with those others to transform the state's dominant political, economic, and moral environment, with its individualist *ethos*, into a political, economic, and moral environment with a more communitarian *ethos* like *Piscopolis*, and thereby help address the crisis of well-being, distress, and dysfunction that has been afflicting the Republic. It is not unreasonable to hope that as we reflect upon our collective experiences with the coronavirus pandemic in a post-Covid-19 world, such a transformation will appear both more attractive and more attainable.

The discussion in various Chapters will also address some important themes and concepts in addition to those mentioned in the above outline, including our proper relationship to our true selves and to God (Chapter 2), liberation from Plato's Cave of illusions and pursuit of the Grail (Chapters 2, 5, 7, and 8), the perspective of Heideggerian phenomenology (Chapters 2, 3, 4, 5, 6, 7, and 8), the nature of good practical reasoning (Chapters 2, 3, and 6), our inescapable mutual interdependence (Chapters 4 and 5), the challenges posed by moral relativism (Chapter 6), the nature and importance of the rule of law and independence of the judiciary and the relationship between law and democracy (Chapter 7), the restoration of civil political conversation (Chapter 8), the concept of cheating (Chapters 3, 4, 5, and 7), and the concept of justice (Chapters 2, 3, 5, 6, and 7).

One final, cautionary note: When *explicating* MacIntyre's thought, although I try always to provide relevant citations to his work, occasionally I interpret (explicitly or implicitly) what he says. When *expanding upon* or *supplementing* his thought, and when *applying* the resulting analysis, I may draw upon (and cite to) the work of others or I may articulate positions of my own. In either case, although the relevant position may not be expressly articulated by MacIntyre himself, unless otherwise noted it nevertheless seems to me to be either implied by or consistent with positions MacIntyre does expressly articulate. While hoping that MacIntyre would approve of these interpretations and positions, I also hope he will forgive any instances in which I may have misinterpreted him, or inappropriately ascribed a given position to him or to his line of thinking.

TWO

COMPOSING THE STORIES OF OUR LIVES

Pursuing Our Good Through Human Flourishing

As indicated in Chapter 1, my thinking about the issues addressed in this book has been greatly influenced by the moral philosopher Alasdair MacIntyre. In particular, I am persuaded that the claims he makes for Thomistic Aristotelianism are largely correct. Over several chapters we will first develop the theoretical justification for these claims (Chapters 2–6). We will then provide a practical justification for them by applying the theory developed in these chapters to the legal profession and the legal conversation in the Republic, thereby illustrating the power of these claims in a real-world context (Chapter 7). After that, we will ask whether and how these claims should inform the political conversation in the Republic (Chapter 8). We begin our consideration of the theoretical justification MacIntyre makes for Thomistic Aristotelianism by exploring in this Chapter MacIntyre's account of how we humans compose the stories of our lives and achieve human flourishing. Then in Chapter 3 we will explore MacIntyre's account of a practice. Participation in various types of practice plays a central role in how we compose our life stories and flourish.

I. Composing the Stories of Our Lives

In his seminal work *After Virtue: A Study in Moral Theory*[1] MacIntyre articulates a "narrative concept of selfhood" in which the self and personal

---

1. ALASDAIR MACINTYRE, AFTER VIRTUE: A STUDY IN MORAL THEORY (3d. ed., 2007) (1981).

identity possess "the unity of a narrative which links birth to life to death."[2] This premodern concept of selfhood is a concomitant of MacIntyre's "particular pre-modern concept of the virtues" as enabling us to make of our lives "one kind of unity rather than another."[3] It is often difficult for us to advertently realize this concept of selfhood and the concomitant concept of the virtues in the conditions of advanced modernity (in both senses of "realize") and thus to "make sense" of our lives in this way.[4] However, it is natural for us to think of ourselves narratively, and doing so is still reflected in many of the ways we think and act even though we may not acknowledge it.[5] Moreover, in a corpus spanning several decades — and most recently in his *Ethics in the Conflicts of Modernity: An Essay on Desire, Practical Reasoning, and Narrative*[6] — MacIntyre has cogently explicated the genealogy of our contemporary moral confusion, and forcefully argued for the superior explanatory and normative power of the traditional conceptions of selfhood and the virtues over any alternative moral approaches in advertently enabling our self-understanding and guiding our decisions and actions.[7]

---

2. *Id.* at 205, 216–18.

3. *Id.* at 203, 205. In this premodern concept of the virtues, "we may understand the virtues as having their function in enabling an individual to make of his or her life one kind of unity rather than another." *Id.* at 203. This is one of three functions of the virtues MacIntyre identifies. We will encounter all three functions in due course.

4. For the reasons why it is often difficult for us to advertently realize these concepts of selfhood and the virtues in the conditions of advanced modernity, both in the sense of envisaging our lives in these terms and in the sense of being able to instantiate them in our actual lives, see *id.* at 204–05 (discussing "the characteristically modern conceptions of selfhood" rooted in the atomistic and individualistic assumptions propagated by modern analytical philosophy, sociology, and existentialism), 226–55 (discussing the concomitant degeneration in the tradition of the virtues and the conceptual transformation of the virtues in modernity). MacIntyre's project seeks to challenge these modern conceptions and to rehabilitate the pre-modern concepts of selfhood and the virtues.

5. *Id.* at 205–06.

6. ALASDAIR MACINTYRE, ETHICS IN THE CONFLICTS OF MODERNITY: AN ESSAY ON DESIRE, PRACTICAL REASONING, AND NARRATIVE (2016).

7. For a brief accessible introduction to MacIntyre's project and some of its initial descriptive and normative claims, see MacIntyre's four-page summary titled *The Claims of After Virtue*, in THE MACINYTRE READER 69–72 (Kelvin Knight, ed., 1998). For an extensive and detailed introduction to, and summary of, MacIntyre's project as it had developed through the late 1990s, see MARK T. MITCHELL, THE LIMITS OF LIBERALISM: TRADITION, INDIVIDUALISM, AND THE CRISIS OF FREEDOM 95–125 (2019). For a similar discussion, in-

A. Our Moral Quest to Live a Good Life in Community

In *After Virtue* MacIntyre makes a foundational twofold claim: In living out the stories of our lives, each of us is the subject of a unique history with "its own peculiar meaning";[8] and yet, we are not the sole authors, but at most only co-authors, of our life stories, which are "part of an interlocking set of narratives" in which "I am part of [others'] story as they are part of mine."[9] This means that our life stories are embedded in the stories of the communities to which we belong.[10] Consequently, we derive our "moral identity" from these communities and their stories, especially from the communities of practice (and their traditions) to which we belong.[11] In short, our moral identity is a social identity and an historical identity; and we can only know what we should do if we can answer the prior question 'Of what story or stories do I find myself a part?'[12] MacIntyre explains that

> I am someone's son or daughter, someone else's cousin or uncle; I am a citizen of this or that city, a member of this or that guild or profession; I belong to this clan, this tribe, this nation. Hence what is good for me has to be the good for one who inhabits these roles. As such, I inherit from the past of my family, my city, my tribe, my nation, a variety of debts, inheritances, rightful expectations and obligations.

---

cluding ways in which MacIntyre clarified, supplemented, or revised some of his initial claims, see Kelvin Knight, *Introduction, in* THE MACINTYRE READER, *supra,* at 1–27; Christopher Stephen Lutz, *Alasdair Chalmers MacIntyre,* Internet Encyclopedia of Philosophy IEP, https://iep.utm.edu/mac-over/; Ted Clayton, *Political Philosophy of Alasdair MacIntyre,* Internet Encyclopedia of Philosophy IEP, https://iep.utm.edu/p-macint/. For a more critical discussion of MacIntyre's project, see JEFFREY STOUT, DEMOCRACY AND TRADITION 118–39 (2004). For a good sense of MacIntyre's current position, see MACINTYRE, CONFLICTS OF MODERNITY, op. cit., at 214–42. For a very helpful summary account integrating many of the elements of MacIntyre's project addressed in the present book, including the elements developed in *Conflicts of Modernity,* published shortly before final submission of the present manuscript to the publisher, see Joseph Dunne, *Learning from MacIntyre about Learning: Finding Room for a Second-Person Perspective?,* 54 J. PHILOS. EDUC. 1147 (2020) (supplementing MacIntyre's conception of personal relationships).

8. MACINTYRE, AFTER VIRTUE, op. cit., at 217.
9. *Id.* at 215, 218.
10. *Id.* at 221.
11. *Id.* at 220–222.
12. *Id.* at 216, 221.

These constitute the given of my life, my moral starting point. This is in part what gives my life its own moral particularity.[13]

Nowadays we might be inclined to say that we have multiple identities, with "identity" being defined as "a deep sense of self in a particular role."[14] Whatever our preferred terminology, in *Conflicts of Modernity* it appears that MacIntyre continues to urge acknowledgment and pursuit of a single, unified identity.[15] Thus, resisting the tendency to live "compartmentalized lives" or, alternatively, "to live somewhat haphazardly," we need to *integrate* the activities in our various roles at any given point in our lives and *rank order* the particular goods or ends they entail[16] — for example, activities and goods in our roles as spouse or significant other, parent, son or daughter, friend, lawyer or law student, member of a worship community and of other local communities, and so on. Otherwise our lives will be marked by excessive conflict and arbitrariness.[17] This means we need to integrate our various "identities" as well; indeed, failure to do so is psychologically unhealthy.[18]

---

13. *Id.* at 220.

14. *See* Patrick Emery Longan, Daisy Hurst Floyd, and Timothy W. Floyd, The Formation of Professional Identity: The Path from Student to Lawyer 4 (2020) (suggesting that we continually add new identities as we acquire new roles in our journey through life).

15. *But see* MacIntyre, Conflicts of Modernity, op. cit., at 240–41 (eschewing pursuit of various issues of personal identity, self-knowledge, and intention in the philosophy of mind in the book).

16. *Id.* at 51–52, 55, 228.

17. MacIntyre, After Virtue, op. cit., at 201–03 (explaining that unless we are able to unify our lives in terms of an overall good, they will be marked by "*too many* conflicts," and "*too much* arbitrariness" in choices, among particular goods).

18. *See* Longan et. al., Professional identity, op. cit., at 4. The authors emphasize the importance of integrating multiple identities for our own psychological health because

> [Y]our senses of yourself in your different roles should not conflict with each
> other in fundamental ways — they should cohere in integrated, mutually en-
> forcing ways. It is unhealthy to be "one person at home" and "another person
> at the office." Psychological research makes it clear that such a lack of integ-
> rity (in the sense of "wholeness") among your various roles is a formula for
> distress and anxiety.

Id. The virtue of integrity in this sense is discussed *infra* notes 88–94 and accompanying text.

In *Conflicts of Modernity* MacIntyre reaches the "single, if complex, theoretical conclusion" that we do well in composing our life stories — we live good lives, we live "rightly and well" — only if and when

(a) We "act to satisfy only those desires whose objects [we] have good reason to desire,"
(b) We are "sound and effective practical reasoners,"
(c) We are "disposed to act as the virtues require," and
(d) We are "directed in [our] actions toward the achievement of [our] final end"[19]

In addition to spending the major part of *Conflicts* elaborating the details of these four propositions or conditions, and addressing actual or potential challengers, MacIntyre also provides four narratives showing how his theoretical conclusion and its four conditions are exemplified "in significant ways" in real lives, specifically in the lives of Vasily Grossman (born in Ukraine, 1905), Sandra Day O'Connor (born in Texas, 1930), C.L.R. James (born in Trinidad, 1901), and Denis Faul (born in Ireland, 1932).[20] According to MacIntyre, such real life examples serve two purposes: They enable us to understand his theoretical conclusion, because understanding "theoretical conclusions in politics and ethics ... is inseparable from knowing how they find application"; and they demonstrate how theoretical generalizations are relevant to self-reflection in real lives, which is especially helpful when those lives have important things to teach us.[21] They serve this latter purpose because the four examples "[are] of agents who are, like the rest of us, not yet fully rational, who are still learning how to act rightly and well, and who therefore are more or less imperfect in all

---

19. *See* MacIntyre, Conflicts of Modernity, op. cit., at 243:

> A single, if complex, theoretical conclusion emerged from the first four chapters of this essay. It is that agents do well only if and when they act to satisfy only those desires whose objects they have good reason to desire, that only agents who are sound and effective practical reasoners so act, that such agents must be disposed to act as the virtues require, and that such agents will be directed in their actions toward the achievement of their final end.

Id. Although the limiting condition "only if and when" expressly refers only to the first proposition, it seems equally applicable to the other three and is so used in the main text.

20. *Id.* at 243–315,

21. *Id.* at 243.

four respects."[22] This suggests that these examples serve a third purpose
as well: not only can such imperfect lives teach us, they can reassure and
encourage us as we pursue our own moral quest to live a good life and do
well in composing our life stories as a narrative unity. And they can help
reconcile us to the reality that our progress will inevitably be gradual, slow,
and uneven — as MacIntyre already told us it would be in *After Virtue*,
when explicitly comparing this halting endeavor to the medieval concept
of a quest:

> The unity of a human life is the unity of a narrative quest. Quests
> sometimes fail, are frustrated, abandoned or dissipated into distrac-
> tion; and human lives may in all these ways also fail. But the only
> criteria for success or failure in a human life as a whole are the crite-
> ria of success or failure in a narrated or to-be-narrated quest.... It is
> in the course of the quest and only through encountering and coping
> with the various particular harms, dangers, temptations and distrac-
> tions which provide any quest with its episodes and incidents that
> the goal of the quest is finally to be understood. A quest is always an
> education both as to the character of that which is sought and in
> self-knowledge.[23]

As MacIntyre stresses, however, the crucial thing about failure is how,
and what, we learn from it.[24] Of course, we are not conscious of our lives as
a narrative or a quest most of the time, and "the narrative structure of our
lives" generally becomes evident only infrequently — for example, when

---

22. *Id.*

23. MacIntyre, After Virtue, op. cit., at 218–19. For a more concrete theoretical understanding of the nature of this quest, including how things can go wrong, see MacIntyre,
Conflicts of Modernity, op. cit., at 1–2, 5, 35–40, 49–59. *See also* Alasdair MacIntyre,
Plain Persons and Moral Philosophy: Rules, Virtues, and Goods (1992), *in* The MacInytre Reader 136–52 (Kelvin Knight, ed., 1998) (describing different episodes in the "failed
quest" of a "plain person," that is, of someone who is not a professional moral philosopher, in the conditions of modernity, mirroring the failed quest of "the larger social order"
in Western culture from the sixteenth century onwards, and urging a response rooted in
Thomistic Aristotelianism). MacIntyre's account of the four lives mentioned above provides
a good experiential sense illustrating this theoretical understanding; *see supra* note 20 and
accompanying text.

24. MacIntyre, Conflicts of Modernity, op. cit., at 40, 223.

we have occasion to tell someone all or part of our life story, or when, at certain critical junctures in our lives, we need to reflect upon how our lives have gone so far in order to make important life-altering decisions or to ask and answer other important questions in life-defining situations. But at these critical junctures "we draw upon our history, upon our knowledge of what we have hitherto done and been, of what we have learned about our capacities and our limitations, about the errors to which we are prone and the resources that we possess."[25]

B. Conditions for Living a Good Life in Community

We must now examine more closely the four conditions in MacIntyre's "single, if complex, theoretical conclusion" we stated above.[26] After considering the first two conditions, we will discuss the fourth condition and then the third. The specific order may be of no great consequence because the four conditions are not independent but are interrelated. Thus: "Spell out any one of them adequately and in so doing you will also have to spell out the other three."[27]

1. Good Reasons for Action

For us to have "good reason" in acting, or in not acting, to satisfy a particular desire, we must be able to do at least three things:

First, we must be able to distinguish between simple desires, including desires for goods, and desires it is *good for us* to satisfy — in other words, to determine which desires and goods conduce to our good and which do not.[28] For example, is it good for me to have an overriding desire for just one thing if failure to achieve it will result in an unhappy life of disappointment, or to want so many different things that I become too distracted and achieve little, or to be so timid in my wants and aspirations that I never adequately use my talents and skills?[29] Or again, is it good for me that I act

---

25. *Id.* at 241. Significantly, MacIntyre observes that "[t]here are different modes of intelligent reflection," and therefore people ask and answer these questions in very different ways — in their actions as well as their words, and in what is unexpressed as well as what is expressed. *Id.*

26. *Supra* note 19 and accompanying text.

27. MacIntyre, Conflicts of Modernity, op. cit., at 243.

28. *Id.* at 32–34, 37–39.

29. *See id.* at 1 (giving these examples).

to satisfy my desire to pursue a particular career, or a life of religious contemplation, or a life of revolutionary politics, or my desire to get married?[30]

Second, we must be able to "make painful choices" among *incompatible*, mutually exclusive desired goods when each good would likely conduce to our good in more or less equal measure.[31] For example, how do I best decide between being a successful athlete and being a useful medical researcher, or between being a good spouse and parent and being a good soldier, when in these cases I cannot be both?[32]

Third, as we have already seen above,[33] we must be able to appropriately rank order *compatible* desired goods when each conduces to our good, in a way that *best* conduces to our good "qua human being" and not just as someone in a particular role. I may know what it is to be good in a particular role and whether it is good for me to be in that role but this does not tell me how it is best for me to arrange my life so that I am living the best life overall.[34] As MacIntyre puts it, "What gives me good reason to integrate the various facets of my life in one way rather than another?"[35] For example, I can be a good lawyer and a good parent and spouse, whether I work as a lawyer for forty hours a week or forty five hours, but what exactly should the balance be? Should I also try to make room in my life to pursue my passion for amateur dramatics or playing in an orchestra? And if I am religious, how much time should I spend in prayer each day or volunteering at my synagogue or mosque or church?[36] And how do the answers to these questions change over time according to circumstances?[37]

---

30. *See id.* at 4 (giving these examples).

31. *Id.* at 222–23.

32. *See id.* at 222 (giving these examples).

33. *Supra* notes 16–17 and accompanying text.

34. MACINTYRE, CONFLICTS OF MODERNITY, op. cit., at 51–52, 55, 227–28. Thus MacIntyre asks: "How is it best for me to live qua human being rather than just qua family member or qua friend or qua student or qua farmer?" *Id.* at 52.

35. *Id.*

36. For another example, see ALASDAIR MACINTYRE, DEPENDENT RATIONAL ANIMALS: WHY HUMAN BEINGS NEED THE VIRTUES 66–67 (1999) ("It may have been best for Gauguin *qua* painter that he went to Tahiti. If it was, it does not follow that it was best for Gauguin *qua* human being or best for him *qua* father"). *But see* MACINTYRE, CONFLICTS OF MODERNITY, op. cit., at 141–46 (acknowledging his discovery that this story about Gauguin is false although it can serve as a fable, and recounting the true story of Oscar Wilde instead).

37. *See* MACINTYRE, CONFLICTS OF MODERNITY, op. cit., at 52 (noting changes over time and through different stages of life). For further discussion of the relationship between de-

MacIntyre is a self-confessed Neo-Aristotelian, or more accurately, a Thomistic Aristotelian (supplementing Aristotle with the insights of St. Thomas Aquinas),[38] and he uses the terms "good," "goods," and "good reasons" accordingly.[39] This means, too, that the goods involved in each of the above three contexts may be individualistic goods, such as the money I earn or the pleasure I derive from a particular activity, or they may be common goods of various types of practices and communities in which we participate, such as "the goods of family, of political society, of workplace, of sports teams, orchestras, and theatre companies," which belong to the relevant community and not the individual alone even though they are essential for my individual good.[40] We will have much more to say about practices and different types of goods in Chapters 3, 4, and 5. We should note, finally, that the word "end" may be substituted for the word "good" when the "good" in question also represents a goal or purpose, as it often does, and we will frequently use it in this sense in this book.

---

sires, goods, and good reasons for action, see *id.* at 8–13. *See also id.* at 2–8 (discussing related matters, including the nature of desires, different ways in which desires may be expressed in actions and motivations, and the relationship between desires and emotions, tastes, affections, biochemical and neurophysiological history, habits, beliefs, and imagination).

38. *Id.* at 31.

39. For discussion of the terms "good," "goods," and "good reasons," and of the types of disagreements about them, including disagreements about rank ordering of "goods," see *id.* at 13–16. For discussion of disagreements between expressivist (and earlier emotivist) accounts of such terms, rooted in psychological stances or states, and Neo-Aristotelian accounts, rooted in claimed facts about human flourishing, as well as their disagreements about how to explain disagreements among differing accounts of these terms, see *id.* at 17–35. At the risk of over-simplification, it seems useful, given their contrasting first premises in psychological states versus claimed facts about human flourishing, to characterize the former accounts as *subjective* and the latter as *objective* (although it should be noted that MacIntyre does not use these terms himself). *See also infra* note 96 (contrasting the dominant *subjective* conception of "happiness" with the *objective* Neo-Aristotelian conception); Chapter 6, notes 100–02, 109 and accompanying text (discussing the expressivist critique of the prevailing secular "Morality" of modernity).

40. *See* MacIntyre, Conflicts of Modernity, op. cit., at 51 (for the quotation). For discussion of common goods of practices in these three contexts, see *id.* at 38, 49 (first context), 223 (second context), 51–52 (third context). For discussion of the differences between individualistic goods belonging to the individual alone and common goods of practices belonging to the relevant community and not just the individual even though they are essential for our individual good, see Chapter 3, notes 73–82 and accompanying text.

2. Good Reasoning

If we are to do these three things well, and thus have "good reason" in acting to satisfy a particular desire, then we must become good "practical reason*ers*."[41] MacIntyre explores the nature and development of good practical reasoning in *Dependent Rational Animals: Why Human Beings Need the Virtues*.[42] Thus, in order to make "judgments about goods ... that we are able to justify rationally to ourselves and others as furnishing us with good reasons for acting in this way rather than that," we must develop our powers as "independent practical reasoners."[43] Specifically, this means that we must develop three essential abilities or capacities:

> [T]he ability to evaluate, modify, or reject our own practical judg-
> ments, to ask, that is, whether what we take to be good reasons for
> action really are sufficiently good reasons, *and* the ability to imagine
> realistically alternative possible futures, so as to be able to make ra-
> tional choices between them, *and* the ability to stand back from our
> desires, so as to be able to enquire rationally what the pursuit of our
> good here and now requires and how our desires must be directed
> and, if necessary, reeducated, if we are to attain it.[44]

These three capacities are interrelated. As MacIntyre explains, "The relationship between the three dimensions is complex. But they all contribute
to a single process of development and a significant degree of failure in
any one of the three areas will be liable to produce or reinforce significant
failure in the others."[45]

The word "independent" in the term "independent practical reasoners"
means that we no longer simply accept what we are taught about goods by
others.[46] It does *not* mean that we henceforth reason entirely alone, outside

---

41. Understandably, then, MacIntyre stresses the role of practical reason in each of these three contexts. *See* the sources cited *supra* in notes 28, 31, 34.

42. ALASDAIR MACINTYRE, DEPENDENT RATIONAL ANIMALS: WHY HUMAN BEINGS NEED THE VIRTUES (1999).

43. *Id.* at 71. *See also id.* at 67 ("Human beings need to learn to understand themselves as practical reasoners about goods, about what on particular occasions it is best for them to do and about how it is best for them to live out their lives").

44. *Id.* at 83.

45. *Id.* at 76.

46. *Id.* at 71.

of relationship with others. To the contrary, in MacIntyre's Neo-Aristotelian account, practical reasoning typically, and "by its nature," involves "reasoning together with others, generally within some determinate set of social relationships."[47] We clearly rely on others when pursuing the common goods of various practices and communities in which we participate.[48] But we usually also rely on others when pursuing our individual goods.[49]

Becoming an independent practical reasoner is a status we generally achieve with the help of others by early adulthood, and it serves us throughout our lives even though we may continue to need others to help sustain us in exercising our reasoning powers.[50] In Chapter 5 we will consider more closely how we develop and are sustained in these powers of independent practical reasoning.

3. Our Final End and the Truth of Our Lives

In judging whether we have "good reason" to satisfy a particular desire through the exercise of good practical reasoning, we should be guided by pursuit of our "final end" or "final good" as we currently understand it.[51]

---

47. *Id.* at 107.

48. MacIntyre, Conflicts of Modernity, op. cit., at 51–52.

49. MacIntyre, Rational Animals, op. cit., at 136, 161. *See also* MacIntyre, Conflicts of Modernity, op. cit., at 51–52 (explaining that even though the ultimate decision regarding what place a particular activity will have in our individual lives may be ours alone, the place we are *able* to give to that activity, and the goods we are able to achieve through it, often depends on what place this activity has in the lives of others and the extent to which we cooperate).

50. *See* MacIntyre, Rational Animals, op. cit., at 96–97 (reiterating the three abilities of an independent practical reasoner and observing that even after "we finally have become independent practical reasoners, generally early in our adult lives ... we continue to the end of our lives to need others to sustain us in our practical reasoning" by having friends or "expert coworkers" in "particular practices" correct our intellectual or moral mistakes).

51. *See* MacIntyre, Conflicts of Modernity, op. cit., at 52–53, 55, 227–29 (characterizing the "final end" or "final good" as "the end of rational activity as such" pursued by a rational agent at very different stages and in very different activities of life, by reference to which she can resolve "a painful conflict between what she wants most on some particular occasion and how she judges it best for her to act," and which we "aim at ... in the course of aiming at achievement of our other ends"). Although MacIntyre presents this characterization in the context of discussing the third type of judgment, its formulation and logic strongly suggest that it applies to all three types of judgment. *See also* MacIntyre, Rational Animals, op. cit., at 85–86 (discussing the ability "to put into question the relationship

This good is a good of a different order from other goods, does not compete with them, and is not a means to some other good that lies beyond it.[52] Instead, other goods are a means to the final good that is our final end, although we do value these other goods in themselves too.[53]

MacIntyre's underlying premise is that although our life stories in community are unpredictable, they are also "partially teleological;" as such, they "have a certain form which projects itself towards our future" and they "aspire to truth."[54] Thus, when we as rational agents seek to realize the narrative unity of our own individual lives in all their unique particularity (again in both senses of "realize"), we are seeking the truth about these lives (including the truth about our mistakes and failures), albeit we undertake this seeking necessarily in relationship with others.[55] But we can only realize the narrative unity of our lives, by appropriately and truthfully integrating our various activities and ordering the particular goods or ends they entail, if "each of us discovers in our lives a certain kind of directedness toward a final end that is our own, toward perfecting and completing the lives that are our own, by living out what in terms of our particular abilities and circumstances we judge to be the best possible life for us,"[56] recognizing of course that these activities, goods, abilities, and circumstances, as well as our understanding of ends and goods, necessarily change over the course of our lives.[57]

The "final end that is our own," then, is partly subjective and partly objective. It is subjective in that the particular shape of our lives depends on "our particular abilities and circumstances"; and it is objective in that this particular shape (and the place in our lives of all the activities and goods that give it this particular shape) are ordered toward a "final good," an "ultimate human good" — the human *telos*, to use the Greek philosophical term — that is rationally desirable as the measure of all other goods in our

---

between my present set of desires and motives and my good. What constitutes a good reason for my doing this rather than that, for my acting from this particular desire rather than that, is that my doing this rather than that serves my good, will contribute to my flourishing *qua* human being").

52. MacIntyre, Conflicts of Modernity, op. cit., at 229.

53. *Id.*

54. MacIntyre, After Virtue, op. cit., at 215–16.

55. MacIntyre, Conflicts of Modernity, op. cit., at 51–52, 54, 56–57.

56. *Id.* at 52–54, 229.

57. *Id.* at 52, 314.

lives.[58] Following Geoff Moore, we might then want to read MacIntyre as conceiving of the "final end that is our own" as our own individual *telos*.[59] As we will see in Part II of this Chapter, this *telos* is to be understood in terms of human flourishing.

4. Nature and Role of the Virtues

If we are to judge whether we have "good reason" in acting to satisfy our desires, through the exercise of good practical reasoning, and guided by pursuit of our *telos* as we currently understand it, we must exhibit certain virtues. Thus, "the virtues are... those [moral and intellectual] qualities that enable agents to identify both what goods are at stake in any particular situation and their relative importance in that situation *and* how that particular agent must act for the sake of the good and the best."[60] Consequently, "[t]o be a good practical reasoner is closely related to being a good human being,"[61] and a "failure in reasoning" is often at the same time "a failure in the exercise of the virtues."[62] There are several different kinds

---

58. *Id.* at 53, 86. Thus

As Aquinas argues powerfully ... , life aimed at the achievement of that final good cannot be a life whose principal aim is the attainment of pleasure, power, political honor, money, or physical, intellectual, moral, aesthetic, or even spiritual excellence, although every one of these is a genuine good. For these are among the goods that have to be ordered.

Id. at 53. *See also id.* at 229 (Aquinas' argument that the final good "cannot consist in the acquisition or possession of money, political honors, reputation, power, health, or pleasure, all of them good in their due place, but none of them our final good").

59. *See generally* GEOFF MOORE, VIRTUE AT WORK: ETHICS FOR INDIVIDUALS, MANAGERS, AND ORGANIZATIONS (2017). Moore speaks of "our own *telos*" throughout his book. *See, e.g., id.* at 41, 59, 79.

60. MACINTYRE, CONFLICTS OF MODERNITY, op. cit., at 190. *See also id.* at 38 (discussing Aristotle's concept of *prohairesis* "as desire informed by reason or as reason informed by desire," thereby promoting human flourishing, and the importance to *prohairesis* of being "rightly disposed by [the] virtues"); MACINTYRE, RATIONAL ANIMALS, op. cit., at 87 (stressing that a child must develop the intellectual and moral virtues "first to redirect and transform her or his desires, and subsequently to direct them consistently towards the goods of the different stages of her or his life"), 97 (emphasizing that "some range of intellectual and moral virtues" is needed to "first achieve and then continue in the exercise of practical reasoning").

61. MACINTYRE, CONFLICTS OF MODERNITY, op. cit., at 190.

62. *Id.* at 191.

of failure.[63] To be educated into the virtues we must recognize the general possibility of such error and combat those errors to which we may be particularly susceptible due to our temperament or social role, including errors due to illusion or various types of unconscious and distorting biases that also represent "obstacles to practical rationality."[64]

The philosopher Nancy Snow provides the following generic definition of a virtue:

> Virtues are character states or dispositions that are entrenched in the sense of being deep-seated parts of someone's personality, and are temporally enduring. Virtues reliably give rise to virtuous actions, that is, actions that are motivated by the desire to act virtuously in the circumstances, and are guided by practical rationality. Virtues in this sense are formed... through habituation.... Ideally, specific virtues, such as courage, generosity, and compassion, become well-integrated components of personality, forming what we would call "character." Practical rationality, as well as appropriate motivation, is essential for virtuous action, yet at some point, virtues should become "second nature," in the sense that possessors of virtue should be able to act virtuously without the need for conscious deliberation about whether and how to act.[65]

And MacIntyre describes the particular, Aristotelian understanding of virtues:

> Virtues are dispositions not only to act in particular ways, but also to *feel* in particular ways. To act virtuously is not, as Kant was later to think, to act against inclination; it is to act from inclination formed

---

63. Examples of such failures include "lack of imagination about the range of [individual and common] goods" involved in a situation, including goods whose achievement may be furthered or impeded in the future, as well as "careless or inept assessment of the harms and dangers to be confronted, insensitivity to the needs of others or to one's own needs, overrating or underrating one's own abilities or the abilities of others, and so on." *Id.*

64. *Id.* at 191–92.

65. Nancy E. Snow, *How Habits Make Us Virtuous, in* DEVELOPING THE VIRTUES: INTEGRATING PERSPECTIVES 135 (Julia Annas, Darcia Narvaez & Nancy E. Snow, eds., 2016).

by the cultivation of the virtues. Moral education is an 'education sentimentale.'[66]

A central goal of MacIntyre's project has been to articulate and defend "a unitary core concept of the virtues" in the Western moral tradition of the virtues.[67] In a pithy description of this "unitary core concept," MacIntyre explains that the virtues are "[those] qualities enabling their possessors to achieve the goods internal to practices,... the goods of a whole human life[,] and the goods of those types of communities in and through which the goods of individual lives are characteristically achieved."[68] We will encounter the first function of the virtues in Chapter 3 and the third function in Chapters 4 and 5. Here, however, we encounter the second function, that is, the role of the virtues in enabling us to understand and pursue our own individual good — our own individual *telos* — as we pursue our moral quests to live a good life and do well in composing our life stories as a narrative unity. Specifically, in this role the virtues are "those dispositions which will... sustain us in the relevant kind of quest for the good, by enabling us to overcome the harms, dangers, temptations and distractions which we encounter, and which will furnish us with increasing

---

66. MACINTYRE, AFTER VIRTUE, op. cit., at 149 (emphasis added). *Cf* ANTHONY T. KRONMAN, THE LOST LAWYER: FAILING IDEALS OF THE LEGAL PROFESSION 75–76 (1993) (explaining that although some "character traits" may have an intellectual dimension, a character trait is essentially an "affective habit" or "a feeling one experiences, without deliberate effort, in a recurrent situation of some kind," provided it is not too trivial (such as love of brandy) or too widely shared (such as fear of death).

67. *See* MACINTYRE, AFTER VIRTUE, op. cit., at 186 (stating this goal). This unitary core concept is a traditional, pre-modern conception of the virtues. For MacIntyre's discussion of degeneration in the tradition of the virtues represented by modern conceptions of the virtues, see *id.* at 226–55. As discussed earlier, *supra* note 4, MacIntyre seeks to dispel these modern conceptions, or rather misconceptions, and to rehabilitate the traditional, pre-modern conception.

68. Alasdair MacIntyre, *A Partial Response to My Critics, in* AFTER MACINTYRE: CRITICAL PERSPECTIVES ON THE WORK OF ALASDAIR MACINTYRE 288 (John Horton & Susan Mendus, eds., 1994). *See also id.* at 284 (Virtues are those qualities that "enable the achievement of three distinct kinds of good: those internal to practices, those which are the goods of an individual life and those which are the goods of community"); MACINTYRE, AFTER VIRTUE, op. cit., at 191, 194–95, 201, 203, 219–20, 221–23 (elaborating on these three functions of the virtues).

self-knowledge and increasing knowledge of the good."[69] But we should always remember that we pursue our individual *telos* within those communities, especially communities of practice, from which we derive our moral identity.[70] This means, of course, that the other two functions of the virtues are also relevant for success in our life quests.[71] In turn, this means that the discussion of the virtues in Chapters 3, 4 and 5 are also relevant for the present discussion. This makes perfect sense because, although analytically distinct, all three functions of the virtues are nevertheless inextricably related in MacIntyre's "*unitary* core concept of the virtues."[72] Thus, we need the virtues to pursue our own individual good — our own *telos* — in our life quests, as well as the common goods of those practices and communities in which we participate that are integral to that quest.

Virtues necessary for all three functions include the four cardinal virtues of courage, temperateness, justice, and prudence, especially as they bear on good practical reasoning.[73] With regard to the function and role

---

69. *Id.* at 219.

70. *See supra* notes 8–14 and accompanying text.

71. And so, in the passage containing the preceding quote, *supra* note 69 and accompanying text, immediately following the passage addressing the unity of our narrative quests, quoted *supra* note 23 and accompanying text, MacIntyre states:

> The virtues therefore are to be understood as those dispositions which will not only sustain practices and enable us to achieve the goods internal to practices, but which will also sustain us in the relevant kind of quest for the good, by enabling us to overcome the harms, dangers, temptations and distractions which we encounter, and which will furnish us with increasing self-knowledge and increasing knowledge of the good. The catalogue of the virtues will therefore include the virtues required to sustain the kind of households and the kind of political communities in which men and women can seek for the good together and the virtues necessary for philosophical enquiry about the character of the good.

MacIntyre, After Virtue, op. cit., at 219.

72. *Id.* at 186 (emphasis added); *see also supra* notes 67–68 and accompanying text for earlier discussion of this "unitary concept."

73. *See* MacIntyre, Conflicts of Modernity, op. cit., at 215–16 (emphasizing the role of virtues such as justice, courage, truthfulness, and prudence in providing reasons by which agents justify their decisions and actions, and avoid "becom[ing] victims of their own disordered or inadequately ordered desires" and thus "unable to achieve those common and individual goods toward which they are directed by their nature as rational agents"); MacIntyre, Rational Animals, op. cit., at 120 (explaining that virtues such as "justice, temperateness, truthfulness, courage, and the like" not only "enable[] us to move from dependence on the reasoning powers of others, principally our parents and teachers, to inde-

of the virtues under consideration here, MacIntyre discusses the example of a "reflective agent" who "experiences a painful conflict between what she wants most on some particular occasion and how she judges it best for her to act."[74] She will ask first, whether what she desires is "genuinely desirable," next, what are the arguments for acting otherwise, and then, in deciding between the alternatives, how the competing goods implicated in the object of her desire and in her judgment should be "rank ordered by a rational agent exercising the virtues of temperateness, courage, justice, and prudence" if she is to act in furtherance of "her final good, as she now understands it."[75]

Most readers are likely already familiar with the four cardinal virtues and we will encounter them throughout the book. However, a brief reminder about the general nature of each one may nevertheless be helpful here. André Comte-Sponville provides some useful definitions and explanations of these four virtues (and several others) in his book *A Small Treatise on the Great Virtues*.[76] The virtue of *courage* is "the capacity to overcome fear."[77] It is "universally admired" although its precise forms and content can vary because "each civilization has its fears and its corresponding forms of courage."[78] Thus, courage can operate in the physical, intellectual, moral, or even psychological spheres. The virtue of *temperance* or *temperateness* is "moderation in sensual desires," and it "allows us to be masters of our pleasure instead of becoming its slaves."[79] We will follow MacIntyre, however, in making explicit that this virtue requires the

---

pendence in our practical reasoning," they "also enable us to participate in relationships of giving and receiving through which our ends as practical reasoners are to be achieved"). We will address relationships of giving and receiving in Chapter 5, Part II, Sections C, D, and E.

74. MacIntyre, Conflicts of Modernity, op. cit., at 54–55.

75. *Id*. at 55.

76. André Comte-Sponville, A Small Treatise on the Great Virtues: The Uses of Philosophy in Everyday Life (1996; tr. Catherine Temerson 2001). The other virtues the author addresses in separate chapters, in addition to courage, temperance, justice, and prudence, include politeness, fidelity, generosity, compassion, mercy, gratitude, humility, simplicity, tolerance, purity, gentleness, good faith, humor, and love. As Comte-Sponville does not believe in God, he does not devote separate chapters to the theological virtues of faith and hope although he does address the theological virtue of charity in his discussion of *agape* love. *Id*. at 286–88.

77. *Id*. at 44.

78. *Id*.

79. *Id*. at 39.

disciplining not only of "desires" but also of "aversions and dispositions."[80] The virtue of *justice* involves giving everyone what is "due" to them, either in the sense of what is "lawful" or in the sense of what is "fair" (equal or justifiably unequal), which may of course not be the same thing at all, as in the case, for example, of an unjust or unfair law.[81]

Courage, temperance, and justice are moral virtues. By contrast, *prudence* or *practical wisdom* is an intellectual virtue, and it is a "precondition" for and "governs" the other virtues because "without it, we cannot know what use to make of the other virtues or how to attain the goal (the good) they put before us."[82] As Comte-Sponville strikingly puts it, "[w]ithout prudence, the other virtues are merely good intentions that pave the way to hell."[83] Indeed, "prudence is the disposition that makes it possible to deliberate correctly on what is good or bad for [humans] (not in itself but in the world as it is, and not in general but in specific situations) and through such deliberation to act appropriately."[84] As such, we will follow MacIntyre again in acknowledging that prudence or practical wisdom is *both* an intellectual virtue *and* a moral virtue.[85] We will elaborate further

---

80. *See, e.g.,* ALASDAIR MACINTYRE, WHOSE JUSTICE? WHICH RATIONALITY? 40 (1988) (referring to "a directed disciplining and transformation of the desires, aversions, and dispositions of the self" when contrasting how the virtue of temperateness operates in the perspective of goods of excellence with how it operates in the perspective of goods of effectiveness). Goods of excellence and goods of effectiveness are discussed further in Chapter 3. *See also* MACINTYRE, RATIONAL ANIMALS, op. cit., at 87–88 (observing that "[t]o have this virtue is not only to know how to avoid the extremes of self-indulgent and even addictive appetite, on the one hand, and of an unappreciative and insensitive puritanism on the other, but also to do so, as Aristotle remarked, with an eye to our own particular circumstances").

81. COMTE-SPONVILLE, GREAT VIRTUES, op. cit., at 62–63, 74, 302 n42.

82. *Id.* at 32.

83. *Id.* at 31.

84. *Id.* at 32.

85. MACINTYRE, CONFLICTS OF MODERNITY, op. cit., at 49–50 (referring to "the moral virtues" as well as "a habit of good practical judgment, the moral and intellectual virtue of prudence"). For MacIntyre's own stress on the central, if not overriding, importance of prudence among the virtues, see *id.* at 49–50, 74, 118, 180–81, 215–18; MACINTYRE, RATIONAL ANIMALS, op. cit., at 106, 111, 125. *See also id.* at 76–77, 92 (emphasizing excellence as an independent practical reasoner and the virtues necessary for such excellence). *See also* MACINTYRE, WHOSE JUSTICE?, op. cit., at 197:

> *Prudentia* perfects those who possess it by providing the kind of control over one's actions which is required for all the virtues.... It is exhibited both in the carrying through of practical reasoning and in the actions which follow

upon the nature of this "governing" virtue in Chapter 3, where we will refer to it as "the master virtue," and also explain why only those who have become independent practical reasoners are capable of practical wisdom.[86]

Before we leave this discussion of the cardinal virtues, we should also note Geoff Moore's explanation for why they are called such:

> [T]he Platonic virtues of Temperance (self-control), Fortitude (courage), Justice, and Practical Wisdom ... are known as *cardinal* virtues (from the Greek for a hinge), in the sense that they provide a core set of virtues from which other sub-virtues might be derived. So, for example, honesty might be understood as a sub-virtue of justice, in that being honest is a way of being fair or just to others.[87]

---

from right reasoning.... Its exercise is inconsistent with overhasty, unconsidered, inconstant, and negligent or careless action, and equally with those simulacra of the virtue of prudence — worldly good sense, caution, and cunning — which are vices and sins ...

Id. (discussing Aquinas' account of prudence).

86. *See* Chapter 3, Part II, Section B. 1 and 3. While the virtue of prudence is distinctive in that it is a precondition for other virtues, Comte-Sponville explains that the virtue of justice is distinctive among the cardinal virtues in another, important respect:

Of the four cardinal virtues, justice is probably the only one that is an absolute good in itself. Prudence, temperance, and courage are virtues only when they serve good ends, either directly or else by furthering other virtues — justice for example — that transcend them or motivate them. Prudence, temperance, and courage in the service of evil or injustice would not be virtues, merely talents or qualities of mind or temperament, to use Kant's expression.

Comte-Sponville, op. cit., at 61.

87. Moore, Virtue at Work, op. cit., at 39–40 (also noting that "Aristotle ... included many other virtues such as wittiness, friendliness, modesty, and magnanimity (generosity of spirit) in his list of virtues"). *See also* MacIntyre, Whose Justice?, op. cit., at 198:

What are accounted other virtues are all in some way parts or aspects of the cardinal virtues, and someone may possess one of the cardinal virtues while not yet having learned how it needs to be exercised in all of those particular areas which are each the province of some one of the subordinate virtues.

Id. (discussing Aquinas' account of the cardinal virtues). Moore also stresses the related point regarding the unity of the virtues:

[I]n the ideal, the truly virtuous individual will possess all of the virtues; there will be a sense of unity about them, a harmony such that their whole life is directed towards their *telos*, and this will occur, hard as it may be, only if all the virtues are possessed and exercised in concert.

In addition to the cardinal virtues, in our life quests we will also come to appreciate the unique role of the virtues of "integrity" and "constancy" in seeking to live our lives as a unity.[88] The virtues of constancy and integrity are closely related to one another. In Moore's pithy formulation: "If integrity is the virtue for consistency across all activities at any particular point in time, then constancy is the virtue which enables consistency over time."[89] MacIntyre elaborates on these two virtues as follows:

> Constancy, like integrity, sets limits to flexibility of character. Where integrity requires of those who possess it, that they exhibit the same moral character in different social contexts, constancy requires that those who possess it pursue the same goods through extended periods of time, not allowing the requirements of changing social contexts to distract them from their commitments or to redirect them.[90]

And he elaborates further upon the virtue of integrity:

> To have integrity is to refuse to be, to have educated oneself so that one is no longer able to be, one kind of person in one social context, while quite another in other contexts. It is to have set inflexible limits to one's adaptability to the roles that one may be called upon to play.[91]

As Moore explains, this means that "we are the same person at work as we are at home, as we are when we are engaging with a practice like medicine (as a patient if not as a nurse, doctor, or consultant)," although we could "appropriately emphasize particular aspects of our character in particular circumstances."[92] Thus, "we are likely to be more efficient at work and more

---

MOORE, VIRTUE AT WORK, *supra*, at 40. *See also* MACINTYRE, WHOSE JUSTICE?, *supra*, at 198 ("Education into each of the cardinal virtues requires the others [although] such education will, while it is in progress, be uneven").

88. MACINTYRE, AFTER VIRTUE, op. cit., at 203, 219.

89. MOORE, VIRTUE AT WORK, op. cit., at 126.

90. *See id.* at 80, 126 (quoting Alasdair MacIntyre, *Social structures and their threats to moral agency*, Philosophy, 74, 3: 318).

91. *See id.* at 81, 126 (quoting Alasdair MacIntyre, *Social structures*, op. cit., at 3: 317).

92. *Id. at 81.*

relaxed at home" but "we would be no less just, no less caring, [and] no less patient."[93] And MacIntyre stresses that in addition to "the qualities of reliability and dependability and the virtue of truthfulness," which are crucial from early life on if good friends and others are to help us develop our virtues and character as fully rational agents, we also need the virtues of integrity and constancy so that they can help us judge "the overall directedness or lack of directedness" in our lives.[94]

II. Achieving Our Good Through Human Flourishing

Success in our life quests — success in composing the stories of our lives so as to satisfy the four conditions for living a good life in community and achieve our final end, our individual *telos* — results in, and indeed consists in, living lives which are justifiably and genuinely excellent, satisfying, and fulfilling; in living lives which are "happy" in the Aristotelian sense of "happiness" (*eudaimonia* for Aristotle, *beatitudo* for Aquinas), that is, "doing well" or "living well."[95] Such *eudaimonia* is a state in which "we finally can have good reason to be satisfied with the outcomes of our lives" when we look back on them, because "we are able to retell the story of our lives, but now truthfully" including being able "to take the true measure of all our failures."[96]

---

93. *Id.* Regarding the importance of integrating our multiple identities through the virtue of integrity, see also *supra* notes 14–18 and accompanying text.

94. MacIntyre, Conflicts of Modernity, op. cit., at 311–14.

95. *Id.* at 52, 54, 229–30. On *eudaimonia* as "doing well" or "living well," see MacIntyre, After Virtue, op. cit., at 148 (referring to Aristotle's notion of *eudaimonia* as "the state of being well and doing well in being well"); Aristotle, The Ethics of Aristotle: The Nicomachean Ethics 63–64, 66–67, 73–76 (J.A.K. Thomson trans., rev. Hugh Tredennick 1976) (the good, the *telos* or "final end," of human beings is "happiness" in the sense of doing well or living well, and this consists in "an activity of [the rational] soul in accordance with virtue").

96. MacIntyre, Conflicts of Modernity, op. cit., at 54. *See also id.* at 193–202 where MacIntyre contrasts (a) the dominant *subjective* conception of happiness as a psychological state of positive feelings in which one is "pleased with, contented with, satisfied with some aspect of one's life … or with one's life as a whole" because one's desires, ordered and expressed as a set of preferences, have been satisfied and one is free of discontentedness, grave apprehensions, and fears, with (b) the *objective* Neo-Aristotelian conception of happiness as requiring an objectively "good reason" or "sufficiently good reason" for feeling pleased, contented, or satisfied with one's life because one is living a life in which "one's powers, physical, moral, aesthetic, and intellectual are developed and educated so that they are directed

For the later, Thomistic Aristotelian MacIntyre, and perhaps even for the earlier Neo-Aristotelian MacIntyre, such a "happy" life is a life of human flourishing, in which we "function well" as human beings. This claim becomes more definite as MacIntyre's views evolve from *After Virtue*[97] through *Dependent Rational Animals*[98] to *Ethics in the Conflicts of Modernity*[99] (although as we will see at the end of Section A below, MacIntyre

---

toward achieving the ends of a rational agent" even though this may entail some justifiable grief, regret, and fear. *Id.* MacIntyre observes that the neo-Aristotelian conception continues to be "embodied in and presupposed by the utterances and activities of nonphilosophical plain persons ... in our everyday practices even when they are inconsistent with the way in which we represent ourselves to ourselves." *Id.* at 201–02. Consequently, unhappiness in the dominant conception is often appropriate and "[t]he good life, the fulfilled life, may be and often is unhappy by the standards of happiness studies." *Id* at 202. Regarding use of the terms *subjective* and *objective*, see *supra* note 39.

97. *See* MACINTYRE, AFTER VIRTUE, op. cit., at 148 (referring to Aristotle's notion of *eudaimonia* as "the state of being well and doing well in being well, of a man's being well-favored in himself and in relation to the divine"), 162–63 (noting disagreements about the nature of "human flourishing and well-being" and the need for any adequate teleological account to "provide ... some clear and defensible account of the *telos*").

98. *See* MACINTYRE, RATIONAL ANIMALS, op. cit., at 112–13 (discussing "flourishing as the human *telos*"). *See also id.* at 64, 67–68, 71 (asserting that to flourish as a member of its particular species, a plant or an animal needs "to develop the distinctive powers that it possesses *qua* member of that species," and this means that humans need to develop their distinctive powers of reasoning and become independent practical reasoners), 66–67, 78–79 (different ascriptions of the term "good" are oriented to the notion of flourishing), 76–77 (referring to "specifically human modes of flourishing" in "very different types of culture and economy and therefore in very different contexts of practice: hunting, farming, mercantile, industrial"), 86 (explaining, when discussing how we become independent practical reasoners, that a good reason for acting from a particular desire is that the action "serves my good, will contribute to my flourishing *qua* human being"), 117 (discussing how market relationships can "contribute to overall flourishing"), 119 (acting "for the sake of ... common goods in order to achieve our flourishing as rational animals").

99. *See* MACINTYRE, CONFLICTS OF MODERNITY, op. cit., at 28–29, 31 (advocating a Neo-Aristotelian and Thomistic account of human flourishing, identifying four components in Aristotle's "core conception of human flourishing," and explaining that "[Aristotle's] core thought is that to flourish is to function well" and that, like machines and nonhuman animals, so also "human agents and human societies ... function well or badly"), 59–62 (contrasting expressivists and Neo-Aristotelians as moral agents with respect to the "narratives of [the]practical history ... through which [they] make themselves as desiring and reasoning animals intelligible to themselves and others," and explaining that "[t]he histories of expressivist agents are primarily histories of their affections, of what they have cared about and of how they came to care about what they now care about" whereas "[t]he histories of

seems to add significant qualification and nuance in this last work).[100] Exactly *how* we flourish, or "function well," as human beings will inevitably depend on the particular culture we inhabit as well as on the particularities of our individual lives even in the same culture, and especially on our differing abilities and circumstances[101] (so that, for example, A would flourish as a doctor but would fail to flourish as a lawyer, and B would flourish as a lawyer but would fail to flourish as a doctor). In all cases, however, we can flourish only by acting as rational agents *to realize our potentialities and develop our powers so as to achieve those goods* that "complete and perfect" our lives,[102] although we may have rational disagreements with one another "about what human flourishing consists in in this or that set of circumstances."[103]

NeoAristotelians are histories of how they succeeded or failed in becoming better judges of what it is for a human being to flourish qua human being and to act accordingly"), 72–76 (discussing rational agents' growing awareness of the facts of human flourishing as they proceed through life and reflect on their reasons for action), 114–15 (discussing the expressivist mistake of assuming that just as it is not possible to establish the "truth" of the moral system of capitalist modernity, the same is true of Neo-Aristotelian claims that judgments about human flourishing can be confirmed by observation as true or false), 82, 107 (referring to virtues and norms of justice necessary for flourishing), 122–23 (discussing how "the characteristic habits of thought of modernity" make it difficult for producers and consumers "to distinguish between what is or could be of genuine value for their lives and their flourishing and what the market invites them to value"), 169, 176, 177, 180, 182 (referring to the flourishing of individuals, families, households, workplaces, and local communities), 224 (noting that human flourishing as rational animals is not restricted to Aristotle's *polis*), 312 (observing that "very different lives [can] give expression to one and the same conception of human flourishing," as demonstrated by the "large differences between the four lives" of Vasily Grossman, Sandra Day O'Connor, C.L.R. James, and Denis Faul whose narratives illustrate the theoretical conclusion MacIntyre reaches in the book). For discussion of these four illustrative narratives, see *supra* notes 20–23 and accompanying text.

100. *See infra* notes 116–19 and accompanying text.

101. MacIntyre, Conflicts of Modernity, op. cit., at 27–28, 30–31, 39, 74.

102. *Id.* at 27–28, 30–31, 39–40.

103. *Id.* at 25–26 (observing that "rational enquiry into and consequent disagreement about what human flourishing consists in in this or that set of circumstances is itself one of the marks of human flourishing"). For a very recent and provocative treatment of the concept of human flourishing, see Kristján Kristjánsson, Flourishing As the Aim of Education: A Neo-Aristotelian View (2020). Kristjánsson "offer[s] a new complex and multi-layered conception of *enchanted flourishing* to replace Aristotle's own (arguably) disenchanted conception." Instead, Kristjánsson's conception "postulat[es] that the flourishing

A. Nature and Conditions of Human Flourishing

Regarding the relevant types of goods, MacIntyre identifies a set of at least eight universal goods that "contribut[e] to a good life, whatever one's culture or social order" and that we can reasonably regard, therefore, as constitutive of human flourishing:[104]

- Good health and a standard of living—food, clothing, shelter—that frees one from destitution;
- Good family relationships;
- Sufficient education to make good use of opportunities to develop one's powers;
- Work that is productive and rewarding;
- Good friends;
- Time beyond one's work for activities good in themselves, athletic, aesthetic, intellectual;
- The ability of a rational agent to order one's life; and
- The ability of a rational agent to learn from one's mistakes.[105]

We should note several points about this catalogue of constituent goods. First, it is a non-exhaustive catalogue; there may be other constituent goods that MacIntyre has not mentioned.[106] For example, although the reference to work that is "rewarding" gestures in this direction, a good that arguably should be more clearly identified is having a sense of purpose and meaning in one's life.[107]

---

agent must have a clear personal sense of meaning or purpose and engage with transpersonal moral ideals." *Id.* at 2.

104. MACINTYRE, CONFLICTS OF MODERNITY, op. cit., at 222. Although MacIntyre does not explicitly state here that these goods are constituent goods of human flourishing, he does claim that they are "constitutive of the good life," and he also seems to allude to such goods elsewhere as "contribut[ing] to our flourishing." *See id.* at 143–44 (discussing aesthetic goods). It therefore seems a reasonable inference to regard these goods as constitutive of human flourishing. In cataloguing these goods, I quote from MacIntyre although formatting the relevant passage as a bulleted list.

105. *Id.* at 222.

106. Thus MacIntyre says that these constitutive goods "are at least eightfold." *Id.*

107. Especially given the centrality of this notion to the argument of this book, I am indebted to Jack Sammons for urging me to make this point explicit in the list of constituent

Second, although it is possible for us to flourish despite the absence of one or more of the constituent goods, we will have to be resourceful in coping with the difficulties resulting from their absence, including recognizing necessary and possible changes in ourselves or in the social and institutional order we inhabit.[108]

Third, the catalogue seems to presuppose the four components of Aristotle's "core conception of human flourishing," specifying various types of human powers, abilities, and capacities, which can perhaps all be regarded as our "powers" broadly understood:

> First, Aristotle recognized the full range of human powers, physical, perceptual, emotional, rational, political, moral, and aesthetic. Secondly, he identified as the distinctively human powers those . . . made possible by the possession of language, notably those powers of practically and theoretically rational agents that enable us not only to reflect on what we are doing and saying or are about to say or do but also to redirect our activities and our enquiries as reason prescribes. Thirdly, there are too those distinctively human abilities, the exercise of which also requires language, that enable us to associate cooperatively with others in ways not open to nonhuman animals. Human beings are by their nature both rational and political animals, and they achieve rational agency in and through their political relationships. Fourthly, our nature is such that we find ourselves directed by our upbringing, if we have been adequately educated, toward ends that we take to be goods and we have some conception, even if initially inchoate, of what it would be for someone to achieve those ends in such a way that their life would be a perfected human life, that they might justly be called *eudaimōn*.[109]

Arguably, it should be made explicit that aesthetic creativity — creativity "in service to beauty in all its many forms and otherwise purposeless al-

---

goods. Sammons Email (September 22, 2020) [on file with author]. *See also* Kristjánsson, Flourishing As the Aim of Education, *supra* note 103.

108. MacIntyre, Conflicts of Modernity, op. cit., at 222.

109. *Id.* at 28–29.

though others may find other purposes in it" — is also among the distinctively human powers.[110]

Fourth, those who flourish or are on the way to flourishing "have those qualities of mind and character that enable them, in the company of others and through their relationships with others, to develop their powers, so that they achieve those goods that complete and perfect their lives."[111] It would seem that by "qualities of mind and character" MacIntyre is referring especially to the intellectual and moral virtues.[112]

Fifth, as we will see in much greater detail in Chapters 3, 4, and 5, in order to flourish, what we need to do, most centrally, is to develop and exercise our powers to achieve the common goods (specifically, internal goods or goods of excellence) of various types of practices and communities in which we participate.[113] We need to discover, therefore, that "it is only through directing themselves toward the achievement of common goods that [rational agents] are able to direct themselves toward the achievement of their own good qua individual."[114]

Sixth, we may fail to flourish for various reasons, some of which are beyond our control, such as malnutrition, injury, or "[p]remature death and disabling illness, crushing poverty and the friendlessness of the excluded and persecuted," but some of which *are* within our control, such as failures to deal appropriately with adversity or to properly develop and exercise our rational powers to make good judgments, act on such judgments, and learn from mistakes.[115]

---

110. Again, I am indebted to Jack Sammons for this thought and for the quoted language. Sammons Email (September 22, 2020) [on file with author].

111. MacIntyre, Conflicts of Modernity, op. cit., at 30.

112. *See* MacIntyre, Rational Animals, op. cit., at 111–12 (explaining that virtuous acts are "worth performing for their own sake [as] constitutive parts of human flourishing").

113. MacIntyre, Conflicts of Modernity, op. cit., at 38, 49–52.

114. *Id.* at 175. *See also id.* at 106–07 (explaining that "individuals ... can achieve their individual goods only through achieving in the company of others those common goods that we share as family members, as collaborators in the workplace, as participants in a variety of local groups and societies, and as fellow citizens"). However, MacIntyre does acknowledge other types of goods that are also "central to our lives" and gives as examples "the goods of affection and friendship and the good of self-knowledge [as well as] the good of light conversation and joking between workmates or groups of casual acquaintances." *Id.* at 52.

115. *Id.* at 39–40, 223–24.

Finally, however, the later MacIntyre of *Conflicts of Modernity*, more explicitly than the earlier Macintyre of *After Virtue*, seems to add a significant qualification and to suggest that the *pursuit* of our flourishing rather than its achievement is what is truly important (or alternatively perhaps, that our flourishing *consists* in its pursuit, at least to a significant extent). Thus, "there are situations in which defeat in achieving particular finite goods, no matter how great, is not a mark of failure," including, for example, situations in which we suffer premature death.[116] Moreover, MacIntyre seems to endorse Aquinas' view that to live a good life we should "continu[e] to rank order particular and finite goods" but should never regard the actual achievement of *any* particular finite good as either necessary or sufficient for our flourishing and for our lives to be complete; instead we should always move forward and leave ourselves "open to a final good beyond all such goods, as good desirable beyond all such goods."[117] Indeed

> To live well is to act so as to move toward achieving the best goods of which one is capable and so as to become the kind of agent capable of achieving those goods. But there is no particular finite good the achievement of which perfects and completes one's life. There is always something more to be attained, whatever one's attainments. The perfection and completion of a life *consists in an agent's having persisted in moving toward and beyond the best goods of which she or he knows*. So there is presupposed some further good, an object of desire beyond all particular and finite goods, a good toward which desire tends insofar as it remains unsatisfied by even the most desirable of finite goods, as in good lives it does.[118]

---

116. *Id.* at 230–31 (giving as examples the death of a child, spouse, or friend for whose well-being the agent cares deeply, failure to attain some extraordinary athletic or intellectual goal to which the agent aspires, or an inopportune and untimely death that cuts short the agent's life, and noting Aquinas' view that "we complete and perfect our lives by allowing them to remain incomplete"). *Cf.* MacIntyre, After Virtue, op. cit., at 219 (stating that "a provisional conclusion about the good life for man" is that "the good life for man is the life spent in seeking for the good life for man").

117. MacIntyre, Conflicts of Modernity, op. cit., at 229–31. Thus, in the case of the agent whose life is cut short by an inopportune and untimely death, for example, "[w]hat matters is what the agent was open to at the time of her or his death, not the perhaps great, but finite goods of which the agent was deprived by that death." *Id.* at 231.

118. *Id.* at 315 (emphasis added).

Furthermore, although MacIntyre appears to accept that a non-theist could certainly understand life in these terms, he also seems to endorse Aquinas' view that our truly ultimate final good, the "final and supreme object of desire," is God and our right relationship with God.[119]

B. Our Vocation to Flourish

If we accept MacIntyre's account of human flourishing and his identi-fication of our truly ultimate final good, as discussed above, how might we expand upon these ideas? We might want to begin by articulating an inclusive understanding of God as denoting something like the ground of our being and the deepest truths of our lives — let us call it "the divine."[120] With this inclusive understanding of "God" in place, we can reasonably conclude that our *telos* — our ultimate good, and thus our ultimate pur-pose — is to seek to live well and to flourish as God calls us to do, whether or not we are able to recognize or acknowledge explicitly the source of the call. Moreover, by seeking to respond as best we can to what God is call-ing us to become — to realize (once again in both senses of the word) our true vocation — we are able to realize our authentic identity and the true meaning and purpose of our lives as we compose our life stories, order the goods in our lives, and pursue our flourishing.

But how, then, are we discover or discern our true vocation and what God is calling us to become? We can get a good start on answering this question by recalling Frederick Buechner's helpful and suggestive reflec-tions on discerning the kind of work to which we are called:

---

119. *Id.* at 55–58, 230–31, 315. A virtue ethics focused on the concept of *human* flour-ishing is sometimes faulted for being anthropocentric and insensitive to environmental con-cerns and nonhuman flourishing. However, a virtue ethics focused on human flourishing can readily accommodate these other concerns, as reflection on what is necessary for good health or the full development of aesthetic powers, or what might be involved in our right relationship with God already suggests. I am grateful to Paul Lewis for bringing my atten-tion to this point. We will return to this point at the end of Chapter 4. *See* Chapter 4, note 98 and accompanying text.

120. I am indebted to Jack Sammons for suggesting "the divine" in this formulation and also for the Augustinian idea that the divine "calls because calling is in the nature of being divine." Sammons Email (September 2, 2020). And I am indebted to Gary Simson for emphasizing the importance of adopting an ecumenical approach that does not privilege any individual faith tradition such as Christianity. Simson Phone Conversation (June 12, 2020) [notes on file with author].

There are all different kinds of voices calling you to all different kinds of work, and the problem is to find out which is the voice of God rather than of Society, say, or the Superego, or Self-Interest.

By and large a good rule for finding out is this: the kind of work God usually calls you to is the kind of work (a) that you need most to do and (b) that the world most needs to have done....

... The place God calls you to is the place where your deep gladness and the world's deep hunger meet.[121]

Parker Palmer rephrases the second statement of Buechner's formula even more pithily as finding "the place where your deep gladness meets the world's deep need."[122] And we should note that the formula seems equally applicable to other activities besides work.

Similarly, Geoff Moore emphasizes the importance of work in satisfying the universal human search for meaning — for a sense of connection to a worthy larger purpose and for a sense of "belonging" or having "a place in the world" — while acknowledging that we can and should also seek meaning from other activities, from other "practices," besides work.[123] But work can only provide such meaning if it is both objectively and subjectively *meaningful*, that is, if it is both objectively worthwhile, because it "contribut[es] to the common good," and subjectively fulfilling, because our motivation for doing the work is to contribute to the common good by achieving the "internal goods" of the work.[124] Again, one assumes that the same is also true of other types of practices.

These subjective and objective aspects of meaningful work correspond nicely with the two elements in Buechner's definition of a "calling" — our "deep gladness" and "the world's deep need." Indeed, although Moore does not discuss Buechner, he does suggest that work is only meaningful when it is viewed as a "calling," rather than as a "job" to earn a living or as a "ca-

---

121. FREDERICK BUECHNER, WISHFUL THINKING: A SEEKER'S ABC 118–19 (1973), reproduced at Frederick Buechner, *Vocation* (July 18, 2017), https://www.frederickbuechner.com/quote-of-the-day/2017/7/18/vocation.

122. For this rephrasing, see, e.g., PARKER J. PALMER, LET YOUR LIFE SPEAK: LISTENING FOR THE VOICE OF VOCATION 16 (2000) (quoting BUECHNER, op. cit., at 119).

123. MOORE, VIRTUE AT WORK, op. cit., at 86.

124. *Id.* at 86–87, 89.

reer" to obtain increased pay, promotion, or prestige.[125] When the work is viewed as a job or a career, the primary motivation for engaging in the work is extrinsic, focused on attaining "external goods," but when it is viewed as a calling, the primary motivation is intrinsic, focused on attaining "internal goods" and contributing to the greater common good.[126] And yet again, we can assume that the same applies *mutatis mutandis* to other types of practices as well. In addition, Moore identifies the virtue of constancy, which entails "a commitment over the long term to the goods of the practice," as essential for sustaining a sense of calling in any type of practice.[127] As indicated earlier in this Chapter, we will explore the notions of a practice, internal and external goods, and the greater common good in much more detail in Chapters 3, 4, and 5 (Chapter 6 will contrast the Thomistic Aristotelian community-oriented conception of the greater common good described in these three chapters with the individualist conception of the common good that seems to be the dominant conception in contemporary liberal democratic societies).

At this point, however, several caveats are in order. These caveats are needed because the process of discerning our true calling or vocation, as we seek to realize the meaning and purpose of our lives through our proper flourishing, can be difficult, challenging, and even perilous. We must be careful, therefore, how we understand, and discover, the two elements of our "deep gladness" and "the world's deep hunger (or need)" in the Buechner formula. We must not approach the formula too glibly or mechanically, and we must also understand that it may take us only part of the way. Thus, one caveat is that sometimes our true calling or vocation is not experienced (or at least not immediately experienced) in terms of a positive feeling of inner "gladness" at all but rather as a disturbing inner disruption, a clue

---

125. *Id.* at 88–92.

126. *Id.* Moore simply uses the term "common good." However, he is referring to what in Chapter 3 we call the "greater common good of the broader community" as opposed to the specific "common goods" that are the internal goods of practices and the main text therefore reflects this intended sense. *See* Chapter 3, notes 83–86 and accompanying text. For Moore's explanation of the term "common good," see MOORE, VIRTUE AT WORK, op. cit., at 42–43.

127. *Id.* at 170–71 (using circus directors in an era of declining popularity and financial rewards to illustrate this point). For earlier discussion of the virtue of constancy, see *supra* notes 88–90, 94 and accompanying text.

perhaps being that in the first statement of the formula set out in the passage quoted at the beginning of this section Buechner phrases the first element as "the kind of work... that you *need* most to do."[128] Another, related caveat, echoing and extending Buechner's statement of the problem in the same passage, concerns the risk of listening to our "false selves" exhibiting an inauthentic identity, rather than our "true selves" exhibiting an authentic identity,[129] and the related risk of idolatry.[130] Parker Palmer addresses the relevance of the distinction between the "true self" and the "false self" for the proper discernment of our calling or vocation as follows:

> The figure calling to me all those years was, I believe, what Thomas Merton calls "true self." This is not the ego self that wants to inflate us (or deflate us, another form of self-distortion), not the intellectual self that wants to hover above the mess of life in clear but ungrounded ideas, not the ethical self that wants to live by some abstract moral code. It is the self planted in us by the God who made us in God's own image — the self that wants nothing more, or less, than for us to be who we were created to be.
>
> True self is true friend. One ignores or rejects such friendship only at one's peril.[131]

---

128. Emphasis added. For the full quote, see *supra* note 121 and accompanying text. *See also supra* note 96 (discussing MacIntyre's contrast between the dominant *subjective* conception of happiness and the *objective* Neo-Aristotelian conception of happiness, and noting that consequently unhappiness in the dominant conception is often appropriate).

129. For a detailed exploration of the distinction between the True Self and the False Self that uses religious language and Scriptural citation but that is intended for everyone, see generally RICHARD ROHR, IMMORTAL DIAMOND: THE SEARCH FOR OUR TRUE SELF (2013). For a concise account of the distinction between these two Selves, listing the main characteristics of each one, see *id.* at 189–91. The author explains that he is "writing this book for secular seekers and thinkers, believers and nonbelievers alike, and that huge disillusioned group in recovery from religion itself." *Id.* at xvii.

130. Regarding the risk of idolatry, see, e.g., Timothy W. Floyd, *The Practice of Law as A Vocation or Calling*, 66 FORDHAM L. REV. 1405, 1424 (1998) (discussing the risk of idolatry in the practice of law, that is, "the risk ... of putting my faith in the profession, or a system, or in a group of people, rather than in God"). Such idolatry is likely rooted in the individual and/ or collective ego, or other kind of "false self" identified in the passage from Parker Palmer quoted *infra* note 131 and accompanying text.

131. PALMER, LET YOUR LIFE SPEAK, op. cit., at 68–69. Importantly, the "false self," which is "a largely mental and cultural construct," is not so much bad as it is small and

A further caveat is that both elements in the formula, especially the first, may change over time. All three caveats are consistent with regarding our lives as a continuing, often halting, quest,[132] and with the notion that the achievement of any particular finite good should not necessarily define the end of the quest, because what is truly important is making progress in the quest as we pursue our proper flourishing.[133] And to recur to a theme that is repeated throughout this Chapter, all three caveats also confirm the importance of our social relationships and the insights of knowledgeable others in determining how well or how badly we understand ourselves and the alternatives open to us.[134]

Mixing literary metaphors, our life quest can perhaps be seen as involving an effort to escape the confines of the Cave in Plato's famed Allegory. It will be recalled that those prisoners who have been freed from their enslavement to "shadows of reality," projected onto the Cave wall in front

incomplete. Indeed, our various false selves are even necessary to get started in life. ROHR, IMMORTAL DIAMOND, op. cit., at 27–28, 64–65. Although moving beyond them toward our true self can happen relatively early in life, it seems that it always first requires owning our denied or repressed "shadow self." RICHARD ROHR, FALLING UPWARD: A SPIRITUALITY FOR THE TWO HALVES OF LIFE xvi, 127-36 (2011).

132. See supra notes 22–24 and accompanying text.

133. See supra notes 116–18 and accompanying text.

134. See MACINTYRE, CONFLICTS OF MODERNITY, op. cit., at 158–63 (discussing the role of our social relationships in helping or hindering us in deliberating and choosing appropriately between alternative careers, and how whether we can learn appropriately from others may depend on our individual "motivational set"). See also id. at 155–56 (discussing Bernard Williams' characterization of "an agent's subjective motivational set" as that agent's "desires, dispositions of evaluation, patterns of emotional reaction, personal loyalties, projects, and commitments" and Williams' emphasis that such motivational set is not static but can be affected by the process of deliberation and also change over time).

For further discussion of Buechner's formula and the first caveat, see the post by Ryan Pemberton, Frederick Buechner on Calling: Your Deep Gladness & the World's Deep Hunger (and the comments that follow the post) at http://www.calledthejourney.com/blog/2014/12/17/frederick-buechner-on-calling (December 22, 2014). For further illuminating discussion, see John Dunaway, "God at Work": A Reflection on Vocation, in TOWARD HUMAN FLOURISHING: CHARACTER, PRACTICAL WISDOM, AND PROFESSIONAL FORMATION 134-38 (Mark L. Jones, Paul A. Lewis & Kelly E. Reffitt, eds., 2013); Timothy Floyd, Answering the Call to Service: Vocation and Professional Identity, id. at 139–42. For a more extensive exploration of our calling or life purpose in general, extending beyond work to life as a whole, that will be especially meaningful for religious believers, especially Christian believers, as well as for seeking nonbelievers, see PALMER, LET YOUR LIFE SPEAK, op. cit.; OS GUINESS, THE CALL: FINDING AND FULFILLING THE CENTRAL PURPOSE OF YOUR LIFE (1998).

of them, ascend out of the Cave into the light of the sun, representing the light of the Good, and thereby acquire knowledge of true reality.[135] In the present context, we can follow T.Z. Lavine in applying the Allegory to the question of what is a truly "good life," and thus interpret it as inviting us to respond to a call to come out of the Cave of distracting illusory desires into the light of our true, individual Good.[136] Moreover, just as Plato's Cave dwellers came to understand the central importance of the four cardinal virtues of courage, temperateness, justice, and wisdom for the proper ordering of their souls in living a good life as they journeyed out of the Cave into the light,[137] so we too, as MacIntyre urges, come to understand the central importance of these same virtues in our own life journey.[138]

Returning to the original literary metaphor, we can perhaps also be seen as pursuing an interior Quest for our personal Grail. In an Arthurian version of the famed Legend of the Holy Grail, many Knights of the Round Table embarked upon the Quest, but only three — Sir Perceval, Sir Lancelot, and Sir Galahad — succeeded in entering the Grail Castle and, of these, only Sir Galahad attained the goal of the Quest because only he "possessed the triple gifts of valour, wisdom and virtue" (in the narrower sense of moral rectitude or absence of disordered desire).[139] In the present context, we can follow Joseph Campbell in applying the Grail Legend to

---

135. *See* T.Z. Lavine, From Socrates to Sartre: The Philosophic Quest 27–30, 41–42 (1984) (providing an accessible account of Plato's Allegory of the Cave and identifying several potential contemporary applications of the Allegory). *See also id.* at 31–41 (discussing Plato's theory of knowledge and his image of the divided line, which "present his theory of knowledge diagrammatically, as the cave presented it allegorically").

136. *See id.* at 28–29 (suggesting interpretation of the Allegory "as a devastating criticism" of the superficial and illusory view that "[a] good life is ... one in which we satisfy our [sensual] desires").

137. *See id.* at 49–52, 54–56 (discussing Plato's tripartite theory of the soul in which the virtues of justice, wisdom, courage, and temperateness are critical for the proper ordering of the soul necessary for living a good life of harmonious balance).

138. *See supra* notes 60–88 and accompanying text.

139. There are many versions of the medieval legend of the Quest for the Holy Grail. For an accessible account of the Arthurian version described and quoted in the text, see David Day, King Arthur 128–33 (1999). *See also id.* at 122–28, 133 (discussing the history and the historical context of the Grail Legend). Day takes what is arguably an unduly negative view of the Grail Legend, particularly because of its association with the Order of the Knights Templar and the Crusades. *Id.* at 122, 133. As discussed below, others have applied the Grail Legend much more positively to the interior quest.

the question of pursuing our vocation to flourish, and thus interpret it as "epitomiz[ing] an especially Western spiritual aim and ideal, which is, of living the life that is potential in *you* and was never in anyone else as a possibility." As Campbell suggests, the Legend reflects "the great Western truth: that each of us is a completely unique creature and that, if we are ever to give any gift to the world, it will have to come out of our own experience and fulfilment of our own potentialities, not someone else's."[140] Closely related to this interpretation, others have interpreted the Grail Quest as a quest for the true self discussed above.[141] Applying the Legend in this way, once again we can see the central importance of the four cardinal virtues in our life journey. Thus, in the Arthurian version discussed above, all three Knights exhibited courage, but Sir Perceval lacked wisdom in failing to ask the right questions in the Grail Castle, and Sir Lancelot lacked temperateness and justice in his disordered desire for, and adultery with, King Arthur's wife Guinevere. Only Sir Galahad, then, exhibited all four cardinal virtues and thus attained the Grail.[142]

But as Jack Sammons reminds us with regard to the legal and political conversations, as will be discussed in Chapters 7 and 8 respectively,[143] in the present context too, our proper response and pursuit always retain an element of mystery beyond the power of language to articulate, even to ourselves, although not beyond the power of our experience to acknowledge. In this regard, MacIntyre continues the passage quoted above at the end of Section A, and thereby concludes *Conflicts of Modernity*, by acknowledging: "But here the enquiries of politics and ethics end. Here natu-

---

140. Joseph Campbell, The Power of Myth 150–51 (1988).

141. For an example of an author who interprets it in this way, see Richard Rohr, Quest for the Grail (1994). Drawing not only on the English Arthurian tradition in developing and applying the Grail story but on German and French traditions as well, and focusing on Parsival (or Percival) as the protagonist, the author uses the legend as a masculine myth, albeit with insights for both men and women, and importantly observes that "[p]erhaps we are burdened with rewriting the quest for the Holy Grail in every age and generation." *Id.* at 7, 10.

142. *See* Day, King Arthur, op. cit., at 129–33 (recounting the experiences and comparing the attributes of the three Knights).

143. *See* Chapter 7, notes 59–62 and accompanying text; Chapter 8, notes 32–39 and accompanying text.

ral theology begins."[144] In considering the potential implications of natural theology and our relationship to God for these enquiries,[145] we do well to remember that the practitioners of natural theology include both "rationalists," who "argue that only propositions that can be justified by unaided human reason are candidates for permissible belief," and "hybridists," who "allow that our natural faculties can take us a certain distance[,]... but argue that we must ultimately appeal to revelation and faith."[146]

III. The Perspective of Phenomenology

We can gain additional insight on several important matters discussed in this Chapter, as well as several matters we will discuss in later Chapters, by considering them from a phenomenological perspective.

A. Introducing the Perspective of Phenomenology

Linda Ross Meyer explains that according to Martin Heidegger "to be human is not primarily to reason but, as he puts it, to be in the world and with others."[147] The phrase "not primarily" signifies that our reasoning, while important, is "derivative," taking place within, emerging from, and abstracted on the basis of a pre-existing context in which we already en-

---

144. MacIntyre, Conflicts of Modernity, op. cit., at 315. For a helpful discussion of natural theology, see Andrew Chignell & Derk Pereboom, *Natural Theology and Natural Religion*, Stanford Encyclopedia of Philosophy, https://plato.stanford.edu/entries/natural-theology/.

145. *Supra* note 119 and accompanying text.

146. Chignell & Pereboom, *Natural Theology*, op. cit., at section 1.2. [emphasis omitted]. It is perhaps unclear which camp MacIntyre endorses. For discussion of the development of MacIntyre's philosophy of religion, see Lutz, *Alasdair Chalmers MacIntyre*, op. cit. (section 3. b. i. 1) (tracing the evolution from MacIntyre's early fideism through his atheism to a "mature theism" that "belongs to a rational worldview").

147. Linda Ross Meyer, The Justice of Mercy 27 (2010). I am aware, of course, of the long-standing charges of sympathy for the Nazis, and more recent charges of antisemitism, leveled against Heidegger. To the extent such charges are well-founded, although they might counsel caution in considering certain aspects of Heidegger's thought, they do not justify "throwing out the baby with the bathwater," any more than Aristotle's notorious endorsement of "natural slavery" should be seen as contaminating the rest of that philosopher's thought. For a helpful commentary on all this, see Zühtücan Soysal's book review of Jean-Luc Nancy, The Banality of Heidegger, trans. Jeff Fort (2017), https://reviews.ophen.org/2018/03/07/jean-luc-nancy-the-banality-of-heidegger-review/.

counter and are engaged with the world and one another before — and as — we reason.[148] Drawing upon Heidegger's *Dasein* (being there), or "the ones who are open to Being," Meyer explains further the implications for our understanding of knowledge and truth:

> "Knowing" must be understood as the knowing of *Dasein*. The world, as well as our connection with it, is a *given*, not a problem. There is no universal, timeless, purely rational standpoint, except as an abstraction that is already grounded in our concrete experience with the world.
>
> Our knowledge is temporal, based on *what lets itself be known — what of its own appears to us.* We no longer have to choose between a universe whose truth is "guaranteed" by a philosopher's god who created it and therefore knows objects "as they truly are" (Descartes) and a universe that we "merely posit" and create for ourselves through our own will (Nietzsche). Instead, thought and world are both finite, *appearing in time, given to us.* Knowing and truth concern *what appears to us*, not what is "in itself" apart from us.[149]

To use Heidegger's terminology, when Being is "unconcealed" or "revealed" or "disclosed" in this way, we have knowledge of truth as the uncovering of an aspect of Being that was hidden (*aletheia*), as opposed to truth as the correspondence of words to objective "facts" or coherence among propositions. In addition to explaining the implications for our understanding of knowledge and truth, Meyer also explains the implications for our understanding of thinking, especially the dependence of our thinking upon the practical context in which we find ourselves:

> Thinking from a finite human standpoint means that things have sense for us not when they are disconnected "substances" with "properties," not when they are "ideas" in the mind of God, but when they are in a world in relation to other things. Thinking is our already being in the world — that is, concerned with things around us, enmeshed in a web of relationships among things that *show up for us*

---

148. *Id.* at 27, 33–36, 44.
149. *Id.* at 27–28 (emphasis added in the second paragraph).

as we engage with them and work with them, from past experience to future possibility.... [W]e "get" our world *not through theoretical knowledge but in practice.* The preeminence of practical knowledge is as true for our understanding of people as it is for our understanding of things.[150]

All this means, too, that language, which Heidegger calls "the house of Being," is never "context-free," so that "[m]eaning is always tied both to the past and to the context in which it lives," and any particular thing "[can] be described in thousands of ways, pointing to this or that relation to other things in the (past) world."[151] However, when we become untethered from this pre-existing context in the sense that we forget the "givenness" of Being — the "givenness" of our world and one another — our use of language and reason is apt to go astray, sometimes seriously so. Heidegger provides a striking illustration of how this can happen in his essay *The Question Concerning Technology*, in which he argues that the kind of thinking animating modern physics and modern technology — which Heidegger calls "enframing" — has led human beings to approach the world and even one another in such a way that they are "revealed" as "standing reserve" to be

---

150. *Id.* at 28–29 (emphasis added).

151. *Id.* at 32. Meyer explains and illustrates "this Wittgensteinian perspective on language":

> The description that language — and, by extension, law — will give to an action or thing will depend on which aspect of it is important or salient to us at the moment (i.e., what we are doing with it, how we are involved with it). My grandmother's old oak rocker is a rocker (when I need to distinguish it from an easy chair), a chair (when I tell the movers what I have), a wooden object (when I am concerned about fire danger or termites), a medium brown with a bit of green (when I am redecorating), a movable (to distinguish it from my landlord's property), an antique (when I think about its value on the market), an heirloom (when I ponder its family history), a thing of beauty (when I look up from my computer to watch the afternoon sun play on it), and a soothing motion (when I want to put my child to sleep).

Id. As the reference to law in the above passage suggests, in her book Meyer is especially interested in the implications of Heidegger's (and Emmanuel Levinas's) thought for law, justice, and mercy — in a phenomenology of law, so to speak, that is applicable to criminal law and justice and the approach to punishment. *See id.* at 26–27, 30–36, 41–51 (exploring various aspects of this phenomenology of law in a preliminary way that is then fully developed in the remainder of her book).

ordered according to our wills.[152] As Meyer puts it, instead of "let[ting] beings, including other *Daseins* be [and] unfold before us," we tend "to take them over, remake them, use them, or improve them."[153]

B. Revelation and Natural Theology

But how does all this help provide the additional insight mentioned above? To consider first the notion of ultimately appealing to revelation, Heidegger's phenomenology emphasizes that knowledge and truth, and indeed thinking and reasoning itself, depend upon our pre-existing immersion in a world of Being — in "a web of relationships among things" that "lets itself be known" and that "appears" or "show[s] up" for us. And, of course, the web of relationships in the world of Being that is "unconcealed" or "revealed" or "disclosed" in this way includes relationships among human beings.[154] Although Heidegger's capitalization of the word Being "should not be read to suggest any otherworldly quality," the givenness of Being certainly does not *preclude* the immanence of the divine or the notion of divine giftedness.[155] Indeed, Heidegger considers that the

---

152. Martin Heidegger, *The Question Concerning Technology* in MARTIN HEIDEGGER, BASIC WRITINGS 287–317 (David Farell Krell, ed., 1977), https://www2.hawaii.edu/~free-man/courses/phil394/The%20Question%20Concerning%20Technology.pdf. In this important essay Heidegger explains that

> [M]odern technology... is a revealing. Only when we allow our attention to rest on this fundamental characteristic does that which is new in modern technology show itself to us.... The revealing that rules throughout modern technology has the character of a setting-upon, in the sense of a challenging-forth.... Everywhere everything is ordered to stand by, to be immediately on hand, indeed to stand there just so that it may be on call for a further ordering....We call it the standing-reserve ... Enframing means the gathering together of the setting-upon that sets upon man, i.e., challenges him forth, to reveal the actual, in the mode of ordering, as standing-reserve.... The essence of technology lies in enframing.... As soon as what is unconcealed... concerns man... exclusively as standing-reserve, and man... is nothing but the orderer of the standing-reserve, then he comes to the very brink of a precipitous fall... where he himself will have to be taken as standing-reserve.

Id. at 296–98, 302, 307–08.

153. MEYER, JUSTICE OF MERCY, op. cit., at 38.

154. For Meyer's discussion of Levinas's critique of Heidegger, possible responses to it, and her use of it "as a help to fleshing out our understanding of being-with" one another in the world of Being, see *id.* at 36–41.

155. *See id.* at 189–90 n3 (for the quoted language).

way we talk about God — as "the highest value" for example — degrades "the essence of God," and that thinking in terms of "values" in general (and not only about God) "is the greatest blasphemy that can be thought of in the face of Being" because "[i]t does not let beings be." This happens especially in the modern age when "Being's very 'givenness' hides itself from [us]" due to our "technological thinking" as discussed above, which "leads to the illusion that human will creates, controls, and values all that is."[156]

Moreover, as Sammons emphasizes, even when we try to avoid this type of error and although language offers multiple descriptive possibilities due to its unavoidable dependence on context, there can still remain that which we can experience but cannot adequately describe and sometimes perhaps cannot describe at all. Indeed, the descriptive limitations of language took extreme and dramatic form in the case of Thomas Aquinas himself, who is said to have written nothing more of the *Summa Theologiae* after apparently experiencing a mystical vision three months before his death, considering everything he had written hitherto to be "worth little more than straw" in comparison.[157] Although it is important to emphasize that Catholics do not understand this episode to be a repudiation by Aquinas of his previous work, it would certainly seem to underscore the need for humility in human enquiry and echoes the distinction between "rationalists" and "hybridists"

---

156. *Id.* at 38, 192 n21 (quoting in the first sentence from Martin Heidegger, *Letter on Humanism*, trans. E. Lohner, *in* PHILOSOPHY IN THE TWENTIETH CENTURY 3:294 (William Barrett & Henry D. Aiken, eds., 1962)). *See also* Heidegger, *Question Concerning Technology*, op. cit., where Heidegger continues the passage quoted *supra* note 152:

> Meanwhile, man, precisely as the one so threatened, exalts himself and postures as lord of the earth. In this way the illusion comes to prevail that everything man encounters exists only insofar as it is his construct. This illusion gives rise in turn to one final delusion: it seems as though man everywhere and always encounters only himself. . . . *In truth, however, precisely nowhere does man today any longer encounter himself, i.e., his essence.* . . . The coming to presence of technology threatens revealing, threatens it with the possibility that all revealing will be consumed in ordering and that everything will present itself only in the unconcealdness of standing-reserve.

Id. at 308. 315. The essence of humanity Heidegger emphasizes is *Dasein* who are "open to Being which is given."

157. *See* CARL McCOLMAN, THE BIG BOOK OF CHRISTIAN MYSTICISM: THE ESSENTIAL GUIDE TO CONTEMPLATIVE SPIRITUALITY 115–16 (2010) (discussing this episode when explaining that "[w]e cannot fully and finally capture the fullness of the divine ineffability in mere human language").

discussed at the end of Part II. From a phenomenological perspective, therefore, in the natural theology referenced by MacIntyre, as songwriter Iris DeMent has it, at some point perhaps we must just "let the mystery be."[158]

C. MacIntyre and Moral Formation

A second insight is that MacIntyre's general approach to moral formation can also be described as phenomenological because it is rooted in the

---

158. Iris DeMent, *Let the Mystery Be* (from the album *Infamous Angel*, Philo, 1992), https://www.google.com/search?client=firefox-b-1-d&q=iris+dement+let+the+mystery +be. In this apparently skeptical and indifferentist song Iris DeMent canvasses the extreme disagreement in beliefs about our origins and ultimate destiny, and states that because "no one knows for certain … it's all the same to me" and she will "just let the mystery be." On the other hand, she confesses that "I believe in love and I live my life accordingly." And this, depending on how such "love" is understood, might be tantamount to confessing a belief in God, for in one famous definition God is Love: `Beloved, let us love one another, because love is of God; everyone who loves is begotten by God and knows God. Whoever is without love does not know God, for God is love," 1 John 4: 7–8, (New Am. Rev. ed. 2011). Although originally articulated in an explicitly Christian context, this saying can also be understood more inclusively as one that transcends distinctions among religions and indeed any religious categories. Moreover, such *agape* love itself also retains an element of mystery beyond the power of language to articulate but not beyond the power of our experience to acknowledge. For an accessible survey of *agape* love in eight religious traditions, see SIR JOHN TEMPLETON, AGAPE LOVE: A TRADITION FOUND IN EIGHT WORLD RELIGIONS (1999) (discussing how the ancient Greek concept of *agape* love is manifested in Judaism, Christianity, Islam, Hinduism, Buddhism, Taoism, Confucianism, and Native American Spirituality).

I do not want to wade too far into deep theological waters, in which I am not trained to swim, but James Fowler's seven stages of faith development provide an additional useful resource when trying to grapple with these difficult theological issues. For a helpful summary account of Fowler's seven stages, see Terri Daniel, *Fowler's Stages of Faith* (2016), https://oregonhospice.org/media/PPEDanielStagesofFaith.pdf. For a classic account describing five stages in the development of a mystical spiritual consciousness (which harmonize with Fowler's seven stages) and entail the process of discovering the True Self (as opposed to what the author calls "the surface-self"), see EVELYN UNDERHILL, PRACTICAL MYSTICISM (1915), reproduced at http://www. anglicanlibrary.org/underhill/UnderhillPracticalMysticism.pdf. For an illuminating illustration of how Fowler's seven stages and Underhill's five stages can be applied to promote greater understanding of the human condition, to address existential questions, and to inform practical strategies to solve human problems, see Terri Daniel, *Loss and Trauma as a Path to Spiritual Awareness: Applying Fowler's Stages of Faith Development to the Grief Journey*, https://www.academia.edu/22704838/Loss_and_Trauma_as_a_Path_to_Spiritual_ Awareness_Applying_Fowlers_Stages_of_Faith_Development_to_the_Grief_Journey; Terri Daniel, *Grief as a Mystical Journey: Fowler's Stages of Faith Development and Their Relation to Post-Traumatic Growth*, 71 JOURNAL PASTORAL CARE COUNSEL. 220–29 (2017).

experience of practical reasoning in practices, and not — despite his acceptance of Thomism — as metaphysical or otherwise foundationalist. Thus,
Christopher Stephen Lutz considers that although MacIntyre became a
Thomist "and accepted that the teleology of human action flowed from a
metaphysical foundation in the nature of the human person," nonetheless
he "continues to approach teleology primarily by examining the phenom-
ena by which metaphysical nature manifests itself," so that this teleology
is "discovered through reflection on practice." Consequently, in his ethics
and politics MacIntyre "continues to argue toward an Aristotelian account
of practical reasoning through the investigation of practice" and "to exemplify [a] phenomenological approach to moral education." This "historicist
and phenomenological" Aristotelianism is well illustrated by *After Virtue*,
which "does not define virtue in metaphysical terms as the perfection of
nature [but] in terms of the practical requirements for excellence in human agency, in an agent's participation in practices ... , in an agent's whole
life, and in an agent's involvement in the life of her or his community."[159]

As the discussion proceeds, however, and with Jack Sammons' indispensable help, we will sometimes press the phenomenological perspective
further than MacIntyre does, both descriptively, when considering whether and how far our reasoning may have gone astray or become too limiting, and normatively, by considering what correctives may be required.
Perhaps we might not want to follow Heidegger completely in questioning
the notion of all "valuing" in our reasoning. But we might want to recommend, as a necessary safeguard, that we pause, at least occasionally, to
reflect upon the context provided by our pre-existing immersion in the
world of Being, from which our reasoning — including our reasoning as
Thomistic Aristotelians — emerges, and to ask whether any untoward untethering of our reasoning has occurred because we have forgotten our
pre-existing immersion in Being and whether, therefore, any retethering
is needed. In this regard, sometimes it might be appropriate to engage in a
sort of back and forth between our reasoning and the givenness of Being
until we reach a point of "reflective equilibrium." This procedure indeed
seems consistent with the sort of dialectic between moral traditions that,
as we will see in Chapter 5, MacIntyre himself recommends in the practice of moral enquiry and that can lead to necessary correctives within

---

159. Lutz, *Alasdair Chalmers MacIntyre*, op. cit. (section 4. a. iv., section 5].

these traditions.[160] And it might be especially appropriate when engaging in the legal and political conversations within the Republic, as we will see in Chapters 7 and 8 respectively.

D. Circling Back to Introduce the World of Practice

Here, however, we press the phenomenological perspective further by circling back to revisit, and gain additional insight on, several matters discussed earlier in this Chapter: MacIntyre's premodern concept of selfhood, with a single, unified identity possessing "the unity of a narrative" across the span of our lives; the idea that in pursuing our respective moral quests to live a good life and flourish in community (especially in communities of practice) we are co-authors composing one another's life stories; and the relevance of the distinction between the "true self" and the "false self" for the proper discernment of our calling or vocation as we pursue these quests. We will do this with the aid of Sammons' article *The Art of Self*.[161] And because it is difficult to summarize or paraphrase Sammons — who writes with artistic eloquence himself — without significant loss, we will quote him at some length.

Like MacIntyre, Sammons rejects as "an illusion" the notion of "an untouchable and autonomous core self," with *its* "morals and ethics," that we "impose... upon the world," not in the sense that it does not exist but "that it does not and cannot reflect the reality of anyone's existence."[162] In

---

160. *See* Chapter 5, note 30 and accompanying text; Meyer, Justice of Mercy, op. cit., at 38 (observing that "for Heidegger, the effort to think Being is itself an act of ethics"). One suspects, however, that MacIntyre is unlikely to be impressed by this suggestion. *See* Alasdair MacIntyre, Three Rival Versions of Moral Enquiry: Encyclopaedia, Genealogy, and Tradition 165–69 (1990) (discussing disapprovingly Heidegger's rejection of Aquinas and Heidegger's affinities with the irrationalism of Meister Eckhart).

161. Jack L. Sammons, *The Art of Self and Becoming a Professional*, 68 Mercer L. Rev. 741 (2017). In this lovely article, Sammons is clearly inspired by Heidegger, especially Heidegger's notion that the arts may save us from the "extreme danger" that everything will be revealed only as standing-reserve. Thus, Heidegger asks whether "revealing lays claim to the arts most primally, so that they ... may awaken and found anew our vision of that which grants and our trust in it" through "essential reflection upon technology and decisive confrontation with it," although this would indeed require that the arts be experienced "primally" rather than as (only) "a sector of cultural activity" in which "[a]rtworks [are] enjoyed aesthetically." Heidegger, *Question Concerning Technology*, op. cit., at 316–17.

162. Sammons, *Art of Self*, op. cit., at 746–47, 756–57, 762.

Sammons' phenomenological account such a self is "inauthentic," because "it is almost impossible from the stance of a core self" for us to make our lives our own.[163] Instead, Sammons urges, this inauthentic, "autonomous core self" must be displaced to make way for an authentic, unified "narrative self," in which the story of our lives "offers an existential self, the self of our being," and our "sense of unity and continuity and thus agency ... comes not from the subject but emerges from the ontological reality lying in between subject and object as a cultural construct." In other words, this authentic, unified narrative self "emerg[es] out of our experiences ... that constitute the narrative, experiences which themselves cannot be described only in regards to a subject."[164] But how exactly can this occur when all these experiences happen within the world of Being—a world which includes other selves (other *Dasein*)—that shapes our experiences, and forms our unique self as a multiplicity, through its disclosure to us and through us:

Who we are,... our identity as a self,... is there in our relationship with others. Our existence as a self then is a co-dependent co-existence. Since there are multiple others, multiple ways of relating to each, and all of this is within a constantly ongoing process, we, each one of us, is a multiplicity of selves existing in the form of a single self... [A]round each of us is formed a world: a world of selves, of others, of relationships among all of these, of projects, creations, discoveries, time, a world of meaning, and on and on.... [T]his world has a semiotic nature. It exists in language in other words (and is necessarily social, cultural, and relational in this way as well).... [I]n each self there is the birth of a world to which this self, and this self alone, gives us access. It is a world in which the mystery of our existence is uncovered for us in a unique, a singular way. And thus each self in its multiplicity is unique, is a singularity, for the world will never disclose itself again in the way it does through each of us.[165]

This is true also for our participation in practices:

---

163. *Id.* at 746–47.
164. *Id.* at 753–57.
165. *Id.* at 742, 744.

[E]ach practice... necessarily assumes a form of the self... that is not fixed, always already multiple, always already co-existent, always already co-dependent, always already contingent, always already within a process of constant change, and always already complex and enigmatic — a self which must forever remain a mystery to itself — not as a mystery to be solved but because being a mystery is its nature. Each practice requires for its own excellences that its practitioners mature into a social world of others upon whom their own existence as selves depends. It asks each of its practitioners, in other words, to know yourself, makes a claim about what this means, and this claim is always about a *decentering* of self.[166]

If this multiple, co-existent, co-dependent, contingent, and changing self is to be a "narrative self" with a sense of unity, continuity, and agency, something must "provide a sense of direction," a "teleology of self."[167] And, Sammons claims, this is exactly what our participation in practices does because practices enable us to live authentically as artists "composing" our lives through "the art of self." To understand what this means, however, we must first understand "the origin of art" in both the artist and the materials of the art. Every painting, for example, seems to have its own "truth" in the form of "its own teleology, suggesting to the painter the fittingness of each color, each line, each brush stroke, and suggesting that some of these are not only necessary, but 'inevitable' *for the painting to be what it was meant to become*," and something similar is true for the other types of artistic endeavor as well.[168] What is true for the paintings is also true for the self of the artist who does the painting, and Sammons spells out the implications

---

166. *Id.* at 751–52.
167. *Id.* at 757.
168. *Id.* at 760–61 (emphasis added). Sammons explicates this important idea more fully as follows:

> [T]his sense of things — painting, sculptures, poems, songs, characters, films, symphonic themes, designs, and on and on — somehow emerging from the materials of one's art is there at the origin of art and the origin of art is our origin as well. It is, in other words, how we became human: the way in which... the unique "access" each of us offers first arose.... The work of art which results comes from the artist and yet does not come from the artist. It is neither the product of a subjective intent nor of an objective reality, and the work

of this truth for professionals and aspiring professionals in terms that seem readily applicable to practices more generally:

> Perhaps they... can approach the materials of their practices, including within those "materials" their own experiences, as the materials of an art out of which emerges for each one uniquely a teleology of self—a self they can experience as *who they were meant to become.* Perhaps they will find that in approaching their work with the attitude of an artist that this truth about who I am meant to be is a radical intimacy, something closer than I am to myself....[In this] conception of the self... our selves, in their reality, [are] disclosed to us,... permitting us to live more truthfully, more authentically. *Who you are and are to become, and the meaning you seek in this...* will disclose itself to you through the materials and experiences of your life as a professional when you approach these with the attitude of an artist. As odd as this may sound and as difficult as it may be to accept, I want to insist that this is exactly how the best of professionals — lawyers, judges, doctors, nurses, priests, psychologists, teachers, architects, and others — experience themselves as the professionals they are.[169]

---

reflects this, for it lives, as the self does, in the ontologically puzzling land between the two.

The good painter's experience of painting reflects this ontology: each stroke is measured against that which the painting seems to want to be — was meant to become — and the good painter takes this pushing back of the materials against his or her intentions for the painting very seriously. In a sense, this "pushing back" seems a form of truth [as *aletheia*]about the painting and has that authority for the painter — as it does for the poet, the novelist, the composer, the guitar maker, the stone and brick mason, the wood carver, and any other good artist working carefully, thoughtfully, attentively, respectfully, and humbly with the materials of his or her particular practice of art. Each painting, it seems, has its own teleology, suggesting to the painter the fittingness of each color, each line, each brush stroke, and suggesting that some of these are not only necessary, but "inevitable" for the painting to be what it was meant to become.

Id.

169. *Id.* at 761–62 (emphasis added). For Sammons' comments on the formation of the self of the artist, see *id.* at 760–61. The artist who inspired Sammons' article, and to whom

As we will see in Chapter 3, all of this implicates the relationship of the practitioner to the "internal goods" of the practice.[170]

Sammons' phenomenological account complements the account in this Chapter by providing added dimension in several respects. First, it enhances our understanding of how we form a *self* within a practice, for we now see more clearly that the types of experiences that form us as selves are "disclosed" to us, and through us, in the social world of the practice we inhabit, and these experiences include not only other selves but also the materials of the practice. Second, it enhances our understanding of how we compose our lives as a *unified narrative* self with "a certain kind of directedness toward a final end that is our own" within a practice,[171] for we now see that there is a certain necessity, even inevitability — a teleology — that inheres not only in any given project, as we pursue the "art of the practice" in our daily activities, but also in all our lived experiences, as we pursue the "art of self" within the practice over time.[172] Third, it enhances our understanding of our unified narrative self within the practice as a type of *true* self that can have a sense of vocation, for we now see that this narrative self is an authentic self that is disclosed to us in the social world of the practice and that any inauthentic, "autonomous core self" we seek to "impose … upon the world" of the practice is a false self — a self that must be displaced to make way for the narrative self to emerge from our experiences within the practice. But now other questions arise such as: What is the relationship to one another of the several "true selves" that are formed and disclosed to us within the world of each practice in which we participate? Can these selves be integrated into a single true self and, if so, how does that happen? What is the relationship of the "true self" formed by the practice to the "true self" that is the image

---

the article is dedicated, is Joshua Bishop, "executed by the People of the State of Georgia on March 13, 2016." *Id.* at 741.

170. *See id.* at 749–50 n42 (maintaining that "the reason[s] you seek the internal goods of your practices … return us to the questions of meaning found within a sense of self which the practice requires of you for its own excellences").

171. *See supra* note 56 and accompanying text.

172. Sammons has expressed this latter idea using the metaphor of musical composition: "We 'compose' our lives in the same way that musicians compose, that is we seek to create but also to *discover* which note comes next given what has preceded it." Sammons Email (September 2, 2020) [on file with author].

of God, of the divine, of which Parker Palmer writes and to whose call he urges us to respond in discerning our vocation as we listen to our lives?[173] Related, can the divine and its creativity speak and be disclosed to us in and through the world of the practice and its creations? And how are the divine and its creativity related to the formation, the creation, of our true selves within practices?

Sammons' phenomenological account complements the account in Chapter 2 by illuminating how we compose our lives and pursue our moral quests to live a good life in community as authentic, unified narrative selves within practices, and we will want to carry this phenomenological understanding and sensibility with us as we explore the notion of a practice in greater depth in Chapter 3 and beyond. But we must also carry with us everything else we addressed in Chapter 2, for these matters are relevant not only for our participation *within* practices, but also for composing our lives as a whole *across* practices and thus for the ordering of our lives through our decisions to engage in one type of practice rather than another, either at all or at any given time. To be sure, Sammons maintains that "[i]t is the potential authenticity of th[e] sense of self as a way of life which links our practices to our lives [a]nd not, as MacIntyre argued, our practices fitting, or not, within the narrative unity of human life as a quest." And here Sammons cites to an article by Lia Mela as providing "a good challenge for MacIntyre." [174] But Mela's challenge seems to be rooted in MacIntyre's alleged failure to "identify positively the conception of the good," or at least "criteria according to which rival conceptions of the good can be assessed," that could supply a guiding principle providing direction for the narrative quest — for ordering our lives as a narrative unity.[175] As we have seen in this Chapter, however, in *Conflicts of Modernity* — published several years after Mela wrote her article and not yet available when Sammons wrote his own article — MacIntyre has now provided such a guiding principle that can serve as the measure of the other goods in our lives. This guiding principle is the human *telos* defined in terms of human flourishing (with at least eight constitutive universal goods) and our re-

---

173. *See supra* note 131 and accompanying text.

174. Sammons, *Art of Self,* op. cit., at 749–50 n42 (citing to Lia Mela, *MacIntyre on Personal Identity,* 3(1) PUBLIC REASON 110–13 (2011)).

175. Mela, *Personal Identity,* op. cit., at 109–10.

lationship to the truly ultimate "final good." And so, we will always want to carry forward this phenomenologically grounded principle, together with Sammons' deeper phenomenological approach, as we seek to find a reflective equilibrium between them.

THREE

FLOURISHING IN PRACTICES

Common Goods and the Pursuit of Excellence

Chapter 2 suggested that we flourish and fulfill our life's purpose most centrally by doing the work, and participating in various other activities, other "practices," to which we have been called. In this chapter we consider in greater detail the nature of a practice, what flourishing in a practice entails, and the attributes or qualities of a good practitioner in the practice. In his seminal book *After Virtue* Alasdair MacIntyre famously defines a "practice" as follows:

> By a 'practice' I am going to mean any coherent and complex form of socially established cooperative human activity through which goods internal to that form of activity are realized in the course of trying to achieve those standards of excellence which are appropriate to, and partially definitive of, that form of activity, with the result that human powers to achieve excellence, and human conceptions of the ends and goods involved, are systematically extended.[1]

We need to unpack and analyze the various elements of this rather abstract and dense definition.

---

1. Alasdair MacIntyre, After Virtue: A Study in Moral Theory 187 (3d. ed., 2007) (1981).

I. Practices, Practitioner Communities, and Institutions

The first element in MacIntyre's definition of a practice is that it is a "coherent and complex form of socially established cooperative human activity." MacIntyre gives examples of what does and does not satisfy this element. Thus he suggests that Tic-tac-toe, throwing a football with skill, bricklaying, and planting turnips are not practices (one assumes this is largely because they are insufficiently complex), but the game of football, chess, architecture, farming, the enquiries of various sciences and of history, painting, and music *are* practices.[2] So also are the making and sustaining of family life and, in the ancient and medieval world, the making and sustaining of cities and nations or, in other words, politics in the Aristotelian sense.[3] And so, too, are professional practices, whether the practitioner is engaged in general or specialized practice.

Practitioners in the practice engage in it as part of a community of practitioners who are in relationship with one another (and also with past practitioners) within a constantly evolving living tradition that they shape and reshape — at least when the practice is in good order — sometimes intentionally, perhaps to correct a perceived corruption, and sometimes unintentionally though example.[4] A practitioner's performance is guided by the practitioner community's standards of excellence and is governed by its rules.[5] Moreover, practitioner communities practice in intimate relationship with various types of institutions that bear and sustain the practice.[6]

---

2. *Id.* With respect to bricklaying, presumably MacIntyre is thinking of this activity as performed by construction workers on a building site and not as performed by a master brick mason. *See infra* note 34.

3. MacIntyre, After Virtue, op. cit., at 187–88.

4. *See id.* at 191, 194, 221–23. I am indebted to Jack Sammons for urging me to emphasize this point at the very beginning of the Chapter (and for suggesting some of the language used here), to help combat any tendency readers may have to regard practices as static or as necessarily part of the status quo. Sammons Email (September 3, 2020) [on file with author].

5. MacIntyre, After Virtue, op. cit., at 190.

6. *Id.* at 194. The notion of being part of a community of practitioners who practice in intimate relationship to institutions that bear and sustain the practice may seem misconceived in the case of an artist who paints alone until one considers (a) that the community of practitioners includes both current and past artists from whom the artist learns his or her art of painting and to whom the artist may continue to refer (or with whom the artist may interact) for comparison and inspiration, and (b) that "institutions" also include the artist acting in a particular way (for example, for purposes of billing rather than painting), as well as a complex network of institutions such as art academies and art galleries within

Examples include a university, a farm, or a hospital.[7] And a professional firm (for example, a law firm) or a professional association with regulatory authority (for example, the American Bar Association (ABA)) are also such institutions.

II. Common Goods of the Practice

The second element in MacIntyre's definition of a practice is that by engaging in a practice the practitioner realizes "goods internal to that form of activity... in the course of trying to achieve those standards of excellence which are appropriate to, and partially definitive of, that form of activity."

A. Standards of Excellence and Goods of Excellence

As the formulation of this second element suggests, and as already indicated above, a practitioner's achievement of the "internal goods" of a practice is guided and measured by the practitioner community's standards of excellence (and regulated by the community's rules governing the practitioner's activity). Helpfully, then, in a later work MacIntyre also calls these internal goods "goods of excellence."[8] For the sake of terminological consistency, from now on we will employ this later terminology even when a cited source employs the prior terminology, except when use of this prior terminology is necessary for sense.

Flourishing in a practice consists centrally in attaining these goods of excellence, and what these goods are becomes clearer from MacIntyre's discussion of how the practice of portrait painting in Western Europe developed from the late Middle Ages until the eighteenth century.[9] He identifies two different kinds of goods of excellence. The first is "the ex-

---

which the painter first learns the art and then shares his or her work. The point extends beyond artists, of course, to solo practitioners in any practice. These matters are elaborated further at various points in this Chapter. I am indebted to Jack Sammons for drawing my attention to the puzzling situation of the lone artist. Sammons Email (September 3, 2020) [on file with author].

7. MacIntyre, After Virtue, op. cit., at 222. It should be noted that such institutions may in fact "house" more than one practice. Geoff Moore, Virtue at Work: Ethics for Individuals, Managers, and Organizations 68 (2017).

8. Alasdair MacIntyre, Whose Justice? Which Rationality? 32 (1988).

9. MacIntyre, After Virtue, op. cit., at 189 (discussing internal goods achieved during two sequences of development—from medieval iconography, to fifteenth century

cellence of the products," and these are themselves of two kinds, namely, "the excellence in performance by the painters and [the excellence] of each portrait itself." The second is "the good of a certain kind of life[,] ... [of] the painter's living out of a greater or lesser part of his or her life *as a paint-er*."[10] We can infer from this discussion of portrait paining that practices in general involve three types of goods of excellence — the excellence of the practitioner's performance, the excellence of the product resulting from this performance, and the excellence of the way of life that is lived out as a practitioner in the practice. Of course, although this tripartite taxonomy of goods of excellence is common to all practices at this high level of generality and abstraction, the specific content of these three goods will vary from practice to practice, as the example of portrait painting illustrates. We should also observe that MacIntyre's example of portrait painting is a telling one, gesturing toward a more general truth. Thus, as Jack Sammons has pointed out, "the intrinsic goods of a practice [its goods of excellence] are, in some good measure, understood aesthetically so that we say, for example, 'that's a beautiful job' or 'a beautiful way of working,' and with this is a tie to human creativity."[11]

B. Qualities of Excellence

In order to flourish in a practice by attaining its goods of excellence — excellence in performance, excellence of resulting product, and excellence of the practitioner's way of life — the practitioner will need to become a particular kind of person, one who possesses an ensemble of deeply ingrained and seamlessly integrated qualities or attributes we can call "qualities of excellence."[12] These qualities of excellence also include

---

relative naturalism, to synthesis of naturalistic portrait as icon; and from seventeenth century mythological faces in French painting, to eighteenth century aristocratic faces).

10. *Id.* at 189–90.

11. Sammons Email (September 12, 2020) [on file with author].

12. As we will see *infra* note 102 and accompanying text, MacIntyre equates "external goods" with "goods of effectiveness" and uses the term "qualities of effectiveness" to denote the attributes needed to obtain such goods. However, he does not seem to use the term "qualities of excellence" to denote those attributes needed to obtain "goods of excellence" even though he equates them with "internal goods." The term "qualities of excellence" would seem perfectly appropriate, however, and we will use it even though MacIntyre himself does not seem to do so.

the "master virtue" of prudence or practical wisdom,[13] and they are related in complex ways to qualities or attributes the practitioner has already acquired before entering the practice.[14]

1. Schematic Overview of Qualities of Excellence

Just as the specific content of the goods of excellence varies from practice to practice, so too does the specific content of the corresponding qualities of excellence, including practical wisdom, needed to attain them. However, just as the goods of excellence in all practices share similar taxonomic and other features at a high level of generality and abstraction, so do their corresponding qualities of excellence and practical wisdoms and we can therefore describe them in general terms applicable to all practices. In any practice, then, the qualities of excellence the practitioner must acquire and exhibit include various kinds of theoretical knowledge, cognitive and practical skills, and qualities of character (dispositions, attitudes, values, or virtues), with the overarching "master virtue" of prudence or practical wisdom (*phronesis*) at their apex. Study alone may be sufficient to acquire much of the needed theoretical knowledge but habitual practice and experience are necessary to acquire the required skills and qualities of character, including the "master virtue" of practical wisdom itself. With this understanding, we can expand Nancy Snow's three paradigms for virtue acquisition through habituation and apply them to all three types of qualities of excellence. Thus, agents may acquire theoretical knowledge, skills, and qualities of character, especially virtues, including the "master virtue" of practical wisdom, in any of three ways: automatically and non-consciously while they consciously aim at something else; consciously through their advertent efforts to acquire the quality and their teachers' or mentors' advertent efforts to instruct them in it; and consciously through their total immersion of in a way of life and advertent reflection

---

13. On the importance of prudence or practical wisdom for success in practices and human flourishing, see ALASDAIR MACINTYRE, ETHICS IN THE CONFLICTS OF MODERNITY: AN ESSAY ON DESIRE, PRACTICAL REASONING, AND NARRATIVE 49–50, 74, 118, 215–18 (2016). *See also id.* at 180–81 (importance of practical wisdom for flourishing of communities).

14. For discussion of this relationship in the case of professional practice, see Mark L. Jones, *Practical Wisdom and Vocation in Professional Formation: A Schematic Account, in* TOWARD HUMAN FLOURISHING: CHARACTER, PRACTICAL WISDOM, AND PROFESSIONAL FORMATION 195–96 (Mark L. Jones, Paul A. Lewis, & Kelly E. Reffitt, eds., 2013).

on various situations they encounter, under the guidance of their teachers or mentors.[15]

The master virtue of practical wisdom is a distinctive kind of "practical reasoning" or "practical rationality" (judgment resulting in action). Specifically, practical wisdom is the overarching ability of the expert practitioner, a *phronimos* in the practice, to access, draw upon, and conduct other, particular qualities or attributes — theoretical knowledge, skills, and qualities of character — in a way appropriate to the context so as to do the right thing in the right way at the right time for the right reason in the particular circumstances, for the benefit of the individual, organization, or community being served. In technical matters the practitioner is able to draw on relevant qualities or attributes to demonstrate technical expertise; in moral matters the practitioner is able to draw on relevant qualities or attributes to demonstrate moral expertise; and the practitioner is able to combine both types of expertise to achieve a practically wise outcome.

This overarching ability resolves itself — both in the technical sphere and the moral sphere, as well as in the combined operation of both spheres — into four interrelated abilities. These are the abilities

    (a) To see the world and read situations in a distinctive way,

    (b) To make sound judgments about ends and means (including ends that are a means to other ends)[16] in light of such perceptions, and to do so either intuitively and instantaneously or consciously and deliberately, depending on such factors as complexity, ambiguity, or novelty,

---

15. *See* Nancy E. Snow, *How Habits Make Us Virtuous*, *in* DEVELOPING THE VIRTUES: INTEGRATING PERSPECTIVES 135–56 (Julia Annas, Darcia Narvaez, & Nancy E. Snow, eds., 2016) (discussing three paradigms for virtue acquisition through habituation — non-conscious development of virtuous habits through "goal-dependent automaticity," conscious development of virtuous habits modeled on acquisition of practical skill or expertise, and conscious development of virtuous habits through the Confucian way of the *junzi*). For an application of Snow's tripartite taxonomy of virtue acquisition through habituation to legal education, see Mark L. Jones, *Developing Virtue and Practical Wisdom in the Legal Profession and Beyond*, 68 MERCER L. REV. 833, 838–39, 850–68 (2017).

16. *See* ALASDAIR MACINTYRE, DEPENDENT RATIONAL ANIMALS: WHY HUMAN BEINGS NEED THE VIRTUES 106 (1999) (discussing Aristotle's account of practical reasoning).

(c) To be motivated to translate judgment into action, and then
(d) To act.[17]

In brief, the practically wise practitioner has good judgment and acts well on the basis of that good judgment.

If we are to flourish in a practice, it is clearly important that we move toward acquiring and exercising the practical wisdom of the practice — that we move toward becoming a *phronimos* in the practice.[18] But as we stated in Chapter 2, only those who have become "independent practical rea-

---

17. In the moral sphere these four abilities are the elements of what is known as the Four Component Model of Morality (FCM): moral sensitivity, moral motivation, moral reasoning, and moral implementation. The FCM provides the "moral infrastructure" or "moral technology" necessary to effectuate any approach to morality and ethics, including an approach that stresses a moral actor's virtue and character. However, we will follow the Aristotelian moral tradition in requiring an association with virtue, the human good, and human flourishing for its four interrelated abilities to be regarded as explicating practical wisdom. For a good introduction to the FCM, see Darcia Narvaez, *Wisdom as Mature Moral Functioning: Insights from Developmental Psychology and Neurobiology*, in TOWARD HUMAN FLOURISHING, op. cit., at 35–37 (referring to these abilities as ethical sensitivity, ethical judgment, ethical focus, and ethical action). For more detailed discussion of the FCM, see Muriel J. Bebeau, Stephen J. Thoma & Clark D. Cunningham, *Educational Programs for Professional Identity Formation: The Role of Social Science Research*, 68 MERCER L. REV. 591, 598–608 (2017); Elizabeth C. Vozzola, *The Case for the Four Component Model vs. Moral Foundations Theory: A Perspective from Moral Psychology*, 68 MERCER L. REV. 633, 640–43 (2017). For another excellent account, written for a legal audience, see Clark Cunningham, *Learning Professional Responsibility*, in BUILDING ON BEST PRACTICES: TRANSFORMING LEGAL EDUCATION IN A CHANGING WORLD 282–89 (Deborah Maranville et. al. eds., 2015). *See also* Narvaez, *supra*, at 36–37 (identifying several skills and virtues within the individual components of the FCM). For an illuminating discussion illustrating how these four moral skills or capacities operate when exercising practical wisdom in legal practice, see Daisy H. Floyd, *Practical Wisdom: Reimagining Legal Education*, 10 U. ST. THOMAS L. J. 195, 196–99, 208–11 (2012) (giving several illustrations). For a very helpful synthetic account of practical wisdom, understood as moral expertise, that integrates the Aristotelian moral tradition with the insights of contemporary psychology and neuroscience, see PAUL LEWIS, FAITHFUL INNOVATION: THE RULE OF GOD AND A CHRISTIAN PRACTICAL WISDOM 39–53 (2020). *See also id.* at 28–30 (discussing practical reasoning and contrasting it with theoretical reasoning), 30–32 (identifying important questions and sources that can inform moral deliberation), 147–52 (Appendix addressing practical wisdom in the history of Christian ethics, and discussing in particular the thought of Augustine, Thomas Aquinas, Martin Luther, Stanley Hauerwas, and William F. May).

18. *See supra* notes 12–13 and accompanying text.

soners" are capable of practical wisdom.[19] So this also is essential to our flourishing in the practice. Thus MacIntyre states that:

> What it is for human beings to flourish does of course vary from context to context, but in every context it is as someone exercises in a relevant way the capacities of an independent practical reasoner that her or his potentialities for flourishing in a specifically human way are developed. So if we want to understand how it is good for humans to live, we need to know what it is to be excellent as an independent practical reasoner, that is, what the virtues of independent practical reasoning are.[20]

In Chapter 2 we also set out the three abilities or capacities of independent practical reasoners.[21] Because we must now consider how these three capacities relate to the four abilities that make up the overarching master virtue of practical wisdom, it is useful to set them out again here. These capacities are:

> [T]he ability to evaluate, modify, or reject our own practical judgments, to ask, that is, whether what we take to be good reasons for action really are sufficiently good reasons, *and* the ability to imagine realistically alternative possible futures, so as to be able to make rational choices between them, *and* the ability to stand back from our desires, so as to be able to enquire rationally what the pursuit of our

---

19. *See* Chapter 2, note 86 and accompanying text. *See also* MacIntyre, Rational Animals, op. cit., at 65–67, 71, 105–06 (attaining the goods of excellence of practices essential to human flourishing depends upon developing one's powers as an independent practical reasoner), 76–77, 92, 96 (emphasizing excellence or soundness as an independent practical reasoner and the virtues necessary to achieve it).

20. *Id.* at 76–77 (identifying "hunting, farming, mercantile, industrial" as "very different types of culture and economy and therefore... very different contexts of practice"). *See also id.* at 92 ("The conclusion of sound and effective practical reasoning is an action, that action which it is best for this particular agent to do in these particular circumstances"), 105 ("[T]he exercise of independent practical reasoning is one essential constituent to full human flourishing," and "not to be able to reason soundly at the level of practice is a grave disability"). *But see id.* at 108 ("[T]o flourish to the full extent... possible for a human being," it is necessary "[to] engage in and achieve *some measure of success* in the activities of an independent practical reasoner") (emphasis added).

21. See Chapter 2, note 44 and accompanying text.

good here and now requires and how our desires must be directed and, if necessary, reeducated, if we are to attain it.[22]

Rather than being coterminous with the four abilities, these three capacities seem to be foundational capacities the *phronimos* draws upon when exercising these abilities.

Arguably, then, the first capacity supports the second ability, the second capacity supports the first and second abilities, and the third capacity supports the third and fourth abilities. However, just as we saw in Chapter 2 that the three foundational capacities of an independent practical reasoner are interrelated, so also are the four abilities of the *phronimos* they support, and what was said in Chapter 2 about the interrelationship and development of the former applies equally to the interrelationship and development of the latter: "The relationship between [them] is complex. But they all contribute to a single process of development and a significant degree of failure in any one of [these] areas will be liable to produce or reinforce significant failure in the others."[23] Moreover, at an even deeper level, underlying the three foundational capacities themselves, and thus at the very core or heart of practical wisdom, may be the ability to balance empathy and detachment toward others.[24]

The preceding schematic account of the qualities of excellence focuses on practices and it therefore also applies to politics, at least where politics satisfies the conditions for being a practice (which MacIntyre claims the politics of the modern nation state does not, as we will see further in Chap-

---

22. MacIntyre, Rational Animals, op. cit., at 83.

23. *See* Chapter 2, note 45 and accompanying text (quoting MacIntyre, Rational Animals, op. cit., at 76).

24. *See* Barry Schwartz & Kenneth Sharpe, Practical Wisdom: The Right Way to Do the Right Thing 40–41 (2010) (drawing on Anthony Kronman's work, discussed in Chapter 7, to claim that "[d]oing any practice well demands learning how to balance empathy and detachment in the particular interactions we are having. The ability to balance these two opposites is at the heart of practical wisdom"). The statement in the text refers to moral expertise and holds true also for the fine arts and performing arts to the extent the artist interacts with others including the (anticipated) audience of the artist's work. Also, something analogous may apply to technical expertise insofar as such expertise requires the ability to balance empathy and detachment toward the materials of the practice. I am indebted to Jack Sammons for focusing my attention on the artist's situation. Sammons Email (September 2, 2020) [on file with author].

ter 6).[25] It applies as well *mutatis mutandis* to our moral quest to live a good life and do well in composing our life stories as a narrative unity that we explored in Chapter 2.[26] I provide additional elements for this schematic account of qualities of excellence elsewhere.[27] And later in this Chapter, as well as in Chapter 6, we will elaborate further upon the type of practical rationality, or practical wisdom, which is manifested in seeking to achieve goods of excellence, when we contrast it with the very different type of practical rationality which is manifested in seeking to achieve goods of a very different kind and which represents the dominant practical rationality in contemporary liberal democracies.[28] Here, however, we need to elaborate upon and illustrate those "qualities of character" that are virtues and also illustrate how the "master virtue" of practical wisdom enables a practitioner to respond appropriately to the particular circumstances arising in the practice. The illustrations will be drawn from the professional practices of architecture, law, and medicine. In such professional practice, the possession and exercise of particular virtues and of the "master virtue" of practical wisdom are at the heart of "professional character" and "professional identity."

2. Operational Virtues

In this Section B we have been considering "operational" qualities practitioners must exhibit to attain a practice's goods of excellence in their regular daily activities in accordance with the practice's standards of excellence. In the above schematic overview of these qualities of excellence, qualities of character are described as "dispositions, attitudes, values, or virtues." Although some may use these terms interchangeably to describe the same thing, there may be significant distinctions among them and our focus here will be on "virtues."

---

25. *See* Chapter 5, notes 5–6, 38, 41–42 and accompanying text; Chapter 6, notes 1–4 and accompanying text.

26. *See* Chapter 2, notes 69, 73–75, 82–86, and accompanying text.

27. *See* Mark L. Jones, *Developing Virtue and Practical Wisdom in the Legal Profession and Beyond*, 68 MERCER L. REV. 845–49 (2017); Jones, *Schematic Account*, op. cit., at 193–96; *see also* Mark L. Jones, *Fisherman Jack: Living in "Juropolis" — The Fishing Village of the Law*, 66 MERCER L. REV. 485, 487 (2015).

28. *See infra* notes 116–18, 128–35 and accompanying text; Chapter 6, notes 92–99, 130–39 and accompanying text.

In Chapter 2 we discussed Nancy Snow's generic definition of a virtue as well as MacIntyre's particular, Aristotelian understanding of a virtue and his "unitary core concept of the virtues" in the Western moral tradition of the virtues.[29] We also encountered one function of the virtues in MacIntyre's "unitary core concept," that is, their role in enabling us to understand and pursue our own individual good — our own individual *telos* — as we compose the stories of our lives.[30] Here in Chapter 3 we encounter another function of the virtues in MacIntyre's "unitary core concept," that is, their role in "enabling their possessors to achieve the goods internal to practices" — in other words their role in enabling us to achieve goods of excellence — which is central to our individual quests.[31] And in the present context, we encounter one aspect of that role, that is, virtues functioning among the operational qualities of excellence as "operational" virtues exhibited by a practitioner in his or her daily activities.

Geoff Moore's account of the qualities needed by a hypothetical architect, Elaine, if she is to be a *good* architect illuminates the critical importance of this function of the virtues in daily practice:

> For Elaine to become an architect required that she mastered a whole range of practical knowledge and technical skills. She needed to understand, for example, the properties of different materials, and the way in which these different materials might be combined to create a building, and the various working, leisure, and functional spaces within it. But essential as those skills and knowledge are, it would not in the end make Elaine a *good* architect. For that, she had to learn to be patient with and attentive to clients in order to be sure that she understands their requirements. She needs to be diligent in her work to ensure that mistakes in design or in implementation do not occur. She may on occasion need to be courageous, but also courteous, in standing up for a particular aspect of her design, which

---

29. *See* Chapter 2, notes 65–72 and accompanying text. For MacIntyre's statement of the three functions of the virtues in his "unitary core concept of the virtues" in the Western moral tradition of the virtues, see Alasdair MacIntyre, *A Partial Response to My Critics, in* AFTER MACINTYRE: CRITICAL PERSPECTIVES ON THE WORK OF ALASDAIR MACINTYRE 288 (John Horton & Susan Mendus, eds., 1994).

30. *See* Chapter 2, notes 69, 73–94 and accompanying text.

31. *See* MacIntyre, *Partial Response*, op. cit., at 288 (articulating this role of the virtues).

she knows is necessary but costly, and which it may be difficult to explain to clients. In addition to the knowledge and skills she has gained (and which may very well need to be honed and updated over time), she will need certain qualities of character, certain virtues, to be a good architect. Patience, attentiveness, diligence, courage, and courteousness may well be some of these.[32]

Moore's list of virtues includes two main types of general virtues — those typically related to what Thomas Lickona calls "performance character" (such as diligence) and those typically related to "moral character" (such as patience, attentiveness, courage, and courteousness).[33] As Moore appears to acknowledge, the list is seriously incomplete. But his account does serve to illustrate the nature and function of these virtues, and it also suggests that performance character and moral character, and the virtues that characterize them, are typically interdependent, working together synergistically.[34]

----

32. GEOFF MOORE, VIRTUE AT WORK: ETHICS FOR INDIVIDUALS, MANAGERS, AND ORGANIZATIONS 39 (2017).

33. For discussion of the concept of "performance character," see Thomas Lickona, *Developing the Ethical Thinker and Responsible Moral Agent*, in TOWARD HUMAN FLOURISHING, op. cit., at 43–46 (identifying "performance character attributes such as creativity, curiosity, love of learning, and persistence").

34. For further discussion of the interdependence and synergy between performance character and moral character, *see id.* While bearing in mind this interdependence and synergy, presumably "intellectual virtues" are typically related to performance character and "civic virtues" are typically related to moral character. I am indebted to Jack Sammons for focusing the point about the incompleteness of Moore's list of general virtues. Thus, a good architect must exhibit many additional general virtues to properly consider and be responsive to all relevant constituencies and interests. As Sammons says, "In the practice there is so much more and so many others to be considered: those who will use the building, those who will see and live with the building, those who will build the building, the building's relationship to other buildings, to the natural environment, to the character of the community, and so forth." Sammons Email (September 3, 2020) [on file with author]. *Compare* Sammons' description of the master brick mason in Jack L. Sammons, *Brick Art in Washington Park: Artists in the Public Realm*, MACON MONITOR (March 26, 2015), http://maconmonitor.com/2015/03/26/brick-art-in-washington-park-artists-in-the-public-realm/. Referring to "the five-thousand-year-old tradition of this craft" and to brick work as "art," Sammons explains that a master mason needs

> [N]ot just the required knowledge, skills, and language of bricklaying, but the set of virtues excellence in bricklaying requires: self-discipline, attention to detail, patience, attunement to the world around the construction, and the humility required to let the materials of the craft — the bricks, the trowel, the mortar (or "mud" as it is called), and so forth — speak to you as you work.

Apart from general virtues such as those in Moore's list, the practitioner may also need to exhibit distinctive virtues specific to the particular practice or type of practice to attain the practice's goods of excellence. In the practice of law, for example, in addition to the "master virtue" of professional practical wisdom, the good lawyer must exhibit distinctive professional virtues such as competence, fidelity to the client, fidelity to the law, public-spiritedness, and civility,[35] as well as related virtues of the lawyer as rhetorician.[36] And here too, there are important relationships and synergies between different types of virtues. These distinctive virtues may be profession-specific forms of more general virtues, or they may depend upon, presuppose, and indeed incorporate such virtues, or both. These general virtues include those listed by Moore (patience, attentiveness, diligence, courage, and courteousness) as well as others such as conscientiousness, perseverance, resilience, loyalty, honesty, justice, temperance, empathy, respect for others, compassion, generosity, and so on.[37]

Presumably, these various relationships between different types of virtues conduce to their mutual development and strengthening. Presumably, too, the practitioner's exercise of virtues within one practice (and the character formation attendant upon such exercise) may also contribute to the exercise of virtue within other practices as well.[38] And here we should notice the important role of the virtue of integrity that we encountered in Chapter 2.[39]

Id. See also supra note 24 (discussing artists in the context of moral expertise).

35. *See generally* Patrick Emery Longan, Daisy Hurst Floyd, and Timothy W. Floyd, The Formation of Professional Identity: The Path from Student to Lawyer (2020); Patrick E. Longan, *Teaching Professionalism*, 60 Mercer L. Rev. 659, 666–69 (2009) (discussing these virtues).

36. *See* Jack L. Sammons, *The Georgia Crawl*, 53 Mercer L. Rev., 985, 985–86 (2002); Jack L. Sammons, *Traditionalists, Technicians, and Legal Education*, 38 Gonz. L. Rev. 246 n28 (2002) [quoting from Sammons, *Georgia Crawl*] (identifying at least fifteen such virtues).

37. The distinctive professional virtues of the good lawyer and their relationship to more general virtues are discussed further in Chapter 7, notes 140–48 and accompanying text.

38. *See* Moore, Virtue at Work, op. cit., at 177 (discussing character formation among surgeons and observing that "the development of virtues in one practice is transferable to other practices — we might expect surgeons to display the virtues they have developed in the course of their medical careers, and so to be courageous, humble, wise, and so on in all the other aspects of their lives"). For a more complete list of virtues needed by surgeons, see *infra* note 43.

39. *See* Chapter 2, notes 88–94 and accompanying text.

3. Operation of the "Master Virtue" of Practical Wisdom

To illustrate how the "master virtue" of practical wisdom operates to enable a practitioner to respond appropriately to the particular circumstances arising in the practice, we turn from the practices of architecture and law to the practice of medicine, specifically surgery, and to Moore's discussion of a 2011 study of the practice of surgery, authored by Daniel Hall.[40] In discussing the practical wisdom of good surgeons, Moore quotes Hall's description of what we have called "technical expertise":

> Even the most detailed description of the technical steps of an operation will not prepare the surgeon for the hundreds of small decisions that must be made: Where should I cut? How should I dissect this tissue plane? What instrument should I use? How hard can I push, pull or tear this particular piece of tissue? ... What can I get away with for the sake of expedience and what limits must I not cross?[41]

Technical expertise draws on technical knowledge and technical skills, as well as virtues related to performance character. However, as we saw in subsection 1 above, practical wisdom requires more than technical expertise. It also requires what we have called "moral expertise." In describing this "inescapable moral dimension," Moore again quotes Hall:

> Consciously or subconsciously, each little decision made by surgeons regarding the care of patients is a moral decision. That is to say that surgeons choose among the options available to them because they have particular opinions regarding what would be good (or bad) for their patients. Such choice requires practical wisdom, and the formation of that wisdom involves many years of training alongside surgeons who embody proven practical wisdom.[42]

---

40. Daniel E. Hall, *The Guild of Surgeons as A Tradition of Moral Enquiry*, 36 THE JOURNAL OF MEDICINE AND PHILOSOPHY: A FORUM FOR BIOETHICS AND PHILOSOPHY OF MEDICINE 114 (2011).

41. MOORE, VIRTUE AT WORK, op. cit., at 176 (quoting Hall, *Guild of Surgeons*, op. cit., at 119). *See also id.* at 173 (referring to "good surgeons").

42. *Id.* (quoting Hall, *Guild of Surgeons*, op. cit., at 123).

Moral expertise draws on moral knowledge and moral skills, as well as virtues related to moral character.[43] This "inescapable moral dimension" is especially evident in Hall's discussion of how practical wisdom aims at "achieving something truly worthwhile and important: namely something good," and of how "[a]s such[,] … it functions only in relation to thick notions of what human beings are meant to be and become." He continues:

> In short, the goal of practical wisdom is human flourishing in all the richness that word implies. More than the comparatively thin or limited notions of utilitarian happiness or the socially contracted justice of reciprocal tolerance, Aristotle and MacIntyre develop the concept of human flourishing (*eudaimonia*) as a thick or full notion of genuine happiness, health, integration, and harmony…. For Aristotle and MacIntyre, it is impossible to choose wisely without a clear sense of what it means for human beings to flourish, and all moral action is directed toward this goal. Consciously or not, the best surgeons have clear notions of what it means for their patients to flourish.[44]

In other words, practically wise surgeons serve their patients by using their expertise to do those things that will maximize their specific contribution to a patient's flourishing in the particular circumstances, including of course any limitations necessarily imposed by the patient's condition. In this respect, indeed, "the fellowship of surgeons" is an example of "particular communities engaged in particular practices ordered toward particular notions of human flourishing."[45] It is important to emphasize that Hall is describing "good" surgeons, or indeed even "the best" surgeons, and certainly not those who corrupt the practice because they are more interested in performing a "walletectomy" than they are in contributing to the pa-

---

43. Regarding the virtues needed by good surgeons, Moore explains that while the passage just quoted "picks out one specific virtue — practical wisdom — which… has been called the 'nurse' of all the virtues, the study identified several other virtues also required of surgeons: courage, humility, assertiveness, gentleness, compassion, tact, industriousness, and honesty." *Id.* (citing Hall, *Guild of Surgeons*, op, cit., at 131). However, one of these — industriousness — would seem to be typically related to performance character rather than moral character.

44. *Id.* at 177 (quoting Hall, op. cit., at 124).

45. *Id.* at 175 (quoting Hall, op. cit., at 115).

tient's flourishing (which may, of course, require them to advise the patient to consider non-surgical treatments).[46] Suitably adapted to the particular context, then, we can agree with Moore that Hall's account of the goal of practical wisdom extends beyond surgery, applying to all practices and to the moral conversations between the practitioner in the practice and those served by the practice.[47]

C. Attaining Goods of Excellence and Qualities of Excellence

We can understand both the standards of excellence and the qualities of excellence in terms of the goods of excellence. Recall that these goods of excellence include the excellence of the practitioner's performance, the excellence of the product resulting from this performance, and the excellence of the way of life lived out as a practitioner in the practice.[48] The standards of excellence specify the specific content of these goods and the particular qualities required to attain them. Moreover, because these goods include excellence of performance and way of life, the qualities of excellence (including particular virtues and the "master virtue" of practical wisdom) that are central in such performance and way of life are recursively themselves also among the goods of excellence (although for the sake of clarity or emphasis we will often continue to refer to them separately). This notion seems to be reflected in MacIntyre's discussion of "productive crafts"

---

46. Thus, Hall observes that:

> Without doubt, the character of the surgical profession is not entirely virtuous. Surgical training can and does inculcate vice as well as virtue, and given the ever present and powerful motives for profit and promotion, surgeons may not be as virtuous as they aspire to be. However, the collective and individual failures of surgeons to embody the virtues of their profession do not change the fact that for better or for worse, the practice of surgery requires a practical wisdom that is taught only through experience, and no amount of technical mastery can ever replace the tradition of wisdom that guides surgeons to know when (and when not) to apply the blade.

Hall, *Guild of Surgeons*, op, cit., at 126–27. Moreover, not only do unvirtuous surgeons not contribute to the patient's flourishing; they also do not contribute to their own flourishing except in the most external, contingent sense. For further discussion of the corruption of a practice, see *infra* Part IV, Section C.

47. *See* MOORE, VIRTUE AT WORK, op. cit., at 177–78 (extending Hall's account to "any other practice-based activity").

48. *Supra* notes 10–11 and accompanying text.

such as catching fish or building houses, in which MacIntyre explains that
"[t]he aim internal to such productive crafts, when they are in good order"
is excellent performance that results not only in a "good product" but also
in "the craftsperson [being] perfected through and in her or his activity."[49]

1. Learning About Excellence in the
Tradition of the Practice

As we will see in Part IV when we consider the fourth element in Mac-
Intyre's definition of a practice, an aspiring practitioner discovers the practice's standards, goods, and qualities of excellence after entering the practice.[50] But *how* does an aspiring practitioner discover them? How exactly
does an aspiring practitioner *come to know* what is excellent performance,
what is an excellent product resulting from such performance, and what
is excellent about the way of life that is lived out as a practitioner in the
practice? How does he or she *come to know* what qualities of excellence
are needed to achieve these goods of excellence, and how to acquire these
qualities? How does he or she *come to know* what the practical wisdom of
the practice is, and how to acquire it?

One straightforward answer is that aspiring practitioners learn these
things from the existing community of practitioners, who apply their standards of excellence to guide and measure performance, resulting product,
and way of life, both in advertent instruction and guidance and through
inadvertent example. But where did current practitioners acquire their
own understanding of the standards of excellence, goods of excellence, and
qualities of excellence of the practice? Here again, we can give the same
straightforward answer — they learned these things from those who constituted the community of practitioners when *they* were aspiring practitioners entering the practice. And this means, of course, that we are talking
about a tradition of the practice that is handed on from one generation of
practitioners to the next, albeit always subject to change and evolution at
the hands of the community of current practitioners (as we will see further

---

49. MacIntyre, *Partial Response*, op. cit., at 284. For additional confirmation of this
notion, see MacIntyre, After Virtue, op. cit., at 188 (identifying "the achievement of
a certain highly particular kind of analytical skill, strategic imagination and competitive
intensity" as "goods internal to the practice of chess").

50. *See infra* note 110 and accompanying text.

in Part III when we consider the third element in the definition). As Mac-
Intyre puts it, the practitioners in a practice are "the bearers of a tradition"
of the practice through which the practice is "transmitted and reshaped,"
perhaps even through many generations.[51] Although using the gendered
language that was customary in the mid-twentieth century, Karl Llewellyn
eloquently describes the powerful influence of such tradition generally,
when addressing "the craft tradition in appellate judging":

> [O]ne of the more obvious and obstinate facts about human beings
> is that they operate in and respond to traditions and especially to
> such traditions as are offered to them by the crafts they follow. Tra-
> dition grips them, shapes them, limits them, guides them; not for
> nothing do we speak of *ingrained* ways of work or thought, of men
> *experienced* or case-hardened, of *habits* of mind. Tradition, more-
> over, wreaks these things upon human beings notwithstanding that
> in a very real degree men also make use of the tradition, reshape it
> in the very use, sometimes manipulate it to the point of artifice or
> actual evasion if need, duty, or both, seem so to require.[52]

2. Fundamental Prerequisite Virtues

At this point we encounter a second aspect of the role of the virtues in
"enabling their possessors to achieve the goods internal to practices."[53] If
aspiring practitioners are to learn what they need to learn from the existing practitioner community, they must accept the authority of the practice
and this community's standards of excellence as well as "the inadequacy
of [their] own performance as judged by them";[54] they must "subordi-
nat[e]" themselves in their relationships with current practitioners;[55] and

---

51. MacIntyre, After Virtue, op. cit., at 221.

52. Karl Llewellyn, The Common Law Tradition: Deciding Appeals 53 (1960)
[quoted in Anthony Kronman, The Lost Lawyer: Failing Ideals of The Legal Profession 215 (1993)].

53. For discussion of the first aspect, see *supra* notes 31–47 and accompanying text.

54. MacIntyre, After Virtue, op. cit., at 190 (also observing that "we cannot be initiated into a practice without accepting the authority of the best standards realized so far").

55. *Id.* at 191 (explaining that a practice's goods of excellence "can only be achieved
by subordinating ourselves within the practice in our relationship to other practitioners");
MacIntyre, Rational Animals, op. cit., at 91–92, 99, 107–08 (discussing how apprentices

they must exhibit various general virtues such as justice, courage, honesty, and temperateness in these relationships.[56] With regard to justice, courage, and honesty, aspiring practitioners must, for example, give due deference to the wisdom of current practitioners, courageously expose their inadequacies when learning how to engage in the practice, and honestly accept criticism of those inadequacies and suggestions for improvement.[57] And temperateness is required to be able to stand back from and evaluate one's desires in this process.[58] Something similar may be said about the relationships among current practitioners if they are to continue learning from one another.[59] For similar reasons, too, both aspiring practitioners and current practitioners must accept the authority of the tradition of the practice, enter into a proper relationship with past practitioners, especially "those whose achievements extended the reach of the practice to its present point," and exhibit these same virtues if they are to learn from

---

are dependent upon more expert practitioners, in the relationships of giving and receiving within the practice, to teach them about the goods of excellence of a practice and how to be independent practical reasoners with respect to such goods).

56. MacIntyre, After Virtue, op. cit., at 190–91 (justice, courage, and honesty required to achieve a practice's goods of excellence); MacIntyre, Rational Animals, op. cit., at 87–89, 95–96 ("a certain range of intellectual and moral virtues," including temperateness and honesty, required to become independent practical reasoners), 119–20 (referring to the indispensable role of virtues such as justice, temperateness, truthfulness, and courage in enabling us to become independent practical reasoners in relationships of giving and receiving).

57. See MacIntyre, After Virtue, op. cit., at 191 ("We have to learn to recognize what is due to whom; we have to be prepared to take whatever self-endangering risks are demanded along the way; and we have to listen carefully to what we are told about our own inadequacies and to reply with the same carefulness for the facts").

58. See MacIntyre, Rational Animals, op. cit., at 87–88 (discussing the virtue of temperateness, in particular in relation to the ability of a child "to stand back from her or his desires and evaluate them"). As we have seen, this is one of the capacities of independent practical reasoners; see Chapter 2, notes 43–44 and accompanying text; supra notes 21–22 and accompanying text.

59. See MacIntyre, After Virtue, op. cit., at 191–93 (discussing how virtues such as justice, courage, and honesty are required in the "relationship between those who participate in [a practice]" in order to ensure "the kind of cooperation, the kind of recognition of authority and of achievement, the kind of respect for standards and the kind of risk-taking which are characteristically involved in practices").

the exemplary achievements of past practitioners and the tradition.[60] Of course, there can be tensions among the relevant relationships. For example, even new practitioners, and perhaps even aspiring practitioners, may justifiably criticize a corrupted practice and the current practitioners who have corrupted it because they have fallen away from what is best in the tradition. The deference that is "due" and to whom it is "due" may vary, therefore, depending on the circumstances. We will consider the corruption of a practice further in Part IV, Section C.

We should also not overlook the important role of dialogical virtues in the process of attaining a practice's goods of excellence and qualities of excellence (and more broadly in sustaining the ongoing conversation that is constitutive of the practice),[61] or the importance of virtues of performance character.[62] Moreover, following Jack Sammons' lovely reframing of practices as art, we might perhaps identify as the most fundamental virtue, undergirding and infusing all the others, a particular form of humility, that is, a humility before and a resulting attunement to the materials of the practice, or art.[63]

In Section B.2 we saw that various general virtues and perhaps some practice-specific virtues will be among the "operational" qualities of excel-

---

60. *Id.* at 194. *See also id.* at 190 (observing that "we cannot be initiated into a practice without accepting the authority of the best standards realized so far").

61. I am indebted to Jack Sammons for bringing the point in parentheses to my attention. For a sense of some of these dialogical virtues, see MACINTYRE, RATIONAL ANIMALS, op. cit., at 111 (discussing the virtue of "conversational justice"), 161 (identifying various virtues as prerequisite conditions for a community's shared rational critical enquiry); Mark W. Roche, *Should Faculty Members Teach Virtues and Values? That Is the Wrong Question*, 95 LIBERAL EDUCATION 32, 34–35 (Summer 2009) (identifying thirteen intellectual and moral virtues that necessarily develop through proper participation in college classes and related intellectual pursuits). *See also* Sammons, *Georgia Crawl*, op. cit., at 985–86 (identifying fifteen virtues essential for the practical wisdom of the lawyer as rhetorician). The dialogical virtues identified by MacIntyre, Roche, and Sammons are discussed in Chapter 5, notes 167–76 and accompanying text, Chapter 7, notes 147, 189, 295–310 and accompanying text; Chapter 8, notes 42–46, 49 and accompanying text.

62. *See supra* notes 32–34 and accompanying text.

63. *See* Jack L. Sammons, *Can Law Be Art?*, 66 MERCER L. REV. 527 (2015) (setting forth this approach). For earlier relevant discussion, see Part III, Section D of Chapter 2. In email correspondence, Sammons also proposes "a missing virtue, one related to others but perhaps separate: the virtue of coming to accept the mostly imagined community of practitioners as a 'we' partly definitional of who you are and are to become. It is a virtue at odds with the liberal presumptions in our time." Sammons Email (May 13, 2015) [on file with author].

lence a practitioner must exhibit to attain a practice's goods of excellence in his or her regular daily activities in accordance with the practice's standards of excellence.[64] In the present context, however, the general virtues discussed above function as "fundamental prerequisite virtues" without which it is not possible to discover, attain, and then continue learning about and attaining, the standards, goods, and qualities of excellence in the first place.[65] When functioning in this way, the general virtues have more to do with ensuring the proper conditions for *learning about* these standards, goods, and qualities by establishing and maintaining proper relationships within the practitioner community and with the materials of the practice, than with the *actual demonstration* of excellence in the regular activities of everyday practice. The same general virtue, then, may be exhibited and function as either a "fundamental prerequisite virtue" or an "operational" virtue, depending on the context and the purpose for its exercise. Admittedly, this distinction may be *functionally* artificial to the extent learning about standards, goods, and qualities of excellence occurs in the experiential context of actual practice.[66] However, because the distinction seems *analytically* sound and serves to illuminate different *ways* in which virtues can be exercised in the context of actual practice, we will continue to use it.

In Chapter 5 we will supplement the analysis of prerequisite virtues here when we examine explicitly the role of these and other virtues in the process of developing and sustaining our powers of practical reason within practices.[67]

D. The Ultimate Excellence of the Practice and Its Tradition

Even though the practitioner community embraces and transmits an understanding of the practice and its tradition, we can still ask: where does this understanding come from most *fundamentally*? What is it that *ultimately* determines the specific standards of excellence, goods of excel-

---

64. *See supra* notes 32–37 and accompanying text.

65. *See* Jones, *Developing Virtue and Practical Wisdom*, op. cit., at 842–45 (drawing on this distinction).

66. *See* MacIntyre, Rational Animals, op. cit., at 88–89 (discussing how virtues are "learned in... those contexts of practice in which we learn from others how to discharge our roles and functions").

67. *See* Chapter 5, Part II, Section C.3.

lence, and qualities of excellence of the practice? These questions are really
questions about the point and purpose of the practice, and to answer them
we have to ask a further question: What is the ultimate good, the ultimate
end, of the practice? MacIntyre answers this question in his discussion of
the practice of a "craft," which for our purposes we can assume is synonymous with a "practice." Thus, MacIntyre explains how practitioners of a
craft pursue "some conception of a finally perfected work" that represents
the "shared *telos*" or "final cause" of the craft (the ultimate end or the ultimate reason for the sake of which the craft exists);[68] he also refers to this
shared *telos* as the "ultimate excellence."[69]

To illustrate the nature of such a shared *telos*, ultimate end, or ultimate
excellence, MacIntyre considers the craft or practice of moral enquiry.
Thus, "[t]he *telos* of moral enquiry ... is excellence in the achievement
not only of adequate theoretical understanding of the specifically human
good, but also of the practical embodiment of that understanding in the
life of the particular enquirer."[70] In his most recent book MacIntyre provides other possible examples. He describes "[t]he end of farming" and
"the end of medical practice" as being "to produce food and to sustain
land and farm animals" (farming) and "to restore and maintain the health
of patients" (medical practice).[71] In the same work, however, he articulates
the ends of these two practices somewhat differently when describing "that
end state, the achievement of which in this particular time and place is
the appropriate end" of several listed practices: "the harvesting of a crop
of perfect vegetables and the renewal of the soil each year under unfa-
vorable conditions" (farming); "restor[ing] to health this particular set of

---

68. ALASDAIR MACINTYRE, THREE RIVAL VERSIONS OF MORAL ENQUIRY: ENCYCLOPAE-
DIA, GENEALOGY, AND TRADITION 64 (1990):

> Every craft is informed by some conception of a finally perfected work which
> serves as the shared *telos* of that craft. And what are actually produced as the
> best judgments or actions or objects so far are judged so because they stand
> in some determinate relationship to that *telos*, which furnishes them with
> their final cause.

Id.

69. *Id.* at 62.

70. *Id.* at 62–63. For MacIntyre's characterization of this activity as a "craft," see *id.* at 61
(referring to "philosophical enquiry" as a craft, at least when conceived in certain modes).

71. MACINTYRE, CONFLICTS OF MODERNITY, op. cit., at 227–28 (2016).

patients" (medicine); "the statement of the elegant, significant, and difficult proof" (mathematics); "the insightful performance by an orchestra
of work too often taken for granted, say, Mozart's clarinet music" (music);
and "captur[ing] what is unique in this particular face" (portrait painting).[72] Whether or not MacIntyre intends these as additional examples of
a practice's shared *telos* or ultimate excellence (or at least as examples of
certain aspects of such a shared *telos* or ultimate excellence), they provide
further useful guidance regarding how we might proceed in seeking to
articulate the shared *telos* or ultimate excellence of a practice.

E. Overarching Common Good and Specific Common Goods of the Practice, and Their Relationship to the Greater Common Good

The specific standards of excellence, goods of excellence, and qualities
of excellence in a practice, then, ultimately derive from the shared *telos* or
ultimate excellence that gives the practice its point and purpose.[73] At any
given time the community of practitioners will have a particular understanding of this shared *telos* or ultimate excellence, and all the specific standards, goods, and qualities of excellence will flow from this understanding.
We can call this particular understanding of the ultimate excellence the
overarching common good of the practice and of the practitioner community. It too is a standard and good of excellence of the practice — the practical ultimate standard and good of excellence. All the specific standards,
goods, and qualities of excellence are specific ends or *specific common
goods* of the practice and of the practitioner community which are entailed by, included within, and co-constitutive of the overarching common
good. What was said above regarding how practitioners first discover and
then continue to learn about the specific standards, goods, and qualities of
excellence from the practice community applies equally to how they first
discover and continue to learn about the ultimate excellence and overarching common good of the practice.[74]

---

72. *Id.* at 50.
73. ALASDAIR MacINTYRE, MORAL INQUIRY, op. cit., at 62–64; Jones, *Fisherman Jack*, op. cit., at 492–93.
74. *See supra* Section C.1 and 2.

All these various common goods of a practice are shared goods that benefit and belong to the practitioner community as a whole and not just its members individually.[75] In this regard MacIntyre distinguishes among "different types of human association" and "[r]ival conceptions of the common good [that is] the end of their shared activities."[76] Thus in one type of association

> [T]he common good of [the] association is no more than the sum-ming of the goods pursued by individuals as members of that asso-ciation, just because the association itself is no more than an instru-ment employed by those individuals to achieve their individual ends [which exist]... antecedently to and independently of their member-ship in it.[77]

An example of such an association is "an investment club, by means of which individuals are able to avail themselves of investment opportunities requiring capital sums larger than any one of them possesses."[78] Because such an association lacks shared goods of excellence as common goods, it does not fit the definition of a practice. Moreover, "[p]articipation in and support for such associations is ... rational only so long as and insofar as it provides a more efficient method of achieving ... individual ends than would alternative types of activity."[79] Later in this Chapter we will call the sorts of individualistic goods that are the focus of such an association "ex-ternal goods" or "goods of effectiveness" when discussing their counter-parts in the context of a practice and contrasting them with the practice's goods of excellence.[80]

Very different is a second type of association in which

---

75. MacIntyre, After Virtue, op. cit., at 190–91 ("[I]t is characteristic of [goods of excellence] that their achievement is a good for the whole community who participate in the practice"). *See also id.* at 194 (referring to "cooperative care for common goods of the practice").

76. Alasdair MacIntyre, *Politics, Philosophy, and the Common Good* (1997) *in* The Mac-Intyre Reader 239 (Kelvin Knight, ed., 1998) (observing that "[t]he notion of the common good has been used in so many different ways and for so many different purposes").

77. *Id.* at 239–40.

78. *Id.*

79. *Id.* at 240.

80. *See infra* Part IV, Section A.1.

[T]he good of the association cannot be constructed out of what were the goods of its individual members, antecedently to and independently of their membership in it. In these cases the good of the whole cannot be arrived at by summing the goods of the parts. Such are those goods not only *achieved* by means of cooperative activity and shared understanding of their significance, but in key part *constituted* by cooperative activity and shared understanding of their significance.[81]

Examples of such common goods include "the excellence in cooperative activity achieved by fishing crews and by string quartets, by farming households and by teams of research scientists"[82] — associations that, because they generate shared goods of excellence as common goods, do fit the definition of a practice. Moreover, as our discussion of fishing crews in Chapter 4 will illustrate, the desire to attain such goods of excellence, and allegiance to the practitioner community and its way of life, may make it rational for practitioners to continue supporting and participating in the practice even during times of economic hardship when the individualistic goods of effectiveness are significantly diminished.

In Chapter 2 we saw that when common goods of a practice contribute to the *greater common good* of the broader community, and when the motivation and vocation of the practitioner is to attain such common goods and contribute to the greater common good, then participation in the practice will be viewed as a calling and will be both objectively and subjectively meaningful, which is also important for the practitioner's flourishing in the practice.[83] We now need to consider briefly the relationship between the common goods of practices and the greater common good.

Practices and their practitioners contribute to the greater common good if they promote the flourishing not only of those engaged in the practice but also, and especially, of those the practice serves, as the example of

---

81. MacIntyre, *Common Good*, op. cit., at 240 (emphasis added).

82. *Id.*

83. *See* Chapter 2, notes 107, 123–26 and accompanying text. Of course, in Chapter 2 we were still using the term "internal goods" to refer to goods of excellence and qualities of excellence. For the terminological transition to "goods of excellence," see *supra* note 8 and accompanying text.

the surgeon discussed above illustrates.[84] The broader community's determination of a practice's contribution to the greater common good and the
flourishing of those the practice serves is essentially a political one, "in
the Aristotelian sense" of "political" (being concerned with the common
good), that may change over time, as the example of the tobacco industry
illustrates.[85] Consequently, although the point or purpose of a practice is
found in its shared *telos* or ultimate excellence, and in the overarching
common good that represents the practitioner community's particular understanding of this ultimate excellence at any given time, for the practice
and its practitioner community to flourish within the broader community
this point and purpose, this ultimate excellence and overarching common
good, must remain anchored in broader community acceptance. However,
the broader community does not simply impose its notions of the greater
common good on the practice and its practitioner community from "outside" as it were, because the practice always also seeks to "teach" others its
worth as it "engages in conversation" with the broader culture.[86] We will
explore the nature of the greater common good of the broader community
and its relationship to practitioner communities and their common goods
in greater depth in Chapters 4 and 5.

III. An Evolving Living Tradition

The third element in MacIntyre's definition of a practice is that by engaging in the practice consistent with the second element, "human powers to achieve excellence, and human conceptions of the ends and goods
involved, are systematically extended" within the evolving tradition of
the practice. Thus, "[p]ractices never have a goal or goals fixed for all
time — painting has no such goal nor has physics — but the goals them-

---

84. *See supra* notes 44–47 and accompanying text.

85. MOORE, VIRTUE AT WORK, op. cit., at 87–88 (emphasizing the importance of "appropriate deliberative structures" facilitating the necessary conversations and decisions).

86. *See* Jack L. Sammons, *The Common Good of Practices*, FIU L. REV. 69, 69–70 (2013)
(explaining that: "no practice is completely closed" but for "its own good" and for "its own
continuation and its own flourishing" every practice seeks to teach the broader culture to
appreciate what it offers; that practices "do[] this, primarily, by initiating people into [their]
ways of thinking"; and that "[t]hrough their elaboration, practices bring things into their
own ... and thus tend to connect to the rest of the community's life in ways such that the
practice (and the character it requires) is thought to be worthy").

selves are transmuted by the history of the activity."[87] In other words, as the earlier reference to past practitioners "whose achievements extended the reach of the practice to its present point" already suggests,[88] the practice or craft evolves; and it does so as the practitioner community pursues its shared *telos* or "ultimate excellence" through argument and criticism within the tradition of the practice:

> The standards of achievement within any craft are justified historically. They have emerged from the criticism of their predecessors and they are justified because and insofar as they have remedied the defects and transcended the limitations of those predecessors as guides to excellent achievement within that particular craft. Every craft is informed by some conception of a finally perfected work which serves as the shared *telos* of that craft. And what are actually produced as the best judgments or actions or objects so far are judged so because they stand in some determinate relationship to that *telos*, which furnishes them with their final cause.[89]

And so progress is made in producing judgments, actions, or objects "which are rationally justified as the best so far, in the light of those formulations of the relevant standards of achievement which are rationally justified as the best so far."[90] The type of reasoning or rationality that is specific to a practice or craft is always historically situated and inseparable from the tradition of the practice.[91] And progress in developing the standards of excellence within a tradition of practice occurs by "transcending through criticism and invention the limitations of what had hitherto been reasoned in that tradition."[92] Consequently,

---

87. MacIntyre, After Virtue, op. cit., at 193–94.

88. *See supra* note 60 and accompanying text.

89. MacIntyre, Moral Inquiry, op. cit., at 64.

90. *Id.* (addressing progress in producing "types of judgment or activity" in forms of theoretical or practical intellectual inquiry).

91. *Id.* at 64–65 (1990). *See also id.* at 58–60 (contrasting this conception of reasoning or rationality with the "encyclopaedist" conception which regards reason as "impersonal, universal, and disinterested" and the "genealogist" conception which regards reason as "the unwitting representative of particular interests, masking their drive to power by its false pretensions to neutrality and disinterestedness").

92. MacIntyre, After Virtue, op. cit., at 222.

[W]hen an institution — a university, say, or a farm, or a hospital — is the bearer of a tradition of practice or practices, its common life will be partly, but in a centrally important way, constituted by a continuous argument as to what a university is and ought to be or what good farming is or what good medicine is. Traditions, when vital, embody continuities of conflict.... A living tradition then is an historically extended, socially embodied argument, and an argument precisely in part about the goods which constitute that tradition. Within a tradition the pursuit of goods extends through generations, sometimes through many generations.[93]

Clearly, then, in a practice with a living tradition the specific standards of excellence, goods of excellence, and qualities of excellence are not static but always in a state of dynamic development. Although the ultimate excellence of the practice may be unchanging, the particular understanding of this ultimate excellence — in other words, the practitioner community's overarching common good — may *well* change. And as this happens — as the practice community's overarching common good evolves, or as their understanding of the best way of achieving it evolves — so correspondingly the specific standards, goods, and qualities of excellence that are the specific common goods of the practice will also evolve. As a result, the practice community may well discover, for example, that new qualities of excellence (new knowledge, skills, or qualities of character) are needed in the light of experience. Moreover, as part of this overall process the practitioner community should also remain attentive to how well the common goods of the practice are contributing to the greater common good of the broader community, and to whether or not this contribution could and should be improved upon and necessary adaptations made; otherwise, in an extreme case the practitioner community might even suffer the fate of the tobacco industry.[94]

---

93. *Id.* For an illuminating argument that the reasoning within the tradition of a practice, and the resulting emergence and evolution of the standards of excellence and other norms, are not "subjective" but are determined by "objective considerations," see Jeffrey Stout, Democracy and Tradition 270–76 (2004) (using the sport of soccer as an illustration).

94. *See* Moore, Virtue at Work, op. cit., at 89–90 (emphasizing the importance of "not ... protect[ing] ourselves from 'evaluative criticism'" when reflecting on "the contribu-

Perhaps we could call this process of dynamic development within a practice The Lexus Principle because the original Lexus motto or slogan, "The Relentless Pursuit of Perfection," guiding and inspiring Lexus automobile engineers to achieve ever greater excellence of the Lexus product, enables one readily to grasp the point.[95] And to repeat, the Lexus Principle does not preclude reasoned argument about either the overarching common good or the specific common goods of the practice, or about the relationship of the common goods of the practice to the greater common good of the broader community; indeed, if the tradition of the practice is a living one, it *presupposes* such argument. This, after all, is *how* the practice evolves. Importantly, however, MacIntyre cautions that progress in achieving excellence within the tradition of a practice is rarely "straightforwardly linear," and there may also be "sequences of decline as well as of progress."[96]

One factor complicating this process, and fueling argument in the practitioner community, is that it may not be possible to *adequately* specify the overarching common good, or how to achieve it through specific common goods of the practice, in the abstract, but only when dealing with particular concrete circumstances. Referring to the examples of farming, medical practice, music, and portrait painting discussed above,[97] MacIntyre explains that

> What such examples make clear is that some of our important ends are such that it would be a mistake to think of them as adequately specifiable by us in advance of and independently of our involvement in those activities through which we try to realize them. It is often true that it is only in and through those activities that we arrive at more adequate ideas of how to think about those ends and of how to be guided by them. So a farmer has to arrive through her or his work at a highly particular set of notions about what good farming is on this particular terrain, in this particular climate, with this kind of plough, and this kind of labor force. So a physician is

---

tion which the goods and services we are involved with ... make ... to the common good" as the tobacco industry arguably did).

95. On the original Lexus motto see *Lexus*, Wikipedia, http://en.wikipedia.org/wiki/Lexus (Lexus Slogans).

96. *See* MacIntyre, After Virtue, op. cit., at 189–90 (discussing goods of excellence of the practice of portrait painting).

97. *See supra* notes 71–72 and accompanying text..

concerned to learn through her or his work how to restore and sustain the health of *these* patients, with *these* particular vulnerabilities, through the use of *these* pharmacological and surgical resources. So the musician or the painter may be as surprised as anyone else when the end to which they have directed their activities emerges as *this* performance or *that* portrait.[98]

And what is true of the overarching common good and the specific standards and goods of excellence entailed by and included within it is equally true of the specific qualities of excellence as well. Thus,

> It is not only the conception of such ends that may be unexpectedly transformed in the course of our activities. We too, while developing those skills and qualities of mind and character needed to achieve those ends, may discover that the transformation of ourselves that is involved is significantly different from what we had expected, in part perhaps because of the particularities of our circumstances, but in part because what such virtues as courage, patience, truthfulness, and justice require can never be fully specified in advance.[99]

Consequently,

> [A]s Aquinas emphasized, in the life of practice there are no fully adequate generalizations to guide us, no set of rules sufficient to do the work for us, something that each of us has to learn for her or himself as we move toward the achievement of the ends of our activities and the end of excellence in those activities.[100]

And with this, of course, we return to the crucial role of the "master virtue" of practical wisdom in enabling the practitioner to respond well to the particular circumstances he or she confronts and, as the last quote

---

98. MacIntyre, Conflicts of Modernity, op. cit., at 50–51.
99. *Id.* at 51.
100. *Id.*

suggests, in learning just how important practical wisdom actually is in the life of practice.

These considerations also return us to Jack Sammons' phenomenological account of practices in Chapter 2 (Part III, Section D) and to the notion that there is a certain necessity, even inevitability — a teleology — that inheres both in any given project, as we pursue the "art of the practice" in our daily activities, and in all our lived experiences, as we pursue the "art of self" within the practice over time. And they suggest that not only may it not be possible for us to *adequately* specify the overarching common good, or how to achieve it through specific common goods of the practice, in the abstract, before we deal with particular concrete circumstances. In addition, they suggest that any prior abstract conception we may have of the evolving and changeable overarching common good and its co-constitutive specific common goods (and any such conception we may have of the unchanging ultimate excellence which is abstracted from these), was itself articulated only on the basis of extensive experience in the practice after reflection on such experience by a philosopher of the practice, perhaps occurring even some generations ago.

IV. Other Goods, Their Relationship to Common Goods, and Moral Risk

The fourth and final element in MacIntyre's definition of a practice is not explicit in the definition but is implied by it. This fourth element is the fundamental contrast MacIntyre draws in *After Virtue* between the "internal goods" of a practice and "external goods" such as such as money, power, status, and prestige.[101] In the same subsequent work in which he calls internal goods "goods of excellence" MacIntyre also calls external goods "goods of effectiveness" and, correspondingly, he calls the qualities necessary to attain goods of effectiveness "qualities of effectiveness."[102] The notion behind this terminology seems to be *effectiveness* in using the

---

101. MacIntyre, After Virtue, op. cit., at 188, 194.

102. MacIntyre, Whose Justice?, op. cit., at 32. As discussed *supra* note 12, although MacIntyre uses the term "qualities of effectiveness" for those qualities or attributes needed to achieve "goods of effectiveness," perhaps somewhat mysteriously he does not appear to use the term "qualities of excellence" for those qualities needed to achieve "goods of excellence."

practice as an *instrument* for obtaining external goods.[103] Once again, for the sake of terminological consistency, from now on we will employ this later terminology even when a cited source employs the prior terminology, except when use of this prior terminology is necessary for sense.

A. Goods of Effectiveness and Qualities of Effectiveness: Comparison with Common Goods of the Practice

Just as the specific content of goods and qualities of excellence may vary from practice to practice, so too the specific content of the goods and qualities of effectiveness may vary according to circumstances — for example, in the specific forms of wealth, power, status, or prestige involved or in their specific combination, and in the corresponding specific qualities needed to attain them. But just as goods and qualities of excellence share similar taxonomic and other features with other goods or qualities of excellence in all practices at a high level of generality, so also do goods and qualities of effectiveness in all circumstances at a high level of generality. Moreover, qualities of excellence and qualities of effectiveness are *taxonomically* very similar at a high level of generality because they are both concerned with the attributes or qualities necessary for attaining *goods*. However, because the type of goods is very different in each case, there are corresponding important *substantive* differences between these qualities even at a high level of generality.

1. Goods of Effectiveness

MacIntyre stresses that goods of effectiveness are genuine goods because they are "characteristic objects of human desire, whose allocation is what gives point to the virtues of justice and of generosity" and "no one can despise them altogether without a certain hypocrisy."[104] However, there are at least seven critical differences between such goods and goods of excellence.

---

103. *See* MacIntyre, Whose Justice?, op. cit., at 32 (discussing the ability "both to identify which means will be *effective* in securing [external] goods and to be *effective* in utilizing those means to secure them") (emphasis added).
104. MacIntyre, After Virtue, op. cit., at 196.

First, goods of excellence can only be attained by engaging in, and can only be specified in terms of, a particular practice or type of practice; whereas goods of effectiveness are "externally and contingently attached to... practices by the accidents of social circumstance" and there are always alternative ways of attaining them other than by engaging in the particular practice or type of practice in question.[105]

Second, to flourish in a practice the practitioner requires an adequate amount of goods of effectiveness, but the flourishing itself consists in attaining the goods of excellence of the practice.[106] Goods of effectiveness are not unimportant but, when properly prioritized and ordered, we pursue them not for their own sake but only because they enable us to engage in various practices and attain those goods of excellence that constitute the flourishing that is our individual *telos*.[107]

Third, research suggests that those who are primarily motivated by "intrinsic rewards" (in other words, "goods of excellence") experience levels of greater satisfaction and well-being but those primarily motivated by "extrinsic rewards" (in other words, "goods of effectiveness) experience greater levels of distress and dissatisfaction.[108]

---

105. *Id.* at 188.

106. *See* MacIntyre, Rational Animals, op. cit., at 64–67; MacIntyre, Conflicts of Modernity, op. cit., at 49–50 (flourishing by achieving the goods of excellence of practices). *See also* Aristotle, The Ethics of Aristotle: The Nicomachean Ethics, 63–64, 66–67, 73–76 (J.A.K. Thomson trans., rev. Hugh Tredennick 1976) (the good, the *telos* or "final end," of human beings is "happiness" in the sense of doing well or living well — in other words flourishing — and this consists in "an activity of [the rational] soul in accordance with virtue"); MacIntyre, After Virtue, op. cit., at 148–49 (discussing Aristotle's account of the human good). On the need for an adequate amount of external goods, see Aristotle, Ethics, *supra*, at 79–80, 84–85, 254; *see also id.* at 303–07 (discussing the external good of having friends). *See also* Aristotle, The Politics 253 (Ernest Barker trans., rev. R.F. Stalley, 1995) ("[T]he best way of life, for individuals separately as well as for cities collectively, is the life of goodness duly equipped with such a store of requisites as makes it possible to share in the activities of goodness").

107. Moore, Virtue at Work, op. cit., at 59–60.

108. *See, e.g.*, Longan, *Teaching Professionalism*, op. cit., at 689–90; Daisy Hurst Floyd & Timothy W, Floyd, *Professional Identity and Formation, in* Learning From Practice: A Text For experiential Legal Education 692–93 (Leah Wortham, Alexander Scherr, Nancy Maurer, & Susan L. Brooks, eds.) (3d. ed., 2016) (reviewing research on lawyers).

Fourth, anyone can readily identify and recognize goods of effectiveness, but only those with experience in the practice can identify and recognize goods of excellence.[109]

Fifth, therefore, someone entering a practice often already has an existing desire and goal to attain extrinsic goods of effectiveness, but he or she can only properly appreciate and form a desire and goal to attain intrinsic goods of excellence after entering the practice and discovering these goods.[110]

Sixth, although practitioners compete for both types of goods, goods of effectiveness will belong to individuals alone, generally on a zero sum basis, whereas goods of excellence, which are potentially unlimited, benefit and belong to the practice, the community of practitioners, and the broader community as common goods of the practice and can only belong to individuals insofar as they also belong to others.[111]

Seventh, because institutions bear and sustain practices[112] they are particularly concerned with attaining and distributing goods of effectiveness,[113] whereas the practitioners of the practice are particularly concerned

---

109. *See* MacIntyre, After Virtue, op. cit., at 188–89.

110. *See* MacIntyre, Whose Justice?, op. cit., at 45; Alasdair MacIntyre, *The Theses on Feuerbach: A Road Not Taken, in* The MacIntyre Reader 225–26 (Kelvin Knight, ed., 1998).

111. *See* MacIntyre, After Virtue, op. cit., at 190–91, 194 (goods of effectiveness "are such that the more someone has of them, the less there is for other people," whereas goods of excellence are common goods whose "achievement is a good for the whole community who participate in the practice"); MacIntyre, Rational Animals, op. cit., at 119 (the goods of networks of giving and receiving are genuinely common goods "that can only be mine insofar as they are also those of others"). *See also* MacIntyre, *Common Good* (1997), op. cit., at 239–40 (quoted *supra* notes 76–82 and accompanying text, distinguishing among "[r]ival conceptions of the common good," specifically a common good that is a kind of summing of the separate shares of individuals in goods of effectiveness and a common good that consists in interdependently shared goods of excellence). In commenting on different types of competitiveness, Jack Sammons distinguishes between healthy and unhealthy forms, observing that the healthy form "is towards excellence, which is unlimited, and it serves the practice, the practitioners, and the community." Sammons Email (September 3, 2020) [on file with author].

112. *See supra* notes 6–7 and accompanying text.

113. MacIntyre, After Virtue, op. cit., at 194. Specifically, institutions "are involved in acquiring money and other material goods; they are structured in terms of power and status, and they distribute money, power and status as rewards." *Id.*

with attaining goods of excellence,[114] at least when the practice is "in good order."[115]

2. Qualities of Effectiveness

As indicated at the beginning of this Section, just as a practitioner needs qualities of excellence to attain goods of excellence, so also a practitioner needs qualities of effectiveness to attain goods of effectiveness, and because both sets of qualities are concerned with qualities or attributes for attaining goods, they are very similar taxonomically at a high level of generality. At this level of generality, therefore, we can describe them in very similar terms.[116]

Thus, to attain goods of effectiveness the practitioner needs to acquire and exhibit various kinds of theoretical knowledge, cognitive and practical skills, and qualities of character (dispositions, attitudes, values, or virtues), with a distinctive kind of overarching "practical reasoning" or "practical rationality" (judgment resulting in action) at their apex. This overarching

---

114. Of course, the reader will suspect, correctly, that the relevant separations are not quite as sharp in practice (pun intended) as the text suggests, for at least three reasons. First, there is in fact a complex relationship between goods of excellence and qualities of excellence, on the one hand, and goods of effectiveness and qualities of effectiveness on the other. Second, institutions are often just practitioners of the practice organized, individually or collectively, in a particular way. This is especially true of a "small business" form involving a solo practitioner or just a few partners. Sometimes, of course, the separation between the institution and the practitioner may indeed be much greater, as in a large corporation (or even a partnership) employing many hundreds or even thousands of people in which the practitioners of the practice may be subject to the decisions of distant "managers." Third, then, because practitioners who carry on their practice within sustaining institutions are in fact concerned with attaining both goods of effectiveness and goods of excellence, the crucial question centers on the relative subordination of these distinct types of goods. This question, in turn, is related to the question of whether a practice is "in good order." Each of these three points is discussed further in what follows.

115. *See* MacIntyre, *Partial Response*, op. cit., at 284 (discussing "productive crafts such as farming and fishing, architecture and construction" and explaining that "[t]he aim internal to such productive crafts, *when they are in good order*, is never only to catch fish, or to produce beef or milk, or to build houses" but "to do so in a manner consonant with the excellences of the craft, so that not only is there a good product, but the craftsperson is perfected through and in her or his activity") (emphasis added).

116. Qualities of excellence are described *supra* notes 12–17 and accompanying text.

ability enables the practitioner to access, draw on, and conduct other, particular qualities or attributes in a way appropriate to the context so as to do the right thing in the right way at the right time for the right reason in the particular circumstances, for the benefit of the individual, organization, or community being served. And again, this overarching ability resolves itself—both in the technical sphere and the moral sphere, as well as in the combined operation of both spheres—into the four interrelated abilities

(a) To see the world and read situations in a distinctive way,
(b) To make sound judgments about ends and means in light of such perceptions (either intuitively and instantaneously or consciously and deliberately, depending on such factors as complexity, ambiguity, or novelty),
(c) To be motivated to translate judgment into action, and then
(d) To act.

Despite the substantial *taxonomic and semantic similarity* in the descriptive accounts of qualities of effectiveness and qualities of excellence, there are very significant *substantive differences* in each of the elements described even at a high level of generality and thus regarding: the type of theoretical knowledge, skills, and virtues required; how the world and situations are perceived; the types of ends and means identified in making judgments and thus in what are considered "sound" judgments; the practitioner's motivations; the prerequisites for the ability to act; whom the practitioner is serving; and consequently, what is considered to be the right thing to do, and the right way, the right time, and the right reason to do it. To be sure, there is some degree of overlap between the two sets of qualities so that certain qualities can be both qualities of excellence and qualities of effectiveness.[117] Outside the area of overlap, however, the differences can be striking.[118] This is seen dramatically (but, of course, not only) in the case of those qualities of character which are the virtues. Thus, how the virtues of justice, temperateness, courage, and friendship, for example, are understood in the perspective of the goods of excellence is often

---

117. *See* MacIntyre, Whose Justice?, op. cit., at 32 (giving "steadfastness of purpose" as an example).
118. *Id.*

quite different from how they are understood in the perspective of the goods of effectiveness.[119]

In the perspective of the goods of excellence, "[j]ustice is a disposition to give to each person, including oneself, what that person deserves and to treat no one in a way incompatible with their deserts," and although a community may establish enforceable rules of justice aimed at securing this outcome, including through obedience by the unjust, justice as a virtue can be independently defined before such rules are established.[120] The rules of justice are "defined in terms of merit and desert;" they are justified because they facilitate pursuit of the goods of excellence and the human good, understood as flourishing through "the form of life" that is best for human beings; and their binding force is rooted in the fact that those who break the rules primarily harm themselves, so that punishment for these breaches is intended to educate and thus be for the benefit of the rule-breaker.[121] In the perspective of the goods of effectiveness, by contrast, the concept of justice has no content apart from the enforceable rules and the virtue of justice is simply "the disposition to obey those rules."[122] The rules of justice are defined in terms of reciprocity, specifying "what is to be exchanged for what" (which in turn is determined by the parties' explicit or implicit understanding of their relative bargaining power); they are justified because they facilitate "effective cooperation" with others, in which "each person [is] trying to obtain what he or she wants, whatever it is;" and their binding force is rooted in the fact that those who break

---

119. *See id.* at 32–43 (discussing, with a focus on Homeric and post-Homeric Greece, how the differing perspectives afforded by an allegiance to goods of excellence and an allegiance to goods of effectiveness leads to differing conceptions of the virtues of justice, temperateness, courage, and friendship). MacIntyre identifies the following "types of systematic activity" (or practices) in which "standards of excellence are elaborated and applied":

> They are: warfare and combat; seamanship; athletic and gymnastic activity; epic, lyric, and dramatic poetry; farming both arable and the management of animals; rhetoric; and the making and sustaining of the communities of kinship and the household and later of the city-state. To this list architecture, sculpture, and painting were to be added, as were the intellectual enquiries of mathematics, philosophy, and theology.

Id. at 30.
120. *Id.* at 39.
121. *Id.* at 32–35, 37–38.
122. *Id.* at 39.

the rules "primarily hurt[] others," thereby lessening their prospects of securing needed cooperation, so they bind "only to the extent to which one cannot commit injustice with impunity" and punishment for such breaches is primarily intended to deter.[123]

There are similar or analogous contrasts in the case of temperateness, courage, and friendship. In the perspective of the goods of excellence, temperateness "prescribes ... a directed disciplining and transformation of the desires, aversions, and dispositions of the self," thereby shaping our judgment and motivations regarding goods, so that as far as possible we become capable of excellence in both judgment and performance. In the perspective of the goods of effectiveness, by contrast, temperateness enables us to achieve more efficiently something we already recognize and desire as a good so that we do not frustrate "pursuit of [our] own satisfaction," just as the virtue of justice "overcomes [its] frustration by others."[124] With respect to courage, the perspectives of excellence and effectiveness both value the abilities to endure and confront various harms and dangers, but there are significant differences in "both the range of relevant harms and dangers and what one may be required to sacrifice in confronting them and why" — for example, to achieve excellence as a soldier versus excellence as a poet, or to increase one's wealth versus one's political power.[125] Moreover, focusing again on the element of efficiency, we should perhaps add that in the perspective of the goods of effectiveness, courage enables us to achieve more efficiently something we already recognize and desire as a good (such as glory or fame), whereas in the perspective of goods of excellence, courage enables us to serve a good we only come to know in the performance of the courageous act even when the act is less efficient in terms of effectiveness.[126] In the perspective of the goods of effectiveness,

---

123. *Id.* at 36–38.

124. *Id.* at 40.

125. *Id.*

126. I am indebted to Jack Sammons for helping me articulate this distinction. Focusing on the different types or association (or organization) discussed *supra* notes 75–82 and accompanying text, Sammons illustrates the distinction as follows:

> Courage as a virtue within organizations of effectiveness, like investment clubs, is itself measurable by compliance with what might be called the rules of efficiency and in this way is like justice within the same. So, for example, betting on baseball would be foolhardy and putting the funds in a money market fund an act of timidity. The right place in between, the place of cour-

"friendship is a virtue ... insofar as it is a source of pleasure and utility," whereas in the perspective of the goods of excellence, friendship involves a "mutual regard which arises from a shared allegiance" to the same good(s), and although friends characteristically do enjoy their relationship and are useful to each other, they care for one another primarily because of this shared relationship to the good.[127]

In MacIntyre's account, consistent with these differences regarding the virtues — especially (but not only) the virtue of justice — in the contrasting perspectives of the goods of excellence and the goods of effectiveness is a corresponding difference in the practical reasoning or practical rationalities involved. In the perspective of the goods of excellence, good reasons for action are objectively *good reasons as such* so that "the soundness of a particular practical argument ... is independent of its force for any particular person." In the perspective of the goods of effectiveness, by contrast, good reasons for action depend on the action satisfying a person's subjective desires or needs.[128] The contrast between these practical rationalities becomes even more pronounced when we also take into account differences in other elements, in addition to these differences in understanding of the virtues and the reasons justifying what are considered "sound" judgments — including differences in the necessary theoretical knowledge and skills, in perception, motivations, and prerequisites for action, and in

---

age, is calculable in terms of maximum efficiency. For practices, however, the efficiency of the practitioner or practitioners is often at odds with courage, as it is in the extreme case of soldiers, and acts determined by efficiency alone are not legitimately considered courageous at all. Instead, courage involves a complex balancing of a broad array of concerns, as justice did within a practice. So, for example, and for lawyers, advising a very unpopular criminal defendant with a questionable case to proceed to a full trial might be foolhardy, just as advising a plea might be timid, with a trial bargain being the place of courage in between. Were this decision to be made on the basis of the practitioner's efficiency, it would not be a courageous one but a betrayal of the client and the practice.

Sammons Email (September 3, 2020) [on file with author].

127. MACINTYRE, WHOSE JUSTICE?, op. cit., at 41–42.

128. *See id.* at 43–45 (surveying the differences between these two types of practical reasoning). Here again, MacIntyre does not himself use the terms *objectively* and *subjective*. For discussion of reasons why use of both terms nevertheless seems warranted, see Chapter 2, note 39.

whom the practitioner is serving.[129] In Chapter 6 we will explore further some of these (and other) differences between these two types of practical rationality when we address contexts encouraging the continued exercise of Neo-Aristotelian practical rationality in contemporary liberal demo-cratic societies alongside the practical rationality of constrained prefer-ence maximization, which MacIntyre considers to be the dominant type of practical rationality in such societies.[130] Moreover, this contrast between the two types of practical rationality is why the above account of quali-ties of effectiveness includes no reference to the "master virtue" of prac-tical wisdom (*phronesis*) and similarly no reference to "good judgment" or "acting well." These are terms we might want to stipulate should be reserved for qualities needed to attain goods more directly related both to the flourishing of the practitioner and the flourishing of those whom the practitioner serves.[131] Similarly, MacIntyre's description of the three foun-dational capacities of independent practical reasoners seems restricted to Neo-Aristotelian practical rationality only.

The essential explanation for these differences between qualities of ex-cellence and qualities of effectiveness is related to our earlier discussion

---

129. For MacIntyre's own, more detailed account of the differences between these two types of practical rationality in the same work, see MACINTYRE, WHOSE JUSTICE?, op. cit., at 124–45 (explicating Aristotle's account of practical reasoning or practical rationality), 338–42 (explicating modern practical reasoning or practical rationality focused on prefer-ence satisfaction).

130. *See* Chapter 6, notes 71, 92–99, 130–39 and accompanying text. Regarding differ-ences in the elements identified here, see note 136 and accompanying text (good reasons and sound judgments; prerequisites for action), note 137 and accompanying text (moti-vations to translate judgment into action), note 139 and accompanying text (whom the practitioner is serving).

131. Interestingly, in discussing "organizational virtues" Geoff Moore does not appear to distinguish between virtues in the perspective of goods of excellence and virtues in the perspective of goods of effectiveness. *See* MOORE, VIRTUE AT WORK, op. cit., at 124–25 (dis-cussing the virtues of courage, temperance, justice, and practical wisdom that are necessary both for excellence and "success" and also identifying a fifth virtue, zeal, which "enables the organization to pursue external goods and achieve success to a sufficient degree" and which therefore, while also relevant for the pursuit of excellence, is especially relevant for the pursuit of success). Moore associates "success" with attaining goods of effectiveness, as in the case of a "successful" business, for example. We will associate it with achieving goods of excellence and flourishing in a practice. *See* Chapter 4, notes 49–50 and accompanying text. The concept of "organizational virtues" is discussed further *infra* notes 149–51 and accompanying text.

of different types of associations and their common goods.[132] Thus, in the perspective of the goods of effectiveness, the virtues and practical rationality serve cooperative activity with others that is instrumental to attaining common goods that are *individualistic* and *extrinsic* to the activity, because they are the object of the participants' independent, pre-existing desires and goals.[133] By contrast, in the perspective of the goods of excellence, the virtues and practical rationality serve cooperative activity with others that is instrumental to attaining common goods that are *shared* and *intrinsic* to the activity, because they are *common goods of the practice* that are independent of any pre-existing desires and goals the participants may already have[134] and, indeed, that will transform their desires and goals as they learn to appreciate these intrinsic goods and acquire the qualities necessary to achieve them.[135]

Here again, although the above account of qualities of effectiveness and of the contrast between them and qualities of excellence focuses on the context of practices, it also applies in the context of politics and *mutatis mutandis* in the context of pursuing our individual life quests.

---

132. *See supra* notes 75–82 and accompanying text.

133. MacINTYRE, WHOSE JUSTICE?, op. cit., at 45 ("In the case of the goods of effectiveness any common good at which cooperation aims is derived from and compounded out of the objects of desire and aspiration which the rival participants brought with them to the bargaining process"); *see also* Alasdair MacIntyre, *The Theses on Feuerbach: A Road Not Taken, in* MacINTYRE READER, op. cit., at 225 ("[T]he only available conception of a common good is one constructed from and reducible to conceptions of the goods pursued by various individuals in their attempts to satisfy their desires").

134. MacINTYRE, WHOSE JUSTICE?, op. cit., at 45 ("In the case of the goods of excellence the good which gives point and purpose to the cooperation of individuals on a given occasion is a good independently of and antecedently to the cooperation of those particular individuals; it is for the sake of that good that they come together"); MacIntyre, *Feuerbach*, op. cit., at 225–26 ("Individuals discover in the ends of any such practice goods common to all who engage in it, goods internal to and specific to that particular type of practice, which they can make their own only by allowing their participation in the activity to effect a transformation in the desires which they initially brought with them to the activity").

135. MacIntyre, *Feuerbach*, op. cit., at 226 ("Thus in the course of doing whatever has to be done to achieve those goods, they also transform themselves through what is at once a change in their desires and an acquisition of those intellectual and moral virtues and those intellectual, physical and imaginative skills necessary to achieve the goods of that particular practice").

B. Relationship Between Goods and Qualities of Effectiveness and Common Goods of the Practice

There are striking differences, then, between goods of excellence and goods of effectiveness, and between qualities of excellence and qualities of effectiveness. There is nevertheless also a complex symbiotic relationship between these two sets of goods and qualities. On the one hand, attaining goods of effectiveness usually involves pursuing goods of excellence (and thus demonstrating qualities of excellence), at least to some extent.[136] This is largely because "[t]he achievement of power, wealth, and fame often enough requires as a means the achievement of some kind of genuine excellence."[137]

On the other hand, and conversely, attaining goods of excellence also involves pursuing goods of effectiveness (and thus demonstrating qualities of effectiveness), at least to some extent.[138] As Geoff Moore puts it, an inadequate amount of goods of effectiveness "simply means that the practice is starved of resources, and its practitioners will therefore find the pursuit of excellence difficult if not impossible."[139] This dependency of a practice on adequate goods of effectiveness implicates the relationship between practices and institutions that we have already noted.[140] Thus, although practitioners pursue goods of excellence within practices, such practices "can only be sustained by being provided with institutionalized settings. And the maintenance of the relevant institutional and organizational forms always requires the acquisition and retention of some degree of power and... wealth."[141] To be able to bear and sustain practices and their traditions,[142] institutions are "characteristically and necessarily concerned with... [goods of effectiveness]. They are involved in acquiring money and other material goods; they are structured in terms of power and status, and they distribute money, power and status as rewards."[143]

---

136. MacIntyre, Whose Justice?, op. cit., at 35.

137. *Id.* Moreover, goods of effectiveness facilitate a person's wants and what a person wants may happen to be "genuinely excellent in some way." *Id.*

138. *Id.*

139. Moore, Virtue at Work, op. cit., at 168.

140. *See supra* notes 6–7 and accompanying text.

141. MacIntyre, Whose Justice?, op. cit., at 35

142. MacIntyre, After Virtue, op. cit., at 194, 222.

143. *Id.* at 194.

Indeed, the relationship between practices and institutions, and consequently between goods of excellence and goods of effectiveness, is "so intimate… that institutions and practices characteristically form a single causal order."[144] This is especially evident when, as is frequently the case, institutions are basically the practitioners of the practice organized, individually or collectively, in a particular way.

Both types of relationship between the two sets of goods and qualities (effectiveness and excellence) acquire added dimension from MacIntyre's claim that "the shared making and sustaining of the types of community within which the common good can be achieved — families, farming households, fishing crews, local forms of political community — are activities which themselves have the structure of practices."[145] Because, then, "the making and sustaining of forms of human community… itself has all the characteristics of a practice" and because institutions are a form of human community, therefore the making and sustaining of institutions is also a practice,[146] although, as Geoff Moore observes, this practice is *secondary* to the "core or primary practice" (or practices) an institution serves.[147] Moore himself is particularly concerned with "organizations" (business, as well as statutory and voluntary), which he conceives of as "practice-institution combination[s]" that are "'*essentially* moral spaces'… in which individuals can together pursue excellence and develop their characters, as well as engage in their narrative quest towards their true *telos*, while also contributing to the common good of the community through the excellence of the goods and services which the organization provides."[148]

The first type of relationship between the two sets of goods and qualities — the dependence of goods of effectiveness upon goods of excellence (and qualities of excellence) — receives added dimension because for Moore the above depiction of individuals pursuing excellence within organizations also includes the managers of an organization. Thus managers, too, "have an opportunity, just as do the practitioners in the core practice, to possess and exercise the virtues in pursuit of the [goods of excellence]

---

144. *Id.*

145. MacIntyre, *Partial Response*, op. cit., at 288.

146. MacIntyre, After Virtue, op. cit., at 194.

147. *See* Moore, Virtue at Work, op. cit., at 68–69 (noting that an institution such as a university, for example, may "house" more than one practice).

148. *Id.*

of the secondary practice of making and sustaining the institution."[149] And the second type of relationship between these two sets of goods and qualities — the dependence of goods of excellence upon goods of effectiveness (and qualities of effectiveness) — receives added dimension because the characteristics of a virtuous manager include concern not only with pursuing and distributing goods of effectiveness, but also concern with the flourishing of the core practice and its practitioners and the contribution of such flourishing to the greater common good.[150] Because the characteristics of "a virtuous organization" mirror the characteristics of a virtuous manager, Moore's summary of the former serves to summarize the latter as well:

> [A] virtuous organization is one which will possess and exercise appropriate virtues, and avoid particular vices, in such a way that it pursues a good purpose, focuses on the core practice and its [goods of excellence], seeks to provide meaningful work and so 'perfect' its members, pursues [goods of effectiveness] but only to the extent necessary for the maintenance and development of the core practice, seeks an appropriate mode of institutionalization which is supportive of virtue, and seeks an environment which is conducive of virtue.[151]

In this account of virtuous managers and virtuous organizations engaged in the secondary practice of making and sustaining the institution serving the core practice, we arguably see a third aspect of the role of the virtues in "enabling their possessors to achieve the goods internal to practices."[152] However, the qualifier to pursuing goods of effectiveness in the above quote — "but only to the extent necessary for the maintenance and devel-

149. *Id.* at 70.

150. *See id.* at 110–14 (identifying several characteristics of a virtuous manager in addition to managerial competence). For Moore's discussion of the managerial virtues themselves, see *id.* at 114–16.

151. *Id.* at 123–24. For Moore's full discussion of the characteristics of "a virtuous organization," see *id.* at 118–24. For his discussion of the organizational virtues themselves, see *id.* at 124–31. For the parallels between the characteristics of a virtuous manager and a virtuous organization, see *id.* at 118–19 ("[T]he characteristics of a virtuous organization follow directly from, and to a large extent mirror, those which virtuous managers should be trying to achieve").

152. For discussion of the first and second aspects, see *supra* notes 31–47, 53–67 and accompanying text respectively.

opment of the core practice" — already suggests the existence of a challenge and moral risk for practices and organizations, to which we now turn.

C. The Moral Risk of Corrupting Common Goods, and Role of the Virtues

The complex symbiotic relationship between goods of excellence (and qualities of excellence) and goods of effectiveness (and qualities of effectiveness) may challenge the ability or willingness of practitioners in the practice to distinguish clearly, or to appropriately prioritize, between them in practical everyday decision-making. And this challenge exists both for practitioners of the core or primary practice and for practitioners of the secondary practice of making and sustaining the institution serving the core practice. For both categories of practitioners the resulting moral risk and the capacity to withstand it center on the question of relative subordination: Does the individual or social group in question systematically subordinate goods and qualities of one kind to goods and qualities of the other?[153] Is their primary motivation extrinsic or intrinsic?[154] And the real concern behind *these* questions seems to be that the undue pursuit of goods of effectiveness by the institutions that bear and sustain practices and their traditions always potentially threatens to corrupt these practices and traditions and indeed the institutions themselves.[155]

In a small business involving a solo practitioner or just a few partners, the relevant individual or social group with whom the moral risk originates is the practitioner or group of practitioners of the core practice themselves because they are effectively coterminous with the institution. In a large corporation (or even a large partnership) employing many hundreds or even thousands of people, the relevant social group with whom the moral risk originates may be distant "managers" to whose decisions the practitioners of the core practice may be subject, and the capacity of practitioners of both the core practice and the secondary practice to withstand it may be diminished due to pressures arising within a large hierarchical organization. In either case, however, the "acquisitiveness of the institution"

---

153. MacIntyre, Whose Justice?, op. cit., at 35.

154. *See also* Chapter 2, notes 125–26 and accompanying text for discussion of extrinsic and intrinsic motivations.

155. MacIntyre, After Virtue, op. cit., at 194, 223.

always poses risks for "the ideals and the creativity of the practice," and "the competitiveness of the institution" always poses risks for "the cooperative care for common goods of the practice."[156] These risks are magnified by the "technological enframing of all thought and all things" that predominates in our era, reducing everything — including here the world of the practice (practitioners, activities, those the practice serves, and so on) — to "standing-reserve" to be ordered according to our wills.[157]

A related concern is that the undue pursuit of goods of effectiveness in any given case, or in general, may create a temptation to "cheat," effectively disabling attainment of goods of excellence to a corresponding extent.[158] We can illuminate this point by considering Jack Sammons' very helpful account addressing Bernard Suit's definition of a "game," which Sammons expands and applies to practices.[159] Suits identifies the four elements in his definition of a "game" as follows:

> To play a game is to attempt to achieve a specific state of affairs [prelusory goal], using only means permitted by the rules [lusory means], where the rules prohibit use of more efficient in favour of less efficient means [constitutive rules], and where the rules are accepted just because they make possible such activity [lusory attitude].[160]

---

156. *Id.* at 194. On the other hand, sometimes the acquisitiveness and competitiveness of the institution may actually help protect the common goods of the practice against another kind of risk. Where, for example, the practitioners in a particular institutional setting have, through self-satisfaction and complacency, drifted away from "best practice," the institution may call the practitioners back to pursuing excellence "partly to protect the external goods which derive from the excellence of the internal goods." *See* MOORE, VIRTUE AT WORK, op. cit., at 119–20 (discussing this point).

157. *See* Chapter 2, notes 152–53, 156 and accompanying text. I am indebted to Jack Sammons for articulating this point and for the quoted language. Sammons Email (September 3, 2020) [on file with author].

158. *See* MACINTYRE, AFTER VIRTUE, op. cit., at 188 (giving the example of teaching the game of chess to "a highly intelligent seven-year-old child" using the inducement of candy and explaining that if the child cheats to get the candy the child will be defeating not the teacher but himself or herself).

159. Jack. L. Sammons, *'Cheater!': The Central Moral Admonition of Legal Ethics, Games, Lusory Attitudes, Internal Perspectives, and Justice*, 39 IDAHO L. REV 273 (2003) (drawing upon BERNARD SUITS, THE GRASSHOPPER: GAMES, LIFE, AND UTOPIA (1978)).

160. *Id.* at 277–78 (quoting SUITS, GRASSHOPPER, op. cit., at 41, and explaining that "'[l]usory' is from the Latin word *ludus* meaning game").

In his account Sammons explicates how players who possess the "lusory attitude" respect the "constitutive rules" restricting them to the use of "lusory means" in attempting to achieve the "prelusory goal."[161] For example, those who truly "play the game" when participating in the competitive sport or practice of amateur track athletics want to attain the "prelusory goal" of crossing the finishing line first, but only after complying with the "constitutive rules" restricting them to the "lusory mean" of running on the track.[162] In this way they can attain the "lusory goal" of being "declared the winner" after meeting all the requirements for participating in the sport.[163] But they can only meet these requirements and "win" if they seek to attain its goods of excellence (excellence of performance in running) by exhibiting its qualities of excellence (the skills and virtues involved in running fast or a great distance). Thus, they view this sport from the internal perspective, want to participate in it as an end in itself, and want to perform well in it.[164] By contrast, "cheaters ... have an excess of zeal in seeking to achieve the prelusory goal" of crossing the finishing line first and therefore lack the lusory attitude and are willing to violate the constitutive rules restricting runners to the "less efficient" lusory mean of running on the track, by employing the "more efficient" means of running across the field instead.[165] A cheater "does not view the game from the internal perspective in which the game itself is an end, as Suit's players do, but externally and instrumentally as a means toward some external end."[166] He or she is not focused on performing well but is prepared to forego the sport's goods and qualities of excellence in order to "win" in the sense of crossing the finishing line first by using whatever means necessary, including illegitimate means. But of course, this is not really "winning" at all because the cheater has not met the requirements for competing in the sport.[167]

Sammons expands Suits' definition, suggesting that cheating in a practice may involve violation of any of its "constitutive norms," which include

---

161. For Sammons' detailed explication, see *id.* at 278–80.

162. *See id.* at 278–79 (discussing this example).

163. *Id.*

164. *See id.* at 281, 283 (discussing these three points).

165. *See id.* at 279–80 (discussing "the constitutive rule proscribing running across the field" and Suits' definition of cheaters).

166. *Id.* at 281.

167. *Id.* at 278.

not just rules but more broadly "rules, customs, and other norms arising from the tradition of the practice,"[168] and which therefore would seem to include everything addressed by the practice's standards of excellence. Also, like competitive games, practices "depend for their existence upon … a certain *cooperation* … that creates a hermeneutical community within the game," as well as "an ongoing interpretation of the game's constitutive rules within a conversation among the[] competitors, and an attitude toward other competitors that closely resembles the lusory attitude required to be a player."[169] Moreover, it is important to attend to the ongoing nature of a practice. Thus, cheating over time in the competitive sport of amateur track athletics or in any other practice will erode its goods and qualities of excellence and the relationships that sustain them, whereas observing the constitutive rules, customs, and other norms will maintain and strengthen them. As Sammons explains,

> [W]hat is behind the lusory attitude in our competitive game with its hermeneutical community of players is not just a desire to play the game nor just a desire to win, but a strong desire to play it well. Within this community, this "well" is a question not of the moment but over time, Thus, what must be included in the constitutive conversation about cheating (constitutive this time not of the game but of the community the game requires) is a desire that the game be maintained as one that can be played well over time, one in which the qualities of performance (or "excellences") as understood by the game's community can improve through the continued playing of the game. More simply put, this community must be concerned, for the sake of the game over time, about avoiding any potential corruption of it.[170]

Focusing on the practice of law, specifically the "game" or activity of "representative adversarial advocacy," Sammons uses his broader understanding of cheating in a practice to develop a sophisticated argument that

---

168. *Id.* at 276–77, 284, 288.

169. *Id.* at 282–83. The "constitutive norms" also "includ[e] those agreed upon hermeneutic norms needed for the ongoing interpretation of the constitutive rules, customs, and other norms through which 'cheating' remains understood by the players." *Id.* at 284.

170. *Id.* at 283–84.

the best moral resources for critiquing the conduct of practitioners of a practice are internal to the practice rather than external to it.[171] We will encounter Sammons' analysis of cheating in a practice again in Chapter 5, and then again in Chapter 7 where we will also consider the question of internal versus external critique of a practice.[172]

The practitioners of a practice must be vigilant, then, lest the goods of excellence of the practice (and the qualities of excellence of the practitioner) are corrupted by the undue pursuit of goods of effectiveness and the individual or collective temptation to cheat. To resist this corruption and temptation, and to sustain the goods and qualities of excellence, practitioners will need to exhibit virtues such as justice, courage, truthfulness, temperateness, and practical wisdom in relevant relationships,[173] just as they needed to exhibit several of these same virtues to attain these goods and qualities of excellence in the first place by submitting to the authority of the practice and the tradition of the practice.[174] The relevant relationships may include relationships with other practitioners, those the practice serves, or both.[175] And in this context, too, the dialogic virtues, virtues

---

171. For Sammons' development of this argument, see *id.* at 286–88, 291–304.

172. *See* Chapter 5, notes 88–92 and accompanying text; Chapter 7, notes 41–44, 225–29 and accompanying text.

173. *See* MacIntyre, After Virtue, op. cit., at 191 (emphasizing the importance of the virtues of justice, courage, and honesty for resisting the temptation to cheat), 194, 223 (emphasizing the importance of the virtues of justice, courage, and truthfulness as well as "the relevant intellectual virtues" for resisting the corruption of institutions, practices, and traditions, and also identifying "the virtue of having an adequate sense of the traditions to which one belongs or which confront one" as an additional virtue needed for the last). One should surely also add temperateness in this context. *See* MacIntyre, Rational Animals, op. cit., at 87–88 (emphasizing the importance of acquiring the virtue of temperateness and of learning how to stand back from and evaluate one's desires). It is also reasonable to assume that MacIntyre has practical wisdom in mind when referring to "the relevant intellectual virtues." *See* Moore, Virtue at Work, op. cit., at 124–25 (identifying practical wisdom as "the key *intellectual* virtue" enabling judgments about how to apply particular virtues, including in situations where they conflict, and about how to properly balance excellence and success, which is focused on "external goods," within organizations).

174. *See supra* notes 56–60 and accompanying text.

175. In certain types of practices the pursuit of "prelusory goals" by those the practice serves may also threaten to corrupt the practice. With regard to the practice of law, for example, clients' "instrumental reasons" for "com[ing] to the game" of representative advocacy may be "[to] get the money I am owed, stop the conduct I abhor, permit the conduct I desire, avoid the imprisonment threatened by the state, etc." Sammons, *'Cheater!'*, op. cit., at

of performance character, and a particular form of the virtue of humility surely also have an important role to play.[176] Sometimes, moreover, resisting these corrupting forces involves an appeal to the history of the tradition of the practice to challenge current trends because, as we have already observed, there may be "sequences of decline as well as of progress" in the evolution of a practice.[177] Here again, subject to the same caveat regarding functional artificiality as opposed to analytical soundness, all these virtues are perhaps best conceived in this particular context as "fundamental prerequisite virtues" without which it is not possible to attain and sustain the goods of excellence in the first place, rather than as part of the ensemble of virtues included among the "operational" qualities of excellence needed to attain goods of excellence in everyday practice that were discussed in Part II Section B.[178] Here again, too, we see a fourth important aspect of the role of the virtues in "enabling their possessors to achieve the goods internal to practices."[179]

Exercising such virtues to resist corrupting pressures and temptations is also an important way in which practitioners may discover that exercise of the virtues in the perspective of goods of excellence may bar or otherwise hinder them in attaining goods of effectiveness.[180] Indeed, the virtues, as

---

284–86, 302–03 (discussing the importance of translating "[clients'] intentional goals into the playing of the game" of representative advocacy in a manner acceptable to clients, of involving clients in this game through their "meaningful participation ... in the resolution of their own disputes," and of thereby avoiding "the vicious and stupid"). Something analogous applies in the practice of medicine. Think of the patient who comes to the physician seeking curative or prophylactic relief from a medical condition or an end to physical or emotional pain and is insistent on being prescribed antibiotics, pain killers, or sedatives even though such prescription may be unwise. In such practices, to avoid corruption of the goods and qualities of excellence, practitioners clearly need to exhibit the virtues in their relationships with those the practice serves.

176. *See supra* notes 61–63 and accompanying text.

177. *See supra* note 96 and accompanying text.

178. *See* Jones, *Developing Virtue and Practical Wisdom*, op. cit., at 842–45 (drawing on this distinction). *See further supra* notes 64–66 and accompanying text.

179. For discussion of the first, second, and third aspects, see *supra* notes 31–47 53–67, 149–52 and accompanying text respectively.

180. *See* MacIntyre, After Virtue, op. cit., at 196 (discussing how the virtues of justice, courage, and truthfulness may bar or hinder in this way). And again, one should surely add other virtues too. *See also id.* at 198 ("[C]ultivation of the virtues always may and often does hinder the achievement of those external goods which are the mark of worldly success").

opposed to their "semblance and simulacra," always represent "a potential stumbling block" to the "comfortable ambition" of achieving both goods of excellence *and* wealth, fame, and power.[181] This may help explain a concession Moore appears to make when discussing numerous studies of organizations and practices and articulating his conclusions in the last Part of his book addressing Organizational Virtue Ethics in Practice. Specifically, he seems to concede that his depictions of the virtuous organization and the virtuous manager discussed in the previous section may well be more aspirational than descriptive of current realities in modern liberal democratic states with their capitalist, large-scale market economies (especially those based on Anglo-American capitalism), so that these depictions can only be realized widely in practice through resistance, reform, and perhaps even revolution.[182]

The discussion in this section applies *mutatis mutandis* to a further moral risk that arises when practitioners' primary motivation is extrinsic and goods and qualities of excellence are subordinated to goods and qualities of effectiveness. This is the risk that practitioners may too easily abandon their current position for another one, or even abandon the common goods of the practice altogether to take up an entirely different occupation, especially during times of economic hardship.[183]

---

181. *See id.*at 196 (Thus, "the world being what it contingently is, …although we may hope that we can not only achieve the standards of excellence and the internal goods of certain practices by possessing the virtues *and* become rich, famous and powerful, the virtues are always a potential stumbling block to this comfortable ambition"). It is perhaps not entirely clear whether MacIntyre has in mind the virtues in the perspective of the goods of effectiveness when he refers to the "semblance and simulacra" of the virtues here.

182. *See* MOORE, VIRTUE AT WORK, op. cit., at 141–65 (discussing business organizations and practices in several different sectors, including banking and other financial services, accounting, open source software (OSS), pharmaceuticals, airlines, fair trading, and automobile production, as well as differences between Anglo-American capitalism and capitalism in continental Europe), 166–87 (discussing various types of non-business organizations and practices, including the performing arts (symphony orchestras, circuses, jazz), the health sector (U.K. National Health Service (NHS), surgery, nursing), churches, and journalism), 188–200 (articulating conclusions, including regarding the challenges involved in attempting to realize his depictions in practice, the need for resistance, reform, or even revolution to do so, and the relatively negative consequences financially of succeeding in this endeavor).

183. *See supra* notes 79–82 and accompanying text.

Many of the fundamental concepts addressed in this Chapter are well illustrated, and further elaborated, by the narrative images of fishing crews and the fishing village of *Piscopolis* developed in the next two Chapters.

FOUR

LIVING IN *PISCOPOLIS* PART I

Fishing Crews, Their Common Goods, and Their Everyday Relationships with Other Inhabitants

In Chapters 2 and 3 we saw that we achieve our individual good, flourish, and fulfill our life's purpose by attaining the common goods of practices, engaged in by various practitioner communities, to which we have been called, and by contributing in this way to the greater common good of the broader community. And in Chapter 3 we noted that a practitioner community contributes to the greater common good if it promotes the flourishing not only of those engaged in the practice but also, and especially, of those the practice serves, and that this determination is essentially a political one in the Aristotelian sense of "political."[1]

Chapter 4 and Chapter 5 will draw from and illustrate the matters discussed in Chapters 2 and 3. They will also build upon those Chapters to deepen our understanding in two main respects. First, they will deepen our understanding of flourishing in a practice and of the relationship between the individual practitioner and the practitioner community. Second, they will deepen our understanding of the greater common good (and the range of matters that are the proper subject of "political" determination), and of the relationship between a practitioner community and the broader community. They will do this largely by extending MacIntyre's short and partial account of fishing crews and a fishing village in his 1994 essay *A*

---

1. For earlier consideration of this relationship between the common goods of practitioner communities and the greater common good of the broader community, see Chapter 3, notes 83–86, 94, 96 and accompanying text.

Partial Response to My Critics[2] and by combining this extended account with MacIntyre's account of an ideal *polis* in two other works published in 1997 and 1999,[3] in order to construct an account of life in an imagined fishing village called *Piscopolis*.[4]

This account of life in *Piscopolis* represents a theoretical ideal. But it is an ideal with practical, real world applications and implications. To begin

---

2. For MacIntyre's account of two contrasting types of fishing crew, see Alasdair MacIntyre, *A Partial Response to My Critics, in* AFTER MACINTYRE: CRITICAL PERSPECTIVES ON THE WORK OF ALASDAIR MACINTYRE 284–86 (John Horton & Susan Mendus, eds., 1994).

3. My understanding of MacIntyre's ideal *polis* is largely informed by his accounts of an ideal local community in Alasdair MacIntyre, *Politics, Philosophy, and the Common Good* (1997), *in* THE MACINTYRE READER 246–52 (Kelvin Knight, ed., 1998) and ALASDAIR MACINTYRE, DEPENDENT RATIONAL ANIMALS: WHY HUMAN BEINGS NEED THE VIRTUES 63–154 (1999), and by the commentaries on MacIntyre's accounts in Kelvin Knight, *Introduction, in* THE MACINYTRE READER (Kelvin Knight, ed., 1998) and Ted Clayton, *Political Philosophy of Alasdair MacIntyre*, Internet Encyclopedia of Philosophy IEP, https://iep.utm.edu/pmacint/. In RATIONAL ANIMALS MacIntyre does not use the term *polis* to describe the ideal local community, but he does use this term in *Common Good*.

In addressing the nature of a *polis*, MacIntyre offers an idealized account of life in the ancient Greek *polis* that can best be understood as proceeding from Neo-Aristotelian premises or, in light of the evolution of his views as articulated, for example, in RATIONAL ANIMALS, from the premises of Thomistic Aristotelianism. For MacIntyre's discussion of Aristotle's account of the ideal *polis*, see ALASDAIR MACINTYRE, WHOSE JUSTICE? WHICH RATIONALITY? 103–08 (1988). MacIntyre's own idealized account, of course, is suitably purged of misconceived and flawed social institutions such as slavery, the subordination of women, and the marginalization of artisans, merchants, and farmers. *Id.* at 104–05; ALASDAIR MACINTYRE, AFTER VIRTUE: A STUDY IN MORAL THEORY 158–60 (3d. ed., 2007) (1981); MacIntyre, *Common Good, supra.*, at 250–51. *See also* Clayton, *Political Philosophy, supra* (section 8 on "The Greek Way of Life," discussing MacIntyre's attempt to separate the positive from the negative features of the ancient *polis* in his proposals); Knight, *Introduction, supra*, at 9 (discussing MacIntyre's rejection of Aristotle's metaphysical biology in *After Virtue*). For further discussion of MacIntyre's evolution toward Thomistic Aristotelianism, see Chapter 5, notes 27–32 and accompanying text.

4. As a further stimulus to the imagination the reader may wish to view two video clips of fishing crews and fishing boats and a set of fishing village slides:

https://www.youtube.com/watch?v=Mqt5Zn3iTNQ (at 4:05–8:05)(fishing crew unloading the catch); https://www.youtube.com/watch?v=ByGSMmenPDM (at 0:00–0:40)(fishing boat in rough seas);

https://www.google.com/search?q=mevagissey+cornwall&tbm=isch&ved (Mevagissy in Cornwall, England).

See also Thomas Højrup, *The Common Fisheries Policy Has to Recognize the Needs for Common Goods for Coastal Communities* (2011), http://www.havbaade.dk/thenecessity.pdf (containing vivid visual portrayals of local fishing boats, crews, and villages).

with, the account will reveal important additional features of life in a practice. In Part II of Chapter 6 we will see that even in the modern state there are various types of local communities, including practice communities, which possess some of these features. Chapter 7 will apply what we have learned about life in *Piscopolis* to the legal profession and the legal *polis*. And Chapter 8 will explore possible broader implications for the Republic.

I. Introducing the Fishing Village of *Piscopolis* and Crew Member Drew

At the outset we need to understand the distinctive nature of *Piscopolis* as a local, small-scale community that is relatively isolated and largely self-sufficient. This is truer historically than today, of course. But if the narrative image of life in *Piscopolis* is to have its intended effect, it is important that we make this assumption because, for MacIntyre, only a more or less complete local community can be an ideal *polis* whose inhabitants have the shared politico-ethical commitments that are normative for the argument in this book.[5] We encounter some of these commitments already in Chapter 4. However, we will discuss them as an entirety in Chapter 5, including those necessary for *Piscopolis* to avoid "corruption by narrowness, by complacency, by prejudice against outsiders and by a whole range of other deformities, including those that arise from a cult of local community."[6] MacIntyre is adamant that the modern liberal democratic state is not a *polis*.[7] Moreover, only a *polis* community can resist the destructive influences of the modern liberal democratic state and its capitalist, large-

---

5. *See, e.g.*, MacIntyre, *Common Good*, op. cit., at 248–49 (stressing the importance of a society being (a) small-scale in order to ensure political accountability and widespread political participation aimed at achieving consensus and to avoid the deformations of compartmentalization and role fragmentation, and (b) as self-sufficient as possible in order to resist "the destructive incursions of the state and the wider market economy").

6. MacIntyre, Rational Animals, op. cit., at 142–43 (emphasizing what moral and political philosophers can learn from historical examples of local communities such as "some fishing communities in New England over the past hundred and fifty years[,] ... Welsh mining communities[,] ... farming cooperatives in Donegal, Mayan towns in Guatemala and Mexico, some city states from a more distant past").

7. *See generally* MacIntyre, *Common Good*, op. cit. (discussing several salient contrasts between politics in a *polis* and politics in a modern liberal democratic state).

scale market economy.[8] We will address these destructive influences in Part I of Chapter 6.

For now we should note that as an instance of an ideal *polis*, *Piscopolis* is intermediate between the family and the modern state,[9] exemplifying "[a] form of local community within which the activities of families, work-places, schools, clinics, clubs dedicated to debate and clubs dedicated to games and sports, and religious congregations may all find a place."[10] And its essence is that "each individual's achievement of her or his own good is inseparable both from achieving the shared goods of practices and from contributing to the common good of the community as a whole."[11] Mac-Intyre elaborates upon this inseparability as follows:

> [T[he good of the individual is not subordinated to the good of the community nor vice versa. The individual in order not just to pursue, but even to define her or his good in concrete terms has first to recognize the goods of the community as goods that she or he must make her own. The common good cannot therefore be understood as a summing of individual goods, as constructed out of them. At the same time although the pursuit of the common good of the community is, for all those capable of contributing to it, an essential ingredient of their individual good, the good of each particular individual is more than the common good. And there are of course common goods other than the goods of the overall community: the goods of families and of other groups, the goods of a variety of practices.[12]

This insight about enlightened self-interest is consistent with the discussion in Chapters 2 and 3 and largely explains *why* the inhabitants of *Piscopolis* care about, and are committed to, promoting and pursuing the common goods of practices and the greater common good of the broader community. In other words, using non-MacIntyrean terminology, it explains why they possess and exhibit the general virtue of civic-mindedness

---

8. *Id.* at 248 (quoted *supra* note 5).
9. MacIntyre, Rational Animals, op. cit., at 131.
10. *Id.* at 135.
11. MacIntyre, *Common Good*, op. cit., at 240–41.
12. MacIntyre, Rational Animals, op. cit., at 109

or public-spiritedness and why this virtue pervades all their commitments and relationships, both within and among practices, in addition to any other virtues they may exhibit in particular contexts. Indeed, the pervasiveness of this virtue of civic-mindedness is one of the most distinctive expressions of the prevailing communitarian *ethos* in *Piscopolis*.

It is important to observe, however, that we are here concerned with rational justification, *if the inhabitants were put to the question*, and not necessarily with their actual reasons for everyday decision-making and action.[13] At least in some circumstances, indeed, for the inhabitants of *Piscopolis* to offer, or to seek, such rational justification before acting may even be inconsistent with possessing the virtues and character their commitments and relationships presuppose.[14] It is essential, therefore, to distinguish such rational justification, defining individual good largely in terms of shared common goods of the community, from a rational justification understanding individual good as preference-satisfaction or as reflecting traditional notions of altruism, in which any common good is defined in terms of individual goods.[15] In *Piscopolis* the inhabitants seek the good of others, and thereby achieve their own individual good, because they have acquired and exercise the virtues and the exercise of virtue is always sufficient reason for action in itself.[16] This is a vastly different *ethos* from that of a society where the inhabitants are deficient in virtue and seek each other's good in a calculated way "in some trading of advantage for advantage" such that each "consults the good of others, only because and insofar as it is to her or his good to do so."[17]

---

13. *Id.* at 156–60.

14. *Id. See also id.* at 112–13 (explaining that although the exercise of virtue always provides its own self-justification and thus sufficient reason for action in itself, it may sometimes be appropriate for an individual to explicitly identify the *telos* of human flourishing as "the first premise of her or his practical reasoning").

15. *Id.* at 113–18, 119, 160.

16. *Id.* at 108, 112–13, 158–60. This is presumably subject to qualification regarding the critical role of the "master virtue" of prudence or practical wisdom in the proper exercise of virtue, as discussed in Chapter 2, notes 82–85 and accompanying text. *See also* MacINTYRE, RATIONAL ANIMALS, op. cit., at 106 (referring to "the relevant virtues, and above all the virtue of prudent judgment" when discussing sound reasoning "about what it is best to do here and now").

17. *Id.* at 108.

Our concern with potential rational justification means that we are considering matters from the perspective of all those inhabitants who have become "independent practical reasoners." We have already encountered the concept of an "independent practical reasoner" in Chapters 2 and 3 and we will encounter it again in Chapter 5.[18] To facilitate our understanding of life in *Piscopolis*, the discussion will mainly proceed from the perspective of a member of a fishing crew who was born and raised in *Piscopolis* and whom we will call Drew (Andrew if male, Andrea if female).[19] Chapter 4 examines Drew's daily life and everyday relationships with the other inhabitants of *Piscopolis*, as well as some of Drew's key politico-ethical commitments instantiated in this life and these relationships. Chapter 5 then discusses Drew's participation in the fishing village's political life and Drew's key politico-ethical commitments as a whole. In both Chapters Drew represents all of the independent practical reasoners in *Piscopolis*, and therefore what is said of Drew could be said of any of them, either directly or *mutatis mutandis* (for example, not everyone belongs to a fishing crew).

As discussed at the beginning of this Chapter, we are interested in the practical applications and implications of the theoretical ideal of life in *Piscopolis*. Therefore, we should try to imagine that we are Drew, to identify with Drew's perceptions, values, motivations, and commitments, and to immerse ourselves in the resulting web of Drew's relationships with the other inhabitants of the fishing village. Moreover, we should also try to see ourselves as Drew does — as part of the story of *Piscopolis* and as part of the stories of the various practitioner communities in *Piscopolis* to which Drew belongs.[20] To provide additional perspective and illumination, the discussion will contrast Drew's situation with that of a member of another fishing crew who was born and raised in a very different type of society, one that is much more individualistic and vulnerable to the destructive influences of the liberal democratic state and its capitalist, large-scale market economy, and whom we will call Cash.[21]

---

18. *See* Chapter 2, notes 41–46 and accompanying text, Chapter 3, notes 19–24 and accompanying text, and Chapter 5, notes 45–49 and accompanying text.

19. Saint Andrew is a patron saint of fishermen, http://www.catholic.org/saints/saint. php?saint_id=109.

20. *See* Chapter 2, notes 8–13 and accompanying text.

21. On use of the name Cash for males and females, see https://www.babycenter. com/baby-names-cash-463965.htm(boys);https://www.babycenter.com/baby-names-

Proceeding in this way is inspired by MacIntyre's discussion of fishing crews in his *Partial Response* essay.[22] In the relevant part of this essay MacIntyre concedes his previous "lack of attention to productive practices [or] crafts such as farming and fishing, architecture and construction" and asks us to consider the differences between two types of fishing crew.[23] Although clarifying that these are "ideal types, defining the extremes of a spectrum on which there are many points," MacIntyre also claims it is "beyond doubt" that "there are in fact fishing crews whose lives embody one extreme or the other." [24] And indeed, MacIntyre's account of these two types of fishing crew in *Partial Response* seems to receive striking confirmation in Thomas Højrup's discussion of the experience of Danish fishing crews following Denmark's privatization of fishing quotas, in his study on *Common Goods for Coastal Communities*, which MacIntyre discusses in *Conflicts of Modernity*.[25] As we consider MacIntyre's depiction of these two types of fishing crew, then, we will assume that one of these types corresponds to fishing crews in *Piscopolis*, such as the one to which Drew belongs, and that the other type corresponds to fishing crews elsewhere, such as the one to which Cash belongs.

In the course of the discussion in Chapter 4 and Chapter 5, we will encounter the third function of the virtues in MacIntyre's "unitary core concept of the virtues" in the Western moral tradition of the virtues.[26] In Chapter 2 we encountered the role of the virtues that enables Drew and the other inhabitants of *Piscopolis* to understand and pursue their own individual good as they compose the stories of their lives.[27] In Chapter 3 we encountered the role of the virtues that enables them to achieve the goods

---

cash-232205.htm (girls). These websites indicate the meaning of the name Cash as "strong," "happy," or "graceful," and the first website gives the additional meaning of "wealthy." *See also* http://www.ohbabynames.com/meaning/name/cash/1436.

22. MacIntyre, *Partial Response*, op. cit., at 284–86.

23. *Id.* at 284.

24. *Id.*

25. Højrup, *Common Goods for Coastal Communities*, op. cit., discussed in ALASDAIR MACINTYRE, ETHICS IN THE CONFLICTS OF MODERNITY: AN ESSAY ON DESIRE, PRACTICAL REASONING, AND NARRATIVE 178–82, (2016).

26. For MacIntyre's statement of the three functions of the virtues in this "unitary core concept of the virtues," see MacIntyre, *Partial Response*, op. cit., at 288.

27. *See* Chapter 2, notes 69, 73–94 and accompanying text.

of excellence of practices, which is central to these individual quests.[28] And here, in Chapters 4 and 5, in addition to revisiting these two roles, we encounter the role of the virtues that enables them to achieve "the goods of those types of communities in and through which the goods of individual lives are characteristically achieved," which is also central to their individual quests.[29] We have already seen that the inhabitants of *Piscopolis* possess the general virtue of civic-mindedness or public-spiritedness, which pervades their commitments and relationships and which is therefore relevant for the discussion in both chapters.[30] In addition to this pervasive virtue of civic-mindedness, Chapter 5 will also identify various other "virtues required to sustain the kind of households and the kind of political communities in which men and women can seek for the good together and the virtues necessary for philosophical enquiry about the character of the good."[31]

II. The "Common Practice of Fishing" in *Piscopolis*

As indicated above, the present chapter examines key features of Drew's daily life and everyday relationships with the other inhabitants of *Piscopolis*, as well as key politico-ethical commitments instantiated in this life and these relationships. As a civic-minded inhabitant of the fishing village, Drew cares about and is committed to appropriately promoting and pursuing the common goods of all the practices, and the flourishing of all their practitioner communities and individual practitioners, that make up village life in *Piscopolis* and thereby contributing to the greater common good. What specific commitments does this general commitment entail? We will begin by considering the practice of fishing in Part II of this Chapter. Section 1 discusses the practitioner community that comprises the fishing crew on Drew's particular fishing boat and, more broadly, all the fishing crews in *Piscopolis*. We will refer to their practice as the practice of "catching fish," although MacIntyre's uses the term "fishing." We will reserve this latter term to describe the "common practice of fishing" in which two other practitioner communities are jointly engaged with the fishing crew prac-

---

28. *See* Chapter 3, notes 31–47, 53–67, 149–52, 173–81 and accompanying text.
29. *See* MacIntyre, *Partial Response*, op. cit., at 288 (articulating this third function).
30. *See supra* notes 12–13 and accompanying text.
31. ALASDAIR MACINTYRE, AFTER VIRTUE: A STUDY IN MORAL THEORY 219 (3d. ed., 2007) (1981).

titioner community. Section 2 will then discuss these other two practices. And in Part III we will consider other practices in *Piscopolis* besides fishing.

A. The Practice of Catching Fish

In that part of his *Partial Response* essay seeking to remedy his previous "lack of attention to productive practices [or] crafts such as farming and fishing, architecture and construction"[32] MacIntyre explicates further his concepts of a practice and its goods of excellence. He begins by explaining that

> The aim internal to such productive crafts, when they are in good order, is never only to catch fish, or to produce beef or milk, or to build houses. It is to do so in a manner consonant with the excellences of the craft, so that not only is there a good product, but the craftsperson is perfected through and in her or his activity. This is what apprentices in a craft have to learn. It is from this that the sense of a craft's dignity derives.[33]

It is in elaborating on this statement that MacIntyre asks us to imagine the two contrasting types of fishing crew mentioned above.[34] In one kind of fishing crew, Drew's fishing crew, we can infer that the craft or practice of catching fish is "in good order"[35] because this is

> [A] crew whose members may well have initially joined for the sake of their wage or other share of the catch, but who have acquired from the rest of the crew an understanding of and devotion to excellence in fishing and to excellence in playing one's part as a member of such a crew. Excellence of the requisite kind is a matter of skills and qualities of character required both for the fishing and for achievement of the goods of the common life of such a crew.[36]

---

32. *Id.* at 284.

33. *Id.*

34. *Supra* notes 22–24 and accompanying text.

35. *See supra* note 33 and accompanying text (discussing productive crafts "when they are in good order").

36. MacIntyre, *Partial Response*, op. cit., at 285. In this passage MacIntyre seems to draw a distinction between fishing, or rather catching fish, on the one hand, and playing one's

How should we understand the above two passages? There are several questions. First, what does it mean to say that Drew "ha[s] acquired from the rest of the crew an understanding of and devotion to excellence in fishing" — that Drew doesn't just want to "catch fish" but wants "to do so in a manner consonant with the excellences of the craft, so that not only is there a good product, but [Drew] is perfected through and in her or his activity"? Second, what is involved in "excellence in playing one's part as a member of such a crew [and] achiev[ing] ... the goods of the common life of such a crew" beyond Drew's "excellence in fishing"? Third, what are we to infer from the transformation of "crew members who may well have initially joined for the sake of their wage or other share of the catch" but who then learn to appreciate and become committed to attaining the excellences of the practice?

Turning to the first question, like other crew members Drew wants to flourish in the craft practice of catching fish by achieving the practice's goods of excellence in accordance with its standards of excellence and by contributing in this way to the greater common good of the broader com-

---

part as a member of the crew on the other, and the different excellences involved. However, catching fish would seem to be integral to being a member of the crew. The more accurate distinction, therefore, may be between excellence in fishing and *other* types of excellence involved in being a member of the crew. On the other hand, perhaps MacIntyre has in mind here a related practice involving "the shared making and sustaining of the types of community within which the common good can be achieved [including] fishing crews." *See id.* at 288; MACINTYRE, AFTER VIRTUE, op. cit., at 194 (discussed in Chapter 3, note 145 and accompanying text). *See also infra* note 64 and accompanying text (referring to "the goods to be achieved in attaining excellence in the activities of fishing and in one's role within the crew"). What these other types of excellence might be is discussed *infra* notes 50–55 and accompanying text. Regarding the reference to "other share of the catch" in the quoted passage, MacIntyre describes the practice of share fishing in Denmark as follows:

> Contrast the lives of members of fishing crews in communities where share fishing is practiced, crews who are self-employed, whose fishing grounds are near at hand, and who belong to communities with long experience of this way of life. At Thorupstrand, as Højrup recounts, income from fishing was calculated, after variable costs had been paid, so that 40% was allotted for maintenance and repair of the boat and fishing gear, 20% to the skipper (usually owner of a share of the boat), and 20% each to the second and third crew members. When a loss was incurred, it was divided proportionately. Every member of a crew was therefore a partner in an enterprise, in some communities often a family enterprise ...

MACINTYRE, CONFLICTS OF MODERNITY, op. cit., at 179.

munity.[37] We should note four points about Drew's desires in this regard. First, Drew aims at achieving the practice's overarching common good, which is the fishing crew community's particular understanding of the shared *telos* or ultimate excellence that gives their practice of catching fish its point and purpose and which, as such, is their *practical* ultimate good of excellence.[38] Consistent with MacIntyre's articulations of the ultimate excellence of farming,[39] we can perhaps express the ultimate excellence of catching fish as being "to provide a particular form of nutritious food source, fish, and to do so in a manner that ensures the sustainability of the relevant fishing stock." The fishing community's particular understanding of this ultimate excellence — the overarching common good of their practice — would then relate to the species, sizes, ages, and amounts of fish to be caught over a particular time period. And of course, in providing this nutritious food source to the inhabitants of *Piscopolis* Drew and other members of the fishing crew community want to promote the inhabitants' physical flourishing and well-being and thereby contribute to the greater common good of the broader community.

Second, Drew seeks to achieve the overarching common good of the craft practice of catching fish and thereby contribute to the greater common good by attaining the goods of excellence and drawing upon the qualities of excellence which, together with the standards of excellence, are specific ends or specific common goods of the practice and which flow from and are entailed by, included within, and co-constitutive of this overarching common good.[40] These goods of excellence include the excellence of Drew's performance in the activity of catching fish, the excellence of the catch resulting from Drew's performance, and the excellence of Drew's way of life as a member of the fishing crew.[41] And the qualities of excellence Drew needs to draw upon to attain these goods of excellence (which are also recursively among these goods[42]) include various kinds of attributes — theoretical knowledge, cognitive and practical skills, and qualities of character (dispositions, attitudes, values, or virtues) — with

37. *See* Chapter 3, notes 8–9, 83–86 and accompanying text.
38. *See* Chapter 3, notes 68–74 and accompanying text.
39. *See* Chapter 3, notes 71–72 and accompanying text.
40. *See* Chapter 3, notes 73–74 and accompanying text.
41. *See* Chapter 3, notes 9–11, 48 and accompanying text.
42. *See* Chapter 3, note 49 and accompanying text.

the overarching "master virtue" of practical wisdom at their apex.[43] In the second passage above MacIntyre refers to "skills and qualities of character" but omits mention of "theoretical knowledge." As we saw in Chapter 3, however, such theoretical knowledge is also included among the necessary qualities of excellence.[44]

Third, Drew only discovers the common goods of the craft practice — the practice's overarching common good and all the specific standards, goods, and qualities of excellence which flow from and are entailed by, included within, and co-constitutive of it as specific common goods — after Drew starts to catch fish as an apprentice crew member, gradually learning about them from the rest of the crew as they pass on the tradition of the practice.[45] And for the necessary learning to occur, Drew has to accept the authority of the practice and the tradition of the practice, and also exercise several important prerequisite virtues (as opposed to operational virtues exhibited and demonstrating excellence in Drew's regular daily activities) in his or her relationships with current and past members of the fishing crew community. These virtues include justice, courage, honesty, temperateness, various dialogical and performance character virtues, and humility.[46] The same is true if Drew and other crew members are to continue learning about these things from one another and from the tradition of the practice.[47]

Fourth, as Drew undertakes such continuous learning and pursuit of excellence within this web of relationships, Drew is participating in a craft practice that, like all practices with a living tradition, is continually evolving. The practice's common goods are not static but always in a state of dynamic development and subject to reasoned argument and disagreement among members of the practitioner community, in conversation with the broader community.[48] The fishing crew community's ultimate excellence — "to provide a particular form of nutritious food source, fish, and to do so in a manner that ensures the sustainability of the relevant

---

43. *See* Chapter 3, notes 12–17 and accompanying text; for further elaboration, see notes 18–47 and accompanying text.

44. *See* Chapter 3, notes 14–15 and accompanying text.

45. *See* Chapter 3, notes 50–52, 74 and accompanying text.

46. *See* Chapter 3, notes 56–58, 60–66 and accompanying text.

47. *See* Chapter 3, notes 59–63 and accompanying text.

48. *See* Chapter 3, Part III.

fishing stock" — may be unchanging. But their particular understanding of it — their overarching common good — and of the contribution they make to the greater common good of the broader community in *Piscopolis* may well change: What species of fish? What size? What age? In what amounts? And so forth. As this happens — as the fishing crew community's understanding evolves, or as the best way of achieving it evolves — so correspondingly the standards, goods, and qualities of excellence entailed by, included within, and co-constitutive of the overarching common good as specific common goods of their practice will also evolve. And so, Drew and other members of the fishing crew community may discover, for example, that new knowledge, skills, or virtues are needed in the light of experience.[49]

We turn now to the second question: What is involved in "excellence in playing one's part as a member of such a crew [and] achiev[ing] ... the goods of the common life of such a crew" beyond Drew's own excellence in the activity of catching fish? There are two main points. First, Drew doesn't just want to attain goods of excellence and flourish in the practice of catching fish him or herself but is concerned that other crew members also attain these goods and flourish. Drew understands that Drew's own excellence and flourishing — Drew's own success — in the practice of catching fish is directly dependent on theirs. Thus Drew understands that Drew depends on other crew members who value and attain the goods of excellence to teach Drew what he or she needs to know as an apprentice,[50] to stimulate competition in striving for excellence (a healthy form of competitiveness that contrasts with an unhealthy form focused primarily on goods of effectiveness),[51] to correct Drew's mistakes,[52] and to perform well, perhaps even by saving Drew's life, so that deficiencies in their own performance do not impede Drew's performance. As MacIntyre explains in the continuation of the second passage above, "[t]he dependence of each member on the qualities of character and skills of others will be accompanied by a recognition that from time to time one's own life will be in danger and that whether one drowns or not may depend upon someone

---

49. *See id.*

50. *See supra* note 45 and accompanying text and Chapter 3, notes 50–52, 74 and accompanying text.

51. *See* Chapter 3, note 111 and accompanying text.

52. MacIntyre, Rational Animals, op. cit., at 96–97.

else's courage."[53] The second point emerges from MacIntyre's further continuation of this passage: "And the consequent concern of each member of the crew for the others, if it is to have the stamp of genuine concern, will characteristically have to extend to those for whom those others care: the members of their immediate families."[54] For example, in addition to caring for Drew as a comrade, other crew members will understandably be more willing to risk their lives to save Drew from drowning if they know that their respective families will be provided for and cared for should they lose their life in doing so. And so MacIntyre refers to "a common affliction and common responsibilities" in the case of a death at sea.[55]

We should note that Drew understands that other crew members depend upon Drew's excellence just as Drew depends upon theirs and that they want to promote Drew's excellence and flourishing in the practice just as Drew wants to promote theirs. And this understanding of mutual interdependence is yet another reason for Drew to attain the goods of excellence and flourish himself or herself. In a virtuous circle Drew's own excellence promotes the excellence of other crew members, which further promotes Drew's excellence, which further promotes their excellence, and so on. Similarly, Drew is more willing to take life-endangering risks for other crew members knowing that Drew's family would be provided for and cared for if necessary, just as they are willing to take such risks for Drew knowing that Drew will help provide and care for their own families if necessary.

Let us now consider the third question: What are we to infer from the transformation of "crew members who may well have initially joined for the sake of their wage or other share of the catch" but who then learn to appreciate and become committed to attaining the excellences of the practice? Here again, there are two main points. First, for such crew members the cooperative activity involved in the practice of catching fish has clearly now become instrumental to attaining shared, intrinsic common goods

---

53. MacIntyre, *Partial Response*, op. cit., at 285.

54. *Id.*

55. *Id. See also infra* note 89 and accompanying text. I am indebted to Jack Sammons for emphasizing the importance of comradeship as a motive for taking such risks. Sammons Email (September 4, 2020) (observing that "[t]his, by the way, is also the reason soldiers kill. It is certainly not for country") [on file with author].

that are independent of any pre-existing desires and goals.[56] To be sure, such a transformation is perhaps less likely in Drew's case. Being born and raised in *Piscopolis* Drew is *already* thoroughly imbued with its *ethos* and is therefore less likely to "have initially joined for the sake of the[] wage or other share of the catch,"[57] but it might be true of a newcomer to the community. In any event, what such a transformation or pre-existing commitment to attaining the excellences of the practice implies is that although Drew and other crew members are of course *also* concerned with pursuing goods of effectiveness (because they need adequate resources to be able to attain those goods of excellence in the practice of catching fish and in other practices that constitute the flourishing that is their individual *telos*),[58] nevertheless their *primary* motivation for engaging in the practice in the way they do is intrinsic, and goods and qualities of effectiveness are systematically subordinated to goods and qualities of excellence.[59] Drew and other crew members predominantly care about goods that don't just belong to them but necessarily benefit others as well as themselves.[60]

Second, such a primary motivation and relative subordination of goods will manifest in two main ways. On the one hand, Drew will resist the many different ways in which the common goods of the practice of catching fish can be corrupted,[61] as discussed below with regard to the second type of fishing crew, Cash's fishing crew.[62] On the other hand, Drew will not easily abandon his or her particular fishing crew for another one, or even abandon the common goods of the practice altogether to take up

---

56. *See* Chapter 3, notes 132, 134–35 and accompanying text.
57. *Supra* note 36 and accompanying text.
58. *See* Chapter 3, notes 104, 106–07, 138–39 and accompanying text. In pursuing, and distributing, goods of effectiveness, Drew's fishing crew will be organized in an institutional form, albeit doubtless a rudimentary one. *See* Chapter 3, notes 112–15, 140–44 and accompanying text (discussing the relationship between practices and institutions).
59. *See* Chapter 3, notes 153–54 and accompanying text. *See also* Chapter 3, notes 101–03 and accompanying text (discussing the general nature of goods and qualities of effectiveness), Part IV, Section A.1 (discussing goods of effectiveness in greater detail, including contrasts between goods of effectiveness and goods of excellence), Part IV, Section A.2 (discussing qualities of effectiveness in greater detail, including contrasts between qualities of effectiveness and qualities of excellence).
60. *See* Chapter 3, note 111 and accompanying text.
61. *See* Chapter 3, notes 155–71 and accompanying text.
62. *See infra* notes 78–81 and accompanying text.

another occupation, lured by the offer of higher economic reward. Indeed, Drew will be prepared to endure times of economic hardship when income is low, for as long as possible. He will not be "a rat leaving a sinking ship" and immediately change jobs or flee *Piscopolis*.[63] Both for Drew and other crew members (and for the other inhabitants of *Piscopolis* as well), "the goods to be achieved in attaining excellence in the activities of fishing and in one's role within the crew will, for as long as possible, outweigh the economic hardships of low wages and periods of bad catches or low prices for fish."[64] In sum, Drew has developed an "allegiance to [his or her] fellow crew members and to the way of life of a fishing community" that transcends purely economic concerns.[65] And once again, Drew will exercise certain important virtues to resist any such pressures and temptations, including practical wisdom and the other virtues already mentioned above in connection with Drew's learning about and attaining such common goods in the first place.[66]

We can illuminate matters further by comparing and contrasting the second type of fishing crew, Cash's fishing crew, with respect to the various points discussed above. To begin with, we can infer that in Cash's fishing crew the craft or practice of catching fish is not "in good order"[67] because this is

A fishing crew [that is] organized and understood as a purely technical and economic means to a productive end, whose aim is only or overridingly to satisfy as profitably as possible some market's demand for fish. Just as those managing its organization aim at a high level of profits, so also the individual crew members aim at a high level of reward. Not only the skills, but also the qualities of character valued by those who manage the organization, will be those well designed to achieve a high level of profitability. And each individual at work as a member of such a fishing crew will value those qualities

---

63. *See* Chapter 3, notes 82, 183 and accompanying text.

64. MacIntyre, *Partial Response*, op. cit., at 285.

65. *Id.* at 286.

66. *See* Chapter 3, notes 173–81 and accompanying text; *supra* notes 46–47 and accompanying text.

67. *See supra* note 33 and accompanying text (discussing productive crafts "when they are in good order").

of character in her or himself or in others which are apt to produce a high level of reward for her or himself.[68]

How are we to understand this passage, which seems to presuppose an arrangement corresponding to Geoff Moore's depiction of a business organization that is a "practice-institution combination," in which a "core or primary practice" (here, the practice of catching fish engaged in by Cash and other crew members) is served by "the secondary practice of making and sustaining the institution" (engaged in by management)?[69] What follows from such a heavy emphasis on achieving a high level of profit or other material reward in the particular business organization for which Cash works? Let us first clarify what does *not* follow. It does *not* necessarily follow that Cash, other crew members, and management are not concerned at all with pursuing the common goods of the core practice of catching fish — the practice's overarching common good and all the standards, goods, and qualities of excellence entailed by, included within, and co-constitutive of it as specific common goods — and with contributing thereby to the greater common good, or that they are not concerned at all with flourishing in the practice.[70] This is because, although they are clearly very concerned to attain goods of effectiveness, doing so usually requires pursuing goods of excellence and demonstrating qualities of excellence as well as qualities of effectiveness, at least to some extent.[71] Consequently, we should understand the reference to "skills" and "qualities of character"

---

68. MacIntyre, *Partial Response*, op. cit., at 284–85. MacIntyre describes fishing crew members working for corporations as follows:

> Much deep sea fishing is financed by corporations whose return on their investment depends on the size of the catch and who, in attempting to maximize that return, compete in national and international markets. Their aim is to dominate in the most profitable fishing grounds and to compete successfully in the sale of salted, canned, and frozen fish. To work for such a corporation is to be like any other worker for a typical capitalist enterprise, that is, you are serving *their* ends for the sake of the livelihood of you and yours …

MacIntyre, Conflicts of Modernity, op. cit., at 178–79.

69. For discussion of Moore's account of business and other organizations as "practice-institution combination[s]," see Chapter 3, notes 145–52 and accompanying text.

70. *See supra* notes 37–44 and accompanying text.

71. *See* Chapter 3, notes 136–37 and accompanying text. For discussion of how management in such business organizations can pursue goods of excellence, both in the secondary practice of making and sustaining the institution bearing the "core or primary practice"

valued by crew members and management in the above passage to include both types of qualities.[72] By the same token, Cash's learning situation, first as an apprentice and then as a full crew member, may be similar to that of Drew, again at least to some extent.[73] It also does not necessarily follow that Cash is not concerned at all with the flourishing of other crew members or with the welfare of their families, or again that management is not concerned about such matters.[74]

What *does* follow is that all these concerns for and resulting commitments to the common goods of the practice are more fragile in the case of Cash's fishing crew than in Drew's fishing crew. In the case of Cash's fishing crew the cooperative activity involved in catching fish is instrumental to attaining individualistic common goods that are independent of and extrinsic to this activity, because they are the object of the pre-existing desire and goal to obtain as much money or other material reward as possible.[75] Even though Cash, other crew members, and management are *also* concerned with the pursuit of goods of excellence, nevertheless their *primary* motivation is extrinsic, and goods and qualities of excellence are systematically subordinated to goods and qualities of effectiveness.[76] They predominantly care about goods that necessarily belong to and benefit themselves and only contingently benefit others.[77]

The fragility of their concern for and commitment to the common goods of the practice resulting from such primary motivation and relative subordination of goods, and from the unhealthy form of competitiveness these entail, may manifest in two main ways. On the one hand, there is a greater risk that Cash and others may corrupt these common goods in various ways.[78] They may, for example, be less concerned about the flourishing of all crew members or the welfare of their families.[79] They may be

---

and in promoting the flourishing of practitioners in the core practice, see Chapter 3, notes 149–52 and accompanying text.

72. For discussion comparing and contrasting qualities of effectiveness with qualities of excellence, see Chapter 3, Part IV, Section A.2.

73. *See supra* notes 45–47 and accompanying text.

74. *See supra* notes 50–55 and accompanying text.

75. *See* Chapter 3, notes 132–33 and accompanying text.

76. *See* Chapter 3, notes 153–54 and accompanying text.

77. *See* Chapter 3, note 111 and accompanying text.

78. *See* Chapter 3, notes 155–71 and accompanying text.

79. *See supra* notes 50–55 and accompanying text.

greedy or overly susceptible to organizational pressures rooted in concern for the "bottom line."[80] Consequently, they may succumb to the individual or collective temptation to "cheat" by putting profit or other material reward above quality of performance and resulting product in terms of the type, size, weight, and ages of the catch, by sacrificing the long-term sustainability of the fishing stock in non-sustainable overfishing for short term gain, and perhaps even by lying about such matters.[81] On the other hand, there is a greater risk of abandoning a particular fishing crew or even abandoning the common goods of the practice altogether.[82] Thus, when the level of reward is not high enough, from his or her perspective Cash will have "the best of reasons" for leaving the crew and joining another one, or even taking up another occupation.[83] Similarly, when the level of profits is not high enough, compared to the return on other investments, from their perspective management will have "no good reason not to fire crew members" and owners will have "no good reason not to invest their money elsewhere."[84] None of them, in other words, will have the same degree of loyalty and allegiance to the fishing crew and its way of life that Drew has.[85]

B. The Practices of Boat Building and Net Making

We have discussed the practice of catching fish in which Drew and other members of the fishing crew community are engaged. But of course, they cannot catch fish without fishing boats and fishing nets. This means

---

80. They may even consider that "greed is good." The allusion, of course, is to Gordon Gekko's speech to the stockholders of Teldar Corporation in the 1987 film "Wall Street":

> The point is, ladies and gentleman, that greed — for lack of a better word — is good. Greed is right. Greed works. Greed clarifies, cuts through, and captures the essence of the evolutionary spirit. Greed, in all of its forms — greed for life, for money, for love, knowledge — has marked the upward surge of mankind. And greed — you mark my words — will not only save Teldar Paper, but that other malfunctioning corporation called the USA.

Wall Street (20th Century Fox, 1987).

81. *See supra* notes 39–40 and accompanying text.

82. *See supra* note 63 and accompanying text; Chapter 3, notes 82, 183 and accompanying text.

83. MacIntyre, *Partial Response*, op. cit., at 285.

84. *Id.*

85. *See supra* note 65 and accompanying text.

that that at least two other crafts or practices in *Piscopolis* are involved in and directly contribute to Drew's practice of catching fish — boat building and net making.[86] Like the practice of catching fish, each of these other two distinct practices has an ultimate excellence. The ultimate excellence of boat building might be something like "the building and maintenance of seaworthy vessels designed for the effective pursuit and catching of fish," and that of net making something like "the construction and repair of durable nets designed for the effective catching of fish." Each one also has an overarching common good, which is their practitioners' particular understanding of this ultimate excellence and which entails, includes, and is co-constituted by specific standards, goods, and qualities of excellence (including the practical wisdom of the craft) as specific ends or specific common goods of the practice. And once again, as in the case of any practice with a living tradition, the craft communities' understanding of their respective overarching common good or of the common goods involved in achieving it may evolve through reasoned argument and disagreement.

Although distinct, the three craft communities engaged in their respective practices of catching fish, boat building, and net making combine in and co-constitute a larger craft community jointly engaged in "the common practice of fishing," and the practitioners of all three craft communities directly participate in this common practice. All three practices are ordered to the ultimate excellence and the overarching common good of the common practice (which entails, includes, and is co-constituted by the overarching common good and all the specific common goods of each of them). Given that the activities of the boat builders and the net makers are entirely derived from the activity of the fishing crews, the ultimate excellence and overarching common good of the common practice of fishing would seem to be the same as for the practice of catching fish.[87] Because the three distinct craft practices of catching fish, boat building, and net making are necessarily interdependent and interpenetrating, we can say that in addition to co-constituting the common practice of fishing they co-constitute one another as well, even though their practitioners do not

---

86. Those inclined to question whether net making is a practice may wish to read Sheila Redmond's discussion of net making and baiting in Louisiana fishing. Sheila Redmond, *Nets and Netmaking in the Delta*, FOLKLIFE IN LOUISIANA, http://www.louisianafolklife.org/LT/ Articles_Essays/deltaNets.html.

87. *See supra* notes 38–39 and accompanying text.

directly participate in one another's activities — for example, Drew does not build boats or make nets, and the boat builders and net makers do not catch fish.

The preceding considerations are especially relevant for the analogy we will draw in Chapter 7 between the common practice of fishing (and its three distinct craft practices of catching fish, boat building, and net making), on the one hand, and the common practice of maintaining the rule of law (and its four distinct craft practices of adjudication, lawyering, assisting the legislature, and legal education), on the other. In the present context, however, the most important point is that, just as Drew wants to promote the excellence and flourishing of other crew members, so also Drew wants to promote the excellence and flourishing of the boat builders and net makers. Drew understands that his or her success in the craft practice of catching fish depends directly not only on the excellence of other crew members but also on the excellence of the boat builders and net makers in their respective craft practices. Drew understands, too, that their own success in these practices depends directly upon Drew's excellence and that therefore they want to promote Drew's excellence and flourishing just as Drew wants to promote theirs. And so, there is another virtuous circle arising from their understanding of mutual interdependence. By contrast, although Cash may also have a sense of such mutual interdependence of the three practitioner communities and associated reciprocal desires in their more individualistic society, this sense is unlikely to be as well developed as it is in Drew and the other inhabitants of *Piscopolis* with its distinctive communitarian *ethos.*

III. Other Practices in *Piscopolis* and Broader Interdependencies

Drew's understanding of such mutual interdependence of practices is not limited to other members of the fishing crew community and the two other craft communities directly and jointly engaged in the common practice of fishing but extends much further. As MacIntyre says after observing that the concern crew members have for one another will extend to the members of each other's immediate families:[88]

---

88. *See supra* note 54 and accompanying text.

So the interdependence of the members of a fishing crew in respect of skills, the achievement of goods and the acquisition of virtues will extend to an interdependence of the families of crew members and perhaps beyond them to the whole society of a fishing village.[89]

Indeed, there is much more going on in *Piscopolis* than just fishing. In addition, there are various craft communities of practitioners engaged in other productive crafts or practices — for example, physicians, teachers, plumbers, police officers; there may even be a lawyer or two.[90] Drew does not participate in these practices. However, there are also practitioner communities engaged in other kinds of practices in which Drew *does* participate — for example, the practice of the making and sustaining of family life,[91] the practice of a particular religious community to which Drew belongs, or the practices of various civic communities to which he or she belongs, such as musical, theatrical, or athletic performance, or volunteer fire fighting. Here too, each of these practices is guided by pursuit of an ultimate excellence and by a particular understanding of this ultimate excellence which is its overarching common good and which entails, includes, and is co-constituted by specific standards of excellence, goods of

---

89. MacIntyre, *Partial Response*, op. cit., at 285. MacIntyre completes the passage by stating: "When someone dies at sea, fellow crew members, their families and the rest of the fishing community will share a common affliction and common responsibilities." *Id.* *See supra* note 55 and accompanying text. *See also* Macintyre's continuation of the passage describing share fishing in Denmark, quoted *supra* note 36:

> Every member of a crew was therefore a partner in an enterprise, in some communities often a family enterprise, so that individuals find it difficult not to recognize three related common goods, those of family, crew, and local community, and achieve their own individual ends in and through cooperating to achieve those common goods. In the achievement of those goods, school teachers, boat builders, and pastors all have crucial roles. Such communities do of course vary in many respects. What they share, as Højrup emphasizes, is that their work is not a means to an external end but is constitutive of a way of life, the sustaining of which is itself an end.

MacIntyre, Conflicts of Modernity, op. cit., at 179. *See also id.* at 176–77 (discussing how "the common goods of family, school, and workplace" are understood as interdependent by those "who have begun to think systematically" about flourishing).

90. With respect to teachers, see Chapter 7, note 11 and accompanying text.

91. For discussion of this practice, see MacIntyre, After Virtue, op. cit., at 187–78; MacIntyre, Rational Animals, op. cit., at 133–35.

excellence, and qualities of excellence as specific ends or specific common goods of the practice. And everything that was discussed above with respect to Drew's participation in the practice of catching fish and Drew's role as a member of the fishing crew community applies *mutatis mutandis* to participation in these other practices and other practitioner communities too.[92]

Drew wants to attain the common goods of *all* the practices in which Drew participates and to which Drew has been called, and to promote the excellence and flourishing of all their practitioners, not only because each one is constitutive of Drew's flourishing but also because they are interdependent in ways that may be very real, albeit sometimes difficult to identify and articulate precisely, so that Drew's success in one contributes directly or indirectly to Drew's success in another. For example, as we already observed in Chapter 3, the exercise of virtues within one practice (and the character formation attendant upon such exercise) may also contribute to the exercise of virtue within other practices as well.[93] And the same may be true of other qualities of excellence — other qualities of character (dispositions, attitudes, or values), cognitive and practical skills, and theoretical knowledge.

Drew also wants to promote the excellence and flourishing of practitioners even of those practices in which Drew does not participate him or herself or upon which Drew's success in practices is not directly dependent (as Drew's success in the practice of catching fish, for example, is directly dependent upon the boat builders and net makers). Drew understands just how far and how pervasively the mutual interdependencies in *Piscopolis* extend. Drew understands that his or her success in practices also depends *indirectly* on many other types of practitioners to do their jobs well — physicians to keep Drew well or treat Drew when sick, school teachers to give Drew the education he or she needs, plumbers to make sure Drew doesn't have to contend with a flood at home as well as at work (!), and to do these things also for all those others upon whom Drew depends directly or indirectly. Moreover, Drew wants to promote the excellence and flourishing of the practitioners in other practices in *Piscopolis* not simply because Drew

---

92. *See supra* Part II, Section A.
93. *See* Chapter 3, notes 38–39 and accompanying text.

understands how Drew is dependent upon these practices but also because they have taught Drew to appreciate their worth.[94] But perhaps even more strikingly, Drew's understanding extends beyond goods of excellence to goods of effectiveness also. Thus Drew understands that just as Drew needs adequate resources to sustain Drew's own practices and to purchase products and services from other inhabitants, so too Drew will not be very successful in the practice of catching fish if others cannot sustain their own practices or afford to buy the fish Drew catches. And this explains why Drew wants other inhabitants in *Piscopolis* to acquire adequate goods of effectiveness, especially money, as well as to attain goods of excellence.[95]

Pressing the phenomenological perspective further as discussed in Part III, Section C of Chapter 2, Being may disclose itself to Drew in such a way that it reveals the interconnectedness among things.[96] If Drew possess-

---

94. *See* Chapter 3, note 86 and accompanying text.

95. *See supra* note 58 and accompanying text.

96. Recall Linda Ross Meyer's explanation in Chapter 2 that in Heidegger's phenomenology "things have sense for us ... when they are in a world in relation to other things" and that we are "enmeshed in a web of relationships among things that show up for us as we engage with them and work with them, from past experience to future possibility." *See* Chapter 2, note 150 and accompanying text. For an elaboration of these propositions that provides a good sense of the spatial and temporal interconnectedness in *Dasein's* world, see MICHAEL INWOOD, HEIDEGGER: A VERY SHORT INTRODUCTION 32–35 (1997). Regarding space, Inwood explains:

> What is Dasein's world like? It is not for the most part a world of purely natural entities. The most immediate and obvious denizens of Dasein's world, apart from Dasein itself, are the tools and equipment that it uses for its daily needs, its hammer, for example, the nails and the leather with which it makes shoes. Tools and equipment have their place in a workshop, the immediate environing world of Dasein. But this world points beyond itself to a larger world, to the other Dasein who buy the shoes, and to those who supply the leather. This in turn points to nature, not the nature of the natural scientist, but the cows from which the leather comes and the fields in which they graze.

Id. at 32. Regarding time, and continuing with the example of the hammer in the cobbler's workshop but adding the example of a table in a room, Inwood explains that:

> The table points ahead to the uses that will be made of it, and back to past events — the scratches made by the boys, the book he wrote at it, and so on. The craftsman too, absorbed in his hammering, looks ahead implicitly to the shoe he will have made, to the fresh supply of leather that he needs to order, and back perhaps to his youth when he was taught his skills by his father, from whom he inherited the workshop.

Id. at 35.

es this more profound phenomenological understanding and sensibility, Drew is aware of even broader interdependencies, and understands that his or her flourishing depends not only upon the flourishing of the practitioners of other practices in *Piscopolis* but also upon the flourishing of the fish Drew catches. And Drew understands that the flourishing of the fish in turn depends upon the flourishing of the entire web of life that inhabits Earth's thin, fragile "critical zone" of which the fish and humans are a part.[97] Because of this radical interdependence and Drew's concern for the well-being of future generations, Drew wants to protect and promote the flourishing of the web of life and the health of the planet, and exhibits certain "environmental virtues."[98] Moreover, this ecological sensibility and its associated virtues doubtless help shape and reinforce Drew's understanding of, and disposition toward, all the interdependencies discussed in this Chapter.

Once again Drew's understanding and desires in all these respects are shared and reciprocated by the other inhabitants of the fishing village. And once again, too, although Cash may also have some sense of the extensive

---

97. For a useful introduction to the "critical zone" that exists on the surface of the Earth's crust, see *Mt Lemmon Science Tour: The Critical Zone*, Flandrau Science Center & Planetarium, University of Arizona College of Science (2017), https://www.youtube.com/watch?v=aezWKCQxR5U. I am indebted to Jack Sammons for drawing my attention to these broader interdependencies and to the relevance of Heidegger's phenomenology in addressing them. Sammons Email (September 4, 2020) [on file with author].

98. Regarding "environmental ethics," see Chapter 2, note 119 and accompanying text (discussing criticisms of a virtue ethics focused on the concept of *human* flourishing for being anthropocentric and insensitive to environmental concerns and nonhuman flourishing as well as possible responses to such criticism). For helpful and suggestive exploration of this theme, see, for example, Dominica Dzwonkowska, *Is Environmental Virtue Ethics Anthropocentric?*, 31 J. AG. ENVIRON. ETHIC 723 (2018) (distinguishing among different types of anthropocentrism and explaining how a virtue ethics can accommodate environmental and nonhuman concerns even when focused on human flourishing); Darcia Narvaez, *Ecocentrism: Resetting Baselines for Virtue Development*, ETHICAL THEORY MORAL PRACT. (July 9, 2020) (exploring, from a neurobiological perspective, the importance for healthy human development of "the evolved nest" or "evolved developmental niche," including a proper relationship to the natural world, and stressing the limitations of "anthropocentric virtue" and the necessity for "human wellbeing" of returning to a lost "ecocentric virtue" and attending to "the earth's wellbeing"); Pope Francis, *Laudato Si': On Care for Our Common Home*, United States Conference of Catholic Bishops (2015) (criticizing "misguided anthropocentrism," emphasizing our responsibility to care for the gift of God's creation, and observing that "[l]iving our vocation to be protectors of God's handiwork is essential to a life of virtue").

interdependence of practices and activities in his or her own more individualistic society, such sense is likely much less well developed than it is in
Drew and the other inhabitants of *Piscopolis* with its distinctive communitarian *ethos*.[99] Also, Cash likely lacks Drew's ecological sensibility and "environmental virtues" and instead, due to "technological thinking," regards
the fish and indeed everything else as mere "standing reserve" to be ordered according to human will.[100] These contrasts between Cash and Drew
are also likely related to a difference in their respective worldviews, specifically differences between the predominant worldview of the modern
West — the secular, mechanistic, and materialistic "Cartesian-Newtonian
worldview" — and an ecological, holistic, and more spiritual worldview,
involving a systems approach to the understanding of biological and social
life, that can inform and be integrated with Drew's Thomistic Aristotelian
politico-ethical commitments to which we now turn.[101]

---

99. And so MacIntyre continues the passage describing fishing crew members working
for corporations, quoted *supra* note 68, as follows:

> To work for such a corporation is to be like any other worker for a typical
> capitalist enterprise, that is, you are serving *their* ends for the sake of the
> livelihood of you and yours, and there is only or principally a financial con-
> nection between your work and the ends that you have as member of a family
> or household or as member of a local community.

MacIntyre, Conflicts of Modernity, op. cit., at 179. For an eloquent discussion
of the "blind spot" regarding our interdependence in the modern liberal democratic state
with its individualist *ethos*, see Jenny Odell, *The Myth of Self-Reliance: An Encounter with
Emerson's Essays*, The Paris Review (January 15, 2020) (interrogating in particular Ralph
Waldo Emerson's essay *Self-Reliance*).

100. *See* Chapter 2, notes 152–53 and accompanying text.

101. For further discussion of the contrasts between these two worldviews, see Fritjof Capra, *Turning Point: A Science of Living Systems*, https://www.earthandspiritcenter.
org/wp-content/uploads/2019/10/3-2-Turning-Point-A-Science-of-Living-Systems-Fritjof
-Capra.pdf. *See also* Chapter 1, note 38.

FIVE

LIVING IN *PISCOPOLIS* PART II

*Political Conversation and the Greater Common Good
in the Fishing Village* Polis

In Chapter 4 we focused on particular practitioner communities and their practices in *Piscopolis*, and examined crew member Drew's daily life and everyday relationships with the other inhabitants, as well as some of Drew's key politico-ethical commitments instantiated in this life and these relationships. In doing so we contrasted Drew's situation in an ideal *polis* such as *Piscopolis* with that of Cash, a member of a very different type of fishing crew more subject to the destructive influences of the modern liberal democratic state and its capitalist, large-scale market economy. The particular communities and practices, and the types of commitments and relationships, discussed in Chapter 4 largely co-constitute the daily life of the fishing village as a whole. In Chapter 5 we also consider the fishing village as a whole, this time, however, from the perspective of the larger political community and its common practice of politics, which are co-constituted by the inhabitants and their communities of practice combining and acting in a political capacity. This larger political community forms around the political conversation in which Drew and the other inhabitants who are independent practical reasoners are jointly engaged and through which they carry on their common practice.[1] As before, we will again focus on crew member Drew as representative of all these inhabitants. Chapter 6

---

1. For earlier discussion of the term "independent practical reasoner" with reference to *Piscopolis*, see Chapter 4, note 18 and accompanying text.

will then contrast the very different situation of crew member Cash in the modern liberal democratic state.

I. The Common Practice of Politics, and Political Conversation in *Piscopolis*

Political conversation in *Piscopolis* may occur both in the context of formally held meetings of the village assembly and more informally within the context of activities in particular practices.[2] MacIntyre endorses Aristotle and Aquinas' view that "both ruled and rulers" in a properly ordered *polis* "aim at achieving its common good" and are able to do so because their participation in the *polis* enables them "to order a variety of common and individual goods in their own lives, acquiring those dispositions, the virtues, which direct them toward their final end."[3] The enquiries and practice of politics are concerned with producing citizens who are "good human beings, good at achieving common and individual goods," and those of ethics, viewed as part of politics, with "the qualities of mind and character" necessary to be a good citizen, good at "ruling and being ruled," and a good human being.[4] Focusing on practices, Kelvin Knight describes MacIntyre's view regarding the nature and purpose of politics and political conversation in an ideal *polis* such as *Piscopolis* as follows:

> Like Aristotle, MacIntyre considers people to be essentially political beings. His first principles and final ends are, accordingly, political. Politics is itself a teleologically ordered practice but one concerned with the proper ordering of all other practices within a community. As such, it is a form of enquiry regarding the purpose of all practice.[5]

---

2. *See* ALASDAIR MACINTYRE, DEPENDENT RATIONAL ANIMALS: WHY HUMAN BEINGS NEED THE VIRTUES 129, 141 (1999) (referring to "institutionalized forms of deliberation" accessible to all members of the community who wish to contribute proposals, objections, and arguments, as well as political activity and political reasoning as one aspect of everyday activity and practical reasoning). *See also infra* note 8 and accompanying text (referring to "modes of deliberation, formal and informal").

3. ALASDAIR MACINTYRE, ETHICS IN THE CONFLICTS OF MODERNITY: AN ESSAY ON DESIRE, PRACTICAL REASONING, AND NARRATIVE 176 (2016).

4. *Id.* at 178.

5. Kelvin Knight, *Introduction, in* THE MACINTYRE READER 20 (Kelvin Knight, ed., 1998).

In *Piscopolis* the inhabitants share a wide range of substantive politico-ethical commitments, including the types of commitments discussed
in Chapter 4, that reflect and sustain the politically determined proper
ordering of practices in the fishing village — their proper ordering both
within and among particular practices. These commitments represent the
standards, goods, and qualities of excellence of the common practice of
politics (that is, its common goods). Moreover, they are themselves reflected in and sustained by both their instantiation in the inhabitants' lives
and relationships and the inhabitants' ongoing political consensus, and
are therefore also reflected in and sustained by the standards, goods, and
qualities of excellence (that is, the common goods) of all the particular
practices in *Piscopolis*.[6] Collectively they shape the distinctive communitarian *ethos* of *Piscopolis* and are concrete expressions of the general virtue
of civic-mindedness that pervades all the inhabitants' relationships.[7]

In Chapter 5 we address the full range of the inhabitants' key politico-ethical commitments and thereby also illuminate the proper ordering
of practices their commitments reflect and sustain. Emerging perhaps
many years ago and continuing within the living traditions of the fishing village, these commitments are always subject to further evolution
through reasoned argument in political conversation in the village. Mac-
Intyre elaborates as follows:

> A *polis* is indeed impossible, unless its citizens share at least one lan-
> guage — they may well share more than one — and unless they also
> share modes of deliberation, formal and informal, and a large degree
> of common understanding of practices and institutions. And such a
> common understanding is generally derived from some particular
> inherited cultural tradition. But these requirements have to serve the
> ends of a society in which individuals are always able to put in ques-

---

6. For MacIntyre's own characterization of such shared "moral commitments," see
MACINTYRE, RATIONAL ANIMALS, op. cit., at 156, 161 ("[T]he moral and political relationships... required for... achievement of [the] common good involve [shared] commitments
that are in some respects unconditional not only to a certain range of goods, but also to
those particular others together with whom we attempt to achieve that common good").

7. For discussion of the general virtue of civic-mindedness and its rational justification
rooted in the enlightened self-interest of the inhabitants in *Piscopolis*, see Chapter 4, notes
11–17 and accompanying text.

tion through communal deliberation what has hitherto by custom and tradition been taken for granted both about their own good and the good of the community. A *polis* is always, potentially or actually, a society of rational enquiry, of self-scrutiny."[8]

Central to the "large degree of common understanding of practices and institutions" is "a large degree of shared understanding of goods, virtues, and rules."[9] And as the quoted passage indicates, once again, as in Chapter 4, we are concerned with rational justification, *if Drew and the other inhabitants were put to the question,* and not necessarily with their actual reasons for everyday decision-making and action.[10]

II. Shared Politico-Ethical Commitments

We will now consider the full range of the inhabitants' key politico-ethical commitments. In doing so we must remain mindful that as stated at the beginning of Part I above, political conversation in *Piscopolis* may occur both in the context of formally held meetings of the village assembly

---

8. Alasdair MacIntyre, *Politics, Philosophy, and the Common Good* (1997) *in* THE MAC-INTYRE READER 241 (Kelvin Knight, ed., 1998) (contrasting the political society of a *Volk*, which not only has but is "constituted by" a "shared culture" and whose "essential bonds," being those of "a shared cultural tradition," are "prerational and nonrational"). *See also* MAC-INTYRE, RATIONAL ANIMALS, op. cit., at 157 (examining the steps involved in, and the value of, a "local community" engaging in a process of "rational enquiry" and "critical scrutiny").

9. *See* MacIntyre, *Common Good,* op. cit., at 247–49 (stressing that, for "rational political justification" and "rational politics" in which "individuals [are] able to learn about their individual and common goods" to be possible, and in stark contrast to modern states with their "large-scale so-called free market economies," a society "must have a large degree of shared understanding of goods, virtues, and rules" in addition to being "a relatively small-scale society whose relationships are not deformed by compartmentalization" and having "[g]enuinely free[,] ... local and small-scale markets" that do not presuppose an "individualist" conception of the common good).

10. MACINTYRE, RATIONAL ANIMALS, op. cit., at 156–60; Chapter 4, notes 13–17 and accompanying text. *See also* MacIntyre, *Common Good,* op. cit., at 240 (referring to "questions that may never be explicitly formulated, but which nonetheless receive answers in the way in which individuals live out their lives"), 247, 249 (observing that whether or not articulated at a theoretical level, the large degree of "shared practical understanding of the relationships between goods, rules, and virtues" in the life of societies such as *Piscopolis* "will be embodied in and presupposed by the way in which immediate practical questions receive answers in actions").

and more informally within the context of activities in particular practices. Because our conceptual approach in Chapter 5 is more formal and systematic than our approach in Chapter 4, we will use the more formal term "commitment" and not just active verbs like "wants to" or "seeks to." At various points during the discussion we will repeat or expand upon matters already addressed in earlier Chapters. Such repetition and elaboration are necessary in order to incorporate these matters within a broader, more comprehensive framework of analysis. This framework will also then be applied in Chapters 6 and 7. I hope, therefore, that readers will be understanding and patient when we work through these repetitions and elaborations, and that it will not seem too much like Drew having to sail through heavy seas to reach the fertile fishing grounds.

A. Active Participation in the Political Conversation

We begin with a threshold commitment. Like the other inhabitants Drew is committed to active participation in the political conversation of the fishing village, but why is this? MacIntyre articulates the rational justification for such active participation in three steps.

The *first step* is Drew's quest to achieve his or her individual *telos* and unique form of flourishing through participation in practices in a life lived out as a unity that we examined in Chapters 2 and 3:

> For each individual the question arises: what place should the goods of each of the practices in which I am engaged have in my life? The goods of our productive activities in the workplace, the goods of ongoing family life, the goods of musical or athletic or scientific activity, what place should each have in my life, if my life as a whole is to be excellent?[11]

We already encountered this question in Chapter 2. The reader will recall that it is the third type of decision a person needs to make in judging whether they have "good reason" in acting, or in not acting, to satisfy a particular desire, using good practical reasoning informed by the virtues and guided by their *telos* as they currently understand it.[12] We should re-

---

11. *Id.* at 240.
12. *See* Chapter 2, notes 16–17, 33–37, 41–42, 51, 60 and accompanying text.

member, too, that "goods" in the above passage refers to the "common goods" of practices, and that these include the overarching common good of a practice and all the standards of excellence, goods of excellence, and qualities of excellence entailed by, included within, and co-constitutive of it as specific common goods.[13] The *second step* is Drew's acknowledgment that Drew's quest to achieve his or her *telos* and unique form of flourishing by attaining the common goods of practices in *Piscopolis* is inseparable from, and dependent upon, the individual quests of all the other inhabitants to achieve their own *telos* and unique flourishing in the same way and thus is inseparable from, and dependent upon, the collective quest of each practitioner community to achieve the common goods of their particular practice, as we saw in Chapter 4:

> Yet any individual who attempts to answer this question pertinaciously must soon discover that it is not a question that she or he can ask and answer by her or himself and for her or himself, apart from those others together with whom she or he is engaged in the activities of practices.[14]

And the *third step* is Drew's recognition that the collective pursuit of answers to these questions inevitably implies and requires a collective quest to achieve the greater common good of the entire fishing village of *Piscopolis*:

> So the questions have to be posed: what place should the goods of each of the practices in which *we* are engaged have in *our* common life? What is the best way of life for *our* community?[15]

Consequently, Drew's quest to achieve his or her individual *telos* and unique form of flourishing, and the collective quest of a practitioner community to achieve the common goods of their particular practice, are also inseparable from, and dependent upon, the collective quest of all the in-

---

13. *See* Chapter 3, notes 73–75 and accompanying text.
14. MacIntyre, *Common Good*, op. cit., at 240.
15. *Id.*

habitants to achieve the greater common good and the maximal flourishing of the entire fishing village:

> These questions can only be answered by elaborating a concep-
> tion of the common good of a kind of community in which each
> individual's achievement of her or his own good is inseparable both
> from achieving the shared goods of practices and from contributing
> to the common good of the community as a whole. According to this
> conception of the common good the identification of my good, of
> how it is best for me to direct my life, is inseparable from the identi-
> fication of the common good of the community, of how it is best for
> that community to direct its life.[16]

This means that Drew is necessarily concerned with the political community and involved in the practice of politics in *Piscopolis*:

> Such a form of community is by its nature political, that is to say, it
> is constituted by a type of practice through which other types of
> practice are ordered, so that individuals may direct themselves to-
> wards what is best for them and for the community.[17]

To recur to an example used in Chapter 2, Drew will be unable to pursue
his or her passion for amateur dramatics or for playing in an orchestra
in *Piscopolis* if it is "a community in which the goods of theater [or live
orchestral music] are not given a certain priority in the allocation of communal resources."[18] And such decisions may, of course, involve matters

---

16. *Id.* at 240–41. For MacIntyre's earlier and very similar account of these three steps,
see Alasdair MacIntyre, *A Partial Response to My Critics, in* AFTER MACINTYRE: CRITI-
CAL PERSPECTIVES ON THE WORK OF ALASDAIR MACINTYRE 288 (John Horton & Susan
Mendus, eds., 1994). For the explicit connection to human flourishing, see MACINTYRE,
RATIONAL ANIMALS, op. cit., at 66–67 (observing that judgments about whether someone
is a good practitioner of a practice, whether it is good for that practitioner that the practice
have a particular place in his or her life, and whether it is good for a society that the goods
of that practice have a particular place in its common life are all "judgments about human
flourishing").

17. MacIntyre, *Common Good*, op. cit., at 241.

18. MACINTYRE, RATIONAL ANIMALS, op. cit., at 140–41. *See* Chapter 2, notes 35–37
and accompanying text.

that are controversial and give rise to various kinds of tensions. Indeed, "because local communities are always to some degree imperfect, competing interests are always apt to emerge."[19] For example, in Drew's practice of catching fish, "the means of harvesting certain sea creatures can conflict with the means of harvesting others, or the requirements of the distribution of the catch (give us more blowfish, the Japanese restaurants would say) are not always harmonious with the goods of fishing, and so forth."[20] And so, as MacIntyre says, "[i]t is in and through *political* decisions about these priorities that we determine the range of possibilities open for the shaping of our individual lives."[21]

What are the other politico-ethical commitments, in addition to this commitment to active participation in the political conversation, by which Drew and the other inhabitants "may direct themselves towards what is best for them and for the community"?[22] In the remaining sections we will consider the other substantive commitments that emerge from and are sustained by this conversation, beginning with the inhabitants' most fundamental commitment from which all their other commitments flow.

B. Ultimate Excellence and Overarching Common Good

Most fundamentally, as "a society of rational enquiry, of self-scrutiny,"[23] Drew and the other inhabitants are committed to engaging in rational political conversation that pursues the ultimate excellence or *telos* of their common practice of politics. Resonant with MacIntyre's formulation of the *telos* of moral enquiry, the *telos* of this common practice can be formulated as "a proper theoretical comprehension of the greater common good in light of the specifically human good and its practical embodiment in the life of the *polis* community" (realization in both senses, then).[24] And the inhabitants are committed to the particular un-

---

19. MacIntyre, Rational Animals, op. cit., at 144.

20. I am indebted to Jack Sammons for this example and for the quoted language. Sammons Email (Oct. 24, 2014) [on file with author].

21. MacIntyre, Rational Animals, op. cit., at 141 (emphasis added).

22. MacIntyre, *Common Good*, op. cit., at 241 (quoted *supra* note 17 and accompanying text).

23. *Id.* (quoted *supra* note 8 and accompanying text).

24. For MacIntyre's formulation of the *telos* of moral enquiry, see Chapter 3, note 70 and accompanying text.

derstanding of this ultimate excellence upon which they agree through reasoned argument about it — to the particular theoretical conception of their greater common good in light of the specifically human good they embrace, and the particular arrangements they design for its practical embodiment in their common life.[25] As suggested earlier, this particular understanding — which is their overarching common good — results from an original agreement, perhaps reached many years ago, and it is sustained by instantiation in the inhabitants' way of life and their ongoing political consensus, albeit always subject to continuing evolution through further reasoned argument in political conversation about how best to understand the ultimate excellence.[26] Given its comprehensive scope, focusing on the greater common good of all, the overarching common good of the common practice of politics is synonymous with the greater common good of the entire fishing village.

Perhaps we might speculate that the inhabitants of *Piscopolis* have followed MacIntyre's own intellectual odyssey in their evolving understanding of the ultimate excellence and thus in the evolution of their overarching common good. With regard to their particular theoretical conception of the greater common good in light of the specifically human good, they might have begun, like MacIntyre in *After Virtue*, by favoring the Aristotelian moral tradition as providing the most rational account.[27] They would have subsequently accepted Aquinas' supplementation and correction of Aristotle, as MacIntyre did in *Whose Justice? Which Rationality?* and *Three Rival Versions of Moral Enquiry.*[28] And they would have then espoused an account of Thomistic Aristotelianism along the lines articulated

---

25. *See* Kelvin Knight's definition of politics in the MacIntyrean *polis* as "[t]he practice of reasoning towards, and of implementing" what is "rationally agreed to be the common and highest good for human beings." Knight, *Introduction*, op. cit., at 20.

26. *See supra* note 8 and accompanying text.

27. ALASDAIR MACINTYRE, AFTER VIRTUE: A STUDY IN MORAL THEORY (3d. ed., 2007) (1981). *See id.* at 219, 275 (discussing quest for the good), 277 ("[I]t is the central thesis of *After Virtue* that the Aristotelian moral tradition is the best example we possess of a tradition whose adherents are rationally entitled to a high measure of confidence in its epistemological and moral resources").

28. For MacIntyre's discussion of Aquinas' supplementation and correction of Aristotle (and Augustine) in these two works, see ALASDAIR MACINTYRE, WHOSE JUSTICE? WHICH RATIONALITY? 181–82, 192–98, 205 (1988); ALASDAIR MACINTYRE, THREE RIVAL VERSIONS OF MORAL ENQUIRY: ENCYCLOPAEDIA, GENEALOGY, AND TRADITION 77, 120, 123, 137, 141, 154, 165 (1990)

in MacIntyre's *Dependent Rational Animals* and *Conflicts of Modernity*, further modifying their previous understanding.[29] The inhabitants would have ended up, then, considering this fully developed Thomistic Aristotelianism rationally superior to all rivals, including liberalism, and "the best theory so far" emerging from the "dialectic" among competing moral traditions. Given the absence of neutral standards for comparing moral traditions, the following dense but concise passage, which repays close reading, summarizes the process involved in this "MacIntyrean dialectic" through which the inhabitants imaginatively assume the perspective of the adherents of various competing moral traditions and then arrive at their conclusion regarding the rational superiority of Thomistic Aristotelianism. Thus, at least with respect to matters that are not "incommensurable":

It will ... be possible for adherents of each tradition to understand and to evaluate — by their own standards — the characterizations of their positions advanced by their rivals. And nothing precludes their discovering that these characterizations reveal to them features of their own positions which had hitherto gone unnoticed or considerations which by their own standards they ought to have entertained, but had not. Indeed nothing precludes the discovery that the rival tradition offers cogent explanations of weaknesses, of inabilities to formulate or solve problems adequately, of a variety of incoherences in one's own tradition for which the resources of one's own tradition had not been able to offer a convincing account.

Traditions do on occasion founder, that is, by their own standards of flourishing and foundering, and an encounter with a rival tradition may in this way provide good reasons either for attempting to reconstitute one's tradition in some radical way or for deserting it. Yet ... if in such successive encounters a particular moral tradition has succeeded in reconstituting itself when rational considerations urged upon its adherents either from within the tradition or from without so required, and has provided generally more cogent accounts of its rivals' defects and weaknesses and of its own than those rivals have been able to supply, either concerning themselves or con-

29. *See generally* MACINTYRE, RATIONAL ANIMALS, op. cit.; MACINTYRE, CONFLICTS OF MODERNITY, op. cit.

cerning others, all this of course in the light of the standards internal
to that tradition, standards which will in the course of those vicissi-
tudes have themselves been revised and extended in a variety of
ways, then the adherents of that tradition are rationally entitled to a
large measure of confidence that the tradition which they inhabit
and to which they owe the substance of their moral lives will find the
resources to meet future challenges successfully. For the theory of
moral reality embodied in their modes of thinking and acting has
shown itself to be, in [this] sense, *the best theory so far.*[30]

The inhabitants would be confirmed in their conclusion regarding the
rational superiority of Thomistic Aristotelianism by comparing their narratively lived individual and collective experience with that of the adherents of rival traditions of enquiry,[31] and by a similar comparison regarding

---

30. MACINTYRE, AFTER VIRTUE, op. cit., at xiii–xiv (explaining that when the protago-
nists of a particular moral tradition engage in the dialectic with a rival moral tradition, "[a]
necessary first step" is that they "learn how to think as if one were a convinced adherent
of that rival tradition," and that "[t]o do this requires the exercise of a capacity for philosophical imagination that is often lacking"), 276–77 (setting forth the passage quoted in the
text). For further discussion of the dialectic and the falsity of relativism, see *id.* at xii–xiv;
MARK T. MITCHELL, THE LIMITS OF LIBERALISM: TRADITION, INDIVIDUALISM, AND THE
CRISIS OF FREEDOM 115–17, 120–23(2018). For MacIntyre's reasons for concluding that
Thomistic Aristotelianism rationally defeats all rival "traditions of enquiry," including liberalism, see generally MACINTYRE, WHOSE JUSTICE?, op. cit.; MACINTYRE, MORAL ENQUIRY,
op. cit. For a brief discussion of MacIntyre's evolution from Aristotelianism to Thomistic
Aristotelianism, see Knight, *Introduction,* op. cit., at 19–20. For a longer discussion, see
Gilbert Meilaender, *Dependent Rational Animals: Why Human Beings Need the Virtues and
the MacIntyre Reader,* FIRST THINGS (1999), https://www.firstthings.com/article/1999/10/
dependent-rational-animals-why-human-beings-need-the-virtues-and-the-macintyre-
reader. MacIntyre recognizes that his dialectical argument is incomplete because it does
not examine Jewish, Islamic, Indian or Chinese "traditions of enquiry." MACINTYRE, WHOSE
JUSTICE?, *supra,* at 10–11. He also recognizes that not all objections have yet been met or
problems resolved and that various critics will likely remain unpersuaded by his Thomistic
Aristotelian account of the human good. MACINTYRE, CONFLICTS OF MODERNITY, op. cit.,
at xii–xiii, 207, 216–17, 231.

31. *See* MACINTYRE, CONFLICTS OF MODERNITY, op. cit., at 72–77 (discussing how rational agents who have received the proper moral training and education grow in awareness
of the facts of human flourishing as they proceed through "the realities of their practical
lives" and reflect on their reasons for action), 206–10 (discussing how reflection on their
personal narratives, in particular how they have learned from experience, including from
their mistakes and failures, justify Thomistic Aristotelian rational agents in having confi-

the extent of their own sociological self-knowledge.[32] As such, we can expect Thomistic Aristotelianism to provide the theoretical account of the greater common good in light of the specifically human good upon which Drew and the other inhabitants of the fishing village would continue to agree through rational enquiry if put to the question (including rational engagement with dissenters).[33] They would therefore accept that something like Chapter 2's account of achieving "happiness" in the sense of human flourishing through the development of powers in living a good life in community describes the specifically human good, and they would consider the greater common good of *Piscopolis* to consist in the maximal human flourishing of the whole fishing village.

Regarding the practical arrangements designed to implement this Thomistic Aristotelian conception, the inhabitants would also follow MacIntyre by agreeing that participation in practices is central to their flourishing and would therefore accept this basic premise of Chapter 3. They would agree, too, that all practices in *Piscopolis*, including the common practice of politics itself, must be properly ordered to achieving the goal of maximal human flourishing that is the greater common good of *Piscopolis* and the overarching common good of their common practice. When

---

dence in their judgments and dispositions), 112, 215 (observing that such agents come to understand the need for the virtues only by at least to some extent acquiring the virtues), 215–16 (explaining that how far others, specifically preference maximizers, find Thomistic Aristotelian agents' virtue-based justifications for their decisions and actions compelling depends on how far such others possess the virtues themselves and thus have had their desires educated and transformed).

32. *See id. at* 112–13 (identifying attachment to "one's social and occupational role … [and] to those objects of desire that bind one to one's social role, desires for success, pleasure, and reputation," together with an inability to achieve the necessary detachment rooted in a kind of pride or self-confidence resulting in moral self-deception, as impediments to independent minded rational enquiry and sociological self-knowledge), 211–13 (explaining how structures for distributing money and power can inhibit or distort rational agency by encouraging unquestioning conformity with conventional notions of success that presuppose the legitimacy of established power hierarchies and related material rewards, as well as harmless political satire "substitut[ing]" for effective critique of and resistance to" the established order, and lack of imagination regarding possibilities for transformational social change).

33. *See* MacIntyre, *Common Good*, op. cit., at 251–52 (members of the *polis* should not only tolerate dissent but also engage dissenters in rational conversation about their reasons for dissenting). *See also infra* notes 160–62, 173–75 and accompanying text (discussing this point further).

all these practices are properly so ordered, their common goods together co-constitute this greater common good and overarching common good and are entailed by and included within it.[34]

However, as in the case of any practice with a living tradition, and as indicated above, the inhabitants' ongoing political consensus around their overarching common good does not preclude all future reasoned argument and disagreement about how to understand it or about the common goods involved in achieving it.[35] Indeed, as we noted in Chapter 2, MacIntyre considers that "rational enquiry into and consequent disagreement about what human flourishing consists in in this or that set of circumstances is itself one of the marks of human flourishing."[36] The discussion of Drew's Thomistic Aristotelian commitments must therefore be understood as being subject to this caveat. As suggested in Part III, Section C of that Chapter, it may also be subject to an additional caveat if Drew and the other inhabitants have a more profound phenomenological understanding and sensibility that sometimes causes them to pause to make sure that their Thomistic Aristotelian practical reasoning has not become unduly untethered from the pre-existing world of Being. And if necessary, they will engage in a dialectical back and forth between their practical reasoning and the givenness of Being until they reach a point of "reflective equilibrium" regarding the matter under consideration. Consistent with the discussion at the end of Chapter 4, conceivably this could occur when some unexpected and ominous natural event, to which human beings (including themselves) might have contributed, focuses their attention on the possibility of untethering — for example, when there is a climate-related natural disaster, or the fish are stricken with some unexplained disease (or perhaps when the inhabitants are threatened by a global pandemic!). More generally, conceivably it could occur whenever the inhabitants become concerned that their Thomistic Aristotelian practical reasoning may be

---

34. *See* Knight, *Introduction*, op. cit., at 20–21 (If politics is "[t]he practice of reasoning towards, and of implementing" what is "rationally agreed to be the common and highest good for human beings," then "[i]t would ... be an essential task of politics to combine the different conceptions of the good life that are engendered within different practices").

35. *See supra* notes 8, 26 and accompanying text; Chapter 3, notes 93–100 and accompanying text.

36. MacIntyre, Conflicts of Modernity, op. cit., at 25–26 (partially quoted in Chapter 2, note 103).

inadequate to deal with a particular matter or may somehow cause them to forget their true selves. And this also echoes the distinction between the "rationalists" and the "hybridists" in the practice of natural theology noted at the end of Part II of Chapter 2.

The inhabitants' ongoing search for a proper understanding of the ultimate excellence of the practice of politics is essentially an existential-theological quest for the meaning and purpose of their lives in *Piscopolis*. Like their analogous individual life quests discussed in Chapter 2, therefore, the inhabitants can perhaps be seen as responding to a call to come out of the Cave of distracting illusion into the light of the Good and as pursuing a Quest for the Grail, but in this context they come into the light of their common Good and pursue their collective Grail.[37]

We have already discussed Drew's commitment to active participation in the common practice of politics and Drew's foundational commitment to its overarching common good. Like these two commitments, Drew's remaining substantive commitments reflect and sustain the proper ordering of practices in *Piscopolis*. Moreover, together with Drew's commitment to active participation in politics, they represent the specific standards, goods, and qualities of excellence of the practice of politics which are specific ends or specific common goods of the practice and which (together with the common goods of the particular practices in *Piscopolis*) are entailed by, included within, and co-constitutive of its overarching common good that is the greater common good. These specific common goods all pertain to the inhabitants' excellence in political performance, the excellence of the political product resulting from their performance, and the excellence of the way of life that is lived out in the fishing village *polis*.[38]

As indicated at the beginning of Part II, this Chapter develops a comprehensive framework of analysis. In discussing these remaining commitments, therefore, we will repeat or expand upon some matters already addressed in earlier Chapters to incorporate them within this framework. We will, of course, address several additional matters as well. Importantly, these additional matters include those conditioned by MacIntyre's later

---

37. *See* Chapter 2, notes 135–46 and accompanying text.

38. For discussion of how the standards of excellence and qualities of excellence can both be understood in terms of these goods of excellence, see Chapter 3, notes 48–49 and accompanying text.

growing awareness of our biological nature and human vulnerability, disability, and dependence — an awareness that is especially prominent in *Dependent Rational Animals*.[39] We can introduce this point by noting that given its particular nature as a *fishing* village, in *Piscopolis* the practice of fishing is central to the life and flourishing of the inhabitants. Their practices are ordered accordingly, so that in their religious practice, for example, there are regular prayers for the fishing crews and the singing of hymns such as "Eternal Father Strong to Save" (aka "For Those in Peril on the Sea").[40]

C. Flourishing Through Achieving the Common Goods of Practices

As we noted above, Drew and the other inhabitants would agree that participation in practices (including their common practice of politics) is central to their flourishing and would therefore accept this basic premise of Chapter 3.[41] Consequently, as we saw in Chapter 4, Drew is committed to achieving the common goods of the practice of catching fish and of all the other practices in which Drew participates and to which Drew has been called, and to thereby promoting Drew's flourishing and the flourishing of those the practice serves.[42] Indeed, as we also noted above, the first step in articulating the rational justification for Drew's commitment to active participation in the political conversation in *Piscopolis* was precisely Drew's quest to achieve his or her individual *telos* and unique form of flourishing through participation in practices in a life lived out as a unity.[43]

1. Achieving Powers as an Independent Practical Reasoner

Drew therefore accepts Chapter 3's account of a practice's overarching common good and of the specific standards of excellence, goods of excel-

---

39. *See e.g.,* MacIntyre, Rational Animals, op. cit., at x–xi, 63–79 (chapter 7 on "Vulnerability, flourishing, goods, and 'good'"). MacIntyre concedes that *After Virtue* was mistaken in supposing it was possible to develop an ethics independent of biology. *Id.* at x.

40. For a rendition of this hymn, see, for example, https://www.youtube.com/watch?v=bDjwUzUnNpU.

41. *See supra* notes 33–34 and accompanying text.

42. *See* Chapter 4, notes 37, 91–92 and accompanying text.

43. *See supra* notes 11–13 and accompanying text.

lence, and qualities of excellence which are entailed by, included within, and co-constitutive of the overarching common good as specific common goods of the practice. This means that Drew also accepts the account, among the qualities of excellence, of the overarching ability that is the "master virtue" of practical wisdom possessed by the expert practitioner, or *phronimos* in the practice.[44] In this account, the three abilities or capacities of the independent practical reasoner discussed in Chapter 2 are foundational capacities the *phronimos* draws upon when exercising the four abilities that make up the overarching ability of practical wisdom.[45] We saw that it is therefore essential for Drew to acquire and exercise these capacities if Drew is to flourish in a practice, and that MacIntyre himself emphasizes that doing so is essential for human flourishing.[46]

Drew is committed, then, to achieving powers as an independent reasoner and to becoming a *phronimos* in those practices in which Drew participates. As we saw in Chapter 2, MacIntyre considers that becoming an independent practical reasoner is a status we generally attain with the help of others by early adulthood, and it serves us throughout our lives even though we may continue to need others to help sustain us in exercising our reasoning powers.[47] Although perhaps not entirely clear from MacIntyre's account, it makes sense that Drew must also continue to develop, strengthen, and sometimes perhaps extend, powers as an independent practical reasoner as Drew seeks to draw on these powers in different practice contexts and has to redirect and adapt them to meet new challenges, and we will read MacIntyre accordingly.[48]

We must now consider how Drew achieves and is subsequently sustained in his or her powers of independent practical reasoning in *Pisco-*

---

44. *See* Chapter 3, notes 12–28, 40–47 and accompanying text.

45. *See* Chapter 3, notes 21–24 and accompanying text.

46. *See* Chapter 3, notes 19–20 and accompanying text.

47. *See* MacIntyre, Rational Animals, op. cit., at 96–97 (reiterating the three abilities of an independent practical reasoner and observing that even after "we finally have become independent practical reasoners, generally early in our adult lives … we continue to the end of our lives to need others to sustain us in our practical reasoning" by having friends or "expert coworkers" in "particular practices" correct our intellectual or moral mistakes).

48. This means that we will either be applying MacIntyre's analysis analogously or adopting a broad interpretation of what he says about others helping to sustain us in exercising our powers of practical reasoning. *But see id.* at 113 (referring to "extending our powers of reasoning to different and changing contexts") for possible more direct support of this proposition.

polis. Because they are so central to the discussion in this section, it will be useful at this point to again remind ourselves that the three abilities or capacities of independent practical reasoners are

> [T]he ability to evaluate, modify, or reject our own practical judgments, to ask, that is, whether what we take to be good reasons for action really are sufficiently good reasons, *and* the ability to imagine realistically alternative possible futures, so as to be able to make rational choices between them, *and* the ability to stand back from our desires, so as to be able to enquire rationally what the pursuit of our good here and now requires and how our desires must be directed and, if necessary, reeducated, if we are to attain it.[49]

2. Relationships of Giving and Receiving

Importantly, Drew understands that his or her powers as an independent practical reasoner in *Piscopolis* can only be developed within "a network of ... familial, neighborhood, and craft relationships"[50] that give Drew what Drew needs "to move from dependence on the reasoning powers of others ... to independence in ... practical reasoning."[51] The network, or perhaps more accurately networks,[52] includes, then, "first of all relationships of the family and household, then of schools and apprenticeships, and then of the range of practices in which adults ... engage,"[53]

---

49. *Id.* at 83

50. *Id.* at 108.

51. *Id.* at 99, 120.

52. *Id.* at 122–23 (noting that "we are often members of more than one community and we may find a place within more than one network of giving and receiving. Moreover we move in and out of communities").

53. *Id.* at 107. For discussion of the development of independent practical reasoning within the relationships of giving and receiving, see *id.* at 71–76, 81–83 (exploring in detail the process of developing the three interrelated abilities of independent practical reasoning, including our vulnerabilities to various kinds of disabilities and other obstacles and difficulties that threaten their adequate development—both those shared with other animals and those unique to the human animal—as well as our dependence on others in making the transition "from our infant condition as human animals" to our "emerg[ence] as independent practical reasoners"), 76, 83–91, 99, 107–08 (role of parents and other family members), 89, 91–92, 99 (role of schoolteachers and others teaching elements of various practices to children and young adults), 88–89, 99, 107–08 (role of craft practice practitioners instructing apprentices). *See also id.* at 147–48 (further discussing obstacles to adequate

and within them Drew owes a debt of giving because Drew has received. More specifically,

> We receive from parents and other family elders, from teachers and those to whom we are apprenticed, and from those who care for us when we are sick, injured, weakened by aging, or otherwise incapacitated. Later on others, children, students, those who are in various ways incapacitated, and others in gross and urgent need have to rely on us to give. Sometimes those others who rely on us are the same individuals from whom we ourselves received. But often enough it is from one set of individuals that we receive and to and by another that we are called on to give. So understood, the relationships from which the independent practical reasoner emerges and through which she or he continues to be sustained are such that from the outset she or he is in debt.... [I]t is... in virtue of what we have received that we owe.[54]

As the passage suggests, the giving and receiving in these relationships is "uncalculated" and repayment of the debt is not governed by the principle of reciprocity.[55] Thus, not only may giving be asymmetrical to receiving because Drew may be called on to give to inhabitants of *Piscopolis* quite different from those from whom Drew received, but what Drew must give may be of a quite different nature or disproportionate to what Drew has received.[56] In such relationships of giving and receiving, "generally and characteristically, what and how far we are able to give depends in part on

---

development as an independent practical reasoner). MacIntyre is aware that, historically, "institutionalized networks of giving and receiving" involving "relationships of family and household, of school or apprenticeship in some practice, of local community, and of the larger society" have typically had a "double-character" as both "constitutive means to the end of our flourishing" and as unjust "hierarchies of power" operating as "instruments of domination and deprivation" that often frustrate its achievement. *Id.* at 101–05. This risk is minimized in an ideal *polis* such as *Piscopolis*.

54. *Id.* at 99–101.

55. *See id.* at 117, 120–21, 126, 144 (referring to "uncalculated" giving and receiving and "uncalculating" actions). *See also id.* at 108, 113–18 (contrasting norms of giving and receiving with norms that are based on calculation and preference satisfaction).

56. *Id.* at 100–01, 108, 126.

what and how far we have received,"[57] but it also depends, as we will see below in subsection 3 and in Section E.2, on the virtue of just generosity.

Although Drew is immersed in these ubiquitous relationships of dependence, or perhaps more accurately of interdependence, in *Piscopolis* "from conception to death,"[58] Drew's powers as an independent practical reasoner are largely developed in the context of various practices. We will have more to say about the broader aspects of the networks of giving and receiving in Section E, but here we focus on those relationships of giving and receiving that enable Drew to learn "the elements of various practices," including appreciation for their common goods,[59] to develop the power to reason well about these common goods and about Drew's individual good, and to acquire practical wisdom.[60]

3. Role of the Virtues

Drew is committed to the development and exercise of the virtues necessary for achieving powers as an independent practical reasoner and for discovering, attaining, and continuing to learn about the common goods of practices. In Chapters 3 and 4 we saw that as an aspiring practitioner of a practice (for example, as an apprentice in the practice of catching fish),

---

57. *Id.* at 99. Importantly, MacIntyre recognizes that those who have not received and/ or who have been the victims of individual or systemic wrongs may not be indebted and may indeed be urgently owed. *Id.* at 101–02; *see also supra* note 53 (discussing the "double character" of "institutionalized networks of giving and receiving").

58. *Id.* at 99.

59. *See id.* at 91–92 (explaining that teaching children and young adults "the elements of various practices" involves developing their skills and ability to recognize "the goods internal to each practice … in terms of whose achievement excellence in [the] practice is defined," and describing the virtues distinguishing teachers from apprentices or students as "[t]hose qualities of mind and character that enable someone both to recognize the relevant goods and to use the relevant skills in achieving them"), 99 (including relationships with "teachers and those to whom we are apprenticed" in the "network of relationships of giving and receiving").

60. *See id.* at 106–09 (observing that in MacIntyre's "generally Aristotelian" account, practical reasoning about goods involves "reasoning together with others," usually in a "network of [social] relationships of giving and receiving," including those of apprenticeships and the range of adult practices in society, through which we "first achieve[] and [are] then supported in the status of an independent practical reasoner," and asserting that those lacking the virtues "and above all the virtue of prudent judgment" are unable "to reason soundly about what it is best to do here and now").

Drew must exhibit various general virtues as fundamental prerequisite virtues in his or her relationships with current practitioners — as opposed to operational virtues exhibited in regular daily activities — in order to discover and attain the practice's common goods in the first place. The relevant virtues include but are not limited to justice, courage, honesty, temperateness, and humility.[61] And we saw that the same is true after Drew has fully entered the practice, if Drew and other practitioners are to continue learning about these things from one another.[62]

We now need to supplement the account in Chapters 3 and 4 in three main respects. First, we need to make explicit the link between this account and the process by which Drew achieves and is sustained in his or her powers as an independent practical reasoner. To begin with, it is in the course of, and indeed through, the very process of developing powers as an independent practical reasoner in the practice that Drew discovers its common goods.[63] It is therefore in the "relationships of giving and receiving" between current and aspiring practitioners, within which Drew develops these powers, that Drew must exhibit (and perhaps in some contexts first acquire or at least further develop and strengthen) the fundamental prerequisite virtues needed for effective learning about the practice's common goods whose achievement conduce to Drew's flourishing.[64] Moreover, for Drew to succeed in developing these practical reasoning powers by exhibiting virtues as fundamental prerequisite virtues or as operational

---

61. *See* Chapter 3, notes 53–58, 61–66 and accompanying text; Chapter 4, notes 45–46 and accompanying text.

62. *See* Chapter 3, notes 59, 61–63 and accompanying text; Chapter 4, note 47 and accompanying text.

63. *See* MacIntyre, Rational Animals, op. cit., at 74 ("[T]o learn how to become an independent practical reasoner is to learn how to cooperate with others in forming and sustaining those same relationships that make possible the achievement of common goods by independent practical reasoners").

64. *See id.* at 87–89, 94–96 (discussing the need to exhibit intellectual and moral virtues in social relationships with others on whom we depend to become independent practical reasoners, including temperateness enabling us to stand back from and evaluate our desires, and honesty (especially "truthfulness about ourselves" exercised in self-examination and accountability to others) enabling us to achieve the self-knowledge necessary to imagine different possible futures and avoid self-deception), 99 (characterizing these social relationships as relationships of giving and receiving), 119–20 (referring to the indispensable role of virtues such as justice, temperateness, truthfulness, and courage in enabling us to become independent practical reasoners in relationships of giving and receiving).

virtues involved in the exercise of such powers — and thus for Drew to succeed in discovering the practice's common goods — Drew's teachers must themselves appropriately exhibit the virtues they seek to cultivate in Drew.[65] They must also exhibit several other fundamental prerequisite virtues needed for effective teaching, such as care for the student and the subject matter.[66] And once again, something very similar is true after Drew has fully entered the practice, if Drew and other practitioners are to sustain their own and others' powers of independent practical reasoning and their continued learning about the practice's common goods in the relationships of giving and receiving among current practitioners.[67]

---

65. *See id.* at 88–89 (stressing that "[t]eachers in general — [including] those who instruct apprentices in crafts — have to have in significant measure the [virtues] that they try to inculcate"), 92 (explaining that virtues such as courage, justice, and temperateness distinguishing teachers from apprentices or students are exhibited both "in an agent's practical reasoning" and in response to various types of situations, including courage in knowing when to take risks or be cautious, justice in knowing when to delegate tasks or do them oneself and when to acknowledge desert through praise or blame, temperateness in knowing when to be demanding and when less so, and amiability in knowing when to make a joke or be angry), 97 (emphasizing that "some range of intellectual and moral virtues" is needed not only to "first achieve and then continue in the exercise of practical reasoning" but also "to adequately care for and educate others *so that they first achieve* and are then sustained in the exercise of practical reasoning," and therefore "the virtues are indispensable to human flourishing") (emphasis added).

66. *See id.* at 89–91 (discussing virtues of all good teachers, such as care for the student and the subject matter, and additional virtues they may need depending on the type of teaching required by their role, such as the ability to identify and exclude the talentless in certain types of teaching, for example, musical performance; and the special care and commitment, resilience, and forbearance parents and other family members, especially mothers, need to provide security and recognition for young children as they experience and learn about the world).

To the extent teaching in a particular domain can itself be regarded as a practice, the fundamental prerequisite virtues needed by teachers are simultaneously both prerequisite virtues, when seen from the perspective of the practice for which the teacher is preparing the aspiring practitioner, and operational virtues demonstrating excellence in everyday practice, when seen from the perspective of the practice of teaching. The extent to which teaching can be regarded as a separate practice is discussed further in Chapter 7 in connection with the practice of legal education. *See* Chapter 7, note 11 and accompanying text.

67. *See id.* at 96–97, discussing correction of various kinds of moral and intellectual errors, addressing how "the virtues are indispensable to human flourishing," and observing that

[W]ithout developing some range of intellectual and moral virtues we cannot first achieve *and then continue* in the exercise of practical reasoning; and without having developed some range of those same virtues we cannot ad-

Second, another set of fundamental prerequisite virtues is needed if Drew is to achieve powers as an independent practical reasoner and succeed in discovering a practice's common goods. MacIntyre calls them "the virtues of acknowledged dependence," and the virtues discussed so far — virtues such as "justice, temperateness, truthfulness, courage, and the like" — he calls "the virtues of independence," or alternatively "the virtues of independent rational agency" or "the virtues of rational independence"[68] MacIntyre summarizes the distinction between these two sets of virtues as "those virtues that enable us to function as independent and accountable practical reasoners and those virtues that enable us to acknowledge the nature and extent of our dependence on others."[69] More specifically, the virtues of acknowledged dependence are exhibited within networks of giving and receiving only in relationships that acknowledge the vulnerability, disability, and dependence of "those least capable of independent practical reasoning," such as children or young adults, who have not yet become independent practical reasoners, or those who may never become, or have temporarily or permanently ceased to be, such independent practical reasoners due to sickness or injury, physical or mental disability, or old age.[70] They are therefore always directed toward the *lack or insufficiency* of independent practical reasoning. By contrast, although they may presuppose some types of vulnerability, disability, and dependence as, for example, in the case of children and young adults, the virtues of independence exhibited within networks of giving and receiving are exhibited only in relationships with actual or potential independent practical reasoners. They are therefore always directed toward the *exercise or*

---

equately care for and educate others so that they first achieve *and are then sustained* in the exercise of practical reasoning.

Id. at 97 (emphasis added). *See also* MacIntyre, Conflicts of Modernity, op. cit., at 191–92 (further discussing various kinds of errors, illusions, and biases that impede practical rationality, and their correction in shared deliberation).

68. MacIntyre, Rational Animals, op. cit., at 8–9, 120.

69. *Id.* at 155–56

70. *See id.* at 73, 75, 82, 99–101, 108–09, 127–28, 129–30, 134–35, 145–46, 155–56, 166 (referring to all these various forms of vulnerability, disability, and dependence and the exercise of the virtues of acknowledged dependence in relationships of giving and receiving).

achievement of independent practical reasoning.[71] But MacIntyre regards the virtues of acknowledged dependence as the "necessary counterpart" to the virtues of independence because the former virtues are needed for adequate exercise of the latter, and because both sets of virtues are necessary to actualize human potentialities and promote human flourishing.[72]

Just as we will have more to say about the relationships of giving and receiving in Section E, so we will also have more to say there about the virtues of acknowledged dependence exhibited in such relationships. In the present context, however, we need to notice the role of these virtues in enabling Drew to develop his or her powers of independent practical reasoning in the relationships of giving and receiving within practices in *Piscopolis*. Thus, Drew's teachers must exhibit the composite virtue of "just generosity," which is made up of several different virtues of giving[73] and disposes those who have received to repay the resulting debt by giving in return, and to do so in the uncalculating ways discussed above even when the giving is disproportionate and asymmetrical to the receiving.[74] Drew must exhibit various virtues of receiving, such as appropriate gratitude, which "always involves a truthful acknowledgement of dependence" and thus helps Drew avoid "an illusion of self-sufficiency."[75] And both Drew's teachers as givers and Drew as receiver must exhibit the virtue of "truthfulness in accountability" so that Drew and Drew's teachers can learn

---

71. *See id.* at 8 (associating the "virtues of independent rational agency" with "individual autonomy, ... the capacity for making independent choices"), 120 (observing that the virtues of independence "enable[] us to move from dependence on the reasoning powers of others ... to independence in our practical reasoning [and] to participate in relationships of giving and receiving through which our ends as practical reasoners are to be achieved").

72. *Id.* at 8–9, 120.

73. *See id.* at 120–22 (explaining that the composite virtue of "just generosity" is made up of several virtues, including generosity or liberality, justice, beneficence or doing good, and taking pity or *misericordia*, that it is "the appropriate response" to various kinds of "deprivations," including "deprivations of physical care and intellectual instruction [and] of the attentive and affectionate regard of others," and that it is "the central virtue exhibited in relationships of receiving and giving" and "what is needed to sustain relationships of uncalculated giving and graceful receiving"), 126 (referring to "these virtues of giving").

74. *See supra* notes 54–57 and accompanying text.

75. *Id.* at 126–27. Virtues of receiving include "knowing how to exhibit gratitude, without allowing that gratitude to be a burden, courtesy towards the graceless giver, and forbearance towards the inadequate giver." *Id.* at 126.

what they need to know about one another and Drew can acquire the
self-knowledge necessary for effective learning.[76]

Importantly, the virtues of independence and the virtues of acknowledged dependence serve not only to develop Drew's powers of independent practical reasoning in the relationships of giving and receiving within
practices in *Piscopolis*, but also to create and sustain these relationships
themselves. Thus, those teachers who exhibit virtues of independence and
virtues of giving to help Drew become an independent practical reasoner
also thereby help Drew acquire these same virtues and be disposed to do
the same for others.[77] But to be so disposed Drew must also exhibit the vir-

---

76. *See id.*at 148–51 (explaining that "by having our reasoning put to the question by
others, by being called to account for ourselves and our actions by others ... we learn how
to scrutinize ourselves as they scrutinize us and how to understand ourselves as they understand us," and "[the] elementary truthfulness in our accounts" that we owe to others "so that
they can learn from us and we from them" is "one of the virtues of acknowledged dependence"). *See also id.* at 147–48 (explaining that such accountability enables us to overcome
various unconscious obstacles to learning to speak for ourselves as independent practical
reasoners and acquiring the necessary moral and intellectual virtues, including: a persisting
infantile desire, or resentment at the need, to please others, distortion of reasoning by se-
lective attention that ignores important relevant considerations, and the influence of some
motivating hope or fear). *See also id.* at 95–96 (emphasizing the importance of the virtue
of "honesty, primarily truthfulness about ourselves," exercised in self-examination and accountability to others, in achieving necessary self-knowledge and resisting self-deception).
See also MacIntyre, Conflicts of Modernity, op. cit., at 191–92 (discussing various
kinds of errors, illusions, and biases that impede practical rationality, and their correction
in shared deliberation).

Once again, to the extent teaching in a particular domain can itself be regarded as a practice, the fundamental prerequisite virtues of just generosity and truthfulness in accountability needed by teachers are simultaneously both prerequisite virtues, when seen from
the perspective of the practice for which the teacher is preparing the aspiring practitioner,
and operational virtues demonstrating excellence in everyday practice, when seen from the
perspective of the practice of teaching. The extent to which teaching can be regarded as a
separate practice is discussed further in Chapter 7 in connection with the practice of legal
education. *See* Chapter 7, note 11 and accompanying text.

77. *See* MacIntyre, Rational Animals, op. cit., at 107–08 (stressing the inseparable
link between "the development of those dispositions and activities through which each is
directed towards becoming an independent practical reasoner" in relationships of giving
and receiving and "[t]he making and sustaining of those relationships," because "each of
us achieves our good only if and insofar as others make our good their good by helping
us through periods of disability to become ourselves the kind of human being — through
acquisition and exercise of the virtues — who makes the good of others her or his good").

tues of receiving that avoid the illusion of self-sufficiency and acknowledge the existence of relationships of dependency.[78]

There is a third way in which we need to supplement our earlier account in Chapters 3 and 4 of the role of the virtues in enabling Drew to discover the common goods of a practice, and this is to note what may indeed be the most obvious and traditional reason why the virtues are considered necessary to actualize human potentialities and promote human flourishing. Drew is committed to development and exercise of the virtues in *Piscopolis* not only because the virtues enable Drew and the other inhabitants to achieve and sustain, and then in turn help others to achieve and sustain, their powers of practical reasoning in the relationships of giving and receiving within practices, but also because "without the virtues [they] cannot adequately protect [them]selves and each other against neglect, defective sympathies, stupidity, acquisitiveness, and malice."[79] There is clearly need for such protection against these vices in the context under discussion here — the development and sustaining of Drew's powers of independent reasoning in relationships of giving and receiving within practices[80] — but there is a similar need in several other contexts too, including Drew's exercise of these powers when deliberating about Drew's individual good as discussed in Chapter 2, Drew's attitude toward goods of effectiveness discussed in Section D, Drew's response to the norms of justice and related matters discussed in Section E, Drew's approach to carrying on the political conversation discussed in Section F, and Drew's posture toward the liberal democratic state discussed in Section G. Whatever other

---

78. *See id.* at 127 (explaining that "like virtues of giving, those of receiving are needed in order to sustain just those types of communal relationship through which the exercise of these virtues first has to be learned" because a failure to acknowledge dependence and "remember benefits conferred by others" results in "an illusion of self-sufficiency" that tends to exclude those laboring under it, especially the rich and powerful, from such relationships).

79. *Id.* at 97–98.

80. *See id.* at 97, explaining that

> [I]t may always happen that those on whom we depend may lack the virtues necessary for developing or sustaining our practical reasoning and so by neglect, by well-intentioned, but harmful misdirection, by manipulation or exploitation or victimization, may fail to prevent otherwise avoidable disability or may themselves be the active causes of disability, even on occasion intentionally, and so of defective development.

Id.

reasons Drew may have for being committed to development and exercise of the virtues in these particular contexts, the need for protection against such vices is an additional one.[81]

4. Role of Rules

Drew is committed, then, to achieving and sustaining, and in turn to helping others achieve and sustain, powers as an independent practical reasoner in relationships of giving and receiving within practices in *Piscopolis*. And for these and other reasons Drew is committed to the development and exercise of the necessary virtues. These commitments mean that Drew is also committed to the observance of certain fundamental rules. Such rules include those that prohibit the use of lethal and nonlethal force or threatened force against the innocent or the unjustified taking of others' property, and rules that enjoin the faithful keeping of reasonable promises and honoring other obligations, telling the truth, being punctual, not disclosing confidential information, and being patient with and caring for the needs of others.[82] Drew is committed to the observance of these rules — almost all of which MacIntyre characterizes as rules of natural law[83] — both because they help constitute various virtues (although exhibiting virtues frequently requires judgment that involves more than just rule following)[84]

---

81. *See id.* at 97–98 (characterizing this need as a third reason why "the virtues are indispensable to human flourishing"). *See also id.* at 128 (observing how various kinds of vicious actions such as serious lies, cruelty, treachery, victimization, and exploitation can always destroy the regard we have for one another).

82. *See* MacIntyre, *Common Good*, op. cit., at 247; MACINTYRE, RATIONAL ANIMALS, op. cit., at 110 MACINTYRE, CONFLICTS OF MODERNITY, op. cit., at 56–57 (enumerating such rules).

83. Alasdair MacIntyre, *Plain Persons and Moral Philosophy: Rules, Virtues, and Goods* (1992), *in* THE MACINTYRE READER 139, 142–43 (Kelvin Knight, ed., 1998); MacIntyre, *Common Good*, op. cit., at 247; MACINTYRE, RATIONAL ANIMALS, op. cit., at 111; MAC-INTYRE, CONFLICTS OF MODERNITY, op. cit., at 57. Punctuality might be an exception.

84. *See* MacIntyre, *Plain Persons*, op. cit., at 143 (explaining that we can only learn "how to go beyond the rules in order to judge appropriately in particular circumstances" what the virtues of courage, temperateness, or truthfulness require — judgment which itself also requires the virtue of *phronesis* — after first learning through the rules what these virtues *always* require); MACINTYRE, RATIONAL ANIMALS, op. cit., at 109–11 (discussing how the virtues of trustworthiness and reliability and the virtue of conversational justice require both conformity to rules and right judgment, and explaining that the precepts of the natural law demand not only observance of the rules of natural law but also whatever the virtues of

and thereby and in other ways conduce to Drew's good,[85] and because, just like the virtues themselves, they also serve to sustain the networks of relationships of giving and receiving in *Piscopolis*,[86] Conversely, failing to observe such rules will erode these virtues and networks. And, closing the virtuous circle, proper observance of these rules itself requires Drew to exhibit the virtues of courage, justice, temperateness, and prudence.[87] Here again, the need to observe such rules extends beyond the present context of developing and sustaining powers of independent practical reasoning in relationships of giving and receiving within practices to the other contexts mentioned at the end of the previous subsection.

But Drew is not just committed to observance of these fundamental rules. In addition, Drew is committed to observance of the "constitutive rules" that govern the various practices in *Piscopolis* — their "rules of the game" as it were.[88] Thus, to return to the example discussed in Chapter 3, if Drew participates in the sport of amateur track athletics, Drew will resist any temptation to cheat by violating the constitutive rule restricting runners to running on the track and proscribing running across the field.[89] And as we saw in Chapter 4, Drew will resist the temptation to cheat in the practice of catching fish, by putting profit or other material reward above quality of performance and resulting product in terms of the type, size, weight, and ages of the catch, by sacrificing the long-term sustainability of the fishing stock in non-sustainable overfishing for short term gain, and

---

courage, temperateness, justice, and prudence require). *But see id.* at 93 (suggesting that "no rule or set of rules by itself ever determines how to respond rightly" and "[k]nowing how to act virtuously always involves more than rule following").

85. *See* MacIntyre, *Plain Persons*, op. cit., at 143 (explicating the relationships between rules, virtues, and goods), 139–40, 143–44 (explicating the relationship between rules and our final good).

86. *See id.* at 142–43; MacIntyre, *Common Good*, op. cit., at 247 (stressing the importance of rules in maintaining the relationships and securing the cooperation necessary if we are to learn what we need to learn from one another); MacIntyre, Rational Animals, op. cit., at 109–11 (giving several concrete examples focused on the virtues of trustworthiness and reliability and the virtue of conversational justice); MacIntyre, Conflicts of Modernity, op. cit., at 56–57 (emphasizing that such rules are needed to structure relationships enabling rational agents to engage in shared rational deliberation in the pursuit of individual and common goods).

87. MacIntyre, *Common Good*, op. cit., at 247.

88. *See* Chapter 3, notes 158–61 and accompanying text.

89. *See* Chapter 3, notes 162–67 and accompanying text.

perhaps even by lying about such matters.[90] Although many, if not all, of these instances of cheating may involve violation of the constitutive rules governing the practice of fishing, some of them might involve other types of norms as well or instead.[91] In the present context, however, we are just focused on the significance of "constitutive rules" governing a practice. Here again, Drew is committed to the observance of these rules because observance of these sorts of rules also helps to constitute the virtues, including those distinctive virtues that are specific to a particular practice or type of practice, and to sustain the relationships of giving and receiving within the practice, whereas cheating by violating such rules will erode these virtues and relationships.[92] We will mention the subject of cheating again in Section D below when we address Drew's attitude toward goods of effectiveness.

5. Broader Concerns and Interdependencies

As the preceding discussion already suggests, Drew is not only committed to achieving and sustaining powers as an independent practical reasoner in relationships of giving and receiving within those practices in which Drew participates, and to the development and exercise of the necessary virtues and observance of the necessary rules by the practitioners in these practices. Drew is also committed to realizing the same things for every able and potentially able inhabitant of *Piscopolis*. And Drew wants these things not just because Drew exhibits the pervasive virtue of civic mindedness and the particular virtue of just generosity[93] but also because Drew understands — again if put to the question of rational justification[94] — the extensive and pervasive direct and indirect mutual interdependencies that exist among practices and practitioners in the fishing village.

---

90. *See* Chapter 4, notes 61–62, 81 and accompanying text.

91. *See* Chapter 3, note 168 and accompanying text. For a sense of the types of matters addressed by the constitutive rules governing the practice of fishing, see *Commercial Saltwater Fishing Regulations* (Georgia Dept. of Natural Resources, Coastal Resources Division) (2018), https://coastalgadnr.org/sites/default/files/crd/CommFish/2018CRDCommercial RegsWEBformat.pdf.

92. *See* Chapter 3, notes 169–70 and accompanying text.

93. *See supra* notes 7, 73–74 and accompanying text; *infra* notes 138–47 and accompanying text.

94. *See supra* note 10 and accompanying text.

As we saw in Chapter 4, Drew understands that Drew depends directly on other practitioners of those practices in which Drew participates, such as the practice of catching fish and the broader common practice of fishing. And Drew understands that Drew depends indirectly on the practitioners of many other practices in which Drew does not participate as a practitioner. These other practices have also taught Drew to appreciate their worth. We saw that Drew is therefore committed to promoting pursuit of the common goods of all practices and the flourishing of all practitioners in the fishing village.[95] And here we see this means that every able inhabitant must achieve and be sustained in the status of an independent practical reasoner, must possess and exercise the necessary virtues, and must observe the necessary rules. We also saw in Chapter 4 that Drew wants other inhabitants to acquire adequate goods of effectiveness, especially money, as well as to attain goods of excellence, just like Drew him or herself, but of course the key word here is "adequate."[96] In short, Drew understands that in a very real sense the flourishing of each depends upon the flourishing of all. Moreover, we saw at the very end of Chapter 4 that Drew and the other inhabitants may also possess an ecological sensibility and a related ecological and holistic worldview acknowledging even broader interdependencies, so that "the flourishing of all" includes the flourishing of the entire web of life in the Earth's "critical zone" and requires protecting and promoting the health of the planet.

D. Attitude Toward Goods of Effectiveness

Section B discussed Drew's substantive foundational commitment to achieving the greater common good of maximal human flourishing in *Piscopolis* through the proper ordering of practices and their common goods. And Section C discussed Drew's resulting substantive commitments related to developing powers as an independent practical reasoner in relationships of giving and receiving within practices and to achieving the common goods of those practices in which Drew participates, as well as Drew's commitment to promoting these same things for other able and potentially able inhabitants of the fishing village. In Sections D and E we

---

95. *See* Chapter 4, notes 50–55, 86–94 and accompanying text.
96. *See* Chapter 4, note 95 and accompanying text.

examine several additional substantive commitments implied and necessitated by these preceding commitments.

1. Systematic Subordination of Goods of Effectiveness

As we also saw in Chapter 4, although Drew does pursue goods of effectiveness as well as goods of excellence, Drew's primary motivation for engaging in the practice of catching fish and other practices in *Piscopolis* is intrinsic, and Drew is therefore committed to systematically subordinating goods and qualities of effectiveness to goods and qualities of excellence in these practices.[97] Moreover, Drew wants to preserve the integrity not just of Drew's practices but of all practices, and the way of life of the fishing village. Drew is therefore committed to the systematic subordination of goods of effectiveness in every practice in *Piscopolis* (including the common practice of politics), in order to guard against the moral risks that, as a result of undue concern with economic or other extrinsic considerations, inhabitants of the fishing village might corrupt the common goods of a practice by, for example, succumbing to the individual or collective temptation to cheat, or might too readily abandon a particular practice situation or even the common goods of the practice altogether.[98]

2. Role of the Virtues

As we have seen, Drew is committed to development and exercise of the virtues that are necessary for Drew and the other inhabitants of *Piscopolis* to achieve and sustain their powers of independent practical reasoning in relationships of giving and receiving within practices, and thereby to discover and continue learning about the common goods of these practices.[99] Similarly, Drew is also committed to exhibiting, and to other inhabitants exhibiting, the virtues necessary to exercise their powers of independent reasoning in these relationships to resist any pressures or temptations to weaken or even reverse the shared commitment to the systematic subordination of goods and qualities of effectiveness to goods and qualities of excellence. In Chapters 3 and 4 we saw that Drew must exhibit the same

---

97. *See* Chapter 4, notes 58–60, 92 and accompanying text.
98. *See* Chapter 4, notes 61–63, 78–83 and accompanying text.
99. *See supra* Section C.3.

fundamental prerequisite virtues to resist any pressures or temptations regarding this shared commitment as those needed to discover and attain,
and then continue learning about, the common goods of the practice in
the first place.[100] These "virtues of independence" include but are not limited to the general virtues of justice, courage, honesty, temperateness, and
humility, together with the virtue of practical wisdom.[101]

E. Just Allocation of Goods of Effectiveness and Other Community Resources

As we have also seen in Chapters 3 and 4, even though goods of effectiveness are systematically subordinated to goods of excellence in *Piscopolis*, Drew and the other inhabitants pursue such goods as well as goods
of excellence because practices require adequate resources enabling their
practitioners to pursue excellence, and individual practitioners require adequate resources enabling them to pursue the particular modes of flourishing involved in achieving their own individual *telos*.[102] And although
economic resources are especially critical in this respect, goods of effectiveness are not limited to economic resources but include other kinds of
resources and assets such as status, power, and prestige.[103] Thus, Drew's
fishing crew needs someone to serve as captain, various religious communities need someone to serve as their clerical and lay leaders, and the
fishing village as a whole needs someone to serve as police chief, fire chief,
school principal, mayor, leader of the village assembly, and so on. And all
of these positions inevitably involve the acquisition of status, power, and
prestige — even in a community such as *Piscopolis* with its communitarian
ethos and undoubted associated notions of servant leadership focused on
serving the needs and well-being of those for whom the leader is responsible. Moreover, other types of community resources may be relevant too.
To use the expression current in religious circles, it is not just a question of

---

100. *See* Chapter 3, notes 173–81 and accompanying text; Chapter 4, note 66 and accompanying text.

101. *See* Chapter 3, notes 173, 176 and accompanying text (identifying these virtues);
supra note 68 and accompanying text (discussing MacIntyre's characterization of such virtues as "virtues of independence").

102. *See* Chapter 3, notes 104, 106–07, 138–39 and accompanying text; Chapter 4, note
58 and accompanying text.

103. *See* Chapter 3, notes 101–02 and accompanying text.

treasure, but also of time and talent. For example, just how much time, talent, and treasure should be devoted to musical or theatrical performance instead of training for volunteer fire fighting, or to catching particular kinds of fish as opposed to other kinds? And just what resources should be devoted to caring for children, the elderly, the sick and injured, and those inhabitants with other kinds of disabilities?

1. Norms of Justice and Related Matters

As indicated earlier in the Chapter, "because local communities are always to some degree imperfect, competing interests are always apt to emerge," and decisions about the allocation of goods of effectiveness and other types of community resources may be controversial and give rise to various kinds of tensions.[104] However, in an ideal *polis* such as *Piscopolis* "politics... is not a politics of competing interests" in the way it is in the modern state, and the inhabitants share various commitments centered on the greater common good and designed as far as possible to limit the emergence of such competing interests.[105] Because the relevant commitments and resulting arrangements subordinate "economic considerations... to social and moral considerations,"[106] they can be seen as aspects of, or at least closely related to, the systematic subordination of goods of effectiveness to goods of excellence discussed above. Moreover, all these commitments and arrangements are necessary "if a local community that is a network of giving and receiving is to survive, let alone thrive."[107]

Drew's most critical commitment in this respect is the shared commitment to the norms of justice that govern the allocation of goods of effectiveness and other community resources among the inhabitants. Here we must distinguish between justice for those inhabitants who are, and justice for those inhabitants who are not, independent practical reasoners. Thus, "[b]etween independent practical reasoners the norms will have to satisfy [the] formula for justice ... according to which what each receives is proportionate to what each contributes" — in other words, a justice based on

---

104. *See supra* notes 18–21 and accompanying text.
105. *See* MacIntyre, Rational Animals, op. cit., at 144–45 (discussing "the politics of [local] communities, when they are at their best or are at least moving in the right direction").
106. *Id.* at 145.
107. *Id.*

desert.[108] Indeed, "the basic political question" in local communities like *Piscopolis* concerns "what resources each individual and group needs, if it is to make its particular contribution to the common good" of maximal human flourishing.[109] To the extent such communities are "in good order," it is in everyone's interest "that each should be able to make its contribution."[110] Presumably, determining the answer to this question also requires considering the "political" question we noted in Chapter 3, regarding the extent to which the common goods of a particular practice contribute to the greater common good by promoting the flourishing not only of those engaged in the practice but also, and especially, of those the practice serves.[111] Presumably, too, it also involves considering the further question whether these determinations of proportionate contributions to the greater common good of maximal human flourishing and resulting resource allocations are best determined through centralized decision-making by the village assembly or officials, decentralized local market forces, the mutual care and concern of practice communities for one another in the course of engaging in their respective practices, philanthropy, or some combination of these different mechanisms. And the answer to this question may vary according to what the relevant decision is about.

This same question of appropriate mechanism is also implicated in the case of several corollary commitments that follow from Drew's commitment to this norm of justice (as well as from Drew's commitments to the systematic subordination of goods of effectiveness to goods of excellence and to limiting as far as possible the emergence of competing interests).[112] Thus, Drew is also committed: to ensuring that inequalities of income or wealth are relatively small (because gross inequalities will likely generate conflicts of interest inimical to realizing a common good in social relation-

---

108. *Id.* at 129–30 (identifying this formula as "Marx's formula for justice in a socialist society").

109. *See id.* at 144 (articulating "the basic political question" in such local communities).

110. *Id.*

111. *See* Chapter 3, notes 84–86 and accompanying text.

112. The existence of a range of different possible mechanisms for addressing the matters under consideration here seems consistent with MacIntyre's acknowledgment, when discussing these matters, that "the institutional forms through which such a way of life is realized [are] economically various." MacIntyre, Rational Animals, op. cit., at 145.

188 Professions and Politics in Crisis

ships);[113] to ensuring also that, as far as possible, everyone takes their turn to perform those jobs that are tedious or dangerous (to avoid "another disruptive form of social inequality");[114] to adopting, as necessary, self-imposed limits to the movement of labor (to help ensure the continuity and stability of families and other institutions);[115] and to investing in some types of children's education based on considerations other than economic productivity[116] (presumably, because human flourishing requires more than activity simply as *homo economicus*).[117]

Importantly, as this last commitment already suggests, Drew is committed to further norms of justice that govern the allocation of goods of effectiveness and other community resources, especially care, concern, and attention, among those who are not independent practical reasoners. Thus, "[b]etween those capable of giving and those who are most dependent and in most need of receiving — children, the old, the disabled — the norms will have to satisfy [the] formula ... 'From each according to her or his ability, to each, so far as possible, according to her or his needs.'"[118] The rational justification for Drew's commitment to these further norms of justice is rooted in MacIntyre's claim that in flourishing local communities such as *Piscopolis*, with flourishing networks of giving and receiving, meeting such needs is a critical aspect of the greater common good; Mac-

---

113. *Id.* at 144.

114. *Id.* at 145.

115. *Id.*

116. *Id.*

117. This point recalls the discussion in Part II, Section B and Part III, Section D of Chapter 2 regarding the discerning of our true calling or vocation in life. *See* MacIntyre, Conflicts of Modernity, op. cit., at 172–74 (stressing the importance of developing children's powers and not just skills, especially skills only for the workplace, and asserting that "[a] good school is a place where students, in the course of developing their powers, are able to find a direction that they can make their own" because they have been able to acquire "an adequate sense of the ends that should be theirs" in the course of pursuing the common goods of shared education and their "initiat[ion]" into a range of literary, mathematical, scientific, musical, and athletic practices," and are not simply "autonomous preference maximizers" whose preferences have not been properly educated, on whom others for their own purposes can then seek to impose ends, especially ends related to economic growth, as students "bring their skills to market").

118. Rational Animals, op. cit., at 130 (identifying this formula as "a revised version of Marx's formula for justice in a communist society" and acknowledging that "limited economic resources allow only for its application in imperfect ways").

Intyre even claims that it is the extent to which inhabitants' need provides "reasons for action" that the community flourishes.[119]

It may be relatively easy for Drew to understand the link between meeting such needs and community flourishing in the case of those, such as children or young adults, who cannot yet make, but who will potentially make, the kinds of direct contributions to the greater common good of maximal human flourishing made by independent practical reasoners, and why Drew should therefore be committed to devoting care, concern, and attention, and related community resources — including, as needed, Drew's own "time, talent, and treasure" — to the proper development of these younger inhabitants. An example would be when Drew instructs apprentice fishing crew members who are still developing their powers of independent practical reasoning in the practice of catching fish. Moreover, Drew understands that Drew enjoys the present ability to flourish in this practice because others gave Drew what Drew needed when still developing his or her own powers of independent practical reasoning as an apprentice, as discussed in Section C.[120]

But we may think it is not so easy for Drew to understand the link between meeting such needs and community flourishing in the case of those inhabitants of *Piscopolis* who are "least capable of independent practical reasoning" not just due to extreme youth but, for example, due to permanent sickness or injury, physical or mental disability, or old age,[121] and why Drew should therefore also be committed to devoting similar resources to these inhabitants as well. In fact, however, in *Piscopolis* "the needs of the disabled [are] not a special interest, the interest of one particular group rather than of others, but rather the interest of the whole political society, an interest that is integral to their conception of the common good."[122] Drew knows that it is simply not the case that such inhabitants can make no contribution, or no further contribution, to the greater common good of maximal human flourishing. To begin with, Drew understands that even the radically disabled may still be able to achieve various forms of flourishing themselves; and although these forms may be more limited

---

119. *Id.* at 108–09.
120. *Id.* at 107–08.
121. *Id.* at 73, 99–101, 107–09.
122. *Id.* at 130.

than in the case of independent practical reasoners, opportunities may be expanded by what Drew and others contribute.[123] And the flourishing of those "least capable of independent practical reasoning" is itself "an important index of the flourishing of the whole community."[124] Moreover, Drew understands that such inhabitants may also contribute in important ways to Drew's own flourishing, as well as the flourishing of other inhabitants and indeed of the entire fishing village, by teaching Drew and other inhabitants both about the common good and their own individual good.

Drew's starting point for understanding how this teaching occurs is understanding the nature and extent of our human vulnerability, dependence, and resulting need for receiving. As MacIntyre explains, even as adults we will likely experience some type of disability and become dependent on others:

> [I]t is important to remember that there is a scale of disability on which we all find ourselves. Disability is a matter of more or less, both in respect of degree of disability and in respect of the time periods in which we are disabled. And at different periods of our lives we find ourselves, often unpredictably, at very different points on that scale.[125]

This point is well understood in communities like *Piscopolis*, which constitute "a form of political society in which it is taken for granted that disability and dependence on others are something that all of us experience at certain times in our lives and this to an unpredictable degree."[126] As a result, Drew understands that in order to flourish, it is not enough to achieve and be sustained in powers of independent practical reasoning. In addition, Drew must also "receive and have a reasonable expectation of receiving the attentive care needed when... very young, old and ill, or

---

123. *See id.* at 73, 75, 105, 108–09 (discussing the possibilities and potential for flourishing of those disabled in various ways).

124. *Id.* at 108–09. *See also supra* note 119 and accompanying text.

125. MacIntyre, Rational Animals, op. cit., at 73 (referring to "such conditions as those of blindness, deafness, crippling injury, debilitating disease, or psychological disorder"). *See also id.* at 130, 138, 139, 146 (discussing the likelihood of experiencing various forms of disability "including those of normal aging").

126. *Id.* at 130.

injured."[127] As part of this reasonable expectation of receiving the necessary attentive care, Drew needs to know that others will recognize Drew
as being "the same individual[]" despite any such disability, displaying "a
commitment and a regard that is not conditional upon the contingencies
of injury, disease and other afflictions,"[128] that the attention given to Drew's
needs will be "proportional to the need" and not to any particular communal relationship,[129] and that being ill, getting injured, or becoming old
does not need to be "a source of fear."[130] And, of course, Drew understands
that other inhabitants need to have a similar reasonable expectation of
attentive care and also know these same things regarding themselves, including that they can depend on Drew to be appropriately responsive in
these respects just as Drew can depend on them.[131]

Here we see again, and in sharp relief, the mutual interdependencies
that exist, and are recognized, in a local community such as *Piscopolis*.
Drew understands, then, that *Piscopolis* fits MacIntyre's description of a
community embodying a "determinate set of social relationships" in which

[T]he good of each cannot be pursued without also pursuing the
good of all those who participate in those relationships. For we cannot have a practically adequate understanding of our own good, of

---

127. *Id.* at 108.

128. *Id.* at 73–74, 128.

129. *Id.* at 124.

130. *Id.* at 146. *See also id.* at 143–44 (explaining that it is only justifiable to ask members
of a local community to risk their lives in protecting the community against internal and
external threats to the community's security "if those who accept this risk can be confident
that they, if disabled, or their dependents, if they die, will receive adequate care"). This point
recalls our earlier discussion of members of Drew's fishing crew risking their lives for one
another at sea. *See* Chapter 4, notes 53–55 and accompanying text.

131. The disabled may teach Drew other important lessons as well. *See* MacIntyre,
Rational Animals, op. cit., at 135–40 (explaining that relationships with the disfigured
and disabled may reveal how our powers of practical reasoning may need to be strengthened
by eliminating certain hitherto unnoticed sources of error that obscure important personal
qualities, including qualities such as courage and gracefulness of spirit, which are virtues of
acknowledged dependence exhibited by the disfigured and disabled and which we may need
to learn and practice ourselves in the future, and that even from the radically disabled who
are the most dependent on us we can learn what it means to be answerable for the well-being
of those "wholly entrusted to our care," including as proxies who speak for them, as far as
possible, as they would have spoken for themselves).

our own flourishing, apart from and independently of the flourishing of that whole set of social relationships in which we have found
our place.…So each of us achieves our good only if and insofar as
others make our good their good by helping us through periods of
disability to become ourselves the kind of human being—through
acquisition and exercise of the virtues — who makes the good of others her or his good.[132]

Crucially, then, to echo what was said in our earlier discussion of the networks of giving and receiving in *Piscopolis*,[133] Drew understands that we
do not

> [M]ake[] the good of others [our] good … because we have calculat-
> ed that, only if we help others, will they help us, in some trading of
> advantage. That would be the kind of human being
> who consults the good of others, only because and insofar as it is to
> her or his good to do so, a very different kind of human being, one
> deficient in the virtues, as I have characterized them.[134]

On the contrary, Drew and the other inhabitants respond to the interdependencies in the fishing village as they do, precisely because they have
been educated into the virtues through their participation in the relationships of giving and receiving in *Piscopolis*.[135] They are therefore simply
disposed to act accordingly, without considering that the rational justification for doing so is that they are thereby furthering their own good, and
certainly without engaging in some calculation of reciprocal advantage.[136]

---

132. *Id.* at 107–08.

133. *See supra* note 55 and accompanying text (explaining that the giving and receiving
in the relationships of giving and receiving in *Piscopolis* is "uncalculated" and repayment
of the debt Drew owes by virtue of having received is not governed by the principle of
reciprocity).

134. MacIntyre, Rational Animals, op. cit., at 108.

135. *See id.* at 155–56 (stating, with respect to virtues of independence and virtues of
acknowledged dependence, that "[b]oth the acquisition and the exercise of those virtues
are possible only insofar as we participate in social relationships of giving and receiving").

136. *See id.* at 156–60 (distinguishing between acting in accordance with the virtue of
just generosity because "gross and urgent need [is] sufficient reason to act" and "giv[ing] a
rationally defensible account of the relationship of moral commitment to critical rational

2. Role of the Virtues

Just as Drew is committed to exhibiting, and to other inhabitants of *Piscopolis* exhibiting, the fundamental prerequisite virtues necessary to resist any pressures or temptations threatening the shared commitment to the systematic subordination of goods and qualities of effectiveness to goods and qualities of excellence, so Drew is also committed to exhibiting, and to other inhabitants exhibiting, the virtues necessary to implement the shared commitment (and corollary commitments) to the norms for the just allocation of goods of effectiveness and other community resources among the inhabitants. And Drew may surely have to exhibit the same virtues of independence such as justice, courage, honesty, temperateness, humility, and practical wisdom for this purpose as well, especially where allocation decisions are controversial and give rise to various kinds of tensions,[137] although in this context these virtues will now be exhibited typically as "operational" virtues in the practice of politics. In exercising Drew's powers of independent practical reasoning with regard to such decisions, however, Drew cannot exhibit the virtue of justice as a virtue of independence in isolation from the virtue of just generosity as a virtue of acknowledged dependence. Indeed, for MacIntyre, the virtue of just generosity is "the central virtue" *exhibited* in relationships of giving and receiving and "the central virtue" required to *sustain* such relationships of giving and receiving.[138] And in a community such as *Piscopolis*, with healthy networks of giving and receiving, in which just generosity is a central virtue, the norms of justice discussed above are as they are precisely *because* they are consistent with exercise of this central virtue.[139] And once again, when exhibited in relationships of giving and receiving in this context, the virtue of just generosity is exhibited typically as an operational virtue in the practice of politics, although it also appears as a fundamental prerequisite virtue when teaching children and training apprentices in various practices.[140]

---

enquiry"). *See also* Chapter 4, notes 13–17 and accompanying text; *supra* note 10 and accompanying text.

137. *See supra* notes 100–01 and accompanying text.

138. MACINTYRE, RATIONAL ANIMALS, op. cit., at 120–21

139. *Id.* at 129–30.

140. This is when it is seen from the perspective of the practice for which the teaching is preparatory. However, it may also appear as an "operational" virtue in the practice of

Given the central importance of just generosity at — and as — the heart of the relationships of giving and receiving in MacIntyre's Thomistic Aristotelian account of local communities such as *Piscopolis*, we now need to reinforce and supplement what we have already said about this virtue. To begin with, the virtue of just generosity is a virtue of acknowledged dependence[141] that is "the appropriate response" to various kinds of "deprivations" including "not only deprivations of physical care and intellectual instruction, but also and most of all deprivations of the attentive and affectionate regard of others."[142] It is a composite virtue made up of several different virtues of giving — justice, generosity or liberality, beneficence or doing good, and taking pity or *misericordia* — exhibited in the particular combination appropriate to the circumstances.[143] As with other virtues, Drew and the other inhabitants are educated into the virtue of just generosity through their participation in the networks of giving and receiving in *Piscopolis*,[144] in a process which involves "education of the affections, sympathies, and inclinations."[145] And it is the resulting virtue of just generosity which disposes Drew to give disproportionately to what Drew has received in these networks, to give to those from whom Drew has not received or will not receive, and to give unconditionally in that the measure of giving is largely based on needs, in the ways we have already noted.[146]

As we have also seen, then, the virtue of just generosity disposes Drew to allocate goods of effectiveness and other community resources to the inhabitants of *Piscopolis* not just based on desert, reflecting the contribution

---

teaching. *See supra* note 76.

141. *See supra* notes 68–78 and accompanying text (discussing the "virtues of acknowledged dependence" and the difference between such virtues and "virtues of independence").

142. MacIntyre, Rational Animals, op. cit., at 121–22. Indeed, MacIntyre seems to consider that acting properly from just generosity always "requires us to act from and with a certain kind of affectionate regard" and although we sometimes act from duty, ideally we do so in order to acquire the required inclination. *Id.*

143. *See id.* at 120–21 (explicating these virtues and the relationship among them in the composite virtue of just generosity, emphasizing that different aspects of an action may exemplify different virtues, and observing that "what the virtues require from us are characteristically types of action that are at once just, generous, beneficent, and done from pity"). *See also id.* at 121, 124–25 (apparently associating beneficence and *misericordia* with the virtue of charity).

144. *Supra* note 135 and accompanying text.

145. MacIntyre, Rational Animals, op. cit., at 120–21.

146. *Id.* at 126; *supra* notes 54–57 and accompanying text.

they and their practices make to the greater common good of maximal human flourishing, but also based on need — educating children and training apprentices, for example, or taking care of the radically disabled.[147] Most expansively, however, Drew's just generosity extends beyond long-term relationships with other inhabitants of *Piscopolis* to include relationships of hospitality to passing strangers who arrive in the fishing village community and relationships of assistance to those outside the community who are in extreme and urgent need.[148] Responding to the dire need of others outside the community requires Drew to emphasize the particular virtue of *misericordia* within just generosity, regarding such others as "neighbor" whose distress is Drew's own, to extend communal relationships so as to include them, and to care about their good just as Drew cares about those already within the community.[149] The exercise by Drew and other inhabitants of *misericordia* in this context strengthens the virtue of just generosity and provides them added reassurance undergirding their "reasonable expectation of receiving ... attentive care" when in dire need themselves.[150]

---

147. *See supra* notes 118, 120–21 and accompanying text.

148. MacIntyre, Rational Animals, op. cit., at 123, 126, 128.

149. *Id.* at 124–26. The notion of "imagined communities" is helpful here. In commenting on this point in the text, Jack Sammons considers that "communities are as much imagined as they are real in other ways. Our imagined communities have no need to honor political boundaries and thus if the story of those at furthest remove become part of Drew's story they too are within *Piscopolis*." Sammons Email (September 6, 2020) [on file with author]. However, given the constraints of finite resources, decisions allocating resources among those with legitimate claims to a response must still be made. For a helpful and thoughtful discussion of the relevant issues and considerations involved in making such allocation decisions, and in trying to find an appropriate balance between competing claims from those within the fishing village community and those outside of it, although not one conducted in terms of just generosity, see Rosalind S. Simson, *Effective Altruism and the Challenge of Partiality: Should We Take Special Care of Our Own?, in* Freedom & Society: Essays on Autonomy, Identity, and Political Freedom 198 (Yi Deng, Creighton Rosental, Robert H. Scott, & Rosalind S. Simson, eds., 2021).

150. *See* MacIntyre, Rational Animals, op. cit., at 124 (explaining that therefore "a capacity for *misericordia* that extends beyond communal obligations is itself crucial for communal life"); *supra* note 127 and accompanying text (discussing a "reasonable expectation of receiving ... attentive care" when needed). It may be especially important here to remind ourselves about the critical distinction, recurring throughout this Chapter, between rational justification *if Drew and the other inhabitants were put to the* question and actual reasons for everyday decision-making and action, in which the exercise of virtue is sufficient reason for action in itself. Responding to those in dire need outside the community

In this way, then, responding appropriately to the dire needs of those out-side the community calls forth mutually reinforcing exercises of the virtue of just generosity in relationships of giving and receiving in ways which redound to the benefit of all and which thereby contribute to the greater common good. However, such exercises of *misericordia* by Drew in re-sponse to dire needs, whether of those within the community or those outside the community, are rooted not just in this sort of rational justi-fication related to the greater common good but typically also in Drew's recognition that "this could have been [me]."[151] Although MacIntyre does not seem to use these terms, perhaps a more familiar way to express this latter point is to say that such exercises of the virtue of compassion are rooted, to a considerable extent, in the virtue of empathy.

F. Character, Structuring, and Conduct of
the Political Conversation

As we noted at the beginning of Part I of this Chapter, the inhabitants' shared politico-ethical commitments, which we are examining from the perspective of fishing crew member Drew as representative of indepen-dent practical reasoners in *Piscopolis*, may have emerged many years ago and continue within the living traditions of the fishing village. They reflect and sustain the proper ordering of practices in *Piscopolis*, and they are themselves reflected in and sustained by both instantiation in the inhabi-tants' lives and relationships and the inhabitants' ongoing political consen-

---

simply because the inhabitants are virtuously disposed to do so is very different from them responding to such persons because they calculate that if they do so, they will benefit when they are in dire need themselves. *See* Chapter 4, notes 13–17 and accompanying text; *supra* notes 10, 132–36 and accompanying text. I am indebted to Jack Sammons for alerting me to the need to emphasize the distinction with respect to this particular point in the text. Sam-mons Email (September 6, 2020) [on file with author]. Even with this clarification, however, a full and satisfactory explanation seems to require more, such as the additional recognition, discussed *infra* note 151 and accompanying text, that "this could have been [me]."

151. *See* MacIntyre, Rational Animals, op. cit., at 100, 125, 128 (expressing this no-tion). Drew may be familiar with the Phil Ochs' song *There But For Fortune, on* New Folks, Volume 2 (Vanguard Records 1964), as covered by Joan Baez, *There But for Fortune, on* Joan Baez/5 (Vanguard Records 1964), https://www.azlyrics.com/lyrics/joanbaez/therebutfor fortune.html (lyrics), https://www.youtube.com/watch?v=S4BYOJ1tc-k (performance).

sus.[152] This includes the commitments examined in this Section F and in Section G below, as well as those already examined in Sections A–E above.

To be sure, then, Drew and the other inhabitants "share ... a large degree of common understanding of practices and institutions" in *Piscopolis*, including an "understanding of the relationships between goods, rules, and virtues" entailed in the proper ordering of practices.[153] Political conversation will therefore usually focus on how best to implement the traditional commitments which reflect and sustain such understanding and proper ordering.[154] As we noted at the beginning of Part I, however, the inhabitants' commitments are always subject to further evolution through reasoned argument in their political conversation. Because Drew and the other inhabitants are committed to *Piscopolis* being "always, potentially or actually, a society of rational enquiry, of self-scrutiny," they are committed to engaging in a political conversation in which an inhabitant can always raise questions about "what has hitherto by custom and tradition been taken for granted both about their own good and the good of the community."[155] Indeed, MacIntyre observes that even in the best communities embodying networks of giving and receiving, "the exercise of shared deliberative rationality is always imperfect" and what is important is "the ability through time and conflict to correct ... mistakes and to move beyond ... limitations."[156] And here we should recall MacIntyre's point that "rational enquiry into and consequent disagreement about what human flourishing consists in in this or that set of circumstances is itself one of the marks of

---

152. *See supra* notes 6–9 and accompanying text.

153. MacIntyre, *Common Good*, op. cit., at 241, 247, 249. *See also id.* at 251 (referring to "a large measure of agreement not only on its common good, but on human goods in general"). As noted earlier in this Chapter, *supra* note 10, whether or not explicitly articulated at a theoretical level, such common understanding in the life of societies such as *Piscopolis* "will be embodied in and presupposed by the way in which immediate practical questions receive answers in actions."

154. *See* MACINTYRE, RATIONAL ANIMALS, op. cit., at 156 (referring to "[the] practical understanding of goods, virtues, rules, and relationships which is presupposed by our [shared] commitments"). For MacIntyre's own characterization of these shared moral commitments, see *supra* note 6.

155. MACINTYRE, RATIONAL ANIMALS, op. cit., at 241 (also quoted *supra* note 8 and accompanying text).

156. *Id.* at 144.

human flourishing."[157] We must now consider the structuring and conduct of the political conversation itself.

1. Political Conversation — Contexts, Participation, and Procedures

The shared rational deliberation that is the political conversation through which the common practice of politics is carried on in *Piscopolis* is an extension, or one aspect, of the widely shared, non-fragmented practical rationality that is integral to the networks of giving and receiving in all the various other practices in the fishing village, in which practitioners learn from one another about common goods, the relationship between such common goods and their individual good, and the proper ordering of goods.[158] As we also stated at the beginning of Part I, such political conversation may occur both in the context of formally held meetings of the village assembly and more informally within the context of activities in particular practices.[159]

Focusing on the former context, Drew's commitment to *Piscopolis* always being a society of rational enquiry and self-scrutiny entails corollary commitments regarding both the participation of those inhabitants who are independent practical reasoners in formal political conversation and the procedures for conducting such conversation. Specifically, the "institutionalized forms of deliberation" in *Piscopolis* — typically, meetings of the village assembly — must be accessible to all those inhabitants who wish to contribute proposals, objections, and arguments.[160] Indeed, "no one from whom something might be learned is excluded" from "extended deliberative debate in which there is widespread participation" and those inhabitants who hold political office and those who do not can put one

---

157. MacIntyre, Conflicts of Modernity, op. cit., at 25–26 (partially quoted in Chapter 2, note 103). *See also id.* at 30–31(observing that such disagreement and debate may occur "in everyday circumstances by plain persons arguing together about what to do next for their common good" or "by theorists reflecting on the practical questioning of those plain persons").

158. MacIntyre, *Common Good*, op. cit., at 242–43; MacIntyre, Rational Animals, op. cit., at 140–41.

159. *See supra* note 2 and accompanying text.

160. MacIntyre, Rational Animals, op. cit., at 129.

another to the question.[161] Because it is possible to learn from everyone, this means that "no one is excluded" from such debate, including "individuals and groups who hold ... radically dissenting views on fundamental issues" of human goods, with whom it will be "crucial... to enter into rational conversation."[162] Complementing these norms regarding participation, the procedures for decision-making must also be "generally acceptable."[163] These participatory and procedural norms help ensure that "both deliberation and decisions are recognizable as the work of the whole" as the inhabitants "come through shared rational deliberation to a common mind."[164] In addition to these commitments regarding inhabitants who are independent practical reasoners, Drew's commitment to norms of justice informed by the virtue of just generosity entails a commitment that communal deliberation about what these norms of justice require must include not just independent practical reasoners but also those speaking as a proxy on behalf of "those whose exercise of reasoning is limited or nonexistent."[165]

2. Role of the Virtues

As in the case of various substantive commitments discussed earlier in this Chapter, Drew is committed to exhibiting, and to other inhabitants exhibiting, the virtues necessary to effectuate the commitments regarding the political conversation discussed above. Moreover, in this context and for this purpose of achieving excellence in political conversation, the

---

161. MacIntyre, *Common Good*, op. cit., at 248.

162. *Id.* at 248, 251.

163. MacIntyre, Rational Animals, op. cit., at 129.

164. *Id.*; MacIntyre, *Common Good*, op. cit., at 248. *See also id.* at 239 (contrasting contemporary politics in the modern state in this respect).

165. MacIntyre, Rational Animals, op. cit., at 130. In the case of those who were independent practical reasoners but who can no longer speak for themselves as such because they are now radically disabled, the proxy's role is to speak for the disabled individual just as he or she would have done; and this generally requires the type of knowledge about the disabled person that is rooted in a previously existing relationship of friendship. *Id.* at 139–40. For discussion of how we learn to speak for the radically disabled as their proxy and "friend" by learning "[how] to assume the other's point of view [and] speak with the other's voice" as we make ourselves accountable to one another for our judgments about our own good and the common good in the process of becoming independent practical reasoners, thereby in one sense becoming friends and learning "how to fill the role of proxy," see *id.* at 147–51.

virtues discussed here, like the virtues discussed in Section E.2 above, are exhibited as "operational" virtues that are qualities of excellence of the common practice of politics rather than as fundamental prerequisite virtues necessary for learning about the common goods of this practice in the first place and sustaining them against corruption or abandonment.[166] In addition to the "master virtue" of political prudence or practical wisdom, then, several particular political virtues are needed.

To begin with, Drew and the other inhabitants must exhibit important dialogical virtues in their political conversation if *Piscopolis* is to remain a society of rational enquiry and self-scrutiny. MacIntyre mentions several of the relevant virtues in the following passage:

> It is only because and when a certain range of moral commitments is shared, as it must be within a community structured by networks of giving and receiving, that not only shared deliberation, but shared critical enquiry concerning that deliberation and the way of life of which it is a part, becomes possible. Truthfulness about their shared practical experience, justice in respect of the opportunity that each participant receives to advance her or his arguments, and an openness to refutation are all prerequisites of critical enquiry. And it is only insofar as we all of us treat those virtues as constitutive of our common good, and ascribe to the standards that they require of us

---

166. Of course, as observed in Chapter 3, although this distinction between operational virtues and fundamental prerequisite virtues in the case of virtues that — depending on the context and purpose for exercise of the virtue — can be exhibited as one or the other seems analytically sound, it may be functionally artificial to the extent, for example, that learning about and defending the common goods of a practice occurs in the experiential context of actual practice. *See* Chapter 3, notes 64–66, 178 and accompanying text. This is likely the case with many of the virtues discussed below. For example, Drew may exhibit justice as a dialogical virtue that gives other inhabitants their due by entertaining their views in the context of political conversation about any of the politico-ethical commitments discussed in Part II, which are common goods of the common practice of politics. And in doing so, Drew might be exhibiting justice as an operational virtue, or Drew might be exhibiting it as a fundamental prerequisite virtue when such conversation enables Drew to learn about these commitments from other inhabitants or when the conversation threatens to corrupt or abandon these commitments and therefore requires Drew to defend them.

an authority that is independent of the interests and desires of each of us, that we will be able to engage in genuinely critical enquiry.[167]

The type of justice mentioned in this passage requires "that every relevant voice is heard and that every relevant argument is given its due weight as an argument and not because of the power or influence of whoever it was who advanced it."[168] And it seems to be another instance of what MacIntyre calls "conversational justice."[169] Such "conversational justice" also requires, for example, that "each of us speaks with candor, not pretending or deceiving or striking attitudes, and … that each takes up no more time than is justified by the importance of the point that she or he has to make and the arguments necessary for making it."[170]

Several of the virtues that Mark Roche identifies, when discussing how various intellectual and moral virtues necessarily develop through proper participation in college classes and related intellectual pursuits, would also seem to be relevant in the present context and to overlap with and supplement the virtues identified by MacIntyre.[171] These virtues include temperance (by renouncing other pleasures to prepare well), a particular form of justice (by entertaining the views of others), respect for others and for truth (by engaging in the give and take of discussion), intellectual hospitality (by actively drawing in others and their ideas), diplomacy (by challenging others' views without personal attacks), humility (by recognizing deficiencies in one's own positions), civil courage (by adhering to an unpopular position when convinced it is valid), honesty and integrity (by following the evidence even against interest), discipline and perseverance (by thoroughly thinking through an issue), capacity for flexibility and self-overcoming (by being willing to abandon beliefs in light of the

---

167. MacIntyre, Rational Animals, op. cit., at 161–62.

168. MacIntyre, Conflicts of Modernity, op. cit., at 178 (observing that this requires "a shared recognition of the authority of the precepts of natural law" prohibiting the use of fraud or force to get one's way). For discussion of these precepts of natural law, see *supra* notes 82–83 and accompanying text.

169. MacIntyre, Rational Animals, op. cit., at 111.

170. *Id.*

171. The relevance of these virtues is confirmed by MacIntyre's comparison of "systematic, rational enquiry" in various academic disciplines and in "a politics of the common good." *See* MacIntyre, *Common Good*, op. cit., at 238–39 (discussing Kant's ideals in this regard and contrasting contemporary politics in the modern state).

evidence), and patience and striving (by continuing efforts when tentative answers are inadequate).[172]

Because of the inhabitants' commitment to include, and learn from, all voices in their political conversation, and more specifically to "enter into rational conversation" with inhabitants who dissent, Drew will "cultivate as a political virtue not merely a passive tolerance, but an active and enquiring attitude towards radically dissenting views."[173] Drew's "active and enquiring attitude" toward the dissenting views of other inhabitants will be reflected in how Drew exercises several of the dialogical virtues discussed above. It will also require Drew, when exercising these virtues, to exhibit the capacity for what Anthony Kronman calls "sympathetic detachment" toward such inhabitants — the ability to balance empathy and detachment which, as we saw in Chapter 3, may be at the very core or heart of practical wisdom[174] — and thereby to help maintain "political fraternity" or "political friendship" within the political community in *Piscopolis*.[175]

---

172. Mark W. Roche, *Should Faculty Members Teach Virtues and Values? That Is the Wrong Question*, 95 LIBERAL EDUCATION 32, 34–35 (Summer 2009). The text in parentheses is illustrative, sometimes selecting from several examples given by Roche. *See also* Jack L. Sammons, *The Georgia Crawl*, 53 MERCER L. REV., 985, 985–86 (2002) (identifying fifteen virtues essential for the practical wisdom of the lawyer as rhetorician). The dialogical virtues identified by Roche and Sammons are discussed further in Chapter 7, notes 147, 189, 295–310 and accompanying text; Chapter 8, notes 41–45, 48–49 and accompanying text.

173. MacIntyre, *Common Good*, op. cit., at 251–52. *But see* MACINTYRE, MORAL ENQUIRY, op. cit., at 60 (claiming that "membership in a particular type of moral community, one from which fundamental dissent has to be excluded, is a condition for genuinely rational enquiry and more especially for moral and theological enquiry").

174. *See* Chapter 3, note 24 and accompanying text.

175. *See* ANTHONY T. KRONMAN, THE LOST LAWYER: FAILING IDEALS OF THE LEGAL PROFESSION 93–101 (1993) (discussing "political fraternity" in the political community). Kronman defines "political fraternity" in the political community as "a kind of statesmanship *in pianissimo*" whereby every member of the political community displays an attitude of "sympathetic detachment," meaning that, especially where the alternatives are incommensurable, they will endeavor "to place [themselves] imaginatively in the position of others and to entertain their concerns in the same affirmative spirit they do, while remaining uncommitted to the values and beliefs that give these concerns their force" yet also being open to revising their preliminary views and making a more informed choice among the alternatives. *Id.* Of course, in an ideal local community such as *Piscopolis*, where there is already such a wide range of shared politico-ethical commitments, values, and beliefs among the inhabitants, the capacity for sympathetic detachment as described by Kronman will likely be needed mainly, and perhaps only, with respect to those with radically dissenting views. Political friendship in *Piscopolis* is discussed further *infra* notes 178–79 and accompanying text.

Moreover, in addition to exhibiting these dialogical virtues, we can also expect Drew to eschew the sorts of vices corresponding to a lack of virtue that Roche identifies as impediments to success, such as arrogance (leading to dismissal of worthy arguments), defensiveness or becoming emotional (clouding thought), disproportionate indulgence in worldly things (distracting from necessary focus and concentration), complacency (avoiding necessary effort and discipline), greed (elevating external recognition and sometimes even tempting to dishonesty and fabrication), and lack of motivation (lessening chances for learning).[176]

The political virtues will also include integrity as "the key virtue" of those holding political office in *Piscopolis*. Because they are not fragmented into separate compartmentalized roles, those seeking and holding political office can be judged by their success or failure in pursuing their own good and the common good in an authentic and unified way in various spheres of activity in the fishing village, especially the home and workplace, as well as in politics. The same individuals and groups will encounter one another in these various spheres of activity, and will therefore be familiar with one another's virtues and any vices they may have. And all this means that there can be no "gap between image and reality" and the inhabitants can be judged for who and what they *really* are.[177]

Finally, although the virtues of justice and just generosity are fundamental in ensuring that all voices can be heard in the political conversation, including the voices of dissent and of "those whose exercise of reasoning is limited or nonexistent" speaking through proxies, as well as in ensuring observance of the norms of justice more generally in *Piscopolis* as discussed in Section E above, more fundamental than even these virtues is the virtue of political friendship. Such political friendship both reflects and constitutes the inhabitants' "large degree of common understanding of practices and institutions" and of "the relationships between goods, rules, and virtues" noted at the beginning of this section.[178] As such, it is

---

176. Roche, *Virtues and Values*, op. cit., at 35.

177. *See* MacIntyre, *Common Good*, op. cit., at 248–49 (discussing such features of "small-scale local community politics" and once again contrasting the politics of the modern state in these respects). For discussion of the virtue of integrity, see Chapter 2, notes 88–94 and accompanying text.

178. *Supra* note 153 and accompanying text. *See* MacINTYRE, AFTER VIRTUE, op. cit., at 155 (discussing Aristotle's account of the virtue of friendship as "embod[ying] a shared

the bedrock foundation of everything else in the fishing village, including the general virtue of civic mindedness which pervades all the inhabitants' commitments and relationships in addition to any other virtues they may exhibit in particular contexts such as justice and just generosity.[179] And one might say that the integrity of the political conversation through which Drew and the other inhabitants carry on the common practice of politics in *Piscopolis* is itself sustainable only because it is a conversation among political *friends* who are committed, as true friends are, to seeking one another's good and to doing justice to one another.

G. "External Relations" with the Modern Liberal Democratic State

In addition to all the preceding politico-ethical commitments, Drew and the other inhabitants share a final set of commitments that, for want of a better terminology, we can call "protective commitments" regulating their "external relations" with the modern liberal democratic state and its capitalist, large-scale market economy. The inhabitants' goal in these commitments is to protect *Piscopolis*, as far as possible, from influences that are incompatible with, and destructive of, their shared way of life, common goods, politico-ethical commitments, and communitarian *ethos*, while at

---

recognition of and pursuit of a good," such sharing being "essential and primary to the constitution of any form of community, whether that of a household or that of a city," and explaining that "in a community whose shared aim is the realization of the human good" it is the "wide range of agreement in that community on goods and virtues ... which makes possible the ... bond [of friendship] between citizens which, on Aristotle's view, constitutes a *polis*"). Addressing how there could be a shared vision of the good and a bond of friendship among tens of thousands of adult male citizens in ancient Athens, Macintyre explains that

> The answer surely is by being composed of a network of small groups of friends, in Aristotle's sense of the word. We are to think then of friendship as being the sharing of all in the common project of creating and sustaining the life of the city, a sharing incorporated in the immediacy of an individual's particular friendships.

Id. at 156.

179. *See id.* at 155–56 (explaining that, according to Aristotle, friendship seems to be a more important aim for lawgivers than justice, the reason being that the virtue of justice presupposes a community that has already been constituted by friendship). *Cf.* KRONMAN, LOST LAWYER, op. cit., at 106–08 (stressing the overriding importance of the value of "political fraternity" and its priority over disputed questions of justice in sustaining a political community).

the same time facilitating any necessary interactions and transactions with the state and the market. The same sorts of protective commitments are necessary whether *Piscopolis* is a local community that exists beyond, or more likely nowadays within, the territorial limits of the modern state. We will examine the various features of the liberal democratic state that pose a threat to the survival of local communities such as *Piscopolis* in more detail in Chapter 6. Here we focus on how the inhabitants seek to protect the fishing village against this threat.

1. Central Protective Commitments

The inhabitants' central "protective" commitments relate to two characteristics of the fishing village that we noted when we first introduced *Piscopolis* at the beginning of Chapter 4. Thus Drew is committed to *Piscopolis* remaining a local, small-scale community, and Drew is committed to the fishing village being as self-sufficient as possible.[180] Drew understands that "the state and the market economy are so structured as to subvert and undermine the politics of local community" so that "[b]etween the one politics and the other there can only be continuing conflict."[181] Drew is therefore committed to *Piscopolis* remaining a local, small-scale community with the features discussed in this Chapter and to resisting destructive outside influences that would subvert or undermine these features. More specifically, Drew understands that "[t]he deliberative and other social relationships" of local, small-scale societies such as *Piscopolis* are "systematically violated by some of the most notable effects of large-scale so-called free market economies."[182] Drew is therefore also committed to the fishing village being as self-sufficient as possible in order to insulate and protect the inhabitants' way of life to a significant extent from destructive outside market forces.[183] This means, though, that Drew is prepared to reject "the economic goals of advanced capitalism" and "a consumer society," and the pursuit of unlimited "economic and technological development."[184]

---

180. *See* Chapter 4, notes 4–5 and accompanying text.

181. MacIntyre, *Common Good*, op. cit., at 252.

182. *Id.* at 249.

183. *Id.* at 248; MacIntyre, Rational Animals, op. cit., at 145.

184. MacIntyre, *Common Good*, op. cit., at 250; MacIntyre, Rational Animals, op. cit., at 145.

Drew's rejection of the politics and economics of the liberal democratic state, however, does not mean that Drew is opposed to free markets. But Drew considers that the only genuinely free markets exist in societies of small producers such as *Piscopolis*, who are always able to do productive work and can choose whether or not to participate in the exchanges of markets that are local and small scale.[185] Furthermore, Drew considers that although market participants generally have regard to their own interests, "[m]arket relationships can only be sustained by being embedded in certain types of local nonmarket relationships, relationships of uncalculated giving and receiving, if they are to contribute to overall flourishing, rather than, as they so often in fact do, undermine and corrupt communal ties."[186] And in pursuing their own interests, vendors should charge a "just price" (the price the vendor would consider it just to pay as a buyer), regard the pursuit of profit for its own sake as unjust and the result of disordered desires, and therefore seek to earn only as much money as is necessary to attain their individual and common goods.[187]

Nor does Drew's rejection of the politics and economics of the liberal democratic state mean that Drew is opposed to interacting and transacting with the state and the market when necessary. Drew knows that the inhabitants of *Piscopolis* cannot, and indeed should not, simply ignore or avoid dealing with the modern state, which is "an ineliminable feature of the contemporary landscape," especially as it can provide needed resources and services.[188] Similarly, the inhabitants will sometimes have to secure resources from national or international markets.[189] However, the

---

185. MacIntyre, *Common Good*, op. cit., at 249–50.

186. MacIntyre, Rational Animals, op. cit., at 117.

187. *See* MacIntyre, Conflicts of Modernity, op. cit., at 90–92 (contrasting the views of Aquinas with those of David Hume and Adam Smith, but also noting Smith's view that although the pursuit of increased individual profit also leads to increased productivity and general prosperity, the motive to become as wealthy as possible is based largely on self-deception regarding the benefits of great wealth and power and leads to corruption of our moral sentiments).

188. MacIntyre, *Common Good*, op. cit., at 252; MacIntyre, Rational Animals, op. cit., at 131–32, 133, 142. *See also* MacIntyre, After Virtue, op. cit., at 255 (acknowledging an appropriate role for modern government to vindicate the rule of law, deal with injustice and unwarranted suffering, exercise generosity, and defend liberty).

189. MacIntyre, *Common Good*, op. cit., at 252.

inhabitants should seek to deal with the state and these markets, as far as possible, on their own terms.[190]

On all these matters Drew and the other inhabitants would doubtless find instructive example in the experience of Danish fishing crews following Denmark's privatization of fishing quotas, as described by Thomas Højrup in his study on *Common Goods for Coastal Communities*, which MacIntyre discusses in *Conflicts of Modernity*.[191] We have already drawn on this discussion in Chapter 4 to supplement MacIntyre's depiction of two types of fishing crew in his *Partial Response* essay.[192] Here we continue to draw on this discussion to examine how Denmark's introduction of Individual Transferable Quotas (ITQs) in 2006 impacted the practice of coastal share fishing by Danish fishing crews. Given our focus on the imagined fishing crews of Drew and Cash and the imagined fishing village of *Piscopolis*, this discussion of real world fishing crews and fishing communities seems especially relevant and illuminating, and we will quote from it extensively as we did in the notes in Chapter 4. MacIntyre describes the effect of allocating ITQs to individual fishing boats as follows:

> [The] legislation ... prescribed the allocation of fishing quotas to individual boats, so bringing about the privatization of those quotas and the acquisition of them by investors. Those crew members with no part in ownership of a boat lost out immediately. From now on they worked, if at all, for wages, not for shares [of the catch]. Those with a share in ownership could sell it for more money than they had ever envisaged having, but from then on would be permanently dependent for employment on those outside the community with even more money. A society that had valued common goods would be-

---

190. *See id.* (stressing that when the local community has to secure resources from the nation-state or the market, such dealing should only be, as far as possible, at a price acceptable to the local community). *See also* MacIntyre, Rational Animals, op. cit., at 132 (stressing the importance of weighing the benefits derived from dealing with the government of modern states against the costs of becoming entangled with it).

191. Thomas Højrup, *The Common Fisheries Policy Has to Recognize the Needs for Common Goods for Coastal Communities* (2011), http://www.havbaade.dk/thenecessity.pdf, discussed in MacIntyre, Conflicts of Modernity, op. cit., at 178–82.

192. *See MacIntyre, Partial Response*, op. cit. at 284–86; Chapter 4, note 25 and accompanying text, notes 36, 68, 89, 99.

come a society of individual preference maximizers and profit maximizers.[193]

In other words, many fishing communities that previously had engaged in
share fishing were unable to resist the destructive influences of the Danish
state and market forces unleashed by the system of Individual Transferable
Quotas[194] — a system that was ostensibly justified on the grounds of ensuring sustainability of fishing resources, even though it seems that those
engaged in share fishing were already successfully ensuring sustainability
through their cooperative management of a common resource for shared
benefits.[195]

However, not all fishing communities succumbed to these destructive
forces. MacIntyre continues the story, which is worth retelling in full:

---

193. MACINTYRE, CONFLICTS OF MODERNITY, op. cit., at 179.

194. Højrup explains the pressures:

> When the privatization of the quotas was implemented in 2006 the ...
> fishing village of Lildstrand lost its fleet of similar fishing clinker crafts in
> only one month. After the two first boats were sold to investors from outside
> Lildstrand the rest of the fishermen became afraid that they personally would
> be the last men at the landing place — carrying all the costs of the upkeep of
> the communal facilities necessary for the fishery to take place. One by one
> they therefore decided to sell their boats with the quotas that had just had
> [sic] been allotted to the boat by the Danish state.

Højrup, *Common Goods for Coastal Communities*, op cit., at 42. More broadly, the result
has been that "most of the ... fishing communities in Denmark have only a few boats left or
their fishery has totally disappeared since 2007." *Id.* at 38.

195. *See id.* at 31–32 (explaining that neoliberal economists, with their concept of the
individual *economic man* narrowly pursuing self-interest, and the governmental discourse
they influenced, "did not recognize, [sic] that in a fishery the protection of the right of
catch necessarily and traditionally implies regulation of the maintenance of the resource");
MACINTYRE, CONFLICTS OF MODERNITY, op. cit., at 181–82 (explaining that there are many
examples of communities solving the problems involved in "[t]he management of common
resources for shared benefits — of water needed for irrigation, of pastures for grazing, of
forests for timber" and that such examples serve to falsify economists' conclusions about human beings necessarily being rational preference maximizers). Højrup suggests, moreover,
that the ITQ system is in fact part of a disingenuous effort to deploy the principle of private
property to confiscate coastal communities' common right to catch and thereby facilitate
the capitalist alternative to share fishing. Højrup, *Common Goods for Coastal Communities*,
op. cit., at 28–30, 34, 37–38.

To many in North Jutland, there appeared to be no alternative, but not so in Thorupstrand. There the possibility of retaining share fishing and with it the form of community that it sustained was explored and achieved. A cooperative company that purchased a common pool of quotas was formed.

The purchase was financed by entrance fees and by substantial loans from two local banks. Security for these loans was provided in large part by the common pool of quotas. Twenty families joined the cooperative in which decisions were made democratically, one member, one vote. The families engaged in share fishing jointly assumed responsibility for sustaining the practice of share fishing and with it their way of life. Between 2006 and 2008, years during which the price of a boat rose 1000 percent, they watched others do strikingly well or more often badly in the market frenzy. But the crisis of 2008 had much the same consequences in North Jutland as elsewhere, one of which was a failure of one of the two local banks and with it a demand for the repayment of the loan, something that would have destroyed the cooperative. They avoided this by resorting successfully to the conventional politics of the Danish state, providing a model of political skill for others in similar situations.[196]

Indeed, the experience of the Thorupstrand fishing community led Højrup to propose that "[t]o ensure the environmental, economic and social wellbeing of fisheries, instead of privatizing most of the fishing rights in Europe's home waters, the European Union should secure most collective fishing rights to [such] common quota companies held by living coastal communities."[197]

2. Role of the Virtues

Drew and the other inhabitants are also committed to exhibiting the virtues necessary to honor their protective commitments to keep *Piscopolis* as a local, small-scale community that is as self-sufficient as possible while facilitating any unavoidable and necessary dealings with the state and the market. Here again, the example of the Thorupstrand fishing com-

---

196. MacIntyre, Conflicts of Modernity, op. cit., at 179–80.
197. Højrup, *Common Goods for Coastal Communities*, op cit., at 5.

munity is instructive. MacIntyre considers that the best way to understand what the Thorupstrand fishing community did is in Thomistic Aristotelian terms even though the members of this community did not explicitly think of themselves in this way.[198] Consequently, he considers the four cardinal virtues as being critical to their success:

> The fragile success of the *Thorupstrand Kystfiskerlaug* (Guild of Thorupstrand Coastal Fishermen) was possible only because of qualities of mind and character especially in those who provided the community with leadership and the Guild with an articulate voice: prudence increasingly informed by economic and political know how, justice in the allocation of shares and in the structure of the Guild, courage in taking the right risks in the right way, and temperateness in not being seduced by the promises of the market. Subtract any one of these and you subtract a necessary condition for the community's flourishing. It matters that ... the survival and flourishing of the community depend upon the political prudence that they bring to their continuing engagement with the economics of the market and the politics of the Danish state.[199]

We must now examine more closely the destructive conditions in the liberal democratic state from which Drew and the other inhabitants of *Piscopolis* seek to protect themselves, from which the fishing community in Thorupstrand did succeed in protecting themselves, and from which so many other Danish fishing communities did not, resulting in their transformation from a community with fishing crews like Drew's to a community with crews more like Cash's.

---

198. MacIntyre, Conflicts of Modernity, op. cit., at 182.
199. *Id.* at 180.

SIX

LIVING IN THE LIBERAL DEMOCRATIC STATE

Contrasts and Prospects

In Chapters 4 and 5 we considered the way of life of fishing crew member Drew in the imagined fishing village of *Piscopolis*. Chapter 4 examined Drew's daily life and everyday relationships with the other inhabitants as they engage in various particular practices in the fishing village, considered some of the key politico-ethical commitments Drew shares with the other inhabitants, and contrasted Drew's situation with that of Cash, a member of a fishing crew subject to the destructive influences of the modern liberal democratic state and its capitalist, large-scale market economy. Chapter 5 then considered the common practice of politics in *Piscopolis*, which Drew and the other inhabitants carry on through their political conversation in which they are jointly engaged, and examined the full range of the inhabitants' key shared politico-ethical commitments shaping the communitarian *ethos* of the fishing village. We saw that these commitments are informed by the premises and tenets of Thomistic Aristotelianism, with its emphasis on human flourishing as well as human vulnerability, disability, and dependence, and that they include commitments to develop and exhibit important virtues.

We saw also that the final set of commitments are intended to protect the inhabitants' flourishing way of life and their shared common goods, politico-ethical commitments, and communitarian *ethos* against the incursions and destructive influences of the modern liberal democratic state and its capitalist, large-scale market economy. And when we compared Drew's situation with Cash's situation in Chapter 4, we noticed that although Cash may have some of the same concerns and commitments discussed there as Drew does — a concern for and commitment to the common goods of the practice of catching fish, for example, at least to some extent — these concerns and commitments are more fragile in the case of Cash's fishing crew than in Drew's fishing crew. This is because the primary motive of crew members in the core practice of catching fish, and the primary motive of corporate officers in the secondary practice of making and sustaining the business organization that manages the enterprise, are extrinsic rather than intrinsic. Because crew members and management are primarily concerned to attain extrinsic, individualistic common goods, especially money or other material rewards, rather than shared, intrinsic common goods of the practice, goods and qualities of excellence are systematically subordinated to goods and qualities of effectiveness, with the attendant moral risk of corrupting the common goods of the practice or too readily abandoning them altogether.

Having considered the political, economic, and moral environment of *Piscopolis* which nurtures its communitarian *ethos* in Chapters 4 and 5, we must now consider the dominant political, economic, and moral environment of the modern liberal democratic state which threatens to erode or replace this *ethos* with a vastly different one. This environment and *ethos* explain the diminished regard for the common goods of practices in the case of Cash's fishing crew and why, more generally, Cash does not have the range of politico-ethical commitments that Drew has. Focusing on MacIntyre's account of relevant matters, Part I examines the salient features of the dominant political, economic, and moral environment of the modern liberal democratic state and the *ethos* it promotes. Part II then considers various ways in which the inhabitants of liberal democratic states can still seek to pursue a *Piscopolis*-like way of life to a greater or lesser extent, despite this environment and *ethos*. We postpone until Chapter 8 the question whether we can, and should, also seek transform the dominant political, economic, and moral environment of the liberal democratic state and its associated *ethos* into a political, economic, and moral environment and *ethos* more like *Piscopolis*, and in this way seek to cultivate the liberal democratic state as a "republic of virtue."

I. Dominant Environment of the Modern Liberal Democratic State

Properly understood as referring to the absence of a societal consensus on a Thomistic Aristotelian understanding of the greater common good in light of the specifically human good (albeit admitting of exceptions in the case of certain individuals or groups within society as discussed further in Part II), the following pithy summation by Ted Clayton vividly captures the essential thrust of MacIntyre's critique of the modern liberal democratic state and the striking contrast between such a state and an ideal *polis* like *Piscopolis*:

> MacIntyre argues that today we live in a fragmented society made up of individuals who have no conception of the human good, no way to come together to pursue a common good, no way to persuade one another about what that common good might be, and indeed most of us believe that the common good does not and cannot exist.[1]

For MacIntyre, then, a *polis* such as *Piscopolis*, and not the modern liberal democratic state, is "the kind of political institution that best suits the nature of human beings."[2] Moreover, as we saw at the end of Chapter 4,

---

1. Ted Clayton, *Political Philosophy of Alasdair MacIntyre*, Internet Encyclopedia of Philosophy IEP, https://iep.utm.edu/p-macint/#H11 (at the beginning of section 7 on "Politics in a World without Morality"). Even more vivid is MacIntyre's dramatic thought experiment at the beginning of *After Virtue*, developing the premise for this claim. *See* ALASDAIR MACINTYRE, AFTER VIRTUE: A STUDY IN MORAL THEORY 1–5 (3d. ed., 2007) (1981) (describing an imaginary world in which the natural sciences have suffered a catastrophe as a result of which only "fragments" remain and "the language of natural science, or parts of it at least, continues to be used but is in a grave state of disorder," albeit a disorder that the inhabitants fail to recognize because they have forgotten about both science and the catastrophe, and claiming that the same sort of narrative describes what has happened to us in the moral sphere). For Clayton's discussion of MacIntyre's thought experiment, see Clayton, *supra* (section 3 on "The Current Moral Disorder and Its Consequences"). I am indebted to Jack Sammons for suggesting a reference to MacIntyre's dramatic thought experiment at this point. Sammons Email (September 12, 2020) [on file with author]. For a fascinating collection of essays, including two by MacIntyre himself, providing multiple perspectives on the matters discussed in this Chapter, especially MacIntyre's critique of liberalism and capitalism as well as the Marxist elements in this critique, see VIRTUE AND POLITICS: ALASDAIR MACINTYRE'S REVOLUTIONARY ARISTOTELIANISM (Paul Blackledge & Kelvin Knight, eds., 2011).

2. Kelvin Knight, *Introduction, in* THE MACINTYRE READER 20 (Kelvin Knight, ed., 1998).

we should supplement MacIntyre's critique with an understanding that the dominant environment of the modern liberal democratic state also reflects the "technological thinking" and related Cartesian-Newtonian worldview of the modern West — a combination that conduces to regarding everything and everyone as "standing reserve" to be ordered according to human will and that imperils "the web of life" in Earth's critical zone, threatens the health of the planet, and mortgages the well-being of future generations.

A. Politics

MacIntyre is adamant that the modern liberal democratic state is not a *polis* and that politics in such a state is not a practice. Indeed, his critique of modern politics contrasts sharply with the common practice of politics in *Piscopolis* portrayed in Chapter 5. Although MacIntyre does acknowledge, and welcome, the "series of social and political liberations and emancipations from arbitrary and oppressive rule" which have occurred during the history of modernity and the appropriate role of modern government in vindicating the rule of law, dealing with injustice and unwarranted suffering, exercising generosity, and defending liberty,[3] his critique of modern politics does indeed seem to be a devastating one.

It should be noted that MacIntyre's critique to a large extent precedes the increasing influence, and in some cases even the rise to power, of contemporary "populist" political movements in several Western liberal democracies. This development can arguably be understood, at least partly, as a reaction against at least some of the features of modern politics that MacIntyre critiques, such as the power wielded by the oligarchy of wealthy elites discussed in subsection 1. I do not want to go too far down the rabbit hole of trying to identify all the various factors that have precipitated the development of current populist movements or to canvass the various responses that have been proposed. Suffice it to say that the matter is complex and multi-faceted. This said, I strongly suspect that MacIntyre is unlikely to approve of the nature, goals, and methods of contemporary populism, especially its "right-wing" variants, regarding these movements

---

3. ALASDAIR MACINTYRE, ETHICS IN THE CONFLICTS OF MODERNITY: AN ESSAY ON DESIRE, PRACTICAL REASONING, AND NARRATIVE 123 (2016); MACINTYRE, AFTER VIRTUE, op. cit., at 255.

instead as being yet another symptom of the same political malady he critiques rather than a cure. Consistent, the MacIntyrean prescription for the malady advocated in this book seeks to provide a more radical and more satisfactory solution than those offered either by contemporary populist movements or the responses to them that have so far been proposed.[4]

1. Participation in the Political Conversation[5]

To begin with, then, it is unlikely that Cash participates in the political conversation of the state in the same active way Drew participates in the political conversation of *Piscopolis*, that is, it is unlikely that Cash has a significant role in shaping and making decisions directly affecting the entire political community or relevant parts of it. Unless Cash has successfully run for political office or at least has a leading role in an influential interest group or social movement, the only way for Cash to have a "voice" in the process of shaping and making political decisions of the state will be through voting in the election of candidates for political office or in popular referenda or possibly through participation in the occasional protest. Although it might perhaps be different in the politics of some types of local political community such as a county or city, and although we have learned through hard experience that "every vote counts," Cash's "voice" as expressed through the vote will typically be only one among thousands or even millions (assuming Cash actually votes at all).[6] And so MacIntyre concludes that "[p]oliti-

---

4. I am indebted to Jack Sammons for insisting on the need to be careful when talking about contemporary populism, and in particular to avoid creating the impression that the anti-elitism of contemporary populism, especially in its right-wing forms, somehow suggests that populists value MacIntyrean "common goods," given that such goods "are exactly what populists don't want for these are understood as restraints on ordinary (read selfish) desires." Sammons Email (September 12, 2020) [on file with author]. For a sense of the complex and multifaceted nature of contemporary populism and the various responses to it that have been proposed, see Benjamin Moffitt, *The trouble with anti-populism: why the champions of civility keep losing*, The Guardian (February 14, 2020), https://www.theguardian.com/politics/2020/feb/14/anti-populism-politics-why-champions-of-civility-keep-losing.

5. For discussion of this topic in *Piscopolis*, see Part II, Section A of Chapter 5.

6. For a brief but illuminating discussion tracing the decline of active citizenship and the rise over the last several decades of passive citizenship in its stead, see William F. May, Beleaguered Rulers: The Public Obligation of the Professional 174–77 (2001). *But see* Jeffrey Stout, Blessed Are the Organized: Grassroots Democracy in America (2010) (explicating and evaluating several concrete examples of grassroots democracy).

cally the societies of advanced Western modernity are oligarchies disguised as liberal democracies," with most inhabitants excluded from membership in the wealthy and powerful "set of interlocking... political, financial, cultural, and media elites" who are really in control.[7] The result is that "a small minority of the population ... make politics their active occupation and preoccupation" and a cadre of "professional and semiprofessional politicians" — the "political elites" — mobilize "a huge largely passive majority... only at periodic intervals, for elections or national crises."[8]

Cash not only lacks the same sort of opportunity for active political participation as Drew enjoys in *Piscopolis*. Cash also lacks the same sort of incentive and rational justification for such participation, and therefore likely lacks any commitment to achieving it. This is partly because Cash's lack of opportunity has the effect of discouraging efforts to become more politically engaged, and partly because there is not the same inseparable connection between the achievement of Cash's own individual good and Cash's contribution to the shared greater common good of society

---

7. Alasdair MacIntyre, *Politics, Philosophy, and the Common Good* (1997) *in* THE MAC-INTYRE READER 237 (Kelvin Knight, ed., 1998); MACINTYRE, CONFLICTS OF MODERNITY, op. cit., at 126–27.

8. ALASDAIR MACINTYRE, DEPENDENT RATIONAL ANIMALS: WHY HUMAN BEINGS NEED THE VIRTUES 141 (1999). *See also* MAY, BELEAGUERED RULERS, op. cit. at 177–78 (further discussing the corruption of politics and political discourse through the influence of money and through distorting and manipulative sloganizing, and lamenting constant political campaigning and only occasional governing by political leaders). Jeffrey Stout's "pragmatic version of deliberative democracy," founded upon a tradition of social practices that aim at excellence and cultivate virtue, including the discursive practice of exchanging ethical reasons (both secular and religious) with one another in democratic conversation, does not necessarily negate this assessment, given Stout's own serious concerns about the health of contemporary liberal democracy, including the anti-democratic influence of various oligarchical elites. *See* Chapter 1, notes 47–51 and accompanying text. *See also* STOUT, BLESSED ARE THE ORGANIZED, op. cit., at xiii–xix, 278–90 (offering the concrete examples of grassroots democracy he discusses in the book as an inspiration for ordinary people to organize their various communities in an effort to "take back the country from the plutocrats, militarists, and culture warriors now dominating our politics"). Stout's words "take back the country" and "culture warriors" doubtless had a far different resonance when he wrote them in 2010 than they do for us in 2020 in the era of Trump. As Jack Sammons observes, for Trump "'[t]aking back' now means abandoning all traditions (including those assumed in civility, law, and politics) by treating those as illegitimate restraints on self-serving, capitalistic driven, future denying individualism. These are 'cultural' and elitist according to MAGA". Sammons Email (September 12, 2020) [on file with author].

as a whole. For the dominant conception of the common good in liberal democratic societies is quite different from the conception of the greater common good in *Piscopolis*, and it gives Cash every incentive and rational justification for being a "free rider" who obtains the benefits political authority provides while contributing as little as possible to its costs.[9]

2. Conception of the Common Good[10]

Unlike the inhabitants of *Piscopolis*, the inhabitants of the modern liberal democratic state, the rulers and the ruled, do not constitute "a society of rational enquiry, of self-scrutiny" whose members carry on a common practice of politics and jointly engage in political conversation that seeks "a proper theoretical comprehension of the greater common good in light of the specifically human good and its practical embodiment in the life of the community."[11] Consequently, there is no resulting foundational politico-ethical commitment to an overarching common good of the practice of politics synonymous with the greater common good of liberal democratic society. Hence there can be no generally shared commitment to the promotion of maximal "happiness" in the sense of human flourishing through the proper ordering of practices, in which the inhabitants of liberal democratic states are encouraged to pursue their own individual good and develop their powers through achieving the shared common goods of practices and the greater common good of society as a whole, and in which they engage in continuing rational enquiry into what more precisely this greater common good is and requires. As MacIntyre puts it, "far from being an area of activity in and through which other activities are rationally ordered, [politics] is itself one more compartmentalized sphere from which there has been excluded the possibility of asking those questions that most need to be asked."[12]

This does not mean, however, that liberal democratic politics does not presuppose and give effect to some dominant conception of the human good and the greater common good.[13] But it does mean that these con-

---

9. MacIntyre, *Common Good*, op. cit., at 241–42.

10. For discussion of this topic in *Piscopolis*, see Part II, Section B of Chapter 5.

11. *See* Chapter 5, notes 23–25 and accompanying text.

12. MacIntyre, *Common Good*, op. cit., at 243.

13. As MacIntyre explains, "every political and social order embodies and gives expression to an ordering of different human goods and therefore also embodies and gives

ceptions are very different from the conceptions prevailing in *Piscopolis*, and that they are not arrived at through rational enquiry and sustained through a political consensus subject to continuing rational enquiry in which they can always be challenged through reasoned argument.[14] The dominant conception of the human good appears to be the achievement of "happiness" understood as a psychological state of positive feelings in which individuals are pleased or contented because their desires, which they express through their choices and order as a set of preferences acting as autonomous agents, have been satisfied.[15] In short, "[i]t is to be, to do, and to have, what one wants to be, to do, and to have."[16] And the dominant conception of the common good appears to be the maximization of "happiness" understood in this way — in other words, understood as the maximization of opportunities for individuals to satisfy their preferences — subject to appropriate legal, institutional, and moral constraints, with the state being as far as possible neutral regarding individual choices and preferences and the differing views of the human good they may reflect.[17]

This dominant conception of the common good in light of the human good is consistent with the dominant conception of practical rationality in liberal democracies, which envisages rational agents as maximizing preference satisfaction and which we will encounter again in this Chapter.[18] And it is consistent with MacIntyre's characterization of the dominant

---

expression to some particular conception of the human good." *Id.* at 247. The important question, however, is whether the exercise of political authority "serve[s] the common good and the human good" by enabling "individuals ... to learn about their individual and common goods ... through rational enquiry and debate" and "through practice;" only if it does can claims to the exercise of such political authority be rationally justified. *Id.* at 247–48.

14. *See* Chapter 5, notes 8, 26, 35–36, 155–57 and accompanying text.

15. *See* MacIntyre, Conflicts of Modernity, op. cit., at 134, 184, 193–96, 200 (discussing the expression of desires through autonomous choices, the rank ordering of desires as a set of preferences, and the dominant conception of happiness, and noting the agreement of "individual agents in their everyday lives and social scientific researchers" that "happiness so understood" is "a very great good, perhaps the good").

16. *Id.* at 193.

17. *See id.* at 134–35, 199, 200 (observing the widespread assumption of modern politics and ethics that rational agreement on the human good is impossible, identifying different types of constraints on preference satisfaction, and questioning the maximization of happiness understood as maximization of opportunities for preference satisfaction as "a political ideal" and "the aim of government").

18. *Id.* at 183–84, 193. *See infra* notes 71–72, 92–99, 135–46 and accompanying text.

conception of the common good animating the modern state and economy as being the sort of "individualist" and "minimalist" conception we
encountered in Chapter 3, in which the common good is "the summing of
the goods pursued by individuals" in an association they regard as instrumental to achieving their individual ends.[19] Specifically, the state "provides
a secure social order within which individuals may pursue their own particular ends, whatever they are," and individuals cooperate "to pursue their
own particular ends effectively and ... to sustain the security of the social
order[,] ... all such cooperation [being] a means to their individual ends."[20]
Such a conception of the common good is not, then, as it is in *Piscopolis*,
a conception "where there is the common good of communal political
learning"[21] and where happiness in the sense of positive feelings supervenes on the achievement of flourishing through the rational exercise of
powers.[22] Moreover, although "communitarians" in liberal democratic
states tend to emphasize their rejection of an individualist conception of
the common good and although "communitarian values" are among the
"ragbag of assorted values" that also inform politics in modern liberal democracies, MacIntyre considers that the conception of the common good
espoused by such communitarians "is not at all that of a kind of community of political learning and enquiry ... necessary for individuals to discover
what their individual and common goods are."[23]

19. MacIntyre, *Common Good*, op. cit., at 239–40, 241–42, 250, 252; Chapter 3, notes
76–79 and accompanying text. Jack Sammons makes the interesting observation that "the
common good of Cash's community requires an assumption of constant and unending
growth for the good to be thought common at all. Christian abundance gone astray!" Sammons Email (September 12, 2020) [on file with author].

20. MacIntyre, *Common Good*, op. cit., at 241–42.

21. *Id.* at 243.

22. MACINTYRE, CONFLICTS OF MODERNITY, op. cit., at 201; MACINTYRE, AFTER VIR-
TUE, op. cit., at 197.

23. MacIntyre, *Common Good*, op. cit., at 245–46. Understanding "liberalism" as covering "the whole spectrum of liberalisms from that of American self-styled conservatives
to that of European self-styled social democrats," MacIntyre identifies three main features
distinguishing communitarianism from liberalism — an emphasis on "relationships" as opposed to "rights," on "particular ties to particular groups and individuals" as opposed to
"universal and impersonal principles," and on the importance of achieving certain "irreduc-
ibly social goods" as opposed to individuals determining "her or his own conception of her
or his good." *Id.* at 244. *See also* MACINTYRE, RATIONAL ANIMALS, op. cit., at 142 (asserting
that it is "a mistake, the communitarian mistake, to attempt to infuse the politics of the state
with the values and modes of participation in local community").

The dominant conception of the common good in liberal democratic politics seems consistent, too, with frequently made claims that the goods of the "secure social order" mentioned above[24] — goods such as national security, law and order, transportation and communication, public education, a stable currency, and public welfare — promote the common good.[25] As MacIntyre observes, such "public goods" are enjoyed by and serve the purposes of individuals qua individuals.[26] However, despite his own earlier references to the dominant individualist conception of the common good in the modern state and the related distinction between different types of common good,[27] it appears that MacIntyre now wants to restrict use of the term "common good," at least in the context of politics, to the Thomistic Aristotelian conception only. Thus, he pointedly rejects claims that the provision of public goods serves the common good as "unfortunate rhetoric ... obscuring the difference between public goods and common goods ... enjoyed and achieved ... by individuals qua members of various groups or qua participants in various activities."[28] This rejection may seem to be in tension with MacIntyre's claim that such common goods can still be achieved in an area of activity clearly related to the provision of certain public goods, such as the shared education that can occur in public schools, or the shared common good of a workplace through which such a public good is delivered.[29] MacIntyre would likely respond that, whatever the case may be at the everyday operational level, the establishment and

---

24. *See supra* note 20 and accompanying text.

25. *See* MacIntyre, Conflicts of Modernity, op. cit., at 125, 168 (identifying such claims and such goods).

26. *Id.*

27. *See supra* note 19 and accompanying text (citing to MacIntyre's 1997 publication, *Common Good,* op. cit.); MacIntyre, Rational Animals, op. cit., at 131–33 (asserting in 1999, with respect to the provision of "shared public goods" provided by modern nation-states — both in their aspect as "giant utility companies" and in their aspect as "the guardian of our values" which sometimes invites us to make the ultimate sacrifice — that such shared public goods "are not the common goods of a genuine nation-wide community" and must be distinguished from "the type of common good" in the stronger sense "for which communal recognition is required by the virtues of acknowledged dependence").

28. MacIntyre, Conflicts of Modernity, op. cit., at 168–69.

29. *See id.* at 130–32, 170–72 (discussing how common goods can be achieved in the right kind of workplaces, including workplaces in the public domain such as the British Broadcasting Corporation (BBC)), 172–75 (discussing how common goods can be achieved in the right kind of schools).

SIX | Living in the Liberal Democratic State   221

administration of the *system* in which such a common good is achieved is focused on the individual qua individual,[30] and systemic decisions (including financing decisions) are typically not the result of shared rational deliberation involving those who regard themselves as pursuing their individual good through the achievement of a shared greater common good.[31]

Just as the shared foundational politico-ethical commitment to the overarching common good of the common practice of politics in *Piscopolis* — promotion of the greater common good of maximal human flourishing in the entire fishing village through the proper ordering of practices — entails and includes additional commitments to various other features as specific common ends or common goods of this common practice,[32] so the lack of such an overarching common good, and indeed the lack of such a common practice, in liberal democratic societies entails the absence of these commitments and features, and even in some cases the presence of their diametrical opposites. We have already seen, for example, that the inhabitants of liberal democratic states likely lack Drew's commitment to active political participation, and indeed may well be incentivized to be passive free riders, and we will now consider the various other commitments we examined in Chapter 5.

3. The Common Goods of Practices and Goods of Effectiveness[33]

In contrast to *Piscopolis*, there is no generally shared commitment in modern liberal democratic states to facilitate and encourage ways of life in which their inhabitants can attain the common goods of practices and

---

30. Some scholars such as Michael Sandel might counter that investment in public goods such as quality public schools, reliable public transportation, public health clinics, and other public amenities can also represent an investment in "an infrastructure for civic renewal" providing "common spaces of a shared democratic citizenship" critical to "a new politics of the common good" in which inhabitants of liberal democracies can respectfully "reason together about the meaning of the good life" and navigate "the disagreements that will inevitably arise." MICHAEL J. SANDEL, JUSTICE: WHAT'S THE RIGHT THING TO DO? 261, 263, 267–69 (2009).

31. *See* MACINTYRE, RATIONAL ANIMALS, op. cit., at 131 (explaining that "the distribution of [public] goods by government in no way reflects a common mind arrived at through widespread shared deliberation governed by norms of rational enquiry").

32. *See* Chapter 5, notes 33–34, 38 and accompanying text.

33. For discussion of these topics in *Piscopolis*, see Part II, Sections C and D of Chapter 5.

develop their powers as independent practical reasoners in networks of giving and receiving because doing so is seen as central to their flourishing. Nor, therefore, is there a generally shared commitment that their inhabitants systematically subordinate goods and qualities of effectiveness to goods and qualities of excellence in practices. Correspondingly, liberal democratic states are not committed to ensuring that their inhabitants develop and exhibit the necessary virtues and observe all the necessary rules of natural law and the rules governing practices, or to ensuring that all their inhabitants have sufficient opportunity to attain adequate goods of effectiveness, especially money, to support their flourishing.

It does not follow from the absence of such generally shared commitments that there are no communities of practice in such states which have such commitments, as we will see further in Part II. Indeed, as we already saw in Chapter 4[34] and noted again at the beginning of this Chapter, Cash belongs to such a community of practice within a "practice-institution combination" business organization, specifically the practitioner community engaged in the core practice of catching fish. But again, in the case of Cash's fishing crew, any concern for and commitment to attaining the common goods of the practice is fragile, because even though Cash, other crew members, and management (engaged in the secondary practice of making and sustaining the institution), are *also* concerned with the pursuit of goods of excellence, nevertheless their *primary* motivation is extrinsic, and goods and qualities of excellence are systematically subordinated to goods and qualities of effectiveness. Such communities of practice, then, exist on a spectrum of robustness of concern for and commitment to the common goods of the practice, with the systematic subordination of goods and qualities of effectiveness to goods and qualities of excellence at one end and with the converse at the other end.

Moreover, as MacIntyre shows, not only are substantive issues regarding different ways of life excluded from the political conversation, the effects of governmental activity are not neutral toward these ways of life but undermine some ways and promote others, as seen, for example, in promotion of "the way of life of the fashionably hedonistic consumer" or the virtual disappearance of family or household farming and its replacement

---

34. *See* Chapter 4, note 69 and accompanying text.

by multinational agribusiness.[35] We can now add, as a further example, the virtual disappearance of coastal share fishing in Denmark following privatization of fishing quotas by the Danish state, as discussed in Chapter 5.[36] The destructive effects of the modern state (and as we will see further in Section B, of its so-called free market economy) may result, then, in the weakening of a traditional practice and erosion of its common goods or even the complete disappearance of such practice and its common goods and the way of life associated with them, although presumably technological progress may also create opportunities for the birth of entirely new practices as well.[37]

4. Allocation of Goods of Effectiveness and Other Resources[38]

Unlike in *Piscopolis*, too, in liberal democratic states there are no generally shared commitments to a coherent set of norms concerning justice and related matters and to inhabitants developing and exhibiting the relevant virtues necessary to implement such commitments. Michael Sandel illuminates the problem well:

> To ask whether a society is just is to ask how it distributes the things we prize — income and wealth, duties and rights, powers and opportunities, offices and honors. A just society distributes these goods in the right way; it gives each person his or her due. The hard questions begin when we ask what people are due, and why...
>
> ... [W]e've identified three ways of approaching the distribution of goods — welfare, freedom, and virtue. Each of these ideals suggests a different way of thinking about justice...
>
> ... One says justice means maximizing utility or welfare — the greatest happiness for the greatest number. The second says justice means respecting freedom of choice — either the actual choices people make in a free market (the libertarian view) or the hypothetical

---

35. MacIntyre, *Common Good*, op. cit., at 237–39.

36. *See* Chapter 5, notes 191–95 and accompanying text.

37. For discussion of such creative and productive as well as destructive effects, see MacIntyre, Conflicts of Modernity, op. cit., at 122.

38. For discussion of this topic in *Piscopolis*, see Part II, Section E of Chapter 5.

choices people *would* make in an original position of equality (the liberal egalitarian view). The third says justice involves cultivating virtue and reasoning about the common good.[39]

We can relate the three approaches to justice identified in this passage to our earlier discussion as follows. Thus, the first, utilitarian approach, which "has had an influential career [and] exerts a powerful hold on the thinking of policy-makers, economists, business executives, and ordinary citizens to this day," appears to be reflected in the dominant individualist conception of the common good focused on maximizing preference satisfaction discussed in subsection 2 above, while the second and third approaches appear to represent those moral constraints on this maximizing principle which are based on protection of fundamental rights and freedoms and certain other moral considerations.[40] In addition, the third approach, which "means giving people what they morally deserve — allocating goods to reward and promote virtue" and which "connects justice to reflection about the good life," is an Aristotelian approach similar to the formula for justice among independent practical reasoners in *Piscopolis*, in which goods of effectiveness and other community resources are allocated according to contribution to the common good.[41]

The problem, of course, is that these various ideals or approaches are not unambiguous or mutually compatible. As Sandel explains, "Some of our debates reflect disagreement about what it means to maximize welfare or respect freedom or cultivate virtue. Others involve disagreement about what to do when these ideals conflict."[42] Here Sandel seems to agree with MacIntyre, who considers that political debate about issues of justice reflects incoherent, conflicting, and incommensurable values, just like oth-

---

39. SANDEL, JUSTICE, op. cit., at 19, 260.

40. *See supra* notes 17–19 and accompanying text; *infra* notes 91, 95–99 and accompanying text (dominant conception of common good and moral constraints); SANDEL, JUSTICE, op. cit., at 34 (for the quoted language), 37, 41 (counting and aggregating preferences), 106, 107, 108 (examples of additional references to preferences); MACINTYRE, CONFLICTS OF MODERNITY, op. cit., at 77 (explaining that in recent utilitarian thought "to maximize utility is to maximize preference satisfaction").

41. *See* SANDEL, JUSTICE, op. cit., at 106 (for the quoted language), 193–95 (discussing Aristotle's reasons for advocating the distribution of goods based on contribution to the *polis*).

42. *Id.* at 19.

er moral debate in liberal democracies.[43] The same applies to the related matters regarding income and wealth disparities, responsibility for tedious and dangerous jobs, self-imposed limits on the movement of labor, and children's education, which are the subject of corollary commitments in *Piscopolis*. Like MacIntyre, Sandel favors the third, virtue-based approach to justice focused on the common good (although his understanding of the common good seems significantly different from MacIntyre's), and considers that even though political philosophy cannot definitively resolve such disagreements, it can "bring moral clarity to the alternatives" confronting the citizens in liberal democracies.[44] In this he is probably correct and presumably MacIntyre would not disagree. However, unlike MacIntyre, Sandel arguably may be representative of the communitarianism we discussed in subsection 2, and he seems optimistic, although perhaps only faintly so, about the prospects for "[a] politics of moral engagement" in which respectful political conversation will lead to greater mutual appreciation of differences, and possibly greater agreement and a more just society.[45] On this point, MacIntyre would seem to be even less optimistic than Sandel and to have little or no hope that these different approaches to justice, including the Thomistic Aristotelian approach he himself favors, will be anything more than part of the "ragbag of assorted values" informing contemporary politics in liberal democratic states.[46] Indeed, as we will see further in the next subsection, MacIntyre considers such contemporary politics to be essentially a politics of competing and conflicting interests.[47] Consequently, "the modern state cannot provide a political framework informed by the just generosity needed to achieve the common goods of networks of giving and receiving."[48]

---

43. *See* MacIntyre, After Virtue, op. cit., at 244–54 (discussing disparate views of justice, especially those based on legitimate entitlement and those based on need, noting that both bracket out desert). *See also infra* Section C (discussing Morality in liberal democracies).

44. Sandel, Justice, op. cit., at 19. For Sandel's favored approach, see *id.* at 244–69 (Chapter 10 on "Justice and the Common Good").

45. *Id.* at 268–69.

46. *See supra* note 23 and accompanying text (discussing the "ragbag of assorted values," including "communitarian values," informing politics in modern liberal democracies).

47. MacIntyre, Rational Animals, op. cit., at 131, 144.

48. *Id.* at 133.

5. Character, Structuring, and Conduct of
the Political Conversation[49]

MacIntyre's pessimism regarding the prospects for elevating political conversation above its current parlous and debased state appears to be rooted in his perception that the inhabitants of modern liberal democratic states, unlike the inhabitants of *Piscopolis*, do not share any general commitment to being "always, potentially or actually, a society of rational enquiry, of self-scrutiny."[50] We have already noted several effects resulting from the absence of such a commitment — the pervasive influence of the dominant individualist conception of the greater common good focused on maximizing individual preferences, whatever they may be, within certain constraints; the absence of generally shared commitments to flourishing through attaining the common goods of practices, to promoting and defending associated ways of life, to systematically subordinating goods and qualities of effectiveness to goods and qualities of excellence, to observing a coherent set of norms concerning justice and related matters, and to cultivating the relevant virtues necessary for all these things; and the absence of a generally shared commitment to active participation in the political conversation.

But what *is* the character of this political conversation then? Or perhaps better said, how does it lack character? And how does it risk corrupting the character of those who do become active participants in it? MacIntyre provides a global assessment which incorporates and expands upon various points we have already encountered. He observes that, even though political rhetoric may sometimes suggest otherwise, political conversation in modern liberal democratic states typically excludes philosophical questions.[51] As we have seen, it excludes questions about the value and goodness of alternative ways of life (which would be among the sorts of philosophical questions Michael Sandel would like it to address), and oth-

---

49. For discussion of this topic in *Piscopolis*, see Part II, Section F of Chapter 5.

50. See Chapter 5, notes 8, 23, 155 and accompanying text.

51. *See* MacIntyre, *Common Good*, op. cit., at 235–38 (discussing how such exclusion is a symptom of "the exceptional degree of compartmentalization" in advanced Western societies). Jack Sammons considers that "the letter perfect example" of such exclusion of philosophical questions is how, in the debates for the 2020 Democratic presidential nomination, "the word 'existential' was a way of avoiding talking about the end of Gaia (within the lifetime of my grandchildren)." Sammons Email (September 13, 2020) [on file with author].

er questions raised by radically dissenting voices who seek to mount fundamental challenges.[52] And it is precisely because political conversation typically excludes such questions that it is not, and cannot be, a conversation in which the participants typically engage in "rational enquiry" and "self-scrutiny" and exhibit the political virtues necessary for such enquiry and self-scrutiny.

On the contrary, MacIntyre tells us, political debate in electoral campaigns, legislatures, and government bureaucracies is rarely systematic or in depth, disregards canons of enquiry, fails to follow through an argument's implications, responds to immediate concerns rather than long-term considerations, reflects incoherent and conflicting values, and is influenced by the rich and powerful.[53] While "a set of small-scale academic publics" carry on "the rational discourse of enquiry," political debate, by contrast, "is generally and characteristically the antithesis of serious intellectual enquiry," so that "decisions and policies emerge from a strange *mélange* of arguments, debating points and the influence of money and other forms of established power."[54]

Correspondingly, not only is political prudence or practical wisdom a rarity,[55] few active participants in the political conversation generally and characteristically exhibit conversational justice and other dialogical virtues, including "an active and enquiring attitude" toward dissent. Indeed,

---

52. *See supra* note 35 and accompanying text (regarding the exclusion from political conversation of substantive issues regarding ways of life), notes 30, 44–45 and accompanying text (regarding the types of philosophical questions Sandel would like political conversation to address); MacIntyre, *Common Good*, op. cit., at 237, 243, 251 (discussing the refusal of political actors to acknowledge "serious argument" as opposed to "rhetorical embellishments" when "first principles" are invoked, the exclusion of "the most fundamental issues" and "th[e] questions that most need to be asked" from political conversation and decision, and the absence from the contemporary dominant politics of "an active and enquiring attitude towards radically dissenting views").

53. *Id.* at 238–39, 245. *See also* MacIntyre, Rational Animals, op. cit., at 131; MacIntyre, Conflicts of Modernity, op. cit., at 126–27 (discussing the influence of money on government and on the agenda setting for national politics, and concluding that consequently power in liberal democracies is distributed "in grossly, even grotesquely unequal ways").

54. MacIntyre, *Common Good*, op. cit., at 238–39.

55. For an excellent discussion of political practical wisdom (statesmanship) in modern liberal democracies, see Anthony T. Kronman, The Lost Lawyer: Failing Ideals of the Legal Profession 53–62, 87–108 (1993).

most of them frequently, or even typically, exhibit dialogical vices such as lying and other deceptive rhetorical conduct.[56] Contemporary politicians — the rulers — are often inauthentic, fictional, and reality-concealing constructs (of image makers) who engage in rhetorical self-presentation; and instead of integrity they exhibit "adaptability" as their "key virtue," resulting in broken promises and shifting positions.[57] Moreover, the large size of modern states is not conducive to restoring the integrity of individuals in social relationships that have been deformed by the compartmentalization and fragmentation of advanced modernity.[58] As for the electorate — the ruled — their situation is not particularly conducive to the cultivation of virtuous civic engagement. Thus, although voters enjoy the power of the ballot box, "their votes will not be effective unless they are cast for one of those alternatives defined for them by the political elites."[59] And those political elites, who mobilize the electorate for elections and national crises, present them with "only a highly simplified and impoverished account of the issues" using "modes of presentation ... designed to conceal as much as to reveal."[60] As suggested in subsection 1 above, voters like Cash may not only be discouraged from voting, they also have every rational incentive to be "free riders" who may not even bother to do so.

Most fundamentally of all, because the inhabitants in modern liberal democratic states do not share a "large degree of common understanding of practices and institutions" and of "the relationships between goods, rules, and virtues," they are not bound together by the bedrock virtue of

---

56. *See* MACINTYRE, CONFLICTS OF MODERNITY, op. cit., at 125 (discussing "the ethics-of-the-state," which requires conscientiousness and rectitude from dutiful public servants in government bureaucracies, but which permits their "masters" who govern to be "adept in the arts of successful lying and of concealing their responsibility for, for example, acts of brutality" in the course of providing public goods such as law and order and national security, because "they must be prepared to use whatever means are necessary, while making it appear that they only use such means as are generally thought morally acceptable," and intimating that such conduct is not necessarily rare).

57. MacIntyre, *Common Good*, op. cit., at 236, 238, 245, 249.

58. *See id.* at 235–36, 248–49 (discussing the compartmentalization and fragmentation of roles and norms in "the societies of advanced Western modernity" and stressing that now only local and small-scale societies can prevent such compartmentalization and fragmentation and the resulting deformation of social relationships).

59. *Id.* at 236; *See also* MACINTYRE, CONFLICTS OF MODERNITY, op. cit., at 126 (making a similar point).

60. MACINTYRE, RATIONAL ANIMALS, op. cit., at 141–42.

political friendship.[61] Indeed, instead of being based on friendship and "a matter of genuine moral consensus," politics in modern liberal democracies is riven by divisions and, in MacIntyre's memorable phraseology, is tantamount to "civil war carried on by other means."[62] As such, it is primarily a politics of bargaining and compromise among competing and conflicting interests whose power and persuasiveness are largely determined by money, and not a politics of shared deliberation about common goods in which persuasiveness is determined by "standards independent of the desires and interests" of the participants.[63]

B. Economics

MacIntyre considers that the institutional forms of modern politics represent a systematic rejection of the tradition of the virtues and suggests, therefore, that from the standpoint of this tradition "[m]odern systematic politics, whether liberal, conservative, radical or socialist" should itself be rejected.[64] The modern liberal democratic state is of course intimately related to the capitalist, large-scale market economy which it harbors and promotes with varying degrees of state intervention.[65] In addition to being incompatible with the modern political order, then, the tradition of the virtues is also incompatible with the modern economic order.[66] Indeed, in Chapter 5 we examined two shared commitments by which the inhabitants of *Piscopolis* seek to protect their way of life, common goods, politico-ethical commitments, and communitarian *ethos*, as far as possible, from the destructive effects of both orders, while at the same time facilitating any necessary interactions and transactions with the state and the market.[67] And, once again, the experience of local coastal communities

---

61. *See* Chapter 5, notes 178–79 and accompanying text.

62. MacIntyre, After Virtue, op. cit., at 253.

63. MacIntyre, Rational Animals, op. cit., at 131; MacIntyre, Conflicts of Modernity, op. cit., at 177–78. Related, the virtue of patriotism is significantly compromised because loyalty to country and community becomes detached from obedience to government. MacIntyre, After Virtue, op. cit., at 254.

64. MacIntyre, After Virtue, op. cit., at 255.

65. MacIntyre, Conflicts of Modernity, op. cit., at 124, 127–28, 135.

66. *See* MacIntyre, After Virtue, op. cit., at 254–55 (discussing how the tradition of the virtues is "at variance with central features of the modern economic order" and also "involves a rejection of the modern political order").

67. *See* Chapter 5, notes 180–90 and accompanying text.

engaged in share fishing in Denmark demonstrates what can happen in the absence of such protection.[68]

In Section A above we discussed MacIntyre's account of the salient features of the modern political order. We will now consider his account of the salient features of the modern economic order, bearing in mind that there is a synergistic relationship between these two sets of features. The discussion is structured by MacIntyre's observation that the tradition of the virtues is "at variance with central features of the modern economic order and more especially its individualism, its acquisitiveness and its elevation of the values of the market to a central social place."[69]

1. Individualism

The "individualism" of the modern economic order is clearly reflected in the shared assumption of economic actors that anyone engaging in any kind of market transaction (selling labor and skills, investing, using new machines, buying or growing food, etc.) is seeking a bargain that maximizes their individual benefits relative to their individual costs.[70] The type of reasoning that is based on this assumption — a type of reasoning explicated by decision theorists and game theorists — illustrates "the dominant conception of [practical] rationality in the culture of advanced economies," which envisages rational agents as seeking to maximize their preference satisfaction.[71] Such a culture of individualism and such reasoning also clearly reflect and help constitute the dominant conception of the greater common good in modern liberal democracies we examined in Section A.2. It will be recalled that this is an "individualist" conception in which the common good — envisaged as the maximization of opportuni-

---

68. *See* Chapter 5, notes 191–99 and accompanying text.

69. MacIntyre, After Virtue, op. cit., at 254.

70. *See* MacIntyre, Conflicts of Modernity, op. cit., at 184 (describing this shared assumption).

71. *Id.* For MacIntyre's explication of the rules of reasoning involved in seeking to achieve the goal of maximizing benefits relative to costs when everyone else is assumed to be seeking the same, see *id.* at 184–87 (discussing decision theory and game theory). MacIntyre notes that because rational maximizers in the market will also seek to minimize the cost to themselves of sustaining the large, complex national and international institutional frameworks needed to facilitate market transactions, their political goal will be to ensure that others pay those costs indirectly, resulting in increasing inequalities. *Id.* at 187–88.

ties for constrained preference satisfaction — consists in "the summing of the goods pursued by individuals" in an association they regard as instrumental to achieving their individual ends.[72]

2. Acquisitiveness

The character trait of "acquisitiveness," or *pleonexia*, is among those "qualities of mind and character that are most highly valued" in the modern economic order because they "enable some to outdo others in acquisition and in the making of profits." And there may even be a *duty* to exhibit it so that owners of capital, who mobilize managers and workers, can maximize the return on their investment.[73] Presumably, in the case of Cash's fishing crew, such acquisitiveness may also be among Cash's qualities of character especially valued by management, as well as by Cash and other members of the crew (as a quality of effectiveness as opposed to a quality of excellence).[74] In a "culture of acquisitiveness" in which motives are primarily extrinsic and goods of excellence are systematically subordinated to goods of effectiveness, Cash and other crew members are primarily focused on attaining the greatest amount of money possible, perhaps for management and investors (if crew members' wages, or some component of them, are tied to profitability of the catch as incentive), and in any event for themselves. Clearly, this can lead to a vicious circle (the more they acquire, the more they want) that risks corruption of the common goods of the practice as discussed in Chapter 4.[75]

But there is another vicious circle at work in Cash's life too. For the acquisitiveness of those who want to market certain types of consumer goods to Cash and thereby to relieve Cash of his or her wages is fueled by Cash's own vices of acquisitiveness and intemperateness as a consumer, and vice-versa.[76] Indeed, MacIntyre considers that "the social order of capitalism ... miseducates and wrongly directs desire" toward objects

---

72. *See supra* notes 17, 19 and accompanying text; MacIntyre, *Common Good*, op. cit., at 250 (observing that "the conception of the common good presupposed by large-scale so-called free market economies is necessarily an individualist one, although the 'individuals' are sometimes corporate entities").

73. MacINTYRE, CONFLICTS OF MODERNITY, op. cit., at 127.

74. *See* Chapter 4, notes 68, 71–72 and accompanying text.

75. *See* Chapter 4, notes 75–81 and accompanying text.

76. *See* MacINTYRE, RATIONAL ANIMALS, op. cit., at 88 (discussing such mutual vices).

that rational agents as preference maximizers might want but that rational agents seeking to develop their powers and "directed toward the ends of human flourishing" have "no good reason to want;" and it does so especially through "the seductive rhetoric of advertising and the deceptions of marketing."[77]

3. Centrality of Values of the Market and Impact on Practices

With respect to "elevation of the values of the market to a central social place" in the modern economic order, MacIntyre's most recent work acknowledges, and welcomes, the fact that capitalist investment and technological progress have resulted in increasing standards of living[78] and that "[c]ontinuing economic growth in developing markets" over the past

---

77. MacINTYRE, CONFLICTS OF MODERNITY, op. cit., at 108–09. The problem is even deeper and more extensive than MacIntyre appears to suggest. It is not just that such rhetoric and deceptions manipulate consumers as rational preference maximizers into wanting things they have "no good reason to want." Such rhetoric and deceptions do not in fact value economic individualism or respect consumers as such rational agents but instead regard them as "mere carbon-based units." Moreover, the very concept of the rational preference maximizer is to some extent a fiction that is presumably subject to the same sorts of qualifications regarding illusion and various types of unconscious or distorting biases MacIntyre notes as potential obstacles to Neo-Aristotelian practical rationality when discussing education into the virtues necessary for exercise of such rationality. *Id.* at 191–92; *see also* Chapter 2, note 64 and accompanying text. But even assuming that rational preference maximizers can effectively combat such obstacles once they become aware of them, they may still be unable to distinguish effectively, in thought and action, between their perceived short-term interest and their long-term interest in preference satisfaction and to understand that the former may have to be sacrificed or mitigated for the sake of the latter. They are, then, rational in one way and irrational in another. Their inability and this contradiction are rooted both in the natural human tendency to envisage the short-term more easily than the long-term and in the manipulations of the market and politics. By contrast, due to fundamental differences in their practical rationalities, Neo-Aristotelians are likely to be much more successful than such manipulated preference maximizers in moving along a temporal continuum through the creative exercise of imagination, enabling them to find a proper balance between their short-term and long-term interest in flourishing. For further discussion of the differences between these two types of practical rationality, see *infra* notes 130–39 and accompanying text.; Chapter 3, Part IV, Section A.2. I am indebted to Jack Sammons for focusing me on, and encouraging me to think through, these issues. Sammons Email (September 13, 2020) [on file with author].

78. MacINTYRE, CONFLICTS OF MODERNITY, op. cit., at 99–100.

three decades has substantially reduced the percentage of the population in the poorest countries living in the most extreme poverty.[79] But Mac-Intyre also acknowledges, and does *not* welcome, the continuing "limitations and horrors" of "capitalist modernity," including the destruction or marginalization of traditional ways of life, recurring economic crises and mass unemployment, poverty, hunger, and various forms of exclusion resulting from national and global "structures of inequality."[80] This suggests that MacIntyre would affirm his earlier critique of "large-scale so-called free market economies," at least for the most part:

> Such economies are misnamed 'free markets.' They in fact ruthlessly impose market conditions that forcibly deprive many workers of productive work, that condemn parts of the labor force in metropolitan countries and whole societies in less developed areas to irremediable economic deprivation, that enlarge inequalities and divisions of wealth and income, so organizing societies into competing and antagonistic interests. And under such conditions inequality of wealth ensures inequality in access to the sources of both economic and political power.[81]

In addition, of course, the forces of "impersonal capital" and "institutionalized acquisitiveness" can have a destructive effect on productive practices and on the pursuit and preservation of their common goods.[82] These forces can destroy a practice altogether, as occurs for example when production moves from the context of a practice such as a household to a production line in a factory.[83] Another example is when administra-

---

79. *Id.* at 187 (citing a decline from 43 percent to 21 percent during the period from 1990 to 2010).

80. *Id.* at 99–100, 124, 126–27, 133.

81. MacIntyre, *Common Good*, op. cit., at 249. For MacIntyre's critique of the role of academic economists in championing the concept of the rational agent as preference maximizer, in legitimating capitalism and its resulting inequalities, and in failing to predict capitalism's recurrent crises, rooted especially in the narrowness of their education and approach and the resulting inability to understand the larger political, social, and psychological context, see MACINTYRE, CONFLICTS OF MODERNITY, op. cit., at 101–05.

82. MACINTYRE, AFTER VIRTUE, op. cit., at 227–28.

83. *Id.*

tors and managers in an organization, in which workers had previously worked as a team engaged in a "mode of practice" with shared common goods — shared standards, goods, and qualities of excellence — now so completely impose their own ends and standards on the workers, and dictate the means for achieving them, in the interests of greater efficiency, productivity, or profitability, that the workers no longer have primary responsibility for the quality of the end product.[84] Alternatively, these forces may not destroy but seriously weaken a practice when workers (engaged in the core practice) still have primary responsibility for the quality of the end product, but administrators and managers (engaged in the secondary practice focused on the institution) control the ends and means to the extent that extrinsic motives are primary and goods and qualities of excellence are systematically subordinated to goods and qualities of effectiveness, with the attendant moral risk of corrupting the core practice's common goods. We saw an example of this in the case of Cash's fishing crew.[85] The members of Danish fishing crews who had engaged in coastal share fishing but who now work for corporations may be another example, assuming of course that something of the core practice of catching fish still remains in their activities.[86]

On the other hand, sometimes administrators and managers consider it in the best interests of the business or other organization to sustain an existing "mode of practice" and its common goods, or even introduce a new mode of practice and its goods, in their organization in the interests,

---

84. *See* MacIntyre, Conflicts of Modernity, op. cit., at 130–31 (discussing the example of the British Broadcasting Corporation (BBC)), 170 (common goods of excellence of performance, and excellence of product contributing to the life of the community resulting from such excellent performance), 172 (motives of management). Regarding the BBC, to avoid causing Jack Sammons "great disappointment," it is incumbent upon me to mention the BBC self-parody comedy series W1A, which nicely captures the transformation in the culture at the BBC discussed by MacIntyre. As one reviewer observes, "[the show] does indeed reflect reality.... [A]ll those meetings, the layers of middle management, the gobble-digook, the nonsense job titles etc." Sam Wollaston, *W1A review: 'nibling, not biting, satire,'* The Guardian (April 24, 2015), https://www.theguardian.com/tv-and-radio/2015/apr/24/w1a-review-satire-jeremy-clarkson. I am indebted to Jack Sammons for his brilliant, cool suggestion that I refer to the show at this point. Sammons Email (September 13, 2020) [on file with author].

85. *See* Chapter 4, notes 75–81 and accompanying text.

86. *See* Chapter 4, notes 68, 99 and accompanying text; Chapter 5, notes 191–95 and accompanying text.

for example, of improving workmanship and achieving a higher quality product even if it means sacrificing maximum profitability.[87] MacIntyre seems to conclude, however, that "the inexorable pressure to become, not just profitable, but more and more profitable, does in fact result in most workplaces being quite other than [this]."[88]

C. Morality

The features of the modern political and economic orders described above reflect features of the underlying social order and moral order (or disorder) of advanced modernity. According to MacIntyre, "disruptive and transformative social and moral changes in the late middle ages and the early modern world" resulted in an altered understanding of the "moral rules and precepts" of the tradition of the virtues, which had prevailed and flourished in society before these changes. Specifically, the rules and precepts of this tradition "were once at home in, and intelligible in terms of, a context of practical beliefs and of supporting habits of thought, feeling, and action" in which "moral judgments were understood as governed by impersonal standards justified by a shared conception of the human good." But with the loss of this context and justification due to the above changes,

---

87. *See* MacIntyre, Conflicts of Modernity, op. cit., at 130–31, 170–71 (discussing the example of the Japanese automobile industry in which groups of workers, working together as a production team responsible for the entire production process of a car and engaging in shared deliberation and decision-making focused on achieving an excellent product through excellent performance in accordance with standards of excellence, replaced individual workers performing single repeated operations on a production line), 171–72 (discussing the example of the Cummins Engine Company which "[o]ver several decades... subordinated the need to achieve higher levels of profitability to the good of making excellent products, and individuals who worked for the company were expected to serve that common good").

88. *Id.* at 172. In this context we should note the role of business educators such as Geoff Moore, who is now Emeritus Professor of Business Ethics at Durham University's Business School in the United Kingdom and whose MacIntyrean book *Virtue at Work* figures prominently at various points in the present book. *See* Geoff Moore, Virtue at Work: Ethics for Individuals, Managers, and Organizations (2017). I am indebted to Jack Sammons for suggesting the need to bring attention to "the entire industry of business educators who, in various ways, try to reconcile goods of effectiveness with common goods and the virtues they require." Sammons Email (September 13, 2020) [on file with author].

these rules and precepts "had to be understood in a new way and assigned some new status, authority, and justification."[89]

1. Modern Secular Systems of "Morality"

Beginning in the eighteenth century, therefore, moral philosophers have tried to provide such an understanding, each one claiming to have devised a secular system of morality providing impersonal standards with abstract, general precepts regarding duties and obligations that constrain and are universally binding on, and knowable by, individuals as such acting as autonomous agents, irrespective of the particular culture or social order they inhabit. Such "Morality" is considered to be "superior to all other moralities [as] the latest and highest stage in the moral history of humankind," and distinguishable from all other areas of activity, including the religious, legal, political, social, economic, and aesthetic.[90] These efforts have resulted in a set of "rival and incompatible accounts" whose adherents disagree with,

---

89. MACINTYRE, AFTER VIRTUE, op. cit., at ix, xi. *See also* the discussion of MacIntyre's dramatic thought experiment at the beginning of *After Virtue*, *supra* note 1. For recent discussion by MacIntyre explicating the relevant changes, see MACINTYRE, CONFLICTS OF MODERNITY, op. cit., at 89–91 (describing the medieval social and moral order presupposed and promoted in the thought of Thomas Aquinas, in which, for example, both producers selling directly to consumers and merchants acting as middlemen should regard the pursuit of profit for its own sake as unjust and the result of disordered desires, and therefore seek to earn only as much money as is necessary to attain their individual and common goods), 93–99 (using the insights of Karl Marx to describe how the capitalist economy that developed in the intervening centuries transformed this order so that, for example, labor becomes a commodity, capitalists owning the means of production expropriate the unpaid "surplus value" created by workers, although the appearance of legal contractual relations between employers and workers as free individuals disguises this reality, individuals seeking to satisfy their desires under the altruistic constraints of Morality replace "notions ... of an end, a common good, or the natural law," and capitalism produces various "destructive and self-destructive" effects). For MacIntyre's discussion of the twentieth century Thomist revival, see *id.* at 106–10 (explaining that Thomists criticized both capitalism and Marxism for their respective "gross inequalities" and also stressed that "what is amiss with capitalism is not only what it does to the unemployed and the poor, but also what it does to the rich and to better paid workers and managers," especially by imposing types of social relationships that prevent the achievement of common and individual goods, by miseducating and wrongly directing desires, and by encouraging the vice of acquisitiveness). For MacIntyre's related critique of academic economists as the "defenders of capitalism," see *supra* note 81.

90. MACINTYRE, AFTER VIRTUE, op. cit., at ix–x; MACINTYRE, CONFLICTS OF MODERNITY, op. cit., at 65, 115, 118.

and are unable to persuade, one another regarding the justification and content of morality or the resolution of various types of moral dilemmas. The relevant accounts address Kantian "universalizable and exceptionless moral rules and ... inviolable human rights," utilitarian consequentialism, various versions of contractarianism, and (more recently) virtue ethics as well, and they also include several syntheses combining elements selected from among these different approaches.[91] These differing accounts are also resonant with the different views of Justice discussed in Section A.4 above.

2. Dominant Practical Rationality: Constrained Preference Maximization

As we have seen, in this moral context "practical rationality from the standpoint of the dominant economic and political order" envisages rational agents as seeking to maximize satisfaction of their preferences (that is, their desires ordered as a set of preferences),[92] with many of them extending the cost-benefit based reasoning of "rational maximizers" from the economic context to noneconomic contexts, including politics and perhaps even including aspects of family life such as marriage.[93] And, as we have also seen, this dominant conception of practical rationality is complemented by the dominant understanding of the human good as happiness rooted in the satisfaction of individuals' preferences, and by the dominant conception of the common good as the maximization of opportunities for individuals to satisfy these preferences.[94]

Such preference maximization is not necessarily unconstrained, however. In addition to conditional constraints that take the form of important

---

91. MacIntyre, After Virtue, op. cit., at x; MacIntyre, Conflicts of Modernity, op. cit., at 65–67, 116–17, 138. For a useful overview of several of these accounts, see Paul Lewis, Faithful Innovation: The Rule of God and a Christian Practical Wisdom 24–26 (2020) (discussing three schools of ethics, their inherent limitations, and mutual critique: two schools focused on decision-making — the deontological school, including Kantianism, whose adherents "stress our obligation to abide by and act on universal principles," and the teleological school, including utilitarianism, whose adherents "define right and wrong in relation to consequences" — and one school, the aretaic school, including Aristotelianism, focused on the kind of people we are, whose adherents "focus on character traits such as courage, integrity, generosity and, most important, practical wisdom").

92. See supra notes 18, 71 and accompanying text.

93. MacIntyre, Conflicts of Modernity, op. cit., at 135, 183, 186.

94. See supra notes 15–17 and accompanying text.

commitments to others facilitating mutually beneficial cooperation or that inhere in the structure of a particular relationship,[95] rational maximizers are constrained by several different types of social norms, including norms prescribed by the ethics-of-the-market, the ethics-of-the-state, and the law, which "shape many of our desires, attitudes, and expectations."[96] Importantly, they are also constrained by the norms of Morality, which "limit[s] and to some extent civiliz[es] desire" and "unbridled egoism" by "imposing [additional] constraints on the ways in which and the extent to which [individuals] may attempt to satisfy their desires and to further their interests."[97] These moral constraints relate especially to altruistically acting for the good of others, often contrary to self-interest. Moreover, such altruistic moral considerations may also be incorporated into the formation of preferences in the first place in the form of philanthropic preferences.[98] This latter position echoes MacIntyre's earlier claim that "the liberal order" interprets both religiously based moral views that humans should "obey divine law" and secular moral views as "the expression of preferences."[99]

---

95. MACINTYRE, CONFLICTS OF MODERNITY, op. cit., at 186–87, 188.

96. *Id.* at 135. Regarding "ethics," *see further id.* at 124–25 (discussing the ethics-of-the-state and contrasting the ethics of bureaucratic public servants which, for example, prescribe conscientious performance of duties and prohibit favoritism and corruption, with the ethics of those who govern, which, for example, sometimes permit lying, the concealment of brutality, and rationalizing from the purported consequences of acting otherwise), 127–28 (discussing the ethics-of-the-market, including an emphasis upon "trustworthiness and reliability in promise-keeping"), 128 (observing that both types of ethics "combine maximizing injunctions with injunctions to respect certain rules without regard for the consequences," are required for the effective functioning of the modern state and of national and international markets, and "are in an important way parodies of ethics"). Regarding law, *see further id.* at 135 (observing that the law provides individuals "with some security" when they "deal with each another as rational agents concerned to maximize their own preference satisfaction competitively" in the market, in politics, and even their private lives, because it "provides a stable framework within which they can engage with others, whether as winners or as the more numerous losers," by proscribing the use of fraud and force "to pursue the ends of competitive success" and by making behavior more predictable through legal requirements regarding contracts).

97. *Id.* at 98, 129, 135–36.

98. *Id.* at 98, 115, 184, 188.

99. ALASDAIR MACINTYRE, WHOSE JUSTICE? WHICH RATIONALITY? 342–43 (1988).

3. The Expressivist Critique of "Morality"

Although biology and history may account for a certain degree of consensus in both preferences and constraining normative commitments, the
problem remains of how rational preference maximizers should act in the
range of disagreement.[100] Within this range, what specific norms of Morality inform their moral judgments about whether or not to act to satisfy a
particular desire, and thus operate as moral constraints? How is a selection
to be made from among the competing "rival and incompatible accounts"
of morality we enumerated in subsection 1 above? According to the "expressivist" critique of Morality, the selection will be made on the basis
of "commitments, attitudes, concerns, and feelings" that are "prerational"
and rooted in underlying psychological states of mind.[101] Moreover, this is
true of both moral philosophers (who adhere consistently to their favored
account in attempting to resolve "the inconsistencies in moral discourse"
and moral dilemmas) and everyday moral agents in political and private
life (whose commitments tend to oscillate between more definite versions
of a rule, such as an injunction never to lie or never to torture, and more
indefinite versions subject to exception), however sharp or shrill the disagreements among them may be, and however firm their conviction that
their own moral judgments are correct and others' judgments incorrect.[102]

---

100. *See* MacIntyre, Conflicts of Modernity, op. cit., at 20–21 (discussing the
views of Alan Gibbard).

101. *Id.* at 22–23, 41–42, 67, 138–41. Expressivism applies the same critique, of course,
to religiously-based moral views. *See* MacIntyre, Whose Justice?, op. cit., at 342–43 (referring to emotivism). For MacIntyre's views on how the expressivist critique is incomplete
and can be supplemented and strengthened to mount an even stronger challenge to Morality and Neo-Aristotelianism as well, see MacIntyre, Conflicts of Modernity, op. cit.,
at 31–33, 42–48. For MacIntyre's discussion of emotivism as the precursor to expressivism,
see *id.* at 17–19.

102. *Id.* at 65–68, 116–17, 119. One should note, too, that even if recognition of "multiple rationalities," conditioning the appropriate moral response on the particular situa-
tional or relational context in question, may narrow the range of disagreement, it does not
eliminate it. Regarding the recent trend toward recognizing multiple rationalities, see, for
example, Sigal Samuel, *Is rationality overrated?*, Vox (January 20, 2020) (discussing attempts
to recapture the term "rationality" from behavioral economists and rehabilitate an earlier,
capacious understanding of the term that includes reasonableness, as well as the suggestion
that "rationality ... takes different forms in different times, cultures, and situations"), https://
www.vox.com/future-perfect/2020/1/20/21068423/rationality-behavioral-economics-psy
chology-reasonable-decisions.

In the absence of genuinely convincing reasons for choosing one moral position over another, however, there is a real risk of making the choice that rationalizes satisfaction of particular desires and, unable to offer genuinely convincing reasons which succeed in persuading others, of seeking instead to compel them into accepting one's point of view through manipulation, overt coercion, or deception, as modern politics amply demonstrates.[103] On this point MacIntyre seems equally scathing in his criticism of liberalism and contemporary conservatism. Thus, not only is each of them committed in its own way to a corrosive individualism — liberalism through its "neutral[ity] as between rival conceptions of the human good" and conservatism through "[i]ts commitment to a way of life structured by a free market economy." In addition, whereas liberalism "by permissive legal enactments has tried to use the power of the modern state to transform social relationships," contemporary conservatism "by prohibitive legal enactments now tries to use that same power for its own coercive purposes."[104] Indeed, "conservative moralists, with their inflated and self-righteous unironic rhetoric" have become "one more stock character in the scripted conversations of the ruling elites of advanced modernity."[105]

As illustrated by the examples of lying and torture discussed above, many disagreements tend to involve conflict between "certain conceptions of utility" and "certain conceptions of … individual human rights" and the question "whether or not some violation of this or that right can be justified, if the consequences of that violation for the utility of some set of individuals are taken into account."[106] Once again, MacIntyre acknowledges, and welcomes, the historical role of both types of conceptions in "securing the rights of deprived and oppressed individuals and groups" and in "securing benefits for those who badly needed them, in the field of public health, for example," but he also regards both notions, of utility and

---

103. For discussion of these risks, see Clayton, *Alasdair MacIntyre*, op. cit. (Section 3 on "The Current Moral Disorder and Its Consequences," Section 4 on "The Absence of Meaningful Moral Choices," Section 5 on "Emotivism and Manipulative Social Relations," and Section 7 on "Politics in a World Without Morality").

104. MacIntyre, After Virtue, op. cit., at xiv–xv.

105. *Id.* at xv. The other "notable characters in the cultural dramas of modernity" conducing to manipulative social relations include the therapist, the corporate manager, and the rich aesthete. *Id.* at xv, 23–31.

106. MacIntyre, Conflicts of Modernity, op. cit., at 77.

of a human right, as philosophical fictions.[107] And more generally, then, he agrees with the expressivist critique of Morality. Thus, he considers that

> The dominant shared culture of moral modernity is, on the one hand, one whose assertive and expressive judgments and arguments seem to be just what expressivism says that they are, yet, on the other, also one in which agents are unable to recognize or acknowledge this fact about themselves. So the recurrent rejections of expressivism, not just by academic philosophers but by everyday moral agents, may themselves be an important symptom of that culture's moral condition.[108]

MacIntyre also considers, of course, that Thomistic Aristotelianism provides a moral account that is both superior to Morality and in principle not vulnerable to the same expressivist critique, because it is rooted in "truths concerning matters of fact."[109] Consequently, it provides "better

---

107. *Id.* at 77–78. Specifically, MacIntyre claims that '[t]he notion of utility maximization as a freestanding notion that by itself provides guidance for action is a philosophical fiction" because, whether we conceive of utility in terms of maximizing pleasure and minimizing pain (the earlier view) or in terms of maximizing preference satisfaction (the more recent view), our conception "depends on our prior formation and commitments." *Id.* at 77. Regarding human rights, MacIntyre claims that, although there are indeed "unconditional prohibitions," they cannot be justified by "appeal[ing] to human rights, understood as rights attaching to each and every human individual qua human individual" because "there are no sound arguments for asserting the existence of such rights." *Id.* at 77–78. MacIntyre's claim regarding human rights may seem puzzling to say the least, given that the natural law tradition extends over more than two millennia, and even in classical natural law thinking subjective rights were necessarily implied, and indeed were sometimes explicitly recognized. On the other hand, MacIntyre refers here to identifying the particular "argumentative failure" of specific natural rights theorists from the eighteenth century to the twentieth, and therefore presumably considers that only modern natural rights theories lack "sound arguments" justifying them. This is consistent with his claim, discussed below, regarding the superior moral account and argumentative resources of Thomistic Aristotelianism. For a good discussion of the various theories of "natural rights" or "human rights," see generally DAN EDELSTEIN, ON THE SPIRIT OF RIGHTS (2018).
108. MACINTYRE, CONFLICTS OF MODERNITY, op. cit., at 68.
109. *Id.* at 98–99, 114, 140. *See also id.* at 17–35 (detailing differences between expressivist and Neo-Aristotelian accounts of the terms "good," "goods," "good reasons," and of the rank ordering of goods); Chapter 2, note 39 and accompanying text (discussing these differences).

arguments for doing what justice and the common good require" (and for the moral achievements mentioned above, for example) than appeals to utility or human rights,[110] and better arguments for seeking the good of others than altruism.[111]

II. Pursuing a *Piscopolis*-Like Way of Life in the Modern Liberal Democratic State

What practical conclusions should we draw from the MacIntyrean accounts of life in the imagined fishing village of *Piscopolis* in Chapter 5 and of the salient features of the modern liberal democratic state in Part I above? Specifically, to what extent, and in what social contexts, can we still pursue a *Piscopolis*-like way of life despite inhabiting the dominant political, economic, and moral environment of the modern liberal democratic state and being susceptible to the influence of the individualist *ethos* promoted by that environment? Can we create or discover, and also protect, particular social contexts that provide a *Piscopolis*-like Thomistic Aristotelian political, economic, and moral environment and the communitarian *ethos* it nurtures — or at least important elements of such an environment and *ethos*? To what extent, then, and in what social contexts, can we still flourish and achieve our own good by becoming people of virtue who care

---

110. MacIntyre, Conflicts of Modernity, op. cit., at 78.

111. *See* MacIntyre, Rational Animals, op. cit., at 160 (suggesting that altruism or self-sacrifice may still be a vice involving some form or elements of egoism and that our moral education should instead "transform and integrate [egoistic and altruistic impulses and desires] into an inclination towards both the common good and our individual goods, so that we become . . . those whose passions and inclinations are directed to what is both our good and the good of others").

Paul Lewis proposes a more holistic "model of the moral life" than any of the accounts of Morality, one with three dimensions — the dimension of "character" and the dimension of "conduct" or decision-making, both rooted in the dimension of "moral vision." Lewis, Faithful Innovation, op. cit., at 27–28. *See also id.* at 28–32 (discussing practical reasoning and identifying important questions and sources that can inform moral deliberation within the model), 39–53 (giving a synthetic account of practical wisdom). While Lewis uses this model to provide a framework supporting his own account of Christian ethics and Christian practical wisdom (see especially Parts 2 and 3 of his book), arguably the model could also provide a framework supporting MacIntyre's account of Thomistic Aristotelianism. Any differences between the operation of the model in Lewis's account and in MacIntyre's account could presumably be resolved in theory through application of the MacIntyrean dialectic discussed in Chapter 5, notes 30–32 and accompanying text.

about and pursue the common good in all our practices, including the practice of politics, and share the kinds of politico-ethical commitments shared by Drew and the other inhabitants of *Piscopolis*?

A. MacIntyre's Evolving Understanding of Prospects

MacIntyre's answers to such questions and resulting understanding of prospects for pursuing a *Piscopolis*-like way of life in the modern liberal democratic state have evolved considerably over the several decades since the original publication of *After Virtue* in 1981. Although it is clear from the development of MacIntyre's thinking during this time that he regards the prospects for living such a life to be greater than he first supposed, his most recent work also makes clear the challenges still faced by those seeking to do so:

> [T]he dominant culture ... is inimical to those relationships that sustain and are sustained by the exercise of the virtues.... The exploitative structures of both free market and state capitalism make it often difficult and sometimes impossible to achieve the goods of the workplace through excellent work. The political structures of modern states that exclude most citizens from participation in extended and informed deliberation on issues of crucial importance to their lives make it often difficult and sometimes impossible to achieve the goods of local community. The influence of Morality in normative and evaluative thinking makes it often difficult and sometimes impossible for the claims of the virtues to be understood, let alone acknowledged in our common lives. So too the culture that entertains and distracts makes it often difficult and sometimes impossible to develop those imaginative powers that are of the first importance for living the life of the virtues. We therefore have to live *against* the cultural grain, just as we have to learn to act as economic, political, and moral antagonists of the dominant order.[112]

How, then, can we "live *against* the cultural grain" and "learn to act as economic, political, and moral antagonists of the dominant order"?

---

112. MacIntyre, Conflicts of Modernity, op. cit., at 237–38.

1. Complete Local Communities

One consistent theme in MacIntyre's work has been that we can seek to live a *Piscopolis*-like way of life by finding, or by founding, more or less complete local communities like *Piscopolis*, which are as insulated as possible from the dominant political, economic, and moral environment of the liberal democratic state and its individualist *ethos*. Thus, MacIntyre famously ends *After Virtue* by drawing a parallel between our own times in the West and the decline of the Roman Empire into the Dark Ages, except that "[t]his time ... the barbarians are not waiting beyond the frontiers; they have already been governing us for quite some time," although we do not realize it.[113] And he says that "[w]hat matters at this stage is the construction of local forms of community within which civility and the intellectual and moral life can be sustained through the new dark ages which are already upon us," and that "[w]e are waiting ... for another — doubtless very different — St. Benedict."[114]

This focus on more or less complete local communities continues in MacIntyre's subsequent works,[115] culminating vividly in his most recent work with the depiction of local communities such as the Danish fishing community of Thorupstrand which we considered in Section G of Chapter 5.[116] MacIntyre has contrasted the "rational political justification" for the authority of such communities, and resulting basis for "rational allegiance" to them, with the lack of any such rational justification and basis for such

---

113. MacIntyre, After Virtue, op. cit., at 263.

114. *Id.*

115. *See, e.g.*, MacIntyre, *Common Good*, op. cit., at 240–41, 247–50 (describing the characteristics of small-scale *polis*-like societies in which "individuals are able through practice to learn about their individual and common goods"); MacIntyre, Rational Animals, op. cit., at 130–31, 135 (identifying "some form of local community within which the activities of families, workplaces, schools, clinics, clubs dedicated to debate and clubs dedicated to games and sports, and religious congregations may all find a place" as the form of association intermediate between the nation-state and the family "whose common good is to be both served and sustained by the virtues of acknowledged dependence"), 143–46 (recommending comparative study of both good and bad examples of local community, including the history of New England fishing communities and Welsh mining communities, Irish farming cooperatives, Mayan towns, and ancient city states, and discussing several important characteristics of such local communities).

116. MacIntyre, Conflicts of Modernity, op. cit., at 178–80, 182. *See also id.* at 181 (discussing the implementation of "a politics of common goods" by the almost four thousand inhabitants of the *favela* (slum) of Monte Azul in São Paulo, Brazil).

rational allegiance to the modern state.[117] MacIntyre's identification of four sets of characteristics of such communities that are critical in this respect is deferred to subsection 2 below. MacIntyre's subsequent works illustrate his evolving understanding of prospects for pursuing a *Piscopolis*-like way of life in the modern liberal democratic state by acknowledging that existing instances of this type of local community may already possess important features of a Thomistic Aristotelian-based *polis* life to a greater extent than we might realize.[118] The Danish fishing village of Thorupstrand is a good example. As we saw, MacIntyre considers that the best way to understand what the Thorupstrand fishing community did is in Thomistic Aristotelian terms even though the members of this community did not explicitly think of themselves in this way.[119]

2. Partial Local Communities and Particular Local Practices

The gradual development of a second theme in MacIntyre's work also illustrates his evolving understanding of the prospects for pursuing a *Pis-*

---

117. *See* MacIntyre, *Common Good*, op. cit., at 243 (asserting that because modern states are "the political expression of societies of deformed and fragmented practical rationality" and therefore "the common good of communal political learning" with respect to "those questions that most need to be asked" about the rational ordering of activities is absent from their politics, such states "cannot advance any justifiable claim to the allegiance of their members"), 246–51 (describing the characteristics of small-scale societies forming a "political community that deserves our rational allegiance" because "there is a possibility of rational political justification, and with it a rational politics" in which "individuals [are] able to learn about their individual and common goods"). *See also* MacIntyre, Conflicts of Modernity, op. cit., at 125–27 (questioning theoretical claims seeking to justify and legitimate the authority and powers of the modern state), 176–78 (contrasting the Aristotelian character of the politics of local communities focused on common goods with the politics of the modern state).

118. *See, e.g.,* MacIntyre, Rational Animals, op. cit., at 144:

> What extended comparative study of the varying characteristics of communities that embody networks of giving and receiving may teach us is how better to identify what relationships of the relevant kinds of giving and receiving already exist in our own local community and how perhaps to a greater extent than we have realized there is already a degree of shared recognition of the common good.

Id.

119. *See* Chapter 5, note 198 and accompanying text. The Brazilian *favela* of Monte Azul, discussed *supra* note 116, is another example. MacIntyre, Conflicts of Modernity, op. cit., at 181–82.

copolis-like way of life in the modern liberal democratic state. This is the notion that we can seek to live such a life in existing partial local communities and particular local practices that already possess important *Piscopolis*-like characteristics. This theme is somewhat muted in *After Virtue*, despite the explication and analysis in that book of the basic concepts relevant to a proper understanding of practices. Thus, MacIntyre claims that practices and their internal goods, or goods of excellence, "have ... been removed to the margins of social and cultural life."[120] In his subsequent works, however, MacIntyre seems to retreat from this somewhat stark position and to recognize that existing partial local communities and particular local practices, which have various *polis* characteristics, may play a more central role in contemporary society than he had recognized in *After Virtue*.

Already in his partial response to critics in 1994, MacIntyre conceded his previous lack of attention to "productive crafts such as farming and fishing, architecture and construction."[121] Just a few years later, when writing about the "shared practical understanding of the relationships between goods, rules, and virtues" that is a characteristic of his ideal, local *polis* community,[122] MacIntyre stated that

> This type of shared understanding is one familiar to most of us in a variety of local social contexts. We rely on it in many of the everyday enterprises of family and household life, in schools, in neighborhoods, in parishes, on farms, in fishing crews and in other workplaces, and, that is to say, in all those practices and projects in which immediate decision-making has to presuppose rationally justifiable answers to such questions as 'How does my good relate to the good of others engaged in this enterprise?' and 'How does the good to be achieved through this enterprise relate to the other goods of my and their lives?' Where that understanding is absent, is indeed excluded,

---

120. MacIntyre, After Virtue, op. cit., at 227.

121. Alasdair MacIntyre, *A Partial Response to My Critics, in* After MacIntyre: Critical Perspectives on the Work of Alasdair MacIntyre 284 (John Horton & Susan Mendus, eds., 1994).

122. For earlier reference to the same formulation of this characteristic in *Piscopolis*, see Chapter 5, notes 10, 153 and accompanying text. For detailed discussion of the various aspects of this characteristic in *Piscopolis*, see Part II, Sections A–F of Chapter 5.

is in the activities that have come to be labeled 'politics' in the contemporary meaning of that term.[123]

Related, when calling for comparative studies of good and bad historical examples of more or less complete local communities with a view to learning more about "networks of giving and receiving," MacIntyre seems to speak in general terms applicable not only to existing complete local communities but to partial local communities and particular practices as well. Thus, he considers that such comparative studies of historical communities and their varying characteristics

> [W]ill bring home to us … both the variety of social forms within which networks of giving and receiving can be institutionalized and the variety of ways in which such networks can be sustained and strengthened or weakened and destroyed [and] may teach us … how better to identify what relationships of the relevant kinds of giving and receiving already exist in our own local community and how perhaps to a greater extent than we have realized there is already a degree of shared recognition of the common good.[124]

---

123. MacIntyre, *Common Good*, op. cit., at 248.

124. MACINTYRE, RATIONAL ANIMALS, op. cit., at 143–44. The application of the general language in this passage to existing partial local communities and particular local practices as well as more or less complete local communities is confirmed by extensive use of the first person singular and first person plural in many of the quotations reproduced from RATIONAL ANIMALS in the main text or the notes in Sections C, E, and F of Chapter 5, thereby arguably referring to our own varied circumstances in the modern state and not just to an abstract hypothetical "I" or "We" or the situation of the inhabitants of an ideal more or less complete local community such as *Piscopolis* (although we used the quotations in Chapter 5 for this last purpose). Also instructive on this point is MacIntyre's acknowledgement that his statement "that the practices of giving and receiving informed by particular just generosity are primarily exercised towards other members of our own community" may be misleading because "we are often members of more than one community and … may find a place within more than one network of giving and receiving" and also "we move in and out of communities," and his resulting instruction that "[i]f therefore from now on I continue for simplicity's sake to speak of *the* community or network to which someone belongs, the reader should supply the missing arm of the disjunctions: 'community or communities,' 'network or networks.'" MACINTYRE, RATIONAL ANIMALS, *supra*, at 122–23.

Similarly, in discussing various characteristics of political participation and deliberation — in other words, various characteristics of political conversation — in his ideal, local *polis* community,[125] MacIntyre explains that

> Once again I am not describing something alien to everyday experience. This is a kind of deliberative participation familiar in many local enterprises through which local community is realized. What is less familiar is the claim that these local arenas are now the only places where political community can be constructed, a political community very much at odds with the politics of the nation-state.[126]

And in discussing other characteristics, reflecting the subordination of "economic considerations … to social and moral considerations" in ideal, more or less complete local communities, and the related insulation and protection of such communities from outside market forces as well as their resistance to "the goals of a consumer society,"[127] MacIntyre acknowledges

> [T]he extent to which these norms are to some extent already accepted in a variety of those settings — households, workplaces, schools, parishes — in which resistance to the goals and norms of a consumer society is recurrently generated. And, where such resistance is found, it is characteristically within groups whose social relationships are those of giving and receiving.[128]

In light of the explicit references to the politics and economics of the modern state in the above passages discussing these four sets of characteristics, perhaps unsurprisingly MacIntyre seems to suggest that even partial

---

125. For identification of the relevant characteristics, see Section F of Chapter 5, especially notes 160–64 and accompanying text (discussing these characteristics of political conversation in *Piscopolis*).

126. MacIntyre, *Common Good*, op. cit., at 248. *C.f.* Anthony Kronman, *Living in the Law*, 54 U. Chi. L. Rev. 835, 858–61 (1987) (explaining that "[i]n any given community, politics is the business of attending to the community's overall well-being" and includes "the administration of many private organizations — universities, foundations, and profitmaking corporations — as well as the management of cities, states, and nations").

127. For identification of the relevant characteristics, see Chapter 5, notes 113–16 and accompanying text (discussing these characteristics of *Piscopolis*).

128. MacIntyre, Rational Animals, op. cit., at 145.

communities and particular local practices with such characteristics offer the possibility of rational political justification and rational politics that is lacking in the modern state.[129]

3. Neo-Aristotelian Practical Rationality in Contemporary Society

MacIntyre's most recent work continues this focus on the pursuit and achievement of common goods in existing partial local communities and particular local practices, including the "practices of families, workplaces, schools, clinics, theatres, [and] sports."[130] In addition, however, MacIntyre further develops a third theme, related to the necessary Neo-Aristotelian practical reasoning by rational agents. This theme focuses on the nature of such practical reasoning, the contrast between such practical reasoning and the dominant practical rationality, and the incoherence, tensions, and fractures to which these two types of practical reasoning give rise in members of contemporary society. To begin with, then, MacIntyre encourages Thomistic Aristotelians to answer questions posed by individuals "about how they should understand and evaluate their situation" in contemporary society by

> [I]nviting those with whom they speak to recognize and reflect upon the extent to which in their thinking and acting in families and households, in schools, and in workplaces they already presuppose the truth of some key Aristotelian and Thomistic claims concerning individual and common goods. For that recognition provides a starting point for further enquiry.[131]

As the emphasis upon "recognition" in the above passage suggests, MacIntyre considers that, just as seems to be the case with the inhabitants of the Danish fishing village of Thorupstrand, members of contemporary society in partial local communities and particular local practices may

---

129. *See* MacIntyre, *Common Good*, op. cit., at 247–50 (discussing various such characteristics and their relation to rational political justification and rational politics).

130. MACINTYRE, CONFLICTS OF MODERNITY, op. cit., at 110. *See id.* at 38, 49–52, 110, 169–75 (discussing such communities and practices).

131. *Id.* at 175–76.

have "an often inexplicit and unacknowledged commitment to reasoning in Aristotelian and even Thomistic terms about common goods"[132] and to the related notion of "happiness," according to which they "desire and… act as one has good reason to desire and act" because they are developing and educating their "physical, moral, aesthetic, and intellectual [powers]… toward achieving the ends of a rational agent," in other words toward human flourishing.[133] It is clear, then, that the invitation in the above passage and the "further enquiry" to which it may lead is actually an effort at consciousness raising.

Specifically, it is an effort to raise consciousness about three things. First, it is an effort to help everyday rational agents (that is, "plain persons") "who find themselves in family, school, and workplace directed toward common goods, qua family member, qua student or teacher, qua productive worker, deliberating with others as to how in this particular set of circumstances here and now to act so as to achieve the common good of this particular enterprise," to see that this is in fact what they are doing if they are not yet consciously aware of it.[134]

Second, it is an effort to help such everyday rational agents understand that whereas their own Neo-Aristotelian practical rationality in family, school, or workplace (and presumably other social contexts of practice as well) involves shared deliberation with others about the achievement of common goods, for those exhibiting the dominant practical rationality of constrained preference maximization "family, school, or workplace are milieus in which they have to find their own way forward as individuals under the constraints of their social relationships and of the institutionally imposed routines of [those milieus]."[135] And it is also an effort to

---

132. *Id.* at 204. *See also id.* at 167 (referring to everyday agents "thinking and acting in Aristotelian and Thomistic terms … systematically at odds with those of the dominant culture that they inhabit, commonly without recognizing this").

133. *Id.* at 201–02. MacIntyre does not at this point in the book explicitly mention human flourishing but it would seem from his account of Aristotle's "core conception of human flourishing," which includes exercise of the powers he mentions here, that this is what he intends. *Id.* at 28–29. *See also* Chapter 2, notes 109–10 and accompanying text (discussing MacIntyre's account of Aristotle's "core conception of human flourishing"). Regarding Thorupstrand, see *supra* note 119 and accompanying text; Chapter 5, note 198 and accompanying text.

134. MacIntyre, Conflicts of Modernity, op. cit., at 166–67, 174.

135. *Id.* at 174.

help them understand several additional differences related to this basic difference:

- Whereas Neo-Aristotelians presuppose in their practical reasoning "that there are standards independent of our feelings, attitudes, and choices which determine what is and what is not good [to desire] and that rationality requires an acknowledgment of the authority of those standards," rational preference maximizers presuppose in their practical reasoning that any standards guiding their choices and expression of their desires depend on their own acknowledgment of such standards as autonomous agents, and that "their ability to maximize the satisfaction of their preferences and their need to bargain and negotiate with others will depend in key part on their power, their income and wealth, and the place in the social structure in and from which their uses of power and money impact on others;"[136]
- Whereas Neo-Aristotelians "discover[] ... that it is only through directing themselves toward the achievement of common goods that they are able to direct themselves toward the achievement of their own good qua individual" through the rank ordering in their lives of the common and individual goods they acknowledge, rational preference maximizers who "pursue only their own individual goods ... discover that the onus has been placed on them to find for themselves, if they can, motivating reasons for setting themselves to succeed or fail as someone of this particular age group, social class, occupation, and income;"[137]
- Whereas Neo-Aristotelians "are constituted as rational agents in and through their shared deliberations with others concerning the common goods ... they share with those others and their deliberations as to how to give a due place to each good in their individual lives," rational preference maximizers "are constituted as rational agents by their learning first how to arrive at a coherent and relevant set of preferences and then how to implement those preferences in the social world;"[138] and

136. *Id.* at 134, 174–75, 190.
137. *Id.* at 175.
138. *Id.*

- Whereas Neo-Aristotelians "understand themselves as agents some of whose key social relationships are constitutive of their identity as agents," rational preference maximizers "understand themselves as individuals qua individuals whose social relationships are contingent features of their situation, to be evaluated by how far they contribute to the satisfaction of their preferences."[139]

Third, it is an effort to help everyday rational agents in contemporary society understand how so many of us are living "double" or "divided" or "fracture[d]" or "compartmentalized" and "incoherent" lives to the extent we oscillate with "flexibility" not only within constrained preference maximization — for example, "between utilitarian and Kantian arguments" — but more importantly, between this dominant mode of practical rationality in some aspects of our lives and the Neo-Aristotelian mode of practical rationality in other aspects of our lives.[140] But, echoing the passage reproduced at the beginning of this Section, MacIntyre also wants us to understand how challenging it can be in this fragmented context to sustain our ability to continue "thinking and acting in Aristotelian and Thomistic terms" even after we become aware that we are doing so. Thus, everyday rational agents ("plain persons")

[I]nhabit a social world structured to some large degree by the institutions of state, market, and Morality and find themselves in social relationships shaped directly and indirectly by these. It is mostly taken for granted that what they want is what the dominant social institutions have influenced them to want and the practical thinking of those others with whom they engage is for the most part informed by the ethics-of-the-state, the ethics-of-the market, and the norms of Morality. So they continually encounter representations of themselves as individuals envisaged as the institutions of state, market, and Morality envisage them, individuals open to being moved either by other-disregarding competitive ambition and acquisitiveness or

---

139. *Id.* For additional, related differences between these two types of practical rationality, see Chapter 3, Part IV, Section A.2.

140. MacIntyre, Conflicts of Modernity, op. cit., at 166–67, 175, 182–83, 188–89, 190, 202, 204.

by an at least constraining and sometimes self-disregarding care and respect for others.[141]

As MacIntyre suggests, it is vital to be aware of the fracture this represents in order to acquire "the self-knowledge that rational agents need, if they are to judge rightly"[142] and, it should be added, so that they can embrace the kind of shared protective commitments discussed in Section G of Chapter 5 with reference to *Piscopolis*. And this brings us back to fishing crew member Cash and the problem of the moral risk of corrupting the common goods of practices.[143] In Cash's fishing crew the goods of excellence of the practice of catching fish are subordinated to goods of effectiveness. In this perspective, then, Cash appears to be a rational preference maximizer.[144] However, even in Cash's case, we saw at least some degree of commitment, albeit fragile, to the common goods of the practice of catching fish. And in this perspective, Cash also appears to be a Neo-Aristotelian practical reasoner.[145] So here we seem to have an instance of both modes of practical rationality being exhibited by the same rational agent, not in separate aspects of his or her life but in the very same aspect. And as we noted earlier in the Chapter, communities of practice exist on a spectrum of robustness of concern for and commitment to the common goods of the practice, with the systematic subordination of goods and qualities of effectiveness to goods and qualities of excellence at one end and with the converse at the other end.[146] Their place on this spectrum will presumably determine the extent to which practitioners of a practice—both those practitioners engaged in a core practice and management engaged in a secondary practice of making and sustaining the institution within

141. *Id.* at 166–67.
142. *Id.* at 167.
143. *See* Part IV, Section C of Chapter 3 for general discussion of this moral risk.
144. *See* MacIntyre, Conflicts of Modernity, op. cit., at 179 (discussing how following the privatization of fishing quotas by the Danish state in 2006, those who had previously engaged in coastal share fishing would now become employed by corporations and "[a] society that had valued common goods would become a society of individual preference maximizers and profit maximizers," quoted in Chapter 5, note 193 and accompanying text.).
145. *See* Chapter 4, notes 70–74 and accompanying text.
146. For this earlier discussion, see *supra* note 34 and accompanying text.

a "practice-institution combination" business organization — exhibit each type of practical rationality in their practice-related activities.

B. Professional Poleis: Toward Juropolis — The Fishing Village of the Law

This Section will develop a fourth theme — a theme that it seems Mac-Intyre himself has not yet explicitly addressed. Thus, the explicit concern in Section A above has been with local communities and practices, focusing on more or less complete local communities possessing the characteristics of an ideal *polis* such as *Piscopolis*, or on partial local communities and particular local practices that display important *polis*-like characteristics, even though they are not part of a broader local community like *Piscopolis*. We will now explore the claim that the self-regulated professions — for example, the legal and medical professions — can be viewed as professional *poleis*, analogous to a local *polis* community like *Piscopolis*, within which it is possible to pursue a *Piscopolis*-like way of life and possess corresponding politico-ethical commitments, even though they are not local and indeed may be very large, even national in scale.[147]

The premises justifying this claim are twofold. First, the inhabitants of *Piscopolis* and the inhabitants of self-regulated professional *poleis* have a strong sense of identity rooted in the political, economic, and moral environment of the particular *polis* and the communitarian *ethos* it nurtures — local village identity in the case of *Piscopolis* and professional identity in the case of the professions. Indeed, we commonly say that a doctor or a lawyer, for example, has a distinctive "professional identity."[148] Of course, members of the professions usually do in fact practice their profession in

---

147. MacIntyre does gesture in the direction of a large scale industry in his discussion of the Japanese and American automobile industries. MACINTYRE, CONFLICTS OF MODERNITY, op. cit., at 130–32, 170–72. And others have claimed that a practice can be national in scale. For an early, pioneering example of such a claim made with regard to the legal profession, see Timothy W. Floyd, *The Practice of Law as a Vocation or Calling*, 66 FORDHAM L. REV. 1405, 1419 & n51 (1998) (claiming that despite its large size and heterogeneity, the modern American legal profession satisfies MacIntyre's definition of a practice).

148. For an in-depth exploration of professional identity, see *Educational Interventions to Cultivate Professional Identity in Law Students: A Symposium of the Mercer Law Review*, 68 MERCER L. REV. 579, 579–875 (2017) (exploring various aspects of professional identity formation in general, and the process of professional identity formation in several different professional fields in particular, including law, medicine, the ministry, and the military).

some particular locality and increasingly, moreover, within a particular professional sub-specialty. While these contingencies may intensify their sense of professional identity and modulate it in a particular key, arguably the basic melody remains the same for all members of the profession wherever they are and whatever they do. Arguably, too, those served by the professions can also be regarded as inhabitants of the professional *poleis* to the extent — in the case of the legal and medical professions, for example — they identify themselves as clients, or more broadly as subjects of the legal system who enjoy rights and owe duties under human law; or as patients, or more broadly as physical beings who enjoy health and well-being, and face threats to their health and well-being, under natural laws. In this perspective, then, the inhabitants of the various professional *poleis* are inhabitants of the liberal democratic state combining and acting in a distinctive capacity. Thus, the professional *poleis* represent liberal democratic society, or particular elements of this society, viewed through a particular lens.

Second, and related, the jurisdictional boundary represented by the ability of a profession to self-regulate is functionally like the geographical and sociological boundary secured by the protective commitments of a local community such as *Piscopolis*. In principle (and we should emphasize "in principle") it enables the inhabitants of these professional *poleis* to maintain their own distinctive identity and limit the destructive impact of the dominant political, economic, and moral environment of the modern liberal democratic state, which they also inhabit, and their susceptibility to the individualist *ethos* promoted by that environment. Of course, it is another question whether and to what extent such a professional *polis* does limit this impact and maintain this identity. Indeed, if MacIntyre and those of us involved in professional education have the story right, this is one of the central challenges currently facing the self-regulated professions and their *poleis*.

In Chapter 7 we will explore this fourth theme by focusing on the legal *polis*, which we will call *Juropolis*, and by considering whether members of the legal profession have the same sorts of shared commitments as Drew and the other inhabitants of *Piscopolis*. To keep the discussion manageable, the focus will be on *Juropolis* as it manifests in the United States. The exploration in Chapter 7 is intended to be illustrative, in two senses. First, although focusing on the legal profession, it is intended to illustrate an approach and methodology that can be applied to any national, self-regu-

lated profession, and indeed to any local social context with *polis* characteristics, in which we can pursue a *Piscopolis*-like way of life and thus "live
against the cultural grain" and "learn to act as economic, political, and
moral antagonists of the dominant order."[149] Second, although our focus
is only on the legal profession, we will not examine each one of the legal
profession's distinct craft communities engaged in their distinct practices
to the same extent — as we will see, there are at least four such distinct
communities and practices — nor will we even examine in detail every
aspect of the two such communities and practices (practicing lawyers and
legal educators) to which we will direct most of our attention. The exploration is intended, then, less as a comprehensive and exhaustive analysis of
the legal *polis* and more as a suggestive stimulus to the moral imagination
and to further thought and enquiry that can readily expand the analysis as
needed. As such, readers may — and indeed doubtless will — disagree with
at least some parts of the account given in Chapter 7. Of course, any such
disagreement befits us as "a society of rational enquiry, of self-scrutiny."[150]

This stimulus to the moral imagination and to further thought and
enquiry is intended to be challenging. It proposes *Juropolis* — the fishing
village of the law — as a desirable ideal, just as the imagined fishing village
of *Piscopolis* is proposed as a desirable ideal. Doubtless *Juropolis* is imperfect, as everything human is. Therefore, we need to ask ourselves questions
such as: To what extent do we already realize the way of life of *Juropolis*
(again, in both senses of "realize")? To what extent do we still need to realize it? To what extent is the ideal under stress? To what extent do we want
to defend it? These more general questions, and the many specific questions elaborating on them we will ask during the discussion in Chapter 7,
are intended to challenge us to reflect upon how we can enhance lawyers'
and law students' prospects for living a meaningful, purposeful, and fulfilling life — a flourishing life — through the work to which we have been
called, and in this way enhance our prospects for achieving professional
well-being, and for avoiding and alleviating the lawyer and law student

---

149. MacIntyre, Conflicts of Modernity, op. cit., at 238 [quoted *supra* note 112
and accompanying text].

150. *See* Chapter 5, note 8 and accompanying text.

distress and dysfunction that currently ails the legal profession and rightly receives so much attention nowadays.[151]

The exploration in Chapter 7 also necessarily raises a question that is more overtly political and that we take up in Chapter 8: Should members of the legal profession in various ways, including by working with like-minded members of other self-regulated professions and with others too, seek to transform the dominant political, economic, and moral environment of the modern liberal democratic state with its individualist *ethos* into a political, economic, and moral environment with a more communitarian *ethos* like *Piscopolis*, and thereby seek to cultivate the liberal democratic state as a "republic of virtue"? This question challenges us to reflect upon how we can help enhance the prospects for all inhabitants of our Republic to lead a meaningful, purposeful, and fulfilling life — a flourishing life — and in this way enhance our prospects for achieving political well-being and for avoiding and alleviating the political distress and dysfunction that currently ails the Republic and also rightly receives so much attention nowadays. And this question is necessarily raised for members of the self-regulated professions, because our character and values as professionals will inform and shape our character and values as civically engaged citizens concerned about the well-being of the Republic and our fellow citizens. Moreover, as professionals we are unavoidably engaged in a political enterprise in the liberal democratic state by virtue of the public service we provide as a public good, the public power we wield, and the public responsibility we owe to do good work under the social contract allowing us the privilege of self-regulation.[152] The political nature of this public service, power, and responsibility is especially evident and intense in the case of the community of legal professionals in *Juropolis*. Consequently, we should reflect upon how we can best perform and defend the political role that is necessarily ours in any event.

---

151. *See* Chapter 1, notes 20–33 and accompanying text.

152. *See* May, Beleaguered Rulers, op. cit., at 6, 12, 14–15, 21 (2001); William M. Sullivan, Work and Integrity: The Crisis and Promise of Professionalism in America 4–5, 15–18 (2d. ed., 2005) (discussing this public service, power, and responsibility, the social contract allowing the privilege of self-regulation, and the related notion of a public calling or vocation).

SEVEN

LIVING IN *JUROPOLIS*

Trawling for Justice in the Fishing Village of the Law

Before we embark on our journey through *Juropolis* and explore the shared commitments of its inhabitants, it is important to recall what was said toward the end of the last Chapter: The account in Chapter 7 is intended less as a comprehensive and exhaustive analysis of the legal *polis* and more as a suggestive and exploratory stimulus to the moral imagination and to further thought and enquiry that can readily expand the analysis as needed. As such, readers may — and indeed doubtless will — disagree with at least some parts of the account. But such disagreement befits us as "a society of rational enquiry, of self-scrutiny."[1] It is also helpful to first remind ourselves of some key points about *Piscopolis* discussed in Chapters 4 and 5.

Each practitioner community engaged in a particular practice in *Piscopolis* pursues an ultimate excellence of that particular practice and has a particular understanding of it which is their overarching common good and which entails, includes, and is co-constituted by specific standards, goods, and qualities of excellence as specific ends or common goods of the practice. These specific common goods pertain to the practitioners' excellence in performance, excellence of the product resulting from their performance, and excellence of the way of life that is lived out in the practice. The particular practices include the craft practice of catching fish, as well as the craft practices of boat building and net making which, together with the practice of catching fish, combine in and co-constitute a larg-

---

1. *See* Chapter 5, note 8 and accompanying text.

er craft community engaged in the common practice of fishing in which the practitioners of all three craft communities directly participate. All three craft practices are ordered to the ultimate excellence and the overarching common good of the common practice of fishing (which entails, includes, and is co-constituted by the common goods of each of them and which seems to be synonymous with the overarching common good of the practice of catching fish, given that the activities of the net makers and boat builders are entirely derived from the activity of the fishing crews). Because the three distinct craft practices of catching fish, boat building, and net making are necessarily interdependent and interpenetrating, in addition to co-constituting the common practice of fishing, they co-constitute one another as well, even though their practitioners do not directly participate in one another's activities — for example, fishing crews do not build boats or make nets, and the boat builders and net makers do not catch fish. And as in the case of any practice with a living tradition, the craft communities' agreement on and commitment to their respective overarching common goods does not preclude further reasoned argument or disagreement about how to understand them or about the common goods involved in achieving them.[2]

The larger political community of *Piscopolis* and its common practice of politics are co-constituted by the inhabitants and their communities of practice combining and acting in a political capacity. This larger political community forms around the political conversation in which those inhabitants who are independent practical reasoners are jointly engaged and through which they carry on their common practice. Such political conversation may occur both in the context of formally held meetings of the village assembly and more informally within the context of activities in particular practices. As "a society of rational enquiry, of self-scrutiny," the inhabitants of *Piscopolis* are committed to engaging in rational conversation that pursues the ultimate excellence or *telos* of their common practice, which is the realization of the greater common good in light of the specifically human good. And they are committed to the particular understanding of this ultimate excellence upon which they agree through reasoned argument. In *Piscopolis* this particular understanding, which is the overarching common good of their common practice, is maximal hu-

---

2. *See* Chapter 4, notes 37–38, 40–41, 48–49, 86–87, 90–92 and accompanying text.

man flourishing to be achieved through their participation in practices and the proper ordering of these practices, including the common practice of politics itself, to this goal. And when these practices are properly so ordered, their common goods together co-constitute this greater common good and overarching common good and are entailed by and included within it. Again, however, as in the case of any practice with a living tradition, the inhabitants' agreement on, and their commitment to, their overarching common good does not preclude further reasoned argument or disagreement about how to understand it or about the common goods involved in achieving it.[3]

Like their shared commitment to their overarching common good, the inhabitants' other shared politico-ethical commitments reflect and sustain the proper ordering of practices in *Piscopolis*, are themselves reflected in and sustained by both their instantiation in the inhabitants' lives and relationships and the inhabitants' ongoing political consensus, and are therefore also reflected in and sustained by the standards, goods, and qualities of excellence (that is, the common goods) of all the particular practices in *Piscopolis*. Moreover, these other commitments represent the standards, goods, and qualities of excellence of the common practice of politics that are *specific* ends or common goods of the practice and that (together with the common goods of the particular practices in *Piscopolis*) are entailed by, included within, and co-constitutive of its overarching common good which is the greater common good. These specific common goods pertain to the inhabitants' excellence in political performance, excellence of the political product resulting from their performance, and excellence of the way of life that is lived out in the fishing village *polis*.[4]

In the order in which they were discussed in Chapter 5, the inhabitants' key politico-ethical commitments or sets of commitments relate to: their active participation in the political conversation in *Piscopolis*; pursuit of their ultimate excellence and overarching common good; their flourishing through achieving the common goods of practices; their attitude toward goods of effectiveness, involving the systematic subordination of such goods to goods of excellence; the just allocation of goods of effectiveness and other community resources; the character, structuring, and conduct

---

3. *See* Chapter 5, notes 1–2, 23–26, 33–36 and accompanying text.

4. *See* Chapter 5, notes 5–8, 38 and accompanying text.

262 Professions and Politics in Crisis

of the political conversation; and the "external" relations of *Piscopolis* with the modern liberal democratic state and its large-scale market economy.[5] Collectively, the inhabitants' commitments and exercise of the many virtues they entail in particular contexts shape the distinctive communitarian *ethos* of *Piscopolis* and are concrete expressions of the general virtue of civic-mindedness that pervades all the inhabitants' relationships.[6]

Before we examine whether members of the legal profession have the same sorts of shared politico-ethical commitments as the inhabitants of *Piscopolis*, we must introduce the common practice in which they all participate through four distinct types of practice communities and legal practices, and discuss the nature of the legal conversation in which they are all engaged.

I. The Common Practice of Maintaining the Rule of Law, and Legal Conversation in *Juropolis*

In *Piscopolis* the larger political community and its common practice of politics are co-constituted by the inhabitants and their communities of practice combining and acting in a political capacity. This larger political community forms around the political conversation in which the inhabitants who are independent practical reasoners are jointly engaged and through which they carry on their common practice. Similarly, in *Juropolis* the larger legal community and its common practice of maintaining and living by the rule of law are co-constituted by inhabitants of the liberal democratic state combining and acting in a legal capacity. Thus, the professional *polis* of *Juropolis* represents liberal democratic society viewed through a legal lens. Focusing on those inhabitants of *Juropolis* who are legal professionals, the practitioner community of legal professionals as a whole forms around the legal conversation in which they are jointly engaged and through which they carry on that part of the common practice of maintaining and living by the rule of law in the liberal democratic state for which they have special responsibility, that is, the part that involves "maintaining the rule of law."[7] As we saw at the end of Chapter 6, they are

---

5. *See* Chapter 5, Part II, Sections A–G respectively.

6. *See* Chapter 5, note 7 and accompanying text.

7. *C.f.* ANTHONY T. KRONMAN, THE LOST LAWYER: FAILING IDEALS OF THE LEGAL PROFESSION 134–35 (1993) (observing that lawyers and judges are engaged in the "common

unavoidably engaged in a political enterprise as well. The political signifi-cance of the legal conversation derives in particular from the way in which the public good it provides operates as an alternative to the use of force both by individuals and by the state.

The practitioner community of legal professionals as a whole is guided by an ultimate excellence — social peace in the liberal democratic state through the realization of justice for its inhabitants — and by a particular understanding of this ultimate excellence which is their overarching com-mon good, to be achieved through the participation of legal professionals in legal practices and the proper ordering of these practices, including the common practice, to this goal. This overarching common good entails, includes, and is co-constituted by specific standards, goods, and qualities of excellence as specific ends or specific common goods of the common practice. These specific common goods of the common practice are the common goods of the four distinct types of law craft practices discussed below and pertain to the legal professionals' excellence in legal perfor-mance, excellence of the legal product resulting from their performance, and excellence of the way of life that is lived out in "the fishing village of the law." In the above formulation of the ultimate excellence, social peace is not the point and purpose of realizing justice; however, they are two sides of the same coin because law and justice are always an alternative to force and violence.

Legal conversation in *Juropolis* may occur both in the context of spe-cially held meetings open to all members of the profession, such as those of the American Bar Association (ABA), and also in the context of activ-ities in particular practices. Moreover, because the public good provided by the legal conversation means that the practitioner community of legal professionals is unavoidably engaged in a political enterprise, we can view the legal conversation also as a distinctive type of political conversation, and the common goods of the common practice of maintaining the rule of law and of the four law craft practices also as the common goods of a coterminous common *political* practice.

---

enterprise" or "common practice" of maintaining or producing the rule of law). Kronman regards lawyers and judges as having different roles within one common practice. We will reframe these different roles as distinct practices which, together with two additional distinct practices, combine in and co-constitute the common practice of maintaining the rule of law.

A. The Four Law Craft Communities and Their Practices

At least four distinct craft communities of legal professionals, engaged in distinct practices, combine in and co-constitute the practitioner community of the legal profession as a whole and its common practice of maintaining the rule of law. This is partially analogous to the way in which the inhabitants of *Piscopolis* and their communities of practice combine in and co-constitute the larger political community and the common practice of politics of the fishing village. (The analogy is only partial because, unlike the common practice of politics in *Piscopolis*, the common practice of maintaining the rule of law is not an autonomous practice with specific common goods of its own but rather a composite of the four law craft practitioner communities. Another, more complete analogy is discussed below, although it is not one that is focused on a rhetorical conversation.)

The four distinct craft communities of legal professionals and their practices are as follows: Judges are engaged in the practice of adjudication, in which they decide disputes between litigants in an impartial manner.[8] Lawyers are engaged in the practice of lawyering, or representing clients, in which they counsel clients and, if necessary, speak for them as advocates of their interests and on their behalf.[9] Legislative counsel are engaged in the practice of assisting the legislature, in which they draft legislation and provide ancillary services to lawmakers.[10] And academic lawyers are engaged in the practice of legal education, in which they teach law students

---

8. *See id.* at 121 (defining the "law job" of adjudication).

9. *See id.* at 121–22 (defining the "law jobs" of counseling and advocacy). Representing clients is understood broadly also to include in-house counsel and lawyers representing government entities and non-profit organizations.

10. There may be an attorney-client relationship between legislative counsel and members of the legislature. However, the role and function of lawyers drafting legislation as a formal source of law and the type of attorney-client relationship involved are so distinctive that we can regard legislative counsel as engaged in a distinct practice separate from other lawyers representing clients. To keep the discussion manageable, we will not also consider lawyers acting in a similar capacity for the Executive Branch, but the issues and analysis would be analogous. For some sense of the practice of legislative counsel, see, for example, http://legcounsel.house.gov/ (U.S. House of Representatives); http://www.slc.senate.gov/index.htm (U.S. Senate); https://www.legis.ga.gov/joint-office/legislative-counsel (Georgia); http://legislativecounsel.ca.gov/home (California).

and generate legal scholarship influencing lawyers and judges.[11] Broadly speaking, the practices of all four craft communities involve centrally some type of translation of intentional goals: Judges translate litigants' intentional goals, rooted in their legal claims, into the administration of justice. Lawyers translate clients' intentional goals, rooted in their various social activities, into the language of *Juropolis*. Legislative counsel translate legislators' intentional goals, rooted in their political activity, into the language of *Ju-*

---

11. For a lovely description of this traditional role of academic lawyers, see KRONMAN, LOST LAWYER, op. cit., at 109–21, 266–67. *See also id.* at 219–23 (discussing Karl Llewellyn's account of the role of the legal scholar).

It seems that MacIntyre does not regard teaching as a practice. Alasdair MacIntyre & Joseph Dunne, *Alasdair MacIntyre on Education: In Dialogue with Joseph Dunne*, 36 J. PHIL. ED. 1, 5 (2002) ("[T]eaching itself is not a practice, but a set of skills and habits put to the service of a variety of practices"). Whatever may be true of apprenticeship in other practices, including catching fish, it is reasonable to regard legal education as a distinct practice, in particular due to the rather clear institutional and functional divide between legal education and the practice of lawyering that developed, rightly or wrongly, after the era of apprenticeship in the office of a lawyer. There are several possible ways to justify this position: (1) One way, reflecting a criticism that MacIntyre is sometimes insufficiently granular in giving examples of practices, is to argue that it is not teaching or education that is the practice but particular types of teaching or education that are distinct practices, including legal education. *See* Paul Hager, *Refurbishing MacIntyre's Account of Practices*, 45 J. PHIL. ED. 545, 548–52, 559 (2011) (canvassing such arguments). (2) A second way is to accept teaching or education as the relevant category but to argue that it is a practice that, like theology, is internal to other practices. I am indebted to Jack Sammons for this suggestion. Sammons Email (October 24, 2014) [on file with author]. For Sammons' development of this claim regarding theology, see Jack L. Sammons, *Afterwards: Four Concerns*, 53 MERCER L. REV. 1159 (2002); *infra* note 69. Presumably, then, this cross-cutting practice would take the distinct form of legal education within our common practice and perhaps even within the other three distinct practices. (3) A third way is to argue that teaching or education is itself a common practice that, whether or not internal to other practices, is constituted by distinct practices of teaching and education, including legal education. It is quite conceivable, then, that the distinct practice of legal education could co-constitute two common practices, the common practice of teaching or education, and our common practice in *Juropolis*. The second and third ways might perhaps even entail thinking in terms of a separate *polis* of professional educators that intersects and overlaps with other professional *poleis* in various ways. On all this *compare* H. PATRICK GLENN, LEGAL TRADITIONS OF THE WORLD: SUSTAINABLE DIVERSITY IN LAW 345–48, 349–51 (3d. ed. 2007) (discussing the multiplicity of internal and cross-cutting lateral traditions within complex legal traditions). For additional perspectives on teaching as a practice, and on MacIntyre's views regarding the matter, see EDUCATION AND PRACTICE: UPHOLDING THE INTEGRITY OF TEACHING AND LEARNING (Joseph Dunne & Pádraig Hogan, eds., 2004) (also reproducing the Dunne-MacIntyre dialogue cited above).

ropolis as a formal source of law. And academic lawyers translate the intentional goals of the inexpert, rooted in their need to learn, into expertise.[12]

Each law craft community and practice has a distinct role, then, in maintaining the rule of law. Thus, each practice has its own ultimate excellence and an overarching common good, which is the craft community's particular understanding of this ultimate excellence and which entails, includes, and is co-constituted by specific standards, goods, and qualities of excellence as specific ends or specific common goods of the practice. And each practice is ordered to the ultimate excellence and overarching common good of our common practice (which entails, includes, and is co-constituted by the common goods of each of them). Each practice also has its own living tradition within the broader common law tradition of the common practice. We will address the ultimate excellences and overarching common goods of the common practice and of the four distinct law craft practices in greater detail in Sections B and C of Part II respectively.

But now we should observe that a second analogy with practices in *Piscopolis* suggests itself. Thus, the way that the four distinct law craft communities and their respective practices combine in and co-constitute the community of legal professionals as a whole and its common practice of maintaining the rule of law is also analogous to the way in which the three fishing craft communities of fishing crews, boat builders, and net makers and their respective practices combine in and co-constitute the larger craft community engaged in the common practice of fishing. We will see later that because the judiciary ultimately decides any legal issue, the practice of adjudication has the closest practical relationship of all four craft practices to the ultimate excellence and overarching common good of the common practice, the role of the judge is a central focus of all of them, and in practice the other three practices are largely ordered to the ultimate excellence and overarching common good of the practice of adjudication. This is, of course, analogous to the way in which all three fishing craft practices are ordered to the ultimate excellence and overarching common good of one of them, namely the practice of catching fish.

---

12. For discussion of the translation done by lawyers, see Jack. L. Sammons, *'Cheater!': The Central Moral Admonition of Legal Ethics, Games, Lusory Attitudes, Internal Perspectives, and Justice*, 39 IDAHO L. REV 273, 284–86 (2003); Jack L. Sammons, *Justice as Play*, 61 MERCER L. REV. 517, 543–44 (2010).

Moreover, the analogy is strengthened by the consideration that, just as the three distinct fishing craft practices are necessarily interdependent and interpenetrating, and therefore co-constitute one another in addition to co-constituting the common practice of fishing, even though their practitioners do not directly participate in one another's activities, so also the four law craft practices are necessarily interdependent and interpenetrating, and therefore co-constitute one another in addition to co-constituting the common practice of maintaining the rule of law, even though their practitioners also do not directly participate in one another's activities. For example, lawyers representing clients do not adjudicate and judges do not represent clients, even though they may be in the same courtroom, and academic lawyers do not ajudicate or represent clients when teaching law students in the classroom (experiential education in a law school clinic is clearly different in this regard).

How might this analogy work metaphorically? Here's one way: The four law crafts are together "trawling for justice," with each one making its distinct contribution to this joint quest as it plays its distinct role in the common practice of maintaining the rule of law in *Juropolis*. The fishing crews are made up of both the judges trying to capture justice for the litigants appearing before them and the practicing lawyers trying to capture justice for their clients by persuading the judges to cast their nets in a particular location (and like different fishing crews, the practicing lawyers compete with one another for their share of the catch, especially if one thinks of the fishing crews over time making multiple castings of the net). The net makers are the judges who ruled in previous cases and legislative counsel, who each provide (re)sources that must be skillfully deployed for the capturing. And the boat builders are the academic lawyers who help get the practicing lawyers and judges to the fishing grounds where justice may be found. Moreover, just as it is important for those engaged in the common practice of fishing to sustain this natural resource, so also it is important for those engaged in the common practice of maintaining the rule of law to sustain the legal conversation.[13]

---

13. I am indebted to Jack Sammons for articulating this part of the analogy. Sammons Email (October 24, 2014) [on file with author].

B. Nature of the Legal Conversation

Do we, the community of legal professionals as a whole, display those "deliberative" characteristics that MacIntyre considers essential for the existence of a *polis*?[14] Specifically, do we carry on our legal conversation in a shared language and employ shared formal and informal modes of deliberation? It would certainly seem so, as even a brief reflection on the specialized language of the law and legal institutions such as courts and legal procedures will confirm. In our deliberations, do we also "share... a large degree of common understanding of practices and institutions," including an "understanding of the relationships between goods, rules, and virtues"? We will consider the extent to which we do so in Part II. Although our various shared understandings derive from our inherited common law tradition, do we regard *Juropolis* as "always, potentially or actually, a society of rational enquiry, of self-scrutiny," so that "individuals are always able to put in question through communal deliberation what has hitherto by custom and tradition been taken for granted both about their own good and the good of the community"? Once again, this question seems to call for an affirmative answer, at least in principle. We are, after all, "a rhetorical community" characterized by "a culture of argument."[15] In a very real sense our practice is a constant argument, a legal conversation, about how to understand our overarching common good and about the common goods involved in achieving it. The current urgent conversation about lawyer distress, dysfunction, and well-being powerfully illustrates this point.[16]

Of course, this latter conversation is only one conversation, one strand if you will, within a much larger legal conversation that is constitutive of our common practice. We might say, then, that each of the four law craft practices represents a distinct group of voices, which carries on its own

14. *See* Chapter 5, notes 8–9 and accompanying text.

15. *See* Jack L. Sammons, *The Radical Ethics of Legal Rhetoricians*, 32 VAL. U. L. REV. 93, 94 (1997) (explaining that "*[l]egal* rhetoric is a particular form of rhetoric located within a particular rhetorical community with its own particular culture. Thus, lawyering is a particular rhetorical practice with its own unique set of excellences"); Jack L. Sammons, *Justice as Play*, 61 MERCER L. REV. 517, 520 ("The tradition whose origins we will be exploring here is the tradition of legal rhetoric, of legal casuistry, and of the emergence of a culture of argument supporting the art of this casuistry").

16. *See* Chapter 1, notes 20–33 and accompanying text; Chapter 6, note 151 and accompanying text.

conversation constitutive of its particular practice but which also thereby participates in and co-constitutes the larger conversation; and of course there are multiple, often discordant, voices and individual conversations within each group. Justice Breyer conveys the flavor of the larger legal conversation vividly in a 2007 colloquy with Justice Scalia:

> I usually think, and I think Justice Scalia does too, that in the United States, and this is perhaps unique to the United States, or almost, law is not really handed down from on high, even by the Supreme Court. Rather, it emerges. And we're part of it; the courts are part of it, but only part. And what really survives over time is the result, I tend to think, of a conversation — I think that's the right word — conversation among judges, among professors, among law students, among members of the bar, because you need people to put things together, you need people to decide cases, you need people to tell you how it works out in practice. And out of this giant, messy, unbelievably messy conversation emerges law. And that means you have to have the conversation. And then I think *we* participate in it, even at a general level, not just when we're deciding cases.[17]

And as Jack Sammons explains when addressing "the justice carried by the legal conversation," by which he means the individual legal conversation in which "a particular legal dispute was resolved through the conversation for which [the lawyers as advocates] are primarily responsible":

> [W]e are not discussing the state's creation and enforcement of social rules (and whether or not they are just ones), but the process by which the meanings of those rules are determined for their enforcement: a conversational process that operates as a restraint on the state's use of force, as a reduction of the general to the particular, and as a continuation of the rhetorician's ancient fear of written law.[18]

---

17. *Constitutional Relevance of Foreign Court Decisions,* American University, http://www.c-spanvideo.org/program/185122-1 (January 13, 2005) (Colloquy between Justice Breyer and Justice Scalia), at 24:55 minutes.

18. Sammons, *Play,* op. cit., at 517–19.

More precisely, the focus of the legal conversation is on adjudication, specifically "upon the moment when the judge is persuaded."[19] Sammons' emphasis upon this moment is resonant with the observation we made above that each of the other three law craft practices is in practice largely ordered to the ultimate excellence and overarching common good of the practice of adjudication because the judge's role in ultimately deciding any issue is a central focus of each of them. And so, with Sammons' focus on this moment of judicial persuasion, law/justice "emerges" out of, or alternatively we might say law/justice "happens" in, Justice Breyer's "giant, messy, unbelievably messy conversation" among legal professionals in *Juropolis*.[20]

We can obtain additional insight into the nature of the legal conversation in *Juropolis* by considering what MacIntyre has to say about the nature of conversation in general, and by recalling what he says about stories as discussed in Chapter 2. Thus, MacIntyre asserts that conversation is "[t]he most familiar type of context in and by reference to which speech-acts and purposes are rendered intelligible."[21] Indeed, "conversation, understood widely enough, is the form of human transactions in general" and deeds "speak" as much as do words.[22] And these conversations are complex:

---

19. Jack L. Sammons, *The Missing Poetry of Legal Rhetoric: A Phenomenological Inquiry*, point 10 (2014) [unpublished manuscript on file with author].

20. *Supra* note 17 and accompanying text. Consideration of this moment — and because of the central focus just mentioned, consideration of many of the matters discussed in this Chapter — promises to be significantly enriched by the treatment of judicial decision-making undertaken in a book published just before final submission of the manuscript for the present book. *See* BARRY FRIEDMAN, MARGARET H. LEMOS, ANDREW D. MARTIN, TOM S. CLARK, ALLISON ORR LARSON, & ANNA HARVEY, JUDICIAL DECISION-MAKING: A COURSE-BOOK (2020) (combining the "internal" approach of many law professors with the "external" approach of social scientists in a comprehensive, in-depth approach that systematically examines both the "legal" considerations influencing judicial decision-making, such as "constitutions, statutes, regulations [and] court decisions," and the extra-legal considerations influencing these decisions, including "the ideology of the judge, bargaining dynamics on multi-member courts, and the concern of elected judges for avoiding retribution by the voters," as well as such factors as the impact of different types of lawyers in shaping court dockets, caseload pressures, and challenging facts. *Id.* at v).

21. ALASDAIR MACINTYRE, AFTER VIRTUE: A STUDY IN MORAL THEORY 210 (3d. ed., 2007) (1981).

22. *Id.* at 211 (giving as examples "battles, chess games, courtships, philosophy seminars, families at the dinner table, businessmen negotiating contracts").

[T[hey have beginnings, middles, and endings just as do literary works. They embody reversals and recognitions; they move towards and away from climaxes. There may within a longer conversation be digressions and subplots, indeed digressions within digressions and subplots within subplots.[23]

This certainly seems to be an apt depiction capturing the complexity of the "messy, unbelievably messy" legal conversation[24] except perhaps for the notion that it has a beginning, middle, and end (although this notion would indeed seem to apply to the myriad individual conversations that occur within the broader legal conversation).

Moreover, MacIntyre would surely agree that in the legal conversation we are telling ourselves a story; that our individual stories within this story are interlocking and embedded in others' stories and in this larger story; and that these stories are both unpredictable *and* teleological.[25] Importantly, then, each character in a story "is constrained by the actions of others and by the social settings presupposed by his and their actions."[26] In our own case, of course, *Juropolis* is the relevant presupposed social setting. And perhaps most importantly, MacIntyre would consider that, like other stories, the story being told in the legal conversation "aspire[s] to truth."[27] Presumably this truth must have to do with our commitment to achieve a proper understanding of the ultimate excellence of our common practice, but what kind of truth *is* this exactly? It is, of course, a truth about ourselves, as every kind of truth to which we aspire in our story telling must be, whatever else it might also be.[28] What kind of truth about ourselves it

---

23. *Id.* (indicating that this statement applies *mutatis mutandis* to all forms of "conversation").

24. *Supra* note 17 and accompanying text.

25. *See* Chapter 2, notes 8–13, 54 and accompanying text.

26. MacIntyre, After Virtue, op. cit., at 215.

27. *Id.* at 216 ("A central thesis then begins to emerge: man is in his actions and practice, as well as in his fictions, essentially a story-telling animal. He is not essentially, but becomes through his history, a teller of stories that aspire to truth").

28. And so, the stories we tell ourselves in our religions, which seek truth about the supernatural world, or the stories we tell ourselves in our natural sciences, which seek truth about the natural world, or the stories we tell ourselves in our social sciences, which seek truth about the social world, or the stories we tell ourselves in our moral philosophies,

is, and what else it might also be, are questions explored further in Section B of Part II below.

II. Shared Politico-Ethical Commitments

In Part I we have already drawn a number of comparisons between the fishing village of *Piscopolis* and the legal *polis* of *Juropolis*. But to be really like Drew and the other inhabitants of *Piscopolis*, we must share Drew's perceptions, values, motivations, and commitments, and the resulting relationships with other inhabitants of *Juropolis*. Do we? And what does this entail? We will consider these general questions by focusing on our shared politico-ethical commitments in *Juropolis*. As we do so, we should remember that, if these commitments are like their counterparts in *Piscopolis*, they reflect and sustain the proper ordering of practices in *Juropolis*, are themselves reflected in and sustained by both instantiation in our lives and relationships and our ongoing "political" consensus, and are therefore also reflected in and sustained by the standards, goods, and qualities of excellence of our four law craft practices. And collectively, they shape a distinctive communitarian *ethos* in *Juropolis* and are concrete manifestations of a general virtue of civic-mindedness that pervades all our relationships.

The reader is forewarned that the discussion in Part II alternates between an expository style and an "interrogatory" style that formulates many detailed, specific questions, very often in the first person, both plural and singular. The first personal questions are addressed to every member of the relevant law craft practice(s), including myself, and we should regard them as being asked by the ideal, imagined community of *Juropolis* to which we belong. These questions are neither suggestive of tentativeness regarding the subject of the question nor are they merely rhetorical. On the contrary, they are intended to make the discussion personal and more immediate, challenging us to reflect and calling us to account. In several places the interrogatory style becomes particularly intense, with a barrage of questions that may seem overwhelming and even exhausting. My hope is that readers will try to be both understanding of what I am trying to do in asking these questions and patient with my attempt to do it, howev-

---

which seek truth about the ethical world, are necessarily *also* about us and reveal truths about us, whatever else they might reveal.

er faltering and inadequate this attempt may be. Also, as we explore our shared politico-ethical commitments and respond to the questions posed, we should remember that sometimes we are concerned with rational justification, if we are put to the question, and not necessarily with our actual reasons for everyday decision-making and action.[29]

A. Active Participation in the Legal Conversation[30]

There seems little doubt that, just as Drew and the other inhabitants of *Piscopolis* are committed to active participation in the political conversation of the fishing village, so also the legal professionals who inhabit *Juropolis* are committed to active participation in the legal conversation in the fishing village of the law. This is because our everyday activities involving relationships with other inhabitants necessarily entail such participation. But do we also understand that our individual flourishing in the practice depends upon the proper ordering of legal practices, including the practice in which we personally participate? And do we understand our own role in helping to ensure such proper ordering? In other words, do we also understand that this proper ordering and our own flourishing depend on us personally committing to all the other shared commitments discussed below?

B. Ultimate Excellence and Overarching Common Good of the Common Practice[31]

As we proceed through the discussion in this section, we should ask ourselves a series of questions. We noted above that the legal professionals who inhabit *Juropolis* are "always, potentially or actually, a society of rational enquiry, of self-scrutiny."[32] But am I personally committed to engaging in rational conversation that pursues the ultimate excellence or *telos* of our common practice, which we said was "social peace in the liberal democratic state through the realization of justice for its inhabitants"?[33] And am I committed to the particular understanding of this ultimate excellence the

---

29. *See* Chapter 5, notes 10, 94, 136 and accompanying text.
30. For discussion of this topic in *Piscopolis*, see Part II, Section A of Chapter 5.
31. For discussion of this topic in *Piscopolis*, see Part II, Section B of Chapter 5.
32. *See supra* notes 14–16 and accompanying text.
33. *See supra* note 7 and accompanying text.

practitioner community of legal professionals might agree upon as our overarching common good and to thereby contributing to the greater common good of liberal democratic society, that is, the maximization of "happiness" either in the sense of human flourishing, as we might prefer to conceive of it, or in the sense of preference satisfaction, as the dominant conception would currently have it? Even if I am so committed, how far does such agreement extend? In other words, how far does our overarching common good remain controverted? And is it controverted so extensively or fundamentally that our common practice is under significant stress and even threatened with possible corruption?

1. The Realization of Justice

Let us first consider the notion of realizing justice. The traditional understanding of this notion is ensuring that each person receives what is due to him or her under the law. Anthony Kronman puts it this way:

> Doing justice ... means honoring the rights and enforcing the duties that the law assigns ... This ancient and powerful idea rests on a picture of the law as a distributive order that allots different rights and responsibilities to different individuals. [It is important] to ensure that the distributive scheme established by the law is properly maintained — that those subject to it receive the benefits and burdens the law distributes to them. Justice is the name we give to the condition that results when these distributional requirements are satisfied.[34]

Although this formulation seems relatively uncontroversial, it does not take us very far. It is therefore perhaps more apt as a commentary upon the "realizing justice" component of the ultimate excellence than as the particular understanding of that component in our overarching common good. Our particular understanding of this formulation, which *is* our overarching common good, is much more controversial. We argue about

---

34. KRONMAN, LOST LAWYER, op. cit., at 335. Kronman is here discussing the role of the judge in ensuring the realization of justice but the terms in which he writes can be abstracted from that particular context to apply to the realization of justice component in the ultimate excellence of our common practice.

it constantly. Indeed, as already observed, in a very real sense our practice involves a constant argument, a legal conversation, about how to understand our overarching common good and about the common goods involved in achieving it. Regarding the overarching common good, we argue not only about what particular rights and duties, benefits and burdens are in fact assigned and distributed by the law; we argue about how we should discover this. And the argument has intensified in a post-realist world and under the pressures wrought by profound economic and social changes in the last century or so, especially the last half century.[35] Of course, despite the — in many ways necessary — breakdown of previous social and moral consensus in *Juropolis*, in many cases the answer to the question regarding what rights and duties, benefits and burdens exist under the law may be clear where an issue is addressed by "black letter" law established, for example, by settled precedent or precise and unambiguous statutory provision; but in "hard cases" often the answer may not be clear at all.[36]

---

35. Consulting any of the standard works in Jurisprudence will readily confirm this point. *See, e.g.*, Brian H. Bix, Jurisprudence: Theory and Context (8ᵗʰ ed. 2019). For a very useful discussion of how major jurisprudential schools and movements influence legal reasoning, see Linda H. Edwards, Legal Writing and Analysis (4ᵗʰ ed. 2015), specifically *id.* at 55–63 (describing several forms of legal reasoning — rule-based reasoning, analogical reasoning (analogizing and distinguishing cases), policy-based reasoning, principle-based reasoning, custom-based reasoning, inferential reasoning, and narrative), 235–50 (discussing and evaluating several major schools of American jurisprudence — natural law, formalism, legal realism, legal process, fundamental rights, law and economics, and critical legal theory (critical legal studies, critical race theory, and feminist legal theory) — and explaining how each one relates to various forms of legal reasoning). *See also* Bailey Kuklin & Jeffrey W. Stempel, Foundations of the Law: An Interdisciplinary and Jurisprudential Primer 131–92 (1994) (providing a useful overview of these and other jurisprudential influences upon law, including how they might apply to determine the outcome in an illustrative hypothetical case).

36. In his seminal article *Hard Cases*, Ronald Dworkin explains that the most popular theories of adjudication have distinguished between these two types of cases as follows:

> Judges should apply the law that other institutions have made; they should not make new law. That is the ideal, but for different reasons it cannot be realized fully in practice. Statutes and common law rules are often vague and must be interpreted before they can be applied to novel cases. Some cases, moreover, raise issues so novel that they cannot be decided even by stretching or reinterpreting existing rules. So judges must sometimes make new law, either covertly or explicitly.

Ronald Dworkin, *Hard Cases*, 88 Harv. L. Rev. 1057, 1058 (1975).

One thing that *does* seem clear from the above formulation, however, is that the search for justice is inseparable from the search for law, and that discovering justice is effectively synonymous with discovering law and vice-versa. They are two sides of the same coin. And this equation is neither tautological nor one that necessarily implies a positivism in which law is susceptible only to external normative evaluation. Thus the self-critique involved in the continual argument about our overarching common good enables us to challenge a particular understanding of that common good at any given time by drawing upon powerful and venerable notions in the tradition of our practice such as "the judge is the mouthpiece of the law" ("judex est lex loquens") and "an unjust law is not law" ("lex injusta non est lex"), or perhaps better said "the judge is the mouthpiece of the Law" and "an unjust law is not Law."[37] This now suggests, of course, that the above formulation of the realizing justice component in the ultimate excellence of our practice should be revised to refer to Justice and Law with initial caps: We seek to realize the ideal of Justice, which means that we seek to realize the rights and duties assigned, and the benefits and burdens distributed, under the ideal Law. But are this justice and this law, this Justice and this Law, solely internal to the practice or can they be, in part at least, derived from outside the practice? Well, of course, this is the subject of argument too. Here is not the place to canvass, let alone attempt to resolve, the relevant arguments. This would require a separate book on jurisprudence. What follows instead is a discussion of an idealized account of our overarching common good developed by Jack Sammons — a highly original and provocative account that seems broadly MacIntyrean in spirit but with the greater phenomenological depth anticipated in Part III, Section C of Chapter 2 — which will serve to identify some of the fundamental issues and stimulate further reflection.[38]

---

37. For discussion of these notions in classical common law theory, see Mark L. Jones, *Fundamental Dimensions of Law and Legal Education: An Historical Framework — A History of U.S. Legal Education Phase I: From the Foundation of the Republic Until the 1860s*, 39 J. Marshall L. Rev. 1041, 1103–06, 1113 n265. See also *infra* note 64 and accompanying text.

38. For affirmation of the originality of this account, see Joseph Vining, *Jack Sammons As Therapist*, 66 Mercer L. Rev. 335, 336, 341 (2015) (stating that "[t[here is no one like him" and referring to "[t]he boldness, the originality, the genius" of the "astonish[ing]" way Sammons connects law and music, and to his "beautiful, original, provocative" essays).

Sammons' goal is the "humanizing" one of "[r]eturning law and justice" to "the practical world of legal affairs" by "mov[ing] these away from conceptions of them as power, as technique, as reason, as ethics, as politics, as economics, as audience, as subjective projections, as the hidden prejudices of institutions, and so forth that deny to them the fullness of their being in the world."[39] In such an understanding "the legal conversation offers us an alternative to all those other conversations — the political, the social, the technological, the scientific, the economic, the teleological, the philosophical, the utopian — that seek to define us in some final way."[40] Thus, in asking what reasons we have for "playing our game" of "representative adversarial advocacy" in the practice of lawyering Sammons answers eloquently:

> The answer we would give … is: "for justice." This is not, however, … some "justice" that is external to the practice, could be known without it, and stands in judgment of it. This is not, that is, about some thin external conception of "justice" as a product of our practice — a conception in which the practice is really just a massive inefficiency. Such a conception of justice will not work for us. Nor will it work for our students. We can see its failure all around us in the dissatisfaction so many lawyers have with their own lives.
>
> Instead, this is about a justice that is internal to the practice in the way that beauty is internal to the practices of art. This is about the justice we have in mind when we recognize that communities in which our game is played well are rendered more just merely by the playing. This is about the form of justice that communities without our game know they lack and know it all too well. It is in this justice, this justice that is internal to our practice, that we — lawyers and law students — can find the meaning of our work, or, rather, our play. It is a meaning in which our game is … a self-justifying activity, an end in itself.[41]

---

39. Sammons, *Missing Poetry*, op. cit., at points 35–36.
40. Sammons, *Play*, op. cit., at 549.
41. Sammons, '*Cheater'!*, op. cit., at 303–04. Regarding the focus on "representative adversarial advocacy" within the practice of lawyering, see *id.* at 273 n2.

Sammons explains further that "what is captured in the broad word 'external' is really more of an assertion of superiority by an alternative tradition (in our case a tradition of claims about being traditionless, to describe it harshly) to the internal than it is something somehow broader than it."[42] And as we saw in Chapter 6, MacIntyre considers that the argument about justice within this alternative tradition, which is the tradition of liberalism, reflects incoherent, conflicting, and incommensurable values, just like other moral debate in liberal democracies.[43] There is much more that needs to be said about the dialectic between the moral tradition of our practice and other moral traditions and about the "translation" of external critique into terms internal to our tradition which is part of this dialectic, but again we will not undertake such exploration here.[44]

Perhaps we can make a start, however, as we now turn from those who seek to persuade the legal audience to the legal audience that is to be persuaded, and with this turn also turn to the question about truth we asked at the end of Part I: What kind of truth does the story being told in the legal conversation aspire to? Here Sammons argues for a particular phenomenological understanding of the ultimate excellence, for an overarching common good that not only aspires to a truth *about* ourselves but is also true *to* ourselves. The starting point is a realization (again in both senses) of the limitations revealed by the arguments of the lawyers who seek to persuade:

[T]he lawyers in their competing arguments display for us first the limitations of the materials of the law for resolving the dispute, the limitations of policy, reason, knowledge, and finally, the limitations

---

42. *Id.* at 304 n98.

43. *See* Chapter 6, notes 43, 46 and accompanying text. *See also* Chapter 6, notes 23, 53–54 and accompanying text (further discussing incoherent and conflicting values informing politics in modern liberal democracies), notes 91, 97–108 and accompanying text (further discussing competing "rival and incompatible accounts" of morality in modern liberal democracies).

44. For a similar suggestion gesturing toward this "MacIntyrean dialectic" made by Sammons himself, see Sammons, '*Cheater*'!, op. cit., at 294 n69. For MacIntyre's explication of how such an enquiry might be structured, see MACINTYRE, AFTER VIRTUE, op. cit., at xiii–xiv, 275–77. *See also* Chapter 5, notes 27–32 (for references to MacIntyre's works applying this dialectical approach to the competition between the moral tradition of Thomistic Aristotelianism and rival moral traditions and for MacIntyre's summary of the process).

of language itself. They do so by making the dispute fully human which, ironically, makes our community suddenly alien to itself so that we can, with honesty, decide who we are.[45]

But how exactly do lawyers' arguments have these effects? Characterizing the arguments made by adversarial advocates as necessarily moral ones, Sammons explains that

> Our lawyers' competing moral arguments move us toward a recognition of each dispute as a *unique* disturbance of our identity — an anomalous situation that we cannot adequately address using resources familiar to us from past usage — because it is our identity itself that is in question. Together the lawyers insist that what they have to say for their clients be truly heard as new, as unique, as coming from real people, "real presences," singularities, and of great value because they are so; and the lawyers do this by summoning all of those methods of poetic fiction Aristotle described.[46]

How, then, is the legal audience to respond?

> The judge and jury, we say, are to listen truly and, thus, to treat each case as unique — judge it on its own merits. The judge and jury are not to think about the case instrumentally toward some previously determined objective; they are not to think about our identity as just the product of causes or capable of full description on the basis of effects. The judge and jury are to do nothing that would render the "we" whose definition is at issue static and known, nothing that would render the "persons" appearing before the court anything less than the singularities they are, and nothing that would jeopardize the open and ongoing nature of the conversation.[47]

But a decision must still be made, a judgment must still be rendered, and doing so, Sammons tells us, is "a matter of Aristotelian practical wis-

---

45. Sammons, *Play*, op. cit., at 547.
46. *Id.* at 546–47.
47. *Id.* at 547.

dom — this mysterious improvisational creating that we constantly ask of our judges and jurors and occasionally admire in them too" and that "arises from this particular dispute between these particular people at this particular moment."[48] And most fundamentally it arises from "who 'we' are" as a distinct legal "polity."[49] Sammons says that such a practically wise decision comes after "all voices have been heard."[50] But, as the passage quoted above suggests, for all voices to be truly heard, the legal audience must "listen truly."[51] Therefore, in "legal performance," like a composer or a poet listening for the muse, the legal audience must "listen" for what the law and the legal situation are "saying."[52]

Focusing now on the judicial legal audience, the law cannot be "captured in texts" or "reduced to concepts."[53] Therefore it is necessary to listen through the "opening[s]" in language created by "competing interpretations" in the particular legal conversation.[54] To let the Law speak,[55] and to be open and receptive to hearing what it has to say, requires certain virtues, including "humility, patience, candor, and honesty."[56] In this way,

---

48. *Id.* at 547–48.

49. *Id.* at 546, 548–50.

50. *Id.* at 548.

51. *Supra* note 47 and accompanying text.

52. Sammons eloquently describes the process of this listening and what it involves in two unpublished manuscripts on file with the author. *See* Jack L. Sammons, *Listening to Law* (2012); Sammons, *Missing Poetry*, op. cit.

53. Sammons, *Listening*, op. cit., at 14 (discussing the audience for Greek tragedies and analogizing our judges to this audience). Moreover,

> The law is never the sum of its objective parts; never a matter of a collection of rules, procedures, statutes, opinions, people in certain roles, and so forth anymore than what we call music is just a collection of musical works, instruments, and people in certain roles. When we think of law or music in this way, as we are often tempted to do, they disappear from our perception.

Id. at 10. On the other hand, the point is "not that [we] should not think in technical ways, for the law can be uncovered in these ways as well, but that [we] should 'think' more truthfully than [we] are now doing." *Id.* at 17.

54. *Id.* at 7.

55. *See* Linda L. Berger and Jack L. Sammons, *The Law's Mystery*, 2 BRIT. J. AM. LEGAL STUD. 1, 5 (2013) (explaining that in great judicial opinions the Law speaks through the judge).

56. Sammons, *Listening*, op. cit., at 10–11. *See also id.* at 12 ("The waiting, the patience, the attentiveness, the careful thinking, the hopeful expectation, the honesty, the candor, and our careful preparation for these moments, are a taxing struggle, for such is the way of

it is possible to "know the truth of the matter at stake in a matter of law" and uncover "the essence" that is the justice which "supervenes upon" this always conflicted truth.[57] Thus

> The truth revealed in opinions, as in art, is not truth as a correspondence to something or coherence with something....Instead [it]... is truth as the disclosure (uncovering, deconcealing, unclosedness, *aletheia*, etc.) of an aspect of a world that was concealed from us — using that word "world" as we might say the world of law, the world of baseball, or the world of the waterfront — something, that is, that is already there in a vast network of holistic connections reaching out towards a broad horizon in which to understand a thing truly requires some understanding "of an indefinite number of other things."[58]

Despite being conflicted, when revealed in this way, the truth of the matter may appear "inevitable."[59] This "truth of the matter" and the justice that supervenes upon it, then, flows from our true identity, and listening for it in this way "is... a matter of our being authentic — true, that is, to an identity that is always a work in progress."[60] Because this "truth" of the law

---

truth and, if of truth, of justice"), 15 (explaining that in good judging "judges must approach the law with the respectful virtues — humility, patience, truthfulness, honesty, candor — required of all good artists towards the materials of their art, all of which can be described as getting out of the way of the thing itself"); Jack L. Sammons, *Origin of the Opinion as a Work of Art*, at points 25–26 (stressing the need for the judge to exhibit "reverence for the materials of the law [in] an act of profound humility" if "the law" is "to speak through the opinion") [unpublished manuscript on file with author].

57. Sammons, *Listening*, op. cit., at 4, 12–13.

58. Berger and Sammons, *Mystery*, op. cit., at 6 (quoting JAMES C. EDWARDS, THE PLAIN SENSE OF THINGS: THE FATE OF RELIGION IN AN AGE OF NORMAL NIHILISM 154 (1997)).

59. *See id.* at 8 (discussing "inevitability" in judicial opinions and explaining that "[t]his 'inevitable' is not something predictable, but something that suddenly and often surprisingly appears as that which must be, although you did not know this before its appearance;" thus the opinion "strikes us as something we already knew but did not know, until that moment, that we knew it").

60. Sammons, *Listening*, op. cit., at 14.

and this "identity" cannot be captured in language, they are mysterious.[61] But this mystery is also the source of the law's authority over us:

> [T]he Law is a truthful uncovering of our given identity — to ask by whom it is given is to miss the point — within the legal world and, in it, we discover that our identity, too, is grounded in mystery and uncertainty. Because it is our own identity that is uncovered for us in Law, it is authoritative over us.[62]

What are we to make of Sammons' account? Some, like Linda Berger, worry that the claim to "truth" represents "a potential threat to tolerance, diversity, and ... the humanistic values ... in thinking of the world as rhetorical."[63] On the other hand, the notion that this truth flows from our identity echoes the classical common law notion that the judge acts as the authoritative spokesman of an historical community when the judge expounds, declares, and applies the law as the "common and immemorial

---

61. Berger and Sammons, *Mystery*, op. cit., at 4, 7, 8.

62. *Id.* at 7. Consistent with Sammons' account of the realization of justice, James Boyd White explains that lawyers and judges must respond appropriately to many different types of "voices" to achieve "justice as an institutional matter" or "justice in the law" as opposed to "abstract justice." JAMES BOYD WHITE, KEEP LAW ALIVE 97–98, 103, 105 (2019). Moreover, "if abstract justice is to become real, and not merely abstract, it must itself be wisely, justly, and artfully located in the context of the[] tensions" created by these voices. Indeed, "[i]t is not too much to say that in this process lies the only hope for justice in the law." *Id.* at 105. Echoing our discussion of the disagreements about justice and Morality in Chapter 6 (see Part II, Section A.4 and Part II. C respectively), White explains why this is so:

> We talk about justice *abstractly* when we think about what the world should be like as though we could make it whatever we wanted, writing on a clean slate. Thus we might say that in a just country there would be universal education and health care, no death penalty for crimes, public support for the arts, and women's control over their bodies. These are not self-evident truths, however, and someone might say in response that in a just country education and health care and the arts would all be governed by the market, which is the most efficient and hence just allocator of human goods, that the death penalty would be used in cases of murder, and that women's control of their bodies would never include the killing of a human fetus.

Id. at 103. For further discussion of the types of "voices" that must be heard to achieve justice, and in effect of what it means to "listen" to them, see *infra* notes 94–99 and accompanying text (discussing White's account of "the art of law").

63. Berger and Sammons, *Mystery*, op. cit., at 12.

custom" that represents in some way the "collective wisdom" of this community.[64] And the notion that the identity from which this truth flows "is always a work in progress"[65] echoes MacIntyre's "provisional conclusion" in *After Virtue* that "the good life for man is the life spent in seeking for the good life for man, and the virtues necessary for the seeking are those which will enable us to understand what more and what else the good life for man is."[66] It also echoes his recently stated conclusion that "rational enquiry into and consequent disagreement about what human flourishing consists in in this or that set of circumstances is itself one of the marks of human flourishing."[67]

Whatever one's view of Sammons' lovely ideal, to which we have surely scarcely done justice here, there is, as in *Piscopolis*,[68] something in it of the call to come out of the Cave into the light of the Good, and something too of the Quest for the Grail. In the original Allegory of the Cave in Plato's *The Republic*, the Cave dwellers seek to overcome illusory appearances by engaging in a dialectical conversation that is a philosophical quest to discover a propositional and conceptual truth about Justice, a truth that is abstract and universal. Adapting the Allegory here to apply to Sam-

---

64. For discussion of this point, with references, see Jones, *Historical Framework*, op. cit., at 1104–05.

65. *See supra* note 60 and accompanying text.

66. MACINTYRE, AFTER VIRTUE, op. cit., at 219. Kelvin Knight describes this as MacIntyre's "notoriously 'provisional conclusion.'" Kelvin Knight, *Introduction, in* THE MACINTYRE READER 9–10 (Kelvin Knight, ed., 1998).

67. ALASDAIR MACINTYRE, ETHICS IN THE CONFLICTS OF MODERNITY: AN ESSAY ON DESIRE, PRACTICAL REASONING, AND NARRATIVE 25–26 (2016). MacIntyre's original Neo-Aristotelianism seems to have contemplated a continuing enquiry about the good life and human flourishing. Moreover, as we saw in Chapter 2 and Chapter 5, even though MacIntyre's conclusions about these matters have evolved and become more definite since the original publication of *After Virtue* in 1981, he still considers, as stated in the main text, that "rational enquiry into and consequent disagreement about what human flourishing consists in in this or that set of circumstances is itself one of the marks of human flourishing." *See* Chapter 2, notes 97–103 and accompanying text; Chapter 5, notes 27–36 and accompanying text. There is a clear parallel with the continuing enquiry in the legal conversation regarding what the realization of justice calls for in a particular set of circumstances. Interestingly, MacIntyre's original "provisional conclusion" was predicated on recognition of "tragic conflict" in our lives, which parallels the existence of tragic conflict in the law. MACINTYRE, AFTER VIRTUE, op. cit., at 201, 223–25; Knight, *Introduction*, op. cit., at 9; Sammons, *Missing Poetry*, op. cit., at points 5, 10, and 12.

68. *See* Chapter 5, note 37 and accompanying text.

mons' account, we Cave dwellers in *Juropolis* would seek to overcome the limitations of reductive propositions and conceptions by engaging in a rhetorical conversation that is an existential-theological quest to discover (or, perhaps better said, uncover) the experiential truth about that Justice which supervenes upon the law when the Law speaks to and through the judge — a truth that is about the meaning and purpose of *our* lives in *Juropolis*.[69] By proposing the particular phenomenological understanding of our ultimate excellence and thus the overarching common good that he does, Sammons is inviting us, his fellow inhabitants of *Juropolis*, to join in this existential-theological quest for meaning and purpose. In considering this invitation we should understand that Sammons is not rejecting the need for legal technique and legal reasoning — they have their necessary place, of course — but stressing that they can take us only so far and should never become untethered from the fundamental identity that is our way of being together in the world as an imagined, but experientially very real, legal *polis*. This is consistent with the procedure recommended in Part III, Section C of Chapter 2 and echoes the distinction between the "rationalists" and the "hybridists" in the practice of natural theology noted at the end of Part II of that Chapter.

The reader may wonder why we have focused so much on this one particular account of what "the realization of justice" might mean. There are several reasons. First, Sammons makes a serious and disturbing claim, which we should therefore take seriously and which should perhaps indeed disturb us. The claim is that although his account may seem strange, it only seems this way now because we have concealed from ourselves the

---

69. *See* Jack L. Sammons, *Afterwards*, op. cit., at 1163 (discussing theology as a practice concerned with "a search for ... meaning and significance" and "internal to (and constitutive of)" other practices, including the practice of law, which are therefore of "sacral or religious character"). At their deepest levels, then, arguably all of our enquiries, and the stories in which we make them, are an existential-theological quest for meaning and purpose. Echoing Sammons, perhaps that is why Plato was a poet. For more explicit theology regarding the practice of law, see Timothy W. Floyd, *The Practice of Law as A Vocation or Calling*, 66 FORDHAM L. REV. 1405, 1424 (1998):

> God is in the midst of all that we do as lawyers. The world of law practice — no less than any other place in God's creation — is a sacred place. God constantly calls us to serve God and our neighbors through our work as lawyers, and through that work to become the best people we can be.

Id.

reality of how we do in fact experience the law, and we have concealed this reality from ourselves because we dislike mystery and uncertainty and therefore seek control through conceptualizations.[70] Even more disturbingly, Sammons also claims that "other, instrumental descriptions of the legal conversation — those returning it to force, reducing it to politics, science, or economics, rejecting the idea of fictional truths, and denying the literary nature of justice — reveal the potential threats of injustice that they may well harbor." And these potential threats exist because "each would corrupt the game, limit its ability to civilize, and threaten its continuation by making it, not sacred, merely serious."[71] Indeed, in this context we should not overlook the irony of MacIntyre's observation that the only practical way for the liberal order to resolve conflicts entailed in its inconclusive philosophical debates over principles of justice is to have "the verdicts of its legal system" resolve them "without invoking any overall theory of the human good" but instead allowing "almost any position taken in the philosophical debates of liberal jurisprudence" to be invoked on occasion, with the result that "[t]he lawyers, not the philosophers, are the clergy of liberalism."[72] While Sammons himself may reject "any overall theory of the human good" as yet another corrupting conceptualization, lawyers should rightly be disturbed by any implication that, as "the clergy of liberalism," we may also be the clergy of injustice despite rhetorical claims to be the very opposite.

Second, Sammons' claim that he is describing how we in fact really *experience* the law helps explain Joe Vining's striking conclusion about Sammons' work, in particular about his use of music to illuminate the law:

A judge or lawyer finds the law. We do not say it's something new he made up on the spot. Everyone's attitude toward it would change utterly. What Sammons is doing in this extraordinary series of works looking to music is to take seriously law's authority and our dependence on it. Those newly engaged today in what they call the "empirical study of law" do not take authority seriously, and they are no more realistic than the "legal realists" of various kinds that flour-

---

70. Berger and Sammons, *Mystery*, op. cit., at 4; Sammons, *Listening*, op. cit., at 2.

71. Sammons, *Play*, op. cit., at 549–50.

72. Alasdair MacIntyre, Whose Justice? Which Rationality? 344 (1988).

ished in the last century. It is Sammons rather who is doing empirical work, and at a time when it was never more important.[73]

Third, echoing Justice Breyer's characterization of the legal conversation discussed above,[74] Sammons concedes that the legal conversation he describes is "messy."[75] But perhaps he is correct that his description of it "better reflects the messy reality of our social and moral world."[76] And if it does, then, echoing MacIntyre's critique of "Morality,"[77] "[p]erhaps, this messiness is the price to pay for locating a moral discourse within a real community of practitioners, arguing within a real moral tradition they are trying hard to interpret rather than in the non-existent community of universal moral agents."[78] Fourth, it is possible that Sammons' understanding of the "realization of justice" component of the ultimate excellence offers a more robust assurance than other understandings might do for achieving the ultimate excellence's other component of "social peace," to which we now turn.

2. Social Peace

Recall that the full articulation of the ultimate excellence of our common practice is "social peace in the liberal democratic state through the realization of justice for its inhabitants." We can discuss the "social peace" component more briefly than we did the "realization of justice" component because the particular understanding of this component in our overarching common good in *Juropolis* is arguably much less controversial.

We noted above that lawyers translate clients' intentional goals rooted in their various social activities into the language of *Juropolis*.[79] In other words, lawyers translate clients' intentional goals into the legal conversation. As Sammons explains, "[c]lients with strong and strongly conflicting intentional goals," which they often understand as "principled differences," represent the risk of using force or violence in our communities. Lawyers

---

73. Vining, *Jack Sammons*, op. cit., at 340.
74. *Supra* note 17 and accompanying text.
75. Sammons, *"Cheater!"*, op. cit., at 301.
76. *Id.*
77. *See* Chapter 6, notes 89–91 and accompanying text.
78. Sammons, *"Cheater!"*, op. cit., at 301
79. *See supra* note 12 and accompanying text.

provide an alternative to this potential for force or violence because they translate it into the "literary game" that is the legal conversation, which is always about the community itself, and because they keep clients within the community by speaking for them to the community.[80] The conversation is "insistently social: those who would join it must accept that at issue are differences among an 'us' and not just between a 'you' and a 'them.'"[81] And this "game" that is the legal conversation is sustainable because others, in particular "the political other," acknowledge the authoritative "justice" of the judgments made by judges and jurors.[82] This means, of course, that the common practice of maintaining *and living* by the rule of law in the liberal democratic state, which is the common practice of *all* the inhabitants of *Juropolis* — both the practice community of legal professionals as a whole and those they serve — is also sustainable.

The notion that the law and the legal conversation provide an alternative to force or violence is powerfully captured in the following exchange between Sir Thomas More and his son-in-law William Roper in Robert Bolt's play *A Man for All Seasons*. More has just refused to arrest Richard Rich for being "dangerous" although he has committed no crime:

ROPER.　So now you'd give the Devil benefit of law.

MORE.　Yes. What would you do? Cut a great road through the law to get after the Devil?

ROPER.　I'd cut down every law in England to do that.

MORE.　Oh? And when the last law was down — and the Devil turned around on you — where would you hide, Roper, the laws all being flat? This country's planted thick with laws from coast to coast — Man's laws, not God's — and if you cut them down — and you're just the man to do it — d'you

---

80. Sammons, *"Cheater!"*, op. cit., at 302–03; Sammons, *Play*, op. cit., at 544. For a somewhat different view, see Eugene Garver, *Justice, Play, and Politics*, 66 MERCER L. REV. 345, 348 (2015) (cautioning that "[z]ealous advocates can turn a disagreement into something much more polarized, something that turns out to have more potential for violence than the original dispute," and that "[t]o the extent that law does not involve violence, it is because politics does"). One response to Garver's latter point is that without law there would be even more violence. *See infra* notes 322–27 and accompanying text.

81. Sammons, *Play*, op. cit., at 546.

82. *Id.* at 544.

> really think you could stand upright in the winds that
> would blow then? Yes, I'd give the Devil benefit of law, for
> my own safety's sake.[83]

And it is strikingly demonstrated by the State violence unleashed upon
More himself when he is executed following perjured testimony by the
same Richard Rich — perjured testimony that represents corruption of the
legal conversation of the worst kind, because it involves cheating of the
worst kind. Sammons would urge upon us, however, that while the law and
the legal conversation are indeed reasonably seen as an alternative to force
or violence, they can also be seen, much less despairingly, as "point[ing]
to an ontology not of violence but of harmonious difference — towards a
peace in which difference, indeed tension, is relished as it is, for example,
in music"[84] and in which "[l]aw seeks ... to be a joyful exploration of our
difference, a reflection of 'the polyphony' of our ongoing existence, in Bonhoeffer's words."[85]

C. Flourishing Through Achieving the Common Goods of Practices[86]

In the previous section we considered the ultimate excellence and overarching common good of our common practice of maintaining the rule of
law in the liberal democratic state (or, more broadly, of maintaining and
living by the rule of law in the liberal democratic state). In Part I, Section
A we saw that at least four distinct law craft communities of legal professionals, and their respective practices of adjudication, lawyering, assisting the legislature, and legal education, combine in and co-constitute the
community of legal professionals as a whole and our common practice. We
also saw that each law craft practice has its own ultimate excellence and an
overarching common good, which is the craft community's particular understanding of this ultimate excellence and which entails, includes, and is

---

83. ROBERT BOLT, A MAN FOR ALL SEASONS (1960), ACT I, SCENE 6.

84. Sammons, *Play*, op. cit., at 549 n185; Jack L. Sammons, *The Law's Melody*, 55 VILL. L. REV. 1143, 1159 n78 (2010).

85. Sammons, *Law's Melody*, op. cit., at 1155–56 (citing DIETRICH BONHOEFFER, LETTERS AND PAPERS FROM PRISON: THE ENLARGED EDITION 305 (1972)).

86. For discussion of this topic in *Piscopolis*, see Part II, Section C of Chapter 5.

co-constituted by specific standards, goods, and qualities of excellence as specific ends or specific common goods of the practice. And each law craft practice is ordered to the ultimate excellence and overarching common good of our common practice (which entails, includes, and is co-constituted by the common goods of each of them). Moreover, because the four law craft practices are necessarily interdependent and interpenetrating, they also co-constitute one another in addition to co-constituting the common practice, even though their practitioners do not directly participate in one another's activities.

In subsection 1 of Section C we discuss in a general way the common goods of each of the four distinct law craft practices, including the "master virtue" of practical wisdom. This discussion corresponds roughly to the discussion of similar matters regarding Drew's commitments in *Piscopolis* at the beginning of Section C, and in subsection 1 of Section C, in Chapter 5, although in some respects it also anticipates the discussion of goods of effectiveness in Section D. In subsection 2 we will then discuss some specific matters related to achieving the common goods of the four law craft practices, corresponding to subsections 2–5 of Section C in Chapter 5.

1. Common Goods of the Four Law Craft Practices

As we proceed through the discussion in this subsection, addressing the respective common goods of the four law craft practices of adjudication, lawyering, assisting the legislature, and legal education, we should ask ourselves a series of questions, just as we did when addressing the ultimate excellence and overarching common good of our common practice in Section B: Am I personally committed to engaging in rational conversation that pursues the ultimate excellence or *telos* of my particular law craft practice? Am I also committed to the particular understanding of this ultimate excellence my law craft community might agree upon as the practice's overarching common good? Am I committed to achieving this overarching common good, and the specific common goods which it entails and includes and by which it is co-constituted, and to thereby promoting my own flourishing and the flourishing of those our particular practice serves? (Although it is a question to which we will return later, am I also committed to promoting achievement of the common goods of the other three law craft practices?) Even if I am so committed, how far does my particular craft community's agreement (and as appropriate, the agreement of the legal profession as a whole) on our common goods extend? In other words, how far do our overarching common good and our specific common goods remain controverted? How does their being controverted relate to disagreement about the overarching common good of the common practice, to which each distinct practice is ordered (and/ or to disagreement about the overarching common good of the practice of adjudication, to which the other three practices are in practice also largely ordered, as we already observed in Part I, Section A and as we will again discuss shortly below)? And are the common goods of the practice controverted so extensively or fundamentally that it places them under significant stress? Are they under stress in other ways too and, if so, why this is? And could the degree and types of stress they are under even threaten to corrupt these common goods?

As we proceed, we will address the "master virtue" of practical wisdom possessed by the expert practitioner. When discussing this virtue, our focus will not be on the powers of independent practical reasoning. As we have seen, these powers are foundational capacities the practitioner draws upon when exercising the four abilities that constitute practical wisdom.[87] Instead, our focus will be elsewhere. Specifically, we will draw upon Anthony Kronman's account of the professional character ideal of the lawyer-statesman in his 1993 book *The Lost Lawyer* — an ideal that originated in the nineteenth century and that should of course be understood nowadays in a non-gendered way. Kronman shows how this ideal, which is characterized by the interrelated twin virtues of practical wisdom and public-spiritedness or civic-mindedness, has been under pressure or even assault in the practices of lawyering, adjudication, and legal education.[88]

---

87. *See* Chapter 3, notes 19–23 and accompanying text.

88. *See generally* KRONMAN, LOST LAWYER, op. cit. For Kronman's very useful summary overview of the professional character ideal of the lawyer-statesman, see *id.* at 14–17 (giving a "provisional" and "preliminary" account of the classical nineteenth-century ideal of the lawyer-statesman and its twin virtues of practical wisdom and civic-mindedness). *See also id.* at 370–72 (situating the professional ideal of the lawyer-statesman within the culture of professionalism, which became very influential in the latter part of the nineteenth century, and explaining that the notion of a professional ideal, which developed as a secular successor to the Protestant idea of "a calling, of salvation through work," provided a professional identity rooted in the development of a distinctive professional character, and the basis for finding meaning and personal fulfillment through professional work). Although not every-

It is important to note, however, that when discussing practical wisdom, Kronman has a very particular understanding of this concept in mind. Thus, he is generally referring to what he regards as its "core," that is, the "bifocal" capacity for "sympathetic detachment."[89] Kronman describes this capacity as the capacity to combine two "opposing dispositions":

> Through one lens the alternatives are seen not merely at close range but (in contrast to the attitude of observation) from within, from the normative and affective points of view that the alternatives themselves afford. Through the other lens, each of the alternatives appears at an equally great distance. Anyone who has worn bifocal lenses knows that it takes time to learn to shift smoothly between perspectives and to combine them in a single field of vision. The same is true of deliberation. It is difficult to be compassionate, and often just as difficult to be detached, but what is most difficult of all is to be both at once. Compassion and detachment pull in opposite directions and we are not always able to combine them, nor is everyone equally good at doing so. It is, however, just this combination of opposing dispositions that deliberation demands ...[90]

---

one agrees, Kronman considers that the lawyer-statesman ideal remained highly influential throughout the nineteenth century and most of the twentieth century. *Id.* at 2–3, 11–12, 16, 354. He also considers, however, that the ideal gradually declined in prestige during the twentieth century to the point where it is now dying. *Id.* at 3–4, 12–13, 354. *But see* AM. BAR ASS'N, TEACHING AND LEARNING PROFESSIONALISM, REPORT OF THE PROFESSIONALISM COMMITTEE 5–9 & n21, 31 (1996) (apparently endorsing the lawyer-statesman ideal and quoting from Kronman's discussion of the ideal). For further discussion of the historical influence of the lawyer-statesman ideal on the law craft practices of lawyering, adjudication, and legal education during the nineteenth century, see Jones, *Historical Framework*, op. cit., at 1121–64.

89. *See* KRONMAN, LOST LAWYER, op. cit., at 66–74 (addressing the capacity of combining "compassion and detachment" in the context of first-personal deliberation), 87 (referring to "the contrasting dispositions that constitute the core of practical wisdom"). In several other places throughout the book, when discussing political deliberation, third-personal co-deliberation of lawyer and client, and judicial deliberation, Kronman refers to a combination of "sympathy and detachment" or uses the phrase "sympathetic detachment." See, for example, *id.* at 97–99 (political deliberation), 130–33 (co-deliberation between lawyer and client), 319–20 (judicial deliberation), 326–27 (first-personal, third-personal, and adjudicative deliberation).

90. *Id.* at 72.

Despite Kronman's use of the terms "sympathy" and "compassion," the term "empathy" may more accurately capture the first of these dispositions. As we already noted in Chapter 3, the ability to balance empathy and detachment may underlie the three foundational capacities of independent practical reasoning themselves and, as such, be at the very heart or core of practical wisdom.[91] It is also important to note that when discussing public spiritedness, Kronman is generally referring to what is, in our terminology, a civic-minded commitment to the overarching common good of the relevant practice.[92]

We will also draw upon James Boyd White's account of "the art of law" in his 2019 book *Keep Law Alive* — an account that resonates strongly with Jack Sammons' account of the "realization of justice" in the ultimate excellence and overarching common good of our common practice, discussed in section B above.[93] A "complex art of mind and imagination," the art of law is "the complex intellectual, ethical, and emotional life at the heart of the law."[94] It is a rhetorical and literary activity in which lawyers and judges know how to read, speak, and write "the language of the law" — how to use legal materials such as rules, concepts, cases, and statutes — to create legal meaning when this language "meets the world" in particular, typically problematical, situations, with the primary goal of achieving justice, rather than scientific truth.[95] In practicing their art in a "whole-mined response ... to the realities of our world and to ... the [inherited] materials of law," and with "whole-minded creativity," lawyers and judges must work with "a set of internal tensions, by which the old is made new, over and over

---

91. *See* Chapter 3, note 24 and accompanying text.

92. Thus, one way to express the interrelationship between these two virtues is that deliberating and acting in a particular way (with practical wisdom), procedurally, achieves the relevant overarching common good, substantively, and the disposition to deliberate and act in this way arises out of a civic-minded concern to achieve this substantive overarching common good.

93. *See generally* WHITE, KEEP LAW ALIVE, op. cit.; *see also supra* note 62 and accompanying text (further discussing White's account of achieving "justice as an institutional matter" or "justice in the law" and its consistency with Sammons' account of the "realization of justice" component in the ultimate excellence and overarching common good of our common practice).

94. *Id.* at xiv, 101.

95. *Id.* at 3–8, 41–43, 82–85, 100.

again."[96] Some of these tensions in the law are particularly relevant for lawyers, others for judges, and some for both. But each of these tensions

> [I]s … inherently unstable, that is, not resolvable by reference to fixed rules, principles, or conventions; each is dynamic, not static, thus moving us in new directions that we cannot always anticipate; each is dialogic, acting with the force of competing voices at work in the world or in the self. These tensions interact, to create fault lines that run through every act of full legal analysis. Their management is essential to the work of lawyer or judge.[97]

Some of the "competing voices" that must be managed are the voices of actual "speakers," including: the parties and their lawyers; expert and in-expert witnesses; authoritative official actors speaking through federal or state constitutions, legislation, and judicial decisions; and, depending on the type of case, perhaps unofficial actors such as sociologists, psychologists, philosophers, literary critics, and so on.[98] As we will discuss in greater detail in Section G.2 toward the end of this chapter, the role of

---

96. *Id.* at 3, 81–82, 158.

97. *Id.* at 97–98. White provides the following non-exhaustive summary enumeration of the "structural tensions, or clusters of tensions" and "competing voices at work in the world or in the self" (quoted here but reformatted as continuous text with the addition of roman numerals): (i) between ordinary language and legal language (indeed between language itself, of any kind, and the mute world that lies beneath it); (ii) between a multiplicity of voices, speaking from different positions within the legal order, or outside of it, in a variety of specialized and expert languages; (iii) between opposed lawyers, each of whom seems to resist the other at every point, though in another way they are cooperating deeply; (iv) within each lawyer, whenever she asks what it means for herself and the world that she is acting as she is; (v) between many conflicting but justifiable ways of giving meaning to the rules and principles of law, among which the judge will have to choose; (vi) between the reasoning and intuitive capacities of the judge herself; (vii) between substantive and procedural (or institutional) lines of thought, a tension that runs throughout the law; (viii) between the general and the particular; (ix) between the imperatives of law and justice; (x) between the past and the present, the present and the future, for law lives in time and out of shared experience. *Id* at 97–98.

98. For White's detailed explication of all the various speakers, voices, and tensions, see *id.* at 85–97, 104–05.

294 Professions and Politics in Crisis

these speakers in the process demonstrates how law and democracy are inextricably intertwined in the United States.[99]

Although White does not use the term, the rhetorical and literary activity he describes as "the art of law" can reasonably be regarded as the practical wisdom of the legal profession, viewed as a rhetorical community. Like practical wisdom in general, the lawyer or judge draws on other, more particular qualities of excellence in managing the multiple tensions and "competing voices" discussed above to respond appropriately to the context and particular circumstances of a given situation. And when the practical wisdom that is the "art of law" is properly exhibited, it enables us "to find open and respectful ways of imagining ourselves and each other," and thereby "to imagine justice into reality."[100]

White's art of law ideal complements, and can be combined and integrated with, Kronman's lawyer-statesman ideal to depict a more complete professional character ideal.[101] As the discussion continues, we will see that, like the lawyer-statesman ideal, the art of law ideal is also under pres-

---

99. *See id.* at 121 & n15; *infra* notes 340–42 and accompanying text.

100. *Id.* at 41–43. White concedes this is challenging because we inevitably confront and must come to terms with "impediments" in our nature, culture, language, and "the limits and corruptions of our own minds." *Id.* at 43.

101. White does not call the art of law an "ideal," although he does consider it to be "a matter of character and identity," so that "we must know who we are in reading ... and in writing [law], and what it calls upon us to do and to be." *Id.* at 41–42 (explaining that "[w]e need to know what is distinctive about our history, for good and ill: the nature of the experiment of government of the people, by the people, and for the people, and of the forces that threaten it"). However, it seems clear that a character "ideal" is what he is describing. Thus, he explains that he is depicting

> [T]he positive possibilities of life in the law ... an image of the activity of law at its most demanding and fulfilling, by which we can shape our efforts as we practice or teach it — an image, over the horizon, as it were, which we can keep before us as we do our work, a sense of how things might be if only we could make them so.

Id. at 101. Like any ideal, "these possibilities are not attained automatically, and never fully or perfectly, and sometimes they are corrupted." *Id.* But it can be achieved. Indeed, not only does White claim that his idealistic image of the legal conversation was confirmed when he entered law practice. *Id.* at 82–85. Even more importantly, he considers that the "whole way of thinking and acting with each other" he depicts is one that exists in states, cities, courthouses, and law offices throughout the land, "making up a web of connections that provides much of the informal constitution of our country." It is this that he seeks to keep alive. *Id.* at xvii.

sure or even assault in the various law craft practices that co-constitute our common practice. This means, of course, that lawyerly practical wisdom in the combined, more complete professional ideal is under pressure or assault as well.

a) The Practice of Adjudication. In Section B we described the ultimate excellence or *telos* of our common practice as "social peace in the liberal democratic state through the realization of justice for its inhabitants," which we elaborated as "social peace through realizing the ideal of Justice, that is, realizing the rights and duties assigned, and the benefits and burdens distributed, under the ideal Law." We can reasonably articulate the ultimate excellence of the practice of adjudication — in which judges decide disputes between litigants in an impartial manner and translate litigants' intentional goals, rooted in their legal claims, into the administration of justice — as follows: "To promote social peace by actually effecting the proper distribution of these rights and duties, benefits and burdens and thereby realizing Justice under the Law concretely in the cases coming before them." But just as the realizing justice component of the overarching common good of our common practice is controverted and we disagree about which distribution of rights and duties, benefits and burdens is the proper one, so the overarching common good of the practitioner community responsible for actually effecting this distribution — the judiciary — is necessarily and correspondingly controverted as well. The ultimate excellence and overarching common good of the practice of adjudication are, then, very closely and directly related to the ultimate excellence and overarching common good of the common practice. And this fact is of fundamental importance for all four law craft practices. Thus, as we already anticipated in Part I, Section A, because the judiciary ultimately decides any legal issue, the practice of adjudication has the closest practical relationship of all four craft practices to the ultimate excellence and overarching common good of the common practice, the role of the judge is a central focus of all of them, and in practice the other three practices are therefore largely ordered to the ultimate excellence and overarching common good of the practice of adjudication.[102]

---

102. *See* KRONMAN, LOST LAWYER, op. cit., at 109–21 (discussing the centrality of the case method focusing on appellate judicial opinions in law teaching), 123–25 (explaining that "judges occupy a position of preeminence among those who have a say in determining

Anthony Kronman provides what is in our terms a particular understanding of the ultimate excellence of the practice of adjudication and thus
one view of its overarching common good when he describes the judge's
public-spirited concern with "the good of the community represented by
the laws" — with "the well-being of the larger community of which [the
parties] are members, the community constituted by the laws the parties

---

the application of the law" and therefore "[t]he lawyer's expert knowledge of the law is ...
above all else a knowledge of judicial behavior, of what judges are likely to do when called
upon to say how the law should be applied"), 317–18 (discussing how judges directly hold
a "position of dominant importance" in dispute resolution, and indirectly hold such a position in the practices of legal education and lawyering as well because "the judicial point of
view" necessarily "shapes the outlook" of those engaged in both practices). However, some
readers may understandably question the centrality of the role of the judge in the practice of
transactional lawyering as opposed to litigation-oriented lawyering. For a cogent response,
see WHITE, KEEP LAW ALIVE, op. cit., at 83–84 & n1 (explaining that when the author entered law practice, it confirmed the view he had formed of law at law school, including his
perception that in settling a case by negotiation rather than litigation, the lawyers still imagined the arguments that might be made at a possible trial, and that *the same was true even
when drafting documents* because "the lawyers were always testing what they were writing by
imagining a dispute in court"). Readers who remain unpersuaded regarding the many situations in transactional lawyering where there is *normally* no real prospect of litigation (for
example, in drafting a will or performing a real estate closing, or preparing an application
for a public benefit) may want to consider that, in theory at least, the abnormal is always a
possibility. Moreover, the lawyer is still acting within, and with reference to, a settled legal
framework that is at least partially judicially determined, both in the form of common law
norms and in the form of judicially determined limits regarding the interpretation and
validity of any relevant statutory or regulatory norms. This latter point suggests two related
analogies. First, to recur to our fishing metaphor, if Drew is a transactional lawyer crew
member who tends to the nets (i.e., existing legal materials deployed in arguing and deciding current cases) and to the fish after they have been landed by the crew members who are
judges and litigators (i.e., the outcomes in current cases), can't Drew still see him or herself
as essential to the overall enterprise of "trawling for justice"? Second, there is the wonderful
story about the visitors to NASA during the Apollo era who asked a man in a lab coat what
he did there and he replied "I'm helping to put a man on the moon." It turned out that he
was the janitor. But he was able to imagine how his apparently menial and easily fungible job
was connected to a magnificent larger purpose. *See* Tanveer Naseer, *Forget Passion — Purpose is the Real Spice of Life* (TEDxConcordia, December 17, 2017), https://www.youtube
.com/watch?v=Z-EY84sFT4M (at 8:00 minutes). Wouldn't it be equally wonderful if the
many law students who become transactional lawyers could imagine themselves as being
similarly connected to the magnificent larger purpose of achieving social peace through
the realization of justice by virtue of the necessary role they play in maintaining the overall
system of justice, even though they are (only?) tending to the nets and landed fish as it were?

have invoked to settle their dispute." The judge's overall concern with "the good of the community represented by the laws" encompasses several specific concerns, including concerns for "doctrinal coherence," for "the responsiveness of doctrine to social and economic circumstances," and for "the bonds of fellowship that legal conflict strains but that must be preserved to avoid other, more destructive conflicts."[103] The first two concerns are especially focused on those elements in the overarching common good relevant to the "concrete realization of Justice" component in the ultimate excellence, and the third concern, which relates to what Kronman calls "political fraternity," is especially focused on the element relevant to the "promoting social peace" component.[104] With regard to the specific common goods, particularly the virtues, which are entailed by, included in, and co-constitutive of this overarching common good, and which are needed to achieve it, Kronman especially emphasizes practical wisdom — "a subtle and discriminating sense of how the (often conflicting) generalities of legal doctrine should be applied in concrete disputes" — and "judicial statesmanship." And as we have just seen, he emphasizes the judge's public-spirited concern for "the good of the community represented by the laws" — in other words, the judge's civic-minded commitment to the overarching common good of the practice of adjudication.[105]

The generality of Kronman's formulation of the overarching common good of the practice of adjudication seems flexible enough to accommodate most, if not all, substantive disagreements about it and about the

---

103. KRONMAN, LOST LAWYER, op. cit., at 118.

104. For Kronman's use of the term "political fraternity" to express this third concern, see *id.* at 319, 340–41.

105. *Id.* at 21, 113, 117–18, 319, 342. Although Kronman is discussing "[t]he common lawyer" and not judges specifically in the quoted language on practical wisdom (*id.* at 21), the point seems to apply to judges *par excellence*. Mary Ann Glendon's description of the "conventional understanding" of common law judging is very resonant with Kronman's depiction:

> [T]he common law judge is supposed to be a virtuoso of practical reason, weaving together the threads of fact and law, striving not only for a fair disposition of the dispute at hand but to decide each case with reference to a principle that transcends the facts of that case — all with a view toward maintaining continuity with past decisions, deciding like cases alike, and providing guidance for other parties similarly situated; and all in the spirit of caring for the good of the legal order itself and the polity it serves.

MARY ANN GLENDON, A NATION UNDER LAWYERS: HOW THE CRISIS IN THE LEGAL PROFESSION IS TRANSFORMING AMERICAN SOCIETY 180–81 (1994).

closely related overarching common good of our common practice. Because these overarching common goods are so controverted, so are the specific common goods — the specific standards, goods, and qualities of excellence — they entail, include, and by which they are co-constituted. In her 1994 book *A Nation Under Lawyers*, Mary Ann Glendon, for example, provides one well-known account which in effect addresses the controverted nature of these common goods and which identifies competing judicial ideals and virtues, specifically the "classical" ideal and the rival "romantic" ideal as well as a possible synthesis of both.[106] In describing the "classical" ideal, Glendon explains that "[at] least until the 1970s, judicial hagiography emphasized impartiality, prudence, practical reason, mastery of craft, persuasiveness, a sense of the legal system as a whole, the ability to preserve principled continuity while adapting the law to changed social and economic conditions — and above all, self-restraint."[107] With regard to this last judicial virtue, Glendon explains that

> Three distinct concepts of self-control can be discerned: structural restraint (respecting the limits on judicial power imposed by federalism, the separation of powers, and a court's position in the judicial hierarchy); interpretive restraint (observing the bounds imposed on judicial discretion by precedent, statute, or constitutional text, design, and tradition); and personal restraint (avoiding distortion of the decision-making process by one's own opinion of the parties or the issues).[108]

According to Glendon, beginning in the 1960s "the classical ideal associated with modesty, impartiality, restraint, and interpretive skill" has been challenged by a rival "romantic" ideal presenting "an image of the good judge as bold, creative, compassionate, result-oriented, and liberated from legal technicalities." Such judges "mak[e] their influence felt through fiat and rhetoric, rather than craftsmanship, good sense, and steadiness of temperament" and are "celebrated for their daring, imagination, sensitivity, and zeal for fairness." Although one might think that Glendon has ideo-

---

106. *See generally id.* at 109–73.
107. *Id.* at 118.
108. *Id.*

logically "liberal" judges in mind, her real concern is misplaced judicial assertiveness and arrogance, which she makes clear can be just as much of a concern, and sometimes even more of a concern, with ideologically "moderate" or "conservative" judges.[109] At the time of writing her book in 1994, then, Glendon considered that "classical and romantic attributes are competing for ascendancy, not only throughout the judicial system but within the psyche of nearly every judge" and she hoped for a synthesis resembling the "pragmatic, neoclassical catalogue of judicial virtues" articulated by Judge Richard Posner: "'self-restraint, self-discipline (implying submission to the authority of statutes, precedents, etc.), thoroughness of legal research, power of logical analysis, a sense of justice, a knowledge of the world, a lucid writing style, common sense, openness to colleagues' views, intelligence, fairmindedness, realism, hard work, foresight, modesty, gift for compromise, commitment to reason, and candor.'"[110]

But the common goods of the practice of adjudication have come under stress from another direction as well. In order to achieve the goods of excellence of this practice, especially excellence of the judge's performance and excellence of the product resulting from this performance, the judge must possess three qualities stressed by Kronman: disinterestedness, impartiality, and independence.[111] Clearly, these central virtues would be threatened by any "politicization" of the judiciary, such as arguably occurs when judges fail to exercise due self-restraint under the influence of the "romantic" ideal of judging discussed above, or that occurs when they bow to undue external pressure to conform judicial outcomes to satisfy the wishes, or forestall the criticism, of political actors who appoint, elect, or promote them.[112] In addition, some scholars worry that various devel-

---

109. *Id.* at 111–12, 117, 152.

110. *Id.* at 172–73 [quoting from RICHARD A. POSNER, THE FEDERAL COURTS: CRISIS AND REFORM 220 (1985)].

111. *See* KRONMAN, LOST LAWYER, op. cit., at 113, 118, 121, 323–24 (identifying these qualities).

112. For a useful and concise recent discussion of these latter concerns, see *Judicial Independence: Promoting Justice and Maintaining Democracy*, BOSTON BAR ASSOCIATION JUDICIAL INDEPENDENCE WORKING GROUP 10–15 (August 2019), https://bostonbar.org/docs/default-document-library/judicialindependence_aug2019.pdf?Status=Temp&sfvrsn=2. For a more extended discussion of the issues involved in trying to balance judicial independence and judicial accountability while ensuring judicial quality, see *Symposium: Judicial Professionalism in a New Era of Judicial Selection*, 56 MERCER L. REV. 913 (2005). *See also*

opments in the conduct of the judicial process itself, resulting from the vast increase in the caseload and consequent efforts to enhance judicial efficiency and productivity, also threaten these virtues.[113] One concern is that the growing use of pre-trial management techniques in "managerial judging" increases the risk of "transform[ing] [the judge] prematurely into a partisan of one of the positions involved" as well as the risk of undetected bias.[114] Another, related concern is that the increasing "bureaucratization of the judiciary ... has diminished the sense of personal responsibility judges feel for their decisions and led to greater anonymity in judging."[115]

Kronman shares these concerns but considers that managerial judging and the bureaucratization of the judiciary — the use of subordinates such as clerks, magistrates, and staff attorneys — threaten the master virtue of practical wisdom itself by "stifling [the] deliberative imagination on which the work of judging centrally depends."[116] Specifically, these developments threaten the judge's ability to exhibit the core capacity of sympathetic detachment. This threat matters because

> Judging ... is a deliberative activity that always starts from and returns to the specific facts of a concrete controversy, requires a combination of sympathy and detachment, and often presents the person engaged in it with conflicts between incommensurable goods, while nevertheless requiring him or her to pursue what I have termed the good of political fraternity. These are the characteristics of deliberation generally, and the work of adjudication exhibits them all in an especially pure form. Judging is a paradigm of deliberation, and so here if anywhere in the legal profession practical wisdom ought to be a well-understood and valued trait, especially given the absence,

---

Brendon H. Chandonnet, *The Increasing Politicization of the American Judiciary: Republican Party of Minnesota v. White and Its Effects on Future Judicial Selection in State Courts*, 12 Wm. & Mary Bill Rts. J. 577 (2004) (focusing on judicial selection by election).

113. On the vast increase in the caseload, see Kronman, Lost lawyer, op. cit., at 320–23 (discussing supply and demand for judicial services).

114. *Id.* at 323–24 (discussing the concerns of Judith Resnick).

115. *Id.* at 324–25 (discussing the concerns of Owen Fiss and Joseph Vining).

116. *Id.* at 325.

within the judicial sphere, of those intellectual and material forces that have helped to put this virtue on the defensive elsewhere.[117]

The bureaucratization of the judiciary threatens the ability of judges to exhibit the core capacity of sympathetic detachment because they become more dependent not only on their subordinates' perceptions of the facts of the case but also on the judgments these subordinates reach in making a preliminary evaluation of the litigants' claims.[118] And managerial judging threatens the exercise of judicial statesmanship, which depends on this core capacity, and hence it threatens the preservation of political fraternity. On this point, Kronman eloquently explains how some cases involve the "tragic" conflict of incommensurable claims. In such cases, a judge's exercise of "judicial statesmanship" helps "to preserve the bonds of political fraternity, to strengthen the willingness of opposing groups to continue as members of a common enterprise." The judge displays this statesmanship especially by producing a "commensurating opinion" while making the "extraordinary effort ... to engage incommensurable claims in a way that is faithful to each."[119] Managerial judging, however, "reinforces the tendency of judges to view the claims before them as commensurable" and thereby "dulls the tragic sense" judges need to make this "extraordinary effort."[120] In these and other ways, then, the lawyer-statesman ideal and its central virtues have been undermined even in the practice of judging where one would expect them to be most defended.[121]

---

117. *Id.* at 319–20.

118. *Id.* at 326–31.

119. *Id.* at 339–42.

120. *Id.* at 341–42. For Kronman's detailed explanation of how managerial judging has this effect, see *id.* at 331–37. Here Kronman also seems to suggest, in our terms again, that the managerial judge views the realization of justice component in the ultimate excellence through an economic lens and is therefore motivated by considerations of efficiency to "maximize" the production of justice in a quantitative sense.

121. *See id.* at 318–20 (comparing erosion of the lawyer-statesman ideal and its central virtues in legal education, lawyering, and adjudication), 342–47 (discussing how the increased tendency to fracture appellate courts by writing separate opinions diminishes colleagueship on the bench and further jeopardizes political fraternity), 347–51 (discussing how the role of law clerks in the process of writing opinions contributes to this fracturing and undermines the lawyer-statesman ideal in other ways as well).

Moreover, considering now Kronman's broader description of practical wisdom as "a subtle and discriminating sense of how the (often conflicting) generalities of legal doctrine should be applied in concrete disputes,"[122] this "subtle and discriminating sense" — which the judge exhibits through the judge's particular art within the general "art of law" depicted by White — is seriously imperiled by the cumulative effect of the stresses on the common goods of the practice of adjudication discussed above. These stresses compromise the judge's ability to manage the multiple tensions and "competing voices" present in a given situation, so as to respond appropriately to the context and particular circumstances in an effort to "reconcil[e] the ideal and the real" by "do[ing] justice under the law."[123] In particular, where there are competing reasonable readings of the law, they compromise the judge's ability to keep the voices of the two opposing lawyers "present and alive within [her]" and to "keep her mind open until she has heard it all, thought through it all" (thereby resisting any impulse to reach an overhasty decision), as well as the judge's ability to be guided by her educated and disciplined intuition in a hard case. Like the other tensions, the "strong tension between alternative ways of thinking" cannot be resolved "simply by reference to a rule or practice or phrase or idea, but must be [resolved] afresh, in every case, by an art of judgment."[124] White laments, therefore, that this art is disappearing, being increasingly replaced instead by ideology (for example, on the U.S. Supreme Court) or "whatever version of cost-benefit analysis, or other method or theory, happens to appeal" to the judge.[125]

b) The Practice of Lawyering. We can reasonably articulate the ultimate excellence of the practice of lawyering, or representing clients — in which lawyers counsel clients and, if necessary, speak for them as advocates of their interests and on their behalf, translating client's intentional goals, rooted in their social activities, into the language of *Juropolis* — as follows: "To achieve the client's objectives as far as possible, in an effective

---

122. *See supra* note 105 and accompanying text.

123. For earlier discussion of these tensions and competing voices, see *supra* notes 96–99 and accompanying text. For White's discussion of the judge's effort to "reconcil[e] the ideal and the real" by "do[ing] justice under the law," see WHITE, KEEP LAW ALIVE, op. cit. at 95–96 & n9, 102 n17.

124. *Id.* at 91–93.

125. *Id.* at 115–17, 119–20.

and responsible manner within the framework of the law and in a spirit of public service to promote justice." In their book *The Good Lawyer: Seeking Quality in the Practice of Law*, Douglas Linder and Nancy Levit identify the four models of lawyering developed by Thomas Schaffer and Robert Cochran: client victory (the lawyer as "the acknowledged expert" makes all the choices aimed at achieving a "win" to achieve the client's stated interests); client autonomy (the lawyer as "the hired gun" seeks to achieve the client's interests, with the client making all the choices); client rectitude (the lawyer as "the lawyer-guru" makes all the choices, aimed at "doing the right thing" in the best interests of everyone concerned); and client goodness (the lawyer as "the client's friend" co-deliberates with the client in moral conversation that wrestles with the moral issues involved to achieve the client's true interests, which also encompass the client's relationships within the communities to which the client belongs).[126] Very roughly, in terms of the discussion in Part I, Section C of Chapter 6, one might say that the first and second models are concerned with maximizing the client's preferences, while the third and fourth models attend to the moral constraints on those preferences. Again in our terms, these four models reflect four differing particular understandings of the ultimate excellence of the practice of lawyering, representing differing conceptions of the overarching common good of the practice. Linder and Levit clearly prefer the model of client goodness, as do Schaffer and Cochran.[127]

Kronman also prefers the model of "client goodness" and contrasts it with the model of "client autonomy," although he does not use these same terms and does not discuss the other two models. Thus he claims that, when necessary, in counseling a client a responsible lawyer will help the client clarify or determine his or her objectives and not simply accept them as given.[128] And in determining how to achieve these objectives within the framework of the law, the lawyer might have to predict how a judge may ultimately decide the matter in question and this requires the lawyer to

---

126. DOUGLAS O. LINDER & NANCY LEVIT, THE GOOD LAWYER: SEEKING QUALITY IN THE PRACTICE OF LAW 190–203 (2014) (drawing on THOMAS SCHAFFER & ROBERT COCHRAN JR., LAWYERS, CLIENTS, AND MORAL RESPONSIBILITY (2009)).

127. *Id.* at 193–92. For Linder and Levit's further elaboration of the model of client goodness, see *id.* at 187–93, 206–10.

128. KRONMAN, LOST LAWYER, op. cit., at 128–30, 132–33.

see the matter from the judge's point of view.[129] Moreover, much the same is true when the lawyer is engaging in advocacy on behalf of the client because counseling and advocacy are frequently intertwined, and because a lawyer who can view the matter from the judicial point of view will be able to make more persuasive arguments to the court.[130]

With regard to the specific common goods, particularly the virtues, which are entailed by, included in, and co-constitutive of this overarching common good, and which are needed to achieve it, Kronman again emphasizes the need for practical wisdom and public-spiritedness. Thus, the lawyer can only help the client clarify or determine his or her objectives by exhibiting the virtue of practical wisdom and co-deliberating with the client, in particular by exercising the core capacity of sympathetic detachment in "third-personal deliberation," which views matters from the client's point of view but also with the independent judgment necessary to help the client make a decision in the client's best interests, in this sense acting as "the client's friend."[131] And only lawyers who share the judge's public-spirited devotion to "the good of the legal order as a whole, the good of the community that the laws establish and affirm" — in other words, only lawyers who share the judge's civic-minded commitment to the overarching good of the practice of adjudication — can be "connoisseurs of judging" who excel at seeing matters from the judicial point of view, and thus excel at predicting how a judge is likely to rule and at making the most persuasive arguments to the court.[132]

As White explains it, Kronman's "connoisseurs of judging" do not view a judge as a "bundle of prejudices and beliefs and commitments and character traits" but rather "as an ideal judge, one who is always seeking to do justice under the law."[133] When making an argument to the court, there-

---

129. *Id.* at 123–26, 134–38.

130. *Id.* at 146–49.

131. *Id.* at 130–34.

132. *Id.* at 139–44, 149–50.

133. WHITE, KEEP LAW ALIVE, op. cit. at 96n9. At the same time, lawyers will realistically recognize that a particular judge may in fact be biased for or against their client. *Id.* For Kronman's explanation of why lawyers often cannot predict how a judge will rule, despite awareness of this reality or a clear trend in doctrinal development, see KRONMAN, LOST LAWYER, op. cit., at 135–38. For Kronman's claim that the good lawyer also needs a public-spirited appreciation of "judiciousness" to make persuasive arguments to juries, who have a "special duty of fair-mindedness much like that incumbent on a judge," see

fore, a lawyer should generally speak "out of a kind of truth" and sincerely or authentically "mean what she says," in the sense that the argument is a respectable one — indeed, the "best" one that can be made for the client, not only from the client's point of view but also from the point of view of the law — and therefore an argument that a judge could "decently and honorably" accept.[134] In other words, the lawyer

> [I]s saying that this is the best formulation of her client's case that can be made in our legal language — the one that best serves the most fundamental purposes of law, most fully respects the decisions made by others (legislatures, judges, agencies, private persons) that bear upon the case, and most accurately identifies and interprets the texts that govern it.[135]

The lawyer must also seek to show that the result for which she is arguing is compelled by both the law *and* justice, even though the lawyer on the other side will seek to show otherwise because what the law and justice require is legitimately controverted.[136] (The latter point means, of course,

---

id. at 150–51. For his claim that the good lawyer even needs a public spirited-like "love of cooperation" and of creating "transactional communities" when negotiating on behalf of a client, see *id.* at 151–54.

134. WHITE, KEEP LAW ALIVE, op. cit. at 8–9. The virtue required for this type of sincerity or authenticity is what Jack Sammons calls "[a] very particular form of honesty," *See infra* note 147 and accompanying text. For further discussion of "the accuracy and authenticity of the lawyer's current assertions on behalf of the client," see *infra* note 306 and accompanying text.

135. WHITE, KEEP LAW ALIVE, op. cit. at 8.

136. *Id.* at 9–10. White gives the following example to illustrate the point:

> Suppose ... you are trying to enforce a contractual penalty for nonperformance, which the other side says is too severe to be enforced. You will argue not only that the penalty is permissible under relevant case and statutory law, but that the rule validating it is a just one: it respects the free choices of the contracting parties; it tends to produce efficient results because it encourages the bargained allocation of risk; it makes possible certain high-risk investments by placing the loss on the party whose anticipated benefits are typically highest; and so forth. The lawyer on the other side will maintain not only that a penalty in excess of actual damages is unjust, but that the relevant case and statutory law, properly interpreted, prohibit it at least in this egregious form. And a judge too will struggle to show not only that the penalty is valid or

that the lawyer must try to see things not only from the judicial point of view but also from the opposing counsel's point of view, in order to appreciate the persuasiveness of the opposing arguments and thus to make the most effective arguments for his or her client.[137])

Of course, it is reasonable to ask how well a lawyer can do all this given the changes in the practice of adjudication Kronman and White lament, as discussed in subsection 1a) above. In any event, commitment to the overarching good of the practice of adjudication does not mean that lawyers must never recommend putting the client's interests first, for example by bringing a nuisance lawsuit or breaching a contract too expensive for the other party to enforce; and indeed they may well face dilemmatic situations in this regard, including situations where they need to exhibit the virtue of courage to resist client pressures.[138] In addition to their commitment to the overarching good of the practice of adjudication (albeit with this realistic qualification), acting "in a spirit of public service to promote justice" also means that civic-minded lawyers will contribute to law reform efforts and represent worthy causes and clients *pro bono*.[139]

A vision of good lawyering such as the preceding one suggests a broad view of the specific common goods of lawyering generally. Thus it suggests a capacious understanding of practical wisdom in which the lawyer will access, draw upon, and conduct a broad range of professional attributes (a broad range, then, of theoretical knowledge, skills, and qualities of char-

---

> invalid under existing law, but that the law as he reads it is fair and sensible and proper.

Id.

137. I am indebted to Jack Sammons for reminding me of this vitally important point. Sammons Email (September 18, 2020) [on file with author]

138. KRONMAN, LOST LAWYER, op. cit., at 144–46. *See also* LINDER & LEVIT, GOOD LAWYER, op. cit., at 210. The following observations are suggestive of the balancing involved:

> The good lawyer cares about the client in the most complete sense....Yes, it matters whether or not the client "wins" as a matter of law. Yes, respect for the client's autonomy is important. Yes, it matters whether the client does the right thing. But it also matters — it matters a great deal — that the client becomes the best person he can be.

Id. at 202.

139. *See* KRONMAN, LOST LAWYER, op. cit., at 365 (identifying these two activities when addressing the need to raise "the level of public-spiritedness within the profession").

acter).[140] Thus, Mark Aaronson explains that good judgment requires "the contextual synthesizing and prioritizing of a range of factors, including facts, feelings, values, and general and expert knowledge, all at once."[141] And Roy Stuckey and others refer to "the integrative application of knowledge, skills, and values" necessary for competent lawyering.[142] This good judgment is needed in the courtroom as well as the office.[143] Indeed, the need for lawyerly good judgment is ubiquitous even in "everyday lawyering activities."[144] The practically wise lawyer — the lawyer *phronimos* — has learned, then, to "think like a lawyer" in the broad sense. More than a skill, the "master virtue" of lawyerly practical wisdom "requires nothing less than a transformation of the person, an acquisition of a manner, bearing, and style of thought for life."[145]

---

140. See Chapter 3, notes 12–17 and accompanying text. For one account of the breadth of this range of attributes, see Mark L. Jones, *Fundamental Dimensions of Law and Legal Education: Perspectives on Curriculum Reform, Mercer Law School's Woodruff Curriculum, and . . . "Perspectives,"* 63 MERCER L. REV., 975, 995–1002, 1013–39 (2012).

141. Mark Neal Aaronson, *Thinking Like a Fox: Four Overlapping Domains of Good Lawyering*, 9 CLINICAL L. REV. 1, 32 (2002).

142. ROY STUCKEY ET AL., BEST PRACTICES FOR LEGAL EDUCATION 60 (2007).

143. See Daisy H. Floyd, *Practical Wisdom: Reimagining Legal Education*, 10 U. ST. THOMAS L. J. 195, 196–99 (2012) (giving several illustrations).

144. Aaronson, *Thinking Like a Fox*, op. cit., at 32 [quoted by STUCKEY ET AL., BEST PRACTICES, op. cit., at 68–69]:

> Although skill in legal reasoning is not as closed a process of reasoning as sometimes supposed, everyday lawyering activities are even less subject to formally structured deliberation. The factual situations are almost always fraught with complications, contingencies, and uncertainties. The areas of inquiry have no pre-definable limits and include small and large matters. Whether gathering information, communicating with others, planning courses of action, or contemplating client options, attorneys constantly make judgment calls. A lawyer's reliance on judgment runs the gamut from how to order and frame questions when interviewing or counseling clients, to what research leads to follow, to how to decide major issues of legal strategy, to how to identify and reconcile conflicting moral obligations. What the client regards as the problem may or may not be the problem. There may be a legal solution, but it is not clear that it would be the best solution. In short, in the practice of law, how best to proceed and what exactly to say and do are almost always problematic.

> *Id.*

145. Jack L. Sammons, *Traditionalists, Technicians, and Legal Education*, 38 GONZ. L. REV. 237, 238 (2002–03).

With regard to other, more particular virtues included in this capacious understanding of lawyerly practical wisdom, Pat Longan, Daisy Floyd, and Timothy Floyd identify and analyze five distinctive virtues of the professional lawyer — competence, fidelity to the client, fidelity to the law, public-spiritedness, and civility — in addition to the professional practical wisdom needed to make and implement a decision implicating one or more of these virtues under conditions of inherent uncertainty.[146] And Jack Sammons identifies at least fifteen specific, distinctive virtues, or "habits of thought and being," that are essential for the practical wisdom of the lawyer as rhetorician — essential for the lawyer's particular art within the general "art of law" depicted by White — and that are related to the preceding professional virtues in important ways. These virtues, which are perhaps best conceptualized as dialogical virtues, include:

- The ability to recognize what is shared in competing positions;
- An attentiveness to detail, especially linguistic detail;
- An attentiveness as well to the ambiguities of language;
- A use of these ambiguities both for structuring the conversation and analyzing the issue;
- A focus on text and a markedly different sense of its restraint;
- A rhetorical awareness of the reactions of potential audiences to each competing position and even to each argument;
- An imaginative anticipation of future disputes;
- A realistic assessment of the situation even as a partisan in it;
- A recognition of the persuasive elements of all positions, especially those in opposition to the lawyer's own;
- A very particular form of honesty;
- An insistence on practicality combined with an acceptance of complexity;
- A shying away from broad principles and "proud words";
- A concern with the procedures by which decisions are to be made;

---

146. *See generally* Patrick Emery Longan, Daisy Hurst Floyd, and Timothy W. Floyd, The Formation of Professional Identity: The Path from Student to Lawyer (2020); Patrick E. Longan, *Teaching Professionalism*, 60 Mercer L. Rev. 659, 666–69 (2009) (discussing these virtues).

- An equal concern with the quality of the roundtable conversation itself including a concern that all voices round the table be well heard and considered; and
- An evaluation of positions in terms of an objective hypothetical authoritative decision-maker who serves as stand-in for social judgment, and, thus, a consideration of each proposed course of action from a particular social perspective.[147]

As discussed in Chapter 3, these distinctive virtues may be profession-specific forms of more general virtues, or they may depend upon, presuppose, and indeed incorporate such virtues, or both. These general virtues include patience, attentiveness, diligence, conscientiousness, perseverance, resilience, courage, courteousness, loyalty, honesty, justice, temperance, empathy, respect for others, compassion, generosity, and so on.[148]

---

147. Jack L. Sammons, *The Georgia Crawl*, 53 Mercer L. Rev., 985, 985–86 (2002); Sammons, *Traditionalists*, op. cit., 246 n28 (2002) [quoting from Sammons, *Georgia Crawl*]. In identifying these virtues Sammons hypothesizes a community group composed of members of different professions addressing a difficult and complex problem facing the community. *See also* Linda L. Berger, *A Rhetorician's Practical Wisdom*, 66 Mercer L. Rev. 459, 469–70 (2015) (discussing Sammons' account of these virtues). There are clear relationships between Sammons' list of virtues and the virtues of professionalism, such as competence and civility. Of course, some of the virtues identified by Longan et al. and Sammons are shared by other professions. Longan, *Professionalism*, op. cit., at 666–68; Sammons, *Georgia Crawl*, *supra*, at 986. But, as Sammons notes, "[n]evertheless, …considered collectively [they] can be seen as defining a unique character for lawyers as an ideal." *Id.* For further discussion of Sammons' specific virtues and the more general dialogical virtues identified in Chapter 5, Part II, Section F.2, as well as the relationship of both to the virtues of professionalism, see *infra* notes 295–310 and accompanying text.

148. *See* Chapter 3, notes 35–37 and accompanying text. For more historical and/or jurisprudential treatments of the virtues needed by the good lawyer, in addition to the books by Glendon and Kronman, see Robert Araujo, *The Virtuous Lawyer: Paradigm and Possibility*, 50 Smu L. Rev. 433 (1997); Robert Araujo, *The Lawyer's Duty to Promote the Common Good: The Virtuous Law Student and Teacher*, 40 Tex. L. Rev. 83 (1999); Rosalind Hursthouse, *Two Ways of Doing the Right Thing*, in Virtue Jurisprudence 236 (Colin Farrelly and Lawrence B. Solum, eds., 2008); Robert F. Blomquist, Lawyerly Virtues (2008); Robert F. Blomquist, *The Pragmatically Virtuous Lawyer*, 15 Widener L. Rev. 93 (2009); Michael McGinnis, *Virtue Ethics, Earnestness, and the Deciding Lawyer: Human Flourishing in a Legal Community*, 87 N. D. L. Rev. 19 (2011); Michael McGinnis, *Virtue and Advice: Socratic Perspectives on Lawyer Independence and Moral Counseling of Clients*, 1 Tex. A&M L. Rev. 1 (2013). For more practical treatments, see, e.g., Essential Qualities of the Professional Lawyer (Paul Haskins, ed., 2013); Linder & Levit, Good lawyer, op. cit.;

Considering the matter again in our terms, Kronman claims that his understanding of the overarching common good of the practice of law-yering, and of the specific common goods entailed by, included in, and co-constitutive of this overarching common good — in particular, the virtues of practical wisdom and civic mindedness in the lawyer-statesman ideal — have come under stress in recent decades from two main directions. First, institutional changes in the practice and culture of large corporate law firms have greatly diminished the opportunities for cultivating and exercising the sympathetic detachment that is the core of practical wisdom.[149] Second, and related, a competing "narrow view" of the overarching common good of lawyering and of the specific common goods of the practice has arisen.[150] In this narrower vision, both in counseling and advocacy the lawyer takes the client's objectives as given and acts instrumentally as "merely a specialized tool for effecting his client's desires."[151] Because the client alone decides on ends and the lawyer is only responsible for the means, there is no need for the lawyer to exercise the core capacity of sympathetic detachment in "third-personal deliberation."[152] Moreover,

---

Larry O. Natt Gantt II & Benjamin V. Madison III, *Teaching Knowledge, Skills, and Values of Professional Identity Formation, in* BUILDING ON BEST PRACTICES: TRANSFORMING LEGAL EDUCATION IN A CHANGING WORLD 253, 254–60 (Deborah Maranville et. al., eds., 2015)(referring to various virtues as "values"). For an illuminating comparative perspective from the United Kingdom, see JAMES ARTHUR, KRISTJÁN KRISTJÁNSSON, HYWEL THOMAS, MICHAEL HOLDSWORTH, LUCA BADINI CONFALONIERI & TIAN QIU, VIRTUOUS CHARACTER FOR THE PRACTICE OF LAW: RESEARCH REPORT (The Jubilee Center for Character and Virtues, University of Birmingham (2014), https://core.ac.uk/download/pdf/33303623.pdf.

149. *See* KRONMAN, LOST LAWYER, op. cit., at 271–307 (detailing these changes, including a dramatic increase in firm size, increasing specialization and emphasis on technical expertise, weakening ties between the firm and its lawyers, increased emphasis on moneymaking and decreased emphasis on the intrinsic good of legal craftsmanship and the lawyer's way of life, and lengthening of the working day associated with billable hours). *See also* GLENDON, NATION UNDER LAWYERS, op. cit., at 15–108 *passim* (for further discussion of relevant changes).

150. *See* KRONMAN, LOST LAWYER, op. cit., at 122 (referring to "a particularly narrow view of what counselors and advocates do").

151. *Id.* at 123.

152. *See id.* at 123, 128, 130 (explaining that "[t]he client ... does all of the real deliberating ... decid[ing] what the goal shall be, and whether it is worth pursuing given the legal costs his lawyer has identified," and that "[t]he narrow view attaches no importance to the union of sympathy and detachment in which this capacity [for deliberative wisdom] consists").

although proponents of the narrow view do recognize the need, even in counseling, to predict how a judge may ultimately decide the matter, they consider that lawyers can make such predictions effectively without developing a civic-minded devotion to the overarching good of adjudication.[153] Similarly, White considers there are many lawyers who do not speak "out of a kind of truth" and sincerely or authentically "mean what they say," and who do not think about what justice requires, but instead will say anything to help the client win, although White also considers that this is at considerable cost to both their clients and themselves.[154] A lawyer in this narrower vision is aptly described as a "lawyer-technician" rather than a "lawyer-statesman."[155]

This competing, narrower vision of lawyering suggests a narrower view of the common goods of lawyering generally.[156] Thus it suggests a less capacious understanding of practical wisdom in which the lawyer will access, draw upon, and conduct a narrower range of professional attributes (a narrower range, then, of theoretical knowledge, skills, and qualities of character), including the virtues of lawyer professionalism and the related virtues of the lawyer as rhetorician.[157] And this stressing of the common goods of lawyering may reflect a disruption in the proper balance between

---

153. *Id.* at 125–28, 134, 138.

154. WHITE, KEEP LAW ALIVE, op. cit. at 8–9, 90. Thus, such lawyers "do not allow [themselves] to think at all about the right result, about what justice requires, but only about what arguments will work." But White considers that this may actually hurt the client, because such lawyers forfeit the trust and respect of "sensible judges," who will not listen to them, and it also hurts the lawyers themselves, because they are unable to respect what they do and who they are becoming ethically or morally. *Id.*

155. *See* KRONMAN, LOST LAWYER, op. cit., at 2–4 (explaining that the lawyer-statesman is "not simply an accomplished technician" possessing "technical legal expertise" but is "a person of prudence or practical wisdom as well[,] … a person of good judgment, and not just an expert in the law"), 128 (explaining that on the narrow view the role of the lawyer "may require great technical skill, but it does not demand either practical wisdom or civic-mindedness"). Of course, it is possible to be a "lawyer-technician" and impoverish the lawyer's art by reducing it to a matter of mere technique without necessarily being beholden to clients in the ways described in the text. I am indebted to Jack Sammons for drawing out this distinction among lawyers who reduce lawyering practice to technique. Sammons Email (September 18, 2020) [on file with author].

156. *See generally* GLENDON, NATION UNDER LAWYERS, op. cit., at 15–108 *passim.*

157. *Supra* notes 146–48 and accompanying text. *See* Longan, *Professionalism*, op. cit., at 674, 677 (suggesting some ways in which fidelity to the court and civility might suffer because a lawyer is too beholden to a client).

the practitioner's intrinsic and extrinsic motivations and between goods of excellence and goods of effectiveness.[158] There is clearly cause for concern. First, lawyer professionalism is important for both client and society.[159] But because the mechanisms for enforcing lawyer professionalism are relatively weak, it is essential that lawyers be intrinsically motivated to exhibit it.[160] Second, there is evidence indicating that such intrinsic motivation is diminishing among lawyers. Thus, research suggests that motivations — for "intrinsic rewards" (in other words, "goods of excellence," including the values of professionalism), on the one hand, or for "extrinsic rewards" (in other words, "goods of effectiveness), on the other — correlate with satisfaction and well-being, and with distress and dissatisfaction respectively.[161] In this respect, the extent of lawyer dissatisfaction, dysfunction, and unhappiness revealed by data is troubling, not only because these may themselves weaken intrinsic motivation,[162] but because they may stem from such weakened motivation in the first place.

An undue concern with goods of effectiveness over goods of excellence, then, not only threatens to corrupt the common goods of the practice directly, as discussed further in Section D below, but it also threatens to

---

158. *See id.* at 690–91(discussing "the connection between intrinsic motivations and the values of professionalism" and explaining how "the extrinsically motivated lawyer" is less committed to the virtues of professionalism than "the intrinsically motivated lawyer"); Sammons, *Traditionalists*, op. cit., at 244. Addressing a perceived "real problem of competence: the corruption of the truer excellences of our practice by large firms and large clients," Sammons explains that

> The problem is created by the fact that large firms, in combination with their large clients, devalue the practical wisdom that, according to the traditionalists, is the central constitutive component of our practice and its primary internal good and value. In its place, a narrow specialized expertise delivered by narrow specialized people who are, essentially, fungible as technicians and who must then be rewarded with external goods that, when out of balance with internal goods, corrupt the practice as they would any practice. This is sometimes described under the rubric of the "commercialization of the practice," but commercialization, as a reflection of rampant individual equalitarianism, includes many other forms of corruption as well.

Id. at 244 & n24.

159. Longan, *Professionalism*, op. cit., at 670–73.

160. *Id.* at 679–87.

161. *See* Chapter 3, note 108 and accompanying text (discussing the research showing this correlation);.

162. *See* Chapter 1, notes 23–25, 27 and accompanying text.

corrupt them indirectly because it correlates with lawyer distress and dis-satisfaction that further stresses these common goods. And this stress-ing of the common goods of the practice will doubtless be exacerbated by significant economic challenges in the market for legal services as the U.S. economy experiences the current pandemic-driven economic down-turn, just as it clearly was by the 2007–08 Financial Crisis and consequent Great Recession.[163] Indeed, more than a decade earlier, in 1996, the ABA Professionalism Committee already noted a perceived decline in lawyer professionalism since the 1980s.[164] The Committee identified six preva-lent themes articulated in the relevant literature relating to this perceived decline: (1) Concerns about lawyer competence and lawyer ethics; (2) An undermining of the lawyer's traditional role as independent counselor; (3) Negative consequences resulting from the growing commercialization of law practice in which law practice becomes a business rather than a profession (such as reduction of time available for public service activities and growing dissatisfaction regarding incompatibility with personal val-ues and goals); (4) Perceived adversarial system excesses, including loss of civility; (5) Loss of a sense of lawyers' ultimate purpose as related to serv-ing the public good by mediating between conflicting interests in society; and (6) Loss of a sense of law practice as a "calling."[165]

More hopeful, especially for a certain type of law school graduate, is Kronman's view that "there is reason to believe that a small-town or small-city practice may provide a more congenial setting" than other

---

163. For a good sense of all this, see, e.g., Dan Packel, *Will Law Firms Be Ready When the Next Recession Hits?*, Law Journal Newsletters (July 2018), http://www.lawjournalnewsletters.com/2018/07/01/will-law-firms-be-ready-when-the-next-recession-hits/?slreturn=20190718153218 (detailing developments such as the increasing use of in-house corporate counsel as well as alternative legal service providers to do legal work, declining productivity within law firms, increasing use of contract lawyers by law firms, increasing mobility among law firm partners and clients, and a much more "transactional" relationship between law firms and their partners and clients). *See also* Brian Z. Tamanaha, *Is Law School Worth the Cost?*, 63 J. LEGAL ED. 173, 173–77 (2013); Luz E. Herrera, *Educating Main Street Lawyers*, 63 J. LEGAL ED. 189, 198–99, 200–01 (2013) (giving statistics demonstrating the impact of the economic recession on the job market for lawyers and lawyer salaries as well as the dramatic increase in law school tuition since 2001 and resulting debt burden on law school graduates).

164. ABA, PROFESSIONALISM COMMITTEE REPORT, op. cit., at 2–3.

165. *Id.* at 3–4 (identifying these themes in a different order than the order presented here).

practice settings for those who wish to find the professional identity and achieve the professional fulfillment that will come from living out the law-yer-statesman ideal — an ideal that, interestingly and tellingly, the ABA Professionalism Committee appears to endorse in its 1996 Report.[166] This strongly implies that it is those law schools such as Mercer Law School, whose students will mostly enter small-town or small-city practice, that are best positioned to cultivate the lawyer-statesman ideal and its virtues in their students and to prepare them to practice the lawyer's particular art within the general "art of law."[167]

c) **The Practice of Assisting the Legislature.** We can reasonably ar-ticulate the central component of the ultimate excellence of the practice of assisting the legislature — in which legislative counsel draft legislation and translate legislators' intentional goals, rooted in their political activity, into the language of *Juropolis* as a formal source of law, and also provide ancillary services to lawmakers — as follows: "To draft bills reflecting the will of the legislature using language that is understandable and legally effective." Despite interesting jurisprudential debates over the appropriate balance between the legislative and judicial branches and the fascinating issues of political theory in a democracy that they represent, the fact of the matter is that courts have the last word in determining the meaning and constitutionality of statutes, just as they do on other matters regarding the legal conversation in *Juropolis*. In practice, therefore, even the ultimate ex-cellence and overarching common good of the practice of drafting legisla-tion are ordered to the ultimate excellence and overarching common good of the practice of adjudication. However, the meaning and application of the overarching common good of the practice of adjudication are con-troverted with respect to expressions of legislative will. Specifically, there is substantial disagreement regarding the correct approach to statutory interpretation (textualism, intentionalism, or purposivism, and the proper use of extra-textual materials such as legislative history) and regarding the correct approach to interpretation of the Constitution when determining the constitutionality of statutes (originalism versus more dynamic, evolu-

---

166. KRONMAN, LOST LAWYER, op. cit., at 378–81; ABA, PROFESSIONALISM COMMITTEE REPORT, op. cit., at 5–9 & n21, 31. For further discussion of the ABA Professionalism Com-mittee Report, see Jones, *Perspectives*, op. cit., at 999–1000.

167. *See* Jones, *Perspectives*, op. cit., at 1002–13 (discussing Mercer's Woodruff Cur-riculum).

tionary approaches).[168] Consequently, the particular understanding of the ultimate excellence of the practice of legislative drafting representing the overarching common good of this practice is necessarily and correspondingly controverted as well.

As in the case of judging and lawyering, because the overarching common good of the practice of legislative drafting has come under stress in recent decades, so have the specific common goods entailed by, included in, and co-constitutive of this overarching common good. Uncertainty regarding the interpretative norms that govern how a court should rule on what statutory language means and whether a particular interpretation is unconstitutional, as well as the abusive manipulation of legislative history such as committee reports, aimed at influencing the court, make it much more difficult for legislative counsel drafting legislation to exhibit the qualities of excellence of their particular art within the general "art of law." This is especially (but not only) the case when they have to use language that is deliberately vague or ambiguous to garner sufficient political agreement to ensure passage of a bill.[169] Specifically, one has to question how well a lawyer drafting a statute under such conditions can manage the unique "tensions" White identifies in this form of legal writing, such as tensions among the stated purposes of the area of law or the statute in question, or between the statute and common law and constitutional law, or between the statute and the institutional and behavioral context in which it must be applied.[170] And how well can the lawyer exhibit the special abilities Kronman considers necessary for statutory drafting — the ability to "imagine

---

168. For a good discussion of different approaches to statutory interpretation and the current debates regarding the ascertainment of statutory meaning, see LINDA D. JELLUM & DAVID CHARLES HRICIK, MODERN STATUTORY INTERPRETATION: PROBLEMS, THEORIES, AND LAWYERING STRATEGIES xxv–xxix, 43–51 (2d. ed., 2009). Of course, within any particular state jurisdiction, the approach to statutory interpretation may be more settled. *Id.* at xxviii. The different approaches to constitutional interpretation are apparent from reading any of the standard works on constitutional law. *See, e.g.,* NOAH R. FELDMAN & KATHLEEN M. SULLIVAN, CONSTITUTIONAL LAW (20th ed., 2019).

169. For discussion of the abusive manipulation of legislative history, see, e.g., Elizabeth A. Liess, *Censoring Legislative History: Justice Scalia on the Use of Legislative History in Statutory Interpretation*, 72 NEB. L. REV. 568, 573–74 (1993).

170. *See* WHITE, KEEP LAW ALIVE, op. cit. at 3, 10–21, 81 (specifically addressing the tensions involved in drafting the Model Penal Code but doing so in terms that also apply *mutatis mutandis* to other codes and statutes).

in advance a wide range of possible cases that may arise within [the statute's] orbit and ask how each should be resolved" and the ability then to "find the right words" covering these cases?[171]

But the stress on the common goods and art of legislative drafting is due not only to competing, radically different approaches to statutory and constitutional interpretation and the abuses some of these approaches enable. In addition, the increasing number and complexity of bills that need to be drafted, and the often severe time constraints in which this must be done, clearly have a negative effect as well, although this may be more of a problem with federal legislation than with state legislation.[172] Anyone who has to work with statutory materials, especially federal legislation, is quite familiar with the results.[173]

d) The Practice of Legal Education. We can reasonably articulate the ultimate excellence of the practice of legal education — in which academic lawyers teach law students and generate legal scholarship influencing lawyers and judges, translating the intentional goals of the inexpert, rooted in their need to learn, into expertise — as follows: "To help prepare law students for their lives as practicing lawyers through law teaching and to assist in the understanding, operation, and improvement of the legal system through legal scholarship." And here again, the particular understanding of this ultimate excellence representing the overarching common good of the practice is controverted.

---

171. KRONMAN, LOST LAWYER, op. cit., at 360–62 (discussing the special expertise of the lawyer on a committee consisting of a philosopher, an economist, and a lawyer who are charged with considering and drafting a statute in the area of corporate or commercial law, such as a statute regulating insider trading).

172. For federal legislation, see the comments of the U.S. Senate Office of the Legislative Counsel, http://www.slc.senate.gov/Drafting/drafting.htm (noting increasing volume, time demands, difficulty, and technical complexity).

173. I teach Immigration Law, for example, where the results are sometimes abysmal and can only partly be explained by Congress relying upon the administering agencies to supply the needed clarifications. More generally, continuing this focus on the consumer rather than the producer of the statutory (or regulatory) product, compliance lawyers face special challenges in this regard. I am indebted to Jack Sammons for drawing my attention to this point. Sammons Email (September 18, 2020) [on file with author]. For an introduction to the compliance attorney as a "third option" for a legal career, in addition to litigator and transactional lawyer, see David A. Matta, *The New Career Choice: The Compliance Attorney*, NATIONAL JURIST (February 1, 2018), http://www.nationaljurist.com /smartlawyer/ new-career-choice-compliance-attorney.

We can usefully consider disagreements regarding the first component — to help prepare law students for their lives as practicing lawyers through law teaching — using the conceptual framework or metaphor of the "three apprenticeships of professional education" articulated by William Sullivan and the Carnegie Foundation for the Advancement of Teaching in its Preparation for the Professions Project.[174] Thus, the several studies published in this Project envisage professional training as moving the student through three types of apprenticeships — the cognitive or intellectual apprenticeship (focused on doctrinal knowledge and cognitive skills), the apprenticeship of practice (focused on practical skills), and the apprenticeship of identity or purpose, or apprenticeship of professional formation (focused on values or virtues).[175] It is still generally agreed that law schools should provide the traditional "cognitive or intellectual apprenticeship" in which students acquire doctrinal knowledge and learn the skill of common law legal reasoning through classroom dialogue between

---

174. For general discussion of these three "apprenticeships of professional education," see William Sullivan, *Professionalism and Vocation Across the Professions, in* TOWARD HUMAN FLOURISHING: CHARACTER, PRACTICAL WISDOM, AND PROFESSIONAL FORMATION 108–09 (Mark L. Jones, Paul A. Lewis & Kelly E. Reffitt, eds., 2013); WILLIAM M. SULLIVAN, WORK AND INTEGRITY: THE CRISIS AND PROMISE OF PROFESSIONALISM IN AMERICA 207–10 (2005). For the individual studies in the Carnegie Foundation Preparation for the Professions Project, see CHARLES R. FOSTER, LISA E. DAHILL, LAWRENCE A. GOLEMON, & BARBARA WANG TOLENTINO, EDUCATING CLERGY: TEACHING PRACTICES AND PASTORAL IMAGINATION (2006); WILLIAM M. SULLIVAN, ANNE COLBY, JUDITH WELCH WEGNER, LLOYD BOND, & LEE S. SHULMAN, EDUCATING LAWYERS: PREPARATION FOR THE PROFESSION OF LAW (2007); SHERI SHEPPARD, KELLY MACATANGAY, ANNE COLBY, & WILLIAM M. SULLIVAN, EDUCATING ENGINEERS: DESIGNING FOR THE FUTURE OF THE FIELD (2009); MOLLY COOKE, DAVID M. IRBY, & BRIDGET C. O'BRIEN, EDUCATING PHYSICIANS: A CALL FOR REFORM OF MEDICAL SCHOOL AND RESIDENCY (2010); PATRICIA BENNER, MOLLY SUTPHEN, VICTORIA LEONARD, & LISA DAY, EDUCATING NURSES: A CALL FOR RADICAL TRANSFORMATION (2010).

175. The precise terminology varies across the sources cited *supra* note 174. For example, although the 2007 Carnegie Foundation study on legal education uses the term "apprenticeship of identity and purpose" to describe the third apprenticeship, the other Carnegie studies addressing physicians, nurses, clergy, and engineers use a variety of different terms, including "apprenticeship of professional formation." *See* Neil Hamilton, *Fostering Professional Formation (Professionalism): Lessons from the Carnegie Foundation's Five Studies on Educating Professionals,* 45 CREIGHTON L. REV. 763, 771–74, 794–95 (2012) (for discussion of this terminology and the reasons why Hamilton prefers the term "professional formation").

teacher and student using the Socratic case method.[176] There has also been an increasing consensus on the need to provide a robust "apprenticeship of practice" in which students learn various practical lawyering skills, such as legal writing, counseling, and oral advocacy.[177] However, there appears to be less consensus on the extent to which law schools should also provide an "apprenticeship of identity and purpose," or "apprenticeship of professional formation," in which students learn to acquire the virtues and values of lawyer professionalism, including a commitment to justice, and how to discover personal meaning in the practice of law.[178] Moreover, conceptions

---

176. For discussion of issues, challenges, and trends related to this "cognitive or intellectual apprenticeship," see SULLIVAN ET. AL., EDUCATING LAWYERS, op. cit., at 47–86. The Study characterizes the Socratic case dialogue method as "the legal academy's standardized form of the cognitive apprenticeship" and legal education's "signature pedagogy" (that is, the "key educational practice by which a given field creates a common frame through which it can induct new members," as is "bedside teaching during hospital rounds" in clinical medical training). *Id.* at 50.

177. For a discussion of issues, challenges, and trends related to this "apprenticeship of practice," see *id.* at 87–125. Written in 2007, the Study notes that "it remains controversial within legal education to argue that law schools should undertake responsibility for initiating and fostering this phase of legal preparation" with faculty at many schools "view[ing] courses directly oriented to practice as of secondary intellectual value and importance," but also noting that "there is evidence that this situation is changing" with "signs that education for practice is moving closer to the center of attention in the legal academy." *Id.* at 87–88.

178. For a summary of issues, challenges, and trends related to this "apprenticeship of identity and purpose," see *id.* at 126–61. The Study notes that this apprenticeship encompasses "issues of both individual and social justice" and "the virtues of integrity, consideration, civility, and other aspects of professionalism," as well as the "personal meaning that legal work has for practicing attorneys and their sense of responsibility toward the profession," but that despite the importance and urgency of such matters, "in legal education today, most aspects of [this] ethical-social apprenticeship are subordinate to academic training in case-dialogue method and contested as to their value and appropriateness." *Id.* at 128–29, 132.

For discussion of how law students develop, or further develop, and learn to exhibit various kinds of virtues (including the virtues of the good lawyer discussed in subsection 1 b) above) during their legal education addressing these three apprenticeships, see Mark L. Jones, *Developing Virtue and Practical Wisdom in the Legal Profession and Beyond*, 68 MERCER L. REV., 833, 852–68 (2017) (using Nancy Snow's three paradigms of virtue acquisition through habituation (*see* Chapter 3, note 15 and accompanying text), to categorize law school courses into three groups: those in which virtues necessarily supervene upon a law student's participation in the classroom experience outside of students' or even professors' awareness, as in courses using the Socratic case method of classroom teaching, for example; those in which virtues are consciously cultivated in students through explicit instruction,

of the law teaching component of the overarching common good are also
influenced to some extent by differences of opinion in the legal academy
regarding which model of lawyering is the appropriate one for which law
schools should prepare their students,[179] or regarding the extent to which
law schools should provide additional training beyond purely legal training to prepare their students for lives as citizen-leaders due to the many
different types of civic and political leadership roles that will become open
to them by virtue of their being lawyers.[180]

Some might question the distinctions drawn by the three apprenticeships metaphor, at least with respect to the traditional case method of
classroom teaching, stressing the foundational role of this method in developing law students' practical skills and forming their professional identity, in addition to imparting doctrinal knowledge and developing cognitive skills. This is not so much because law teachers may incorporate some
practical skills training — for example, skill in legal writing — and material addressing professional ethics and other relevant matters into courses
with a "doctrinal" focus. More fundamentally, the "three apprenticeships"
metaphor, although of heuristic value as an analytical construct, risks di-
viding what may already be significantly integrated. Thus, Jack Sammons
observes with respect to first year basic courses such as torts, property,
contracts, and criminal law:

> [T]he "case method" of instruction [is] an interactive reading of cas-
> es with each reading further refined by hypotheticals designed to test
> each reading and sometimes accompanied by a sequencing of cases
> in which a more refined rule emerges. This teaching ... is as much
> about professional identity (including the virtue of seeing good ar-

---

as in courses addressing legal ethics or professionalism, for example; and those in which
virtues are consciously cultivated in students through total immersion in the lawyer's way
of life and conscious guided reflection on the resulting experiences, as in experiential education courses such as externship or a clinic, for example).

179. For some sense of the impact of this issue on law teaching, see SULLIVAN ET. AL.,
EDUCATING LAWYERS, op. cit., at 131–32. For discussion of how these different models of
lawyering were reflected in the disputes between "traditionalists" and "technicians" and how
Mercer's Woodruff Curriculum sought to overcome the shortcomings of each approach by
fusing the best of both of them, see Sammons, *Traditionalists*, op. cit.

180. For further discussion of this issue, see Jones, *"Perspectives,"* op. cit., at 1051–53.

guments on both sides ...) and skills as it is about knowledge — more so, in fact. It is the primary shared shaping experience of lawyers, and the virtues it requires are central to any adequate understanding of what it means to be a lawyer.... [Students] have to become someone different (a different sort of reader, for example, but not just this) ... before they can do what is being asked of them in these courses[,] [acquiring] a certain tolerance of ambiguities, contingencies, and an unspoken respect for that within the law that points beyond us.[181]

As the above passage suggests, the case method serves to develop the several virtues of the lawyer as rhetorician.[182] And Kronman explains how, in addition to doctrinal knowledge and analytical and rhetorical skills, such as spontaneous public speaking, the case method serves to develop law students' moral imagination by cultivating both their capacity for sympathetic detachment and their acquisition of a judge's public-spirited concern for the well-being of the law.[183]

Even more extensively and fundamentally — and thus pressing his phenomenological approach to professional formation as described in Part III, Section D of Chapter 2 even further — Sammons proposes that when teaching the cases law teachers should immerse their students imaginatively in the "relational, contextual, and embodied" world of lawyering practice by, "at least conceptually," locating them within and having them explore all the relationships to the case that "give meaning to those cases, and meaning to those whose work they are." These relationships include the appellate judge, readers of the judge's opinion, the parties and opposing attorneys, the trial judge, the jury, and the community. In this way, the teacher can lead students, "step-by-step, to a love of, indeed a reverence for, the materials and experiences" of the world of lawyering practice and help them develop their authentic, professional selves, which are formed by, and will live amongst, these materials and experiences — professional selves who will also know how to be appropriately critical from within

---

181. Jack Sammons, *Confronting the Three Apprenticeships*, in TOWARD HUMAN FLOURISHING, op. cit., at 156–57 n12. *See also* Jones, *Developing Virtue*, op. cit., at 854–58 (discussing law school courses within Nancy Snow's first paradigm of virtue acquisition through habituation).

182. *See supra* note 147 and accompanying text.

183. KRONMAN, LOST LAWYER, op. cit., at 110–21.

the world of practice they come to inhabit.[184] Along similar lines, White urges that the traditional case method, when practiced properly, invites law students to engage in the "art of law" and "fac[e] the set of tensions" that must be managed in this art.[185] To have this desired effect, however, the cases must be regarded "not simply as instances of theoretical questions or the application of rules, but as pieces of the whole process of legal argument and thought... from the interview with the client to the appeal of an adverse judgment."[186] And White strongly implies that this sort of classroom teaching encourages students to discover the many interesting and challenging "ethical and intellectual possibilities of the lawyer's life," and to evaluate the work of judges as "performances of... the art of reconciling the ideal and the real" and not just by whether the result is politically sound or not.[187]

As we will see below, however, using the case method in the ways discussed above is threatened by developments related to the legal scholarship component of the overarching common good of the practice.[188] In any event, differing conceptions of the law teaching component of the overarching common good necessarily imply correspondingly different views regarding the specific co-constitutive standards, goods, and qualities of excellence it entails and includes as specific common goods — specifically, regarding which courses and experiences should be included in the law school curriculum and what qualifications are needed to teach these courses and provide these experiences. As the curriculum expands, a law school is correspondingly required to expand the range of qualifications possessed collectively by its teaching staff. In addition to differences in the doctrinal knowledge required for teaching particular subject matters in traditional classroom settings, expansion of the curriculum into

---

184. Jack L. Sammons, *The Art of Self and Becoming a Professional*, 68 MERCER L. REV. 741, 762–64 (2017).

185. WHITE, KEEP LAW ALIVE, op. cit. at 100 n13, 102 n17. For discussion of the multiple tensions and "competing voices" that must be managed in practicing the "art of law," see *supra* notes 96–99 and accompanying text.

186. WHITE, KEEP LAW ALIVE, op. cit. at 100 n13.

187. *Id.* at 102 n17 (creating this implication from the context in which law teaching is discussed together with these features of lawyering and adjudication and from the phraseology used in discussing them. Regarding the notion that judges are engaged in "the art of reconciling the ideal and the real," see *supra* note 123 and accompanying text.

188. *See infra* notes 204–09 and accompanying text.

newer areas of teaching such as practical skills training, professionalism, and more intensive experiential education involving real clients requires teachers with a different type of knowledge, skill set, and even, to some extent at least, ensemble of virtues. On this latter point, however, all law teachers should ideally possess and appropriately exhibit the virtues of lawyerly practical wisdom, public spiritedness, professionalism, and rhetorician discussed in subsection 1b) above, as well as the dialogical virtues discussed in Chapter 5, many of which indeed were originally envisaged for the academic context.[189] Differences among law schools regarding the content of the curriculum and the necessary qualifications of teaching staff have been magnified as law schools experiment with different curricular models, and sometimes *radically* different curricular models. One source in 2015 identified "change" as "the dominant characteristic of the current environment."[190]

As law schools began to feel the impact of the 2007–08 Financial Crisis and consequent Great Recession, the law teaching component of the overarching common good and its specific common goods started to come under stress from another, related direction as well. The combination of a decline in the market for lawyering services, the resulting downward trend in students' post-graduation employment prospects, and a high student debt load upon graduation created a perfect storm for protest. The following passage conveys the context:

> In the wake of the Great Recession, legal education experienced significant turmoil. After the recession, law school applications rose to an all-time high in 2010 in keeping with the broad historical pattern — in the face of a difficult job market, returning to school looks appealing to many in the potential applicant pool. But this stability was only temporary.

---

189. *Supra* notes 131–48 and accompanying text; Chapter 5, notes 167–72 and accompanying text.

190. BUILDING ON BEST PRACTICES op. cit., at xxxviii. The many contributions in this source convey a good sense of "the scope and speed of the ongoing changes in legal education" and "the significant currents swirling around U.S. law schools and beyond." *Id.* at xxxvii. *See also* STUCKEY ET AL., BEST PRACTICES op. cit., SULLIVAN ET. AL., EDUCATING LAWYERS, op. cit.

Large law firms, hit hard by the contracting economy, were the sector of legal employment that had driven expanding enrollments. These firms offered substantial starting salaries to new law graduates that made high law school tuition costs financed by debt seem like reasonable investments to prospective students. The new economic pressures were exacerbated by ongoing technological changes that threatened upheavals in the delivery of high-end legal services and drastically affected employment, including electronic discovery review. Firms merged, contracted, and even imploded, leaving many experienced and highly qualified attorneys out of work. Pressured to cut costs, clients of large law firms increasingly refused to pay for work done by new lawyers, which they viewed as paying for the cost of lawyer training. With a significant pool of prospective laterals, large law firms shifted their hiring away from recent law school graduates. Many of those graduates thus found themselves underemployed, or unexpectedly practicing as solos.

In the face of gloomy job prospects, taking on massive debt to finance a law school education no longer made economic sense, and law school applications plummeted for four years in a row in the face of crisis rhetoric.[191]

As part of this "crisis rhetoric," law schools were charged with betraying those students who had little or no prospects of employment requiring a JD degree and with being unduly lured by the pursuit of goods of effectiveness such as financial reward and prestige gained, for example, through a higher ranking in sources such as U.S. News and World Report.[192] Indeed, "[s]candals engulfed several law schools that provided misleadingly rosy and, in some cases, flat out false employment statistics," prompting the American Bar Association (ABA) to tighten its accreditation standards by requiring law schools to provide additional, complete, and accurate information regarding relevant matters.[193] Such serious charges of betrayal

---

191. BUILDING ON BEST PRACTICES, op. cit., at xxxviii.

192. *See, e.g.,* BRIAN Z. TAMANAHA, FAILING LAW SCHOOLS (2012). For Tamanaha's reiteration and updating of his argument and for some responses providing useful perspective on these charges, see *Symposium: Is Law School Worth It?*, 63 J. LEGAL. EDUC. 173–246 (2013).

193. BUILDING ON BEST PRACTICES, op. cit., at xxxviii.

and such serious misconduct by some law schools resulted in serious soul searching in a period of plummeting applications nationally, with many law schools reducing the size of their entering class, or experimenting with the radically different curricular models mentioned above, or both. Thus:

> From the fall of 2010 to the fall of 2013, first-year enrollment dropped 24%, in the face of a decline in applicants of 32%, with the decline most noticeable among younger applicants and those with higher LSAT scores.
>
> The myriad responses to these challenges are pulling legal education in conflicting directions. As influential commentators argued that law school should be reduced in length, some law schools responded by adopting year-round programs that compress courses required to obtain a J.D. degree into two calendar years. At the same time, the bleak job market and law firms' need for trained lawyers led to calls for law schools to produce "practice ready" graduates. In response, most law schools expanded their experiential education offerings, especially those that offer students supervised practice opportunities.[194]

There is also disagreement regarding the proper understanding of the second component of the ultimate excellence — to assist in the understanding, operation, and improvement of the legal system through legal scholarship — and thus regarding this component of the overarching common good. Disagreement centers especially on the extent to which legal academics should focus on producing legal scholarship that serves the needs of the other law crafts as opposed to writing for an audience of other legal academics.[195] Both Kronman and Glendon have been among

---

194. *Id.* at xxxviii–xxxix. Moreover, in 2014 the ABA adopted an accreditation standard requiring all law students to complete at least six credit hours of experiential education (defined as including a clinic, externship, or skills simulations course, or a combination of these). *See id.* (citing to and discussing the relevant ABA accreditation standard).

195. For discussion of this issue, see, e.g., David Hricik & Victoria S. Salzmann, *Why There Should Be Fewer Articles Like This One: Law Professors Should Write More for Legal Decision-Makers and Less for Themselves*, 38 SUFFOLK UNIV. L. REV. 761 (2005) (rejecting the distinction between "theoretical" and "practical" scholarship in favor of a focus on "engaged scholarship" that "addresses problems related to the law, legal system, or legal profession

the vocal critics of recent tendencies in legal scholarship. Thus, Kronman traces the development, in legal scholarship since the late 1800s, of an anti-prudentialist outlook that is hostile to the emphasis on practical wisdom in the lawyer-statesman ideal and associated with the rise of scientific law reform as a competing ideal, as manifested more recently in the law and economics and critical legal studies movements.[196] In addition to similar concerns over the rise of these two movements and movements related to the latter, such as feminist jurisprudence and critical race theory, Glendon laments the development of "advocacy scholarship."[197] Indeed, she considers that advocacy scholarship is not really scholarship at all because "its research is not conducted with an open mind and its results are not presented with a view toward advancing knowledge about the subject treated" but rather to advance and promote a particular interest or cause without engaging with contrary evidence and arguments, and sometimes even without revealing the existence of the author's partisanship.[198]

These developments regarding the legal scholarship component of the overarching common good have placed the co-constitutive standards, goods, and qualities of excellence it entails and includes as specific common goods—and especially the virtues—under increasing stress. Glendon is very concerned, for example, that traditional virtues of legal academics, such as "'scepticism, tolerance, discrimination, urbanity, some—but not too much—reserve towards change, insistence upon proportion, and above all, humility before the vast unknown,'" and especially "thoroughness, evenhandedness, and open-mindedness," are threat-

---

that affect a significant portion of society or the legal community," discussing the shift from "engaged scholarship" to "academic scholarship" and the reasons for this shift, and calling on law professors to produce more engaged scholarship because they are "uniquely situated to fill that need, and doing so is in our best interest"); Erwin Chemerinsky, *Foreword: Why Write?*, 107 MICH. L. REV. 881 (2009) (reviewing the various potential audiences for which legal academics may write, including students, practicing lawyers, judges, government decision-makers, and academics in the law and other disciplines, the various types of writing they may produce, and the various formats in which they may produce it, and concluding that such writing should be considered legal scholarship "if [it] makes a significant, original contribution to knowledge about the law," whatever the audience, type, or format).

196. KRONMAN, LOST LAWYER, op. cit., at 17–26, 165–270.

197. GLENDON, NATION UNDER LAWYERS, op. cit., at 206–15.

198. *Id.* at 208–09.

ened.[199] Moreover, she seems to consider that the threat is exacerbated by a commitment to diversity regarding "gender and minority status," combined with the apparent lack of commitment to "ideological" diversity, resulting in "a surprising degree of consensus on many points of politics, on the practice of law, the primacy of theory, and on constitutional law" on law school faculties in which "cultural conservatives and Republicans of any stripe are a decided minority."[200]

Although some may respond that Glendon has overstated her case by claiming the existence of a neutrality that disguised its own hidden biases and by failing to recognize that the inclusion of non-traditional perspectives on law faculties serves to cultivate the practical wisdom of aspiring and practicing members of a diverse legal profession working within a diverse society, her allegations of a lack of commitment to ideological diversity are troubling. To the extent they are well founded, it would mean that the dialogical virtues and the related political virtue of "an active and enquiring attitude towards radically dissenting views," as they are exhibited in the intellectual pursuit of academic legal scholarship and indeed more generally in the legal academy, are also under stress.[201] In turn, this raises the question regarding how far the legal academy truly regards *Juropolis*, or at least the part of *Juropolis* it inhabits, as "always, potentially or actually, a society of rational enquiry, of self-scrutiny."[202] Already in 1994, however, Glendon detected signs of a possible "counter-reformation" led by "dynamic traditionalists" who might be able to unite theory and practice while building on the contributions of the more recent movements in legal scholarship discussed above.[203] The prospects for such a counter-reformation may be unclear given the hyper-partisanship and polarization that has existed in

---

199. *See id.* at 198, 206 (discussing these qualities) [discussing and quoting from Learned Hand, *Foreword to Williston's 'Life and Law,'* in THE SPIRIT OF LIBERTY: PAPERS AND ADDRESSES OF LEARNED HAND 140, 142 (Irving Dillard ed., 1953)].

200. *See id.* at 215–17 (discussing these "diversity" issues).

201. For discussion of these dialogical virtues, see Chapter 5, notes 167–72 and accompanying text; *supra* note 189 and accompanying text; *infra* notes 295–310 and accompanying text. For discussion of the related political virtue regarding dissent, see Chapter 5, note 173 and accompanying text. I am indebted to Jack Sammons for suggesting that Glendon may have overstated her case, as discussed in the text. Sammons Email (September 21, 2020) [on file with author].

202. *See supra* notes 14, 32 and accompanying text.

203. GLENDON, NATION UNDER LAWYERS, op. cit., at 245–46.

our politics and general culture during the last several years and that has intensified since the 2016 election of Donald Trump as President.

Kronman has somewhat different concerns from Glendon. To use our terminology, he is much more concerned that developments related to the second component of the overarching common good may adversely affect the first component and its specific common goods. As Glendon's reference to a possible "counter reformation" led by "dynamic traditionalists" suggests, in 1994 Glendon was relatively optimistic on this score.[204] By contrast, although Kronman was also writing in the early 1990s, he considered it likely that the recent trends in legal scholarship — in particular the law and economics movement — would unduly infiltrate and adversely affect law teaching and the proper preparation of law students for legal practice throughout the legal academy.[205] In this regard, he observes that law and economics — a movement he considers to be hostile to the lawyer-statesman ideal and its character virtue of practical wisdom because it cannot acknowledge moral incommensurability and "equates judgment with calculation" — not only *in*formed almost every area of law but had *trans*formed teaching in certain fields, including corporations and commercial law, as well as contracts, torts, and property.[206] Writing more than twenty-five years later, White similarly singles out law and economics when expressing his own concerns about the disproportionate influence of "policy and theory abstracted from the life of the law" in presenting the cases in casebooks, and about the corruption of the law teacher's particular art within the "art of law." Thus, he "see[s] a turning away from the law in law schools themselves," which have become to some extent more like "'think tanks' or public policy institutes than ... schools of professional training."[207]

---

204. For Glendon's reasons why she was optimistic, see *id*. at 244–45, 246–50.

205. *See id*. at 243–46 (discussing Kronman's concerns but curiously not mentioning his particular concerns regarding the law and economics movement). For Glendon's arguably more sanguine view of the law and economics movement, see *id*. at 209–10.

206. KRONMAN, LOST LAWYER, op. cit., at 166–67, 267–70. Although Kronman also expresses concern about the influence of the critical legal studies movement, he describes the impact of law and economics as "the single most important change in American legal education in the last twenty-five years." *Id*. at 166–67.

207. WHITE, KEEP LAW ALIVE, op. cit. at 99, 117–18.

To the extent Kronman and White are correct in their assessment of these developments, there is a risk that over time the resulting corruption of legal reasoning will inevitably spread beyond the legal academy to influence the entire legal profession and thus the arguments lawyers make to courts and the opinions generated by judges[208] — something that our discussion of the law craft practices of adjudication and lawyering in subsections 1a) and 1b) above suggests does indeed seem to be occurring. Then, in a vicious circle, some of these judicial opinions themselves become included among the materials for study in the casebooks and classroom teaching. (To recur to our fishing metaphor, the fishing boats begin to take the fishing crews to new fishing grounds where a different type of justice is to be found and, as the crews become increasingly seduced by this change in the catch, the boats return there more and more frequently.) None of this is to deny, of course, that economics and other nonlegal disciplines have a place in the life of the law, but it must be a proper place in which the language of these disciplines is appropriately "translated" into the language of the law.[209]

2. Related Matters

We will now consider the commitments related to achieving the common goods of practices that are discussed in subsections 2–5 of Section C in Chapter 5, as they apply to achieving the common goods of the four law craft practices discussed above. To keep the discussion manageable, our main focus will be on the practices of lawyering and legal education, especially the former, although we will occasionally address all four craft practices, and in any event much of what we say about lawyering or legal education will apply *mutatis mutandis* to the other law craft practices as well.

---

208. *See, e.g.,* KRONMAN, LOST LAWYER, op. cit., at 271–72 (observing that as law students absorb the "disdain for practical wisdom" that is signaled by "the topics and methods" to which their teachers expose them, "the antiprudentialist outlook so prominent in contemporary legal thought spreads throughout the culture of the profession as a whole and comes to have a broader influence on lawyers generally").

209. WHITE, KEEP LAW ALIVE, op. cit. at 104–05, 118 n12, 121 n15. *See also* KRONMAN, LOST LAWYER, op. cit., at 157–58, 358–63, 375–76 (stressing that the lawyer's distinctive expertise is "the art of handling cases" and that the role of non-legal disciplines in practicing this art is a subordinate one).

a) Relationships of Giving and Receiving. As legal professionals inhabiting *Juropolis*, are we committed to ensuring that apprentice lawyers are adequately nurtured within a network or networks of relationships of giving and receiving enabling them to learn "the elements of various practices," including appreciation for their common goods, to develop their powers of independent practical reasoning so that they reason well about these common goods and about their own individual good, and to acquire practical wisdom? In the first instance, of course, this question concerns the practice of lawyering, to which the education and preparation of law students is typically oriented. We might think that the answer is clearly affirmative because most law students receive three years of legal education at law school before they take the state bar exam and because, as we have seen, the purpose of law teaching is to help prepare students for their lives as practicing lawyers — subject, of course, to what we said about the impact of the 2007–08 Financial Crisis and consequent Great Recession as well as certain recent trends in legal scholarship on the common goods of law teaching.[210]

One of the main reasons, however, why the "apprenticeship of practice" and the "apprenticeship of professional formation" have been moving into the legal academy — and one of the main reasons, therefore, why the legal profession continues to argue about the law teaching component of the overarching common good of the practice of legal education and its specific common goods[211] — is significant pressure from the community of practicing lawyers that law schools take more responsibility for these elements of a lawyer's preparation for practice.[212] And one of the main reasons why the practicing bar has been pressuring law schools to take such increased responsibility is that so many practicing lawyers are no longer able or willing to discharge their traditional responsibility of providing these apprenticeships themselves. This certainly seems to be the case regarding the apprenticeship of professional formation as the tradition of mentoring by more experienced members of the practicing bar — and thus this aspect of the networks of giving and receiving within the practice of lawyering — has broken down, especially under the pressures of an "exponential increase in

---

210. *Supra* notes 174, 191–94, 204–09 and accompanying text.

211. For discussion of the "three apprenticeships of professional education" and related arguments about the common goods of the practice of law teaching, see *supra* notes 175–78, 181–90 and accompanying text.

212. Longan, *Professionalism*, op. cit., at 660–61.

the number of lawyers in the last forty years and the rampant commercialism that seems to permeate society generally,"[213] but it seems equally to be the case regarding the apprenticeship of practice as well.

Despite some notable countertrends such as certain state bar mentoring programs and the American Inns of Court associations,[214] the general trend, then, has been for the relevant network of giving and receiving responsible for the apprenticeships of practice and professional formation to shift from the craft community of practicing lawyers to the craft community of academic lawyers. It remains to be seen whether law schools' current efforts at curricular experimentation will yield satisfactory results, and also whether the practicing bar can be effectively integrated into these efforts and thus reintegrated into the network of giving and receiving now increasingly responsible for providing these apprenticeships. Examples of how such integration can occur include the participation of practicing lawyers, as well as judges, as guest speakers and interviewees in courses about the legal profession, as placement supervisors acting in cooperation with full time law school faculty supervisors in externship courses, and as adjunct faculty teaching advanced skills and other overtly practice-oriented courses.[215]

The above reference to "rampant commercialism" also suggests the challenges involved in helping law students learn how to reason well about the common goods of the practice and about their own individual good.

---

213. *Id.* at 673–74.

214. For information on Georgia's model Transition Into Law Practice Program (TILPP), also known as "The Mentoring Program," see https://www.gabar.org/membership/tilpp/. For information on American Inns of Court associations, see http://home.innsofcourt.org/AIC/About_Us/What_Is_an_American_Inn_of_Court/AIC/AIC_About_Us/What_Is_An_American_Inn_of_Court.aspx?hkey=d3aa9ba2-459a-4bab-aee8-f8faca2bfa0f.

215. For example, Pat Longan's "Legal Profession" course at Mercer includes an award-winning component called "Inside the Legal Profession" modeled on the television show "Inside the Actor's Studio" hosted by the late James Lipton. For further discussion of this component, in which "[t]he participants have included big firm lawyers, legal aid lawyers, prosecutors, defense counsel, transactional lawyers, and many others," and of the Gambrell Professionalism Award that it earned from the ABA Standing Committee on Professionalism in 2014, see Patrick Emery Longan, *Further Reflections on Teaching Professionalism: A Thank You Note to Jack Sammons*, 66 Mercer L. Rev. 513, 518–20 (2015). Like many law schools, Mercer also has a robust externship program, in which I teach myself, and numerous practice-oriented courses taught by adjunct faculty members who are full-time practicing members of the legal profession.

This implicates, of course, the balance between intrinsic and extrinsic motivations and between goods of excellence and goods of effectiveness that we already noted when discussing the practice of lawyering and that we will address again in Section D below.

b) Role of the Virtues. Are we committed to exhibiting the virtues necessary to achieve powers as an independent practical reasoner and to discover, attain, and then continue learning about the common goods within our particular law craft practice, in the relevant relationships of giving and receiving? Specifically, if I am a law student and aspiring lawyer, do I exhibit general virtues of independence such as justice, courage, honesty, and temperateness, so that I give due deference to the greater experience and wisdom of my law teachers and supervising legal professionals (in law school clinics or externship field placements, for example), courageously expose my inadequacies when learning how to become a lawyer, honestly accept criticism of these inadequacies and suggestions for improvement, and stand back from and evaluate my desires with temperateness in this process?[216] And among the virtues of acknowledged dependence do I exhibit appropriate gratitude to my teachers and supervisors as a virtue of receiving?[217] If I am a law teacher or supervising legal professional, do I myself exhibit the virtues of independence I seek to cultivate in aspiring lawyers, as well as virtues such as care for the student and subject matter that are necessary for effective teaching?[218] And among the virtues of acknowledged dependence do I exhibit the composite virtue of just generosity, which is made up of several virtues of giving and which disposes me, after I have myself received from others, to repay the resulting debt by giving in return, and to do so in an uncalculating manner and thus even when the giving is disproportionate and asymmetrical to what I received?[219] This last question points to the reason why the breakdown of the tradition of mentoring within the practice of lawyering is so troubling. As Pat Longan explains:

---

216. *See* Chapter 3, notes 56–58 and accompanying text; Chapter 5, notes 61, 68, 71 and accompanying text.

217. *See* Chapter 5, notes 70, 75 and accompanying text.

218. *See* Chapter 5, notes 65–66, 68, 71 and accompanying text.

219. *See* Chapter 5, notes 70, 73–74 and accompanying text.

The third apprenticeship of values and ideals at one time was passed from one generation to the next by senior lawyers who served as mentors. Although that still happens to some extent today, the disproportionate number of younger lawyers, at least for a generation, makes it difficult to have meaningful mentor relationships. Once such a chain is broken, it is difficult to fix it. A lawyer who has matured without the guidance of a mentor, especially in frenzied times of excess commercialism, is unlikely to recognize the need to mentor younger lawyers or have the desire to do so. One primary reason why older lawyers mentor younger lawyers is out of a sense of gratitude for the mentoring they received when they were young. A lawyer who never got it never gives it. Even if they do respond to the exhortations of the bar to act as a mentor, these lawyers are unlikely to pass along the right lessons to the next generation because they never learned them. This lost generation is another reason why it is so important to teach law students about professionalism.[220]

In addition, whether I am a law student and aspiring lawyer, or a law teacher or supervising attorney, do I appropriately exhibit the dialogical virtues, humility and resulting attunement to the materials of the practice, and truthfulness in accountability?[221] Do I also appropriately exhibit any of the virtues already discussed that may be necessary for me to learn from the exemplary achievements of past practitioners and the tradition of the practice?[222] If I am a fully qualified legal professional of a law craft practice, do I exhibit in my relationships with other relevant legal professionals those virtues necessary for me to sustain my powers, and to sustain others in their powers, as an independent practical reasoner within this craft practice and in continued learning about its common goods?[223] And am I committed to development and exercise of the virtues in *Juropolis* not only in the particular ways that are discussed above and discussed below in Sections D, E, F, and G but because, in all these different contexts, the

220. Longan, *Professionalism*, op. cit., at 674–75.
221. *See* Chapter 3, note 61 and accompanying text (dialogical virtues); Chapter 3, note 63 and accompanying text, Chapter 5, note 61 and accompanying text (humility); Chapter 5, note 76 and accompanying text (truthfulness in accountability).
222. *See* Chapter 3, note 60 and accompanying text.
223. *See* Chapter 5, notes 62, 67 and accompanying text.

virtues also protect against the risk that we might fall into vicious ways and be the perpetrator or victim of vicious actions?[224]

c) Role of Rules. In addition to exhibiting the appropriate virtues, are we committed to observing all appropriate rules in this and other relevant contexts? This question is not just about those general rules MacIntyre characterizes as fundamental rules of natural law but also (and perhaps even more immediately and directly important to our work as legal professionals) the constitutive rules governing our particular practices, their "rules of the game" as it were.[225] More specifically, in the practice of lawyering, for example, the rules that govern the activity or "game" of representative adversarial advocacy within the legal conversation include rules of evidence and procedure, and ethical regulations.[226] If I am engaging in this activity — when I am "playing this game" — do I have the lusory attitude, restricting myself to the lusory means permitted by these constitutive rules, so that I truly "play the game" and can achieve the lusory goal of being declared the winner and thus legitimately attain the prelusory goal of, for example, obtaining a judgment in favor of my client?[227] Or am I instead prepared to "cheat" by using "more efficient" means, such as

[S]urreptitiously introducing inadmissible evidence; filing suit for improper purposes;... asserting an unwarranted privilege in an effort to prevent discovery;... not reporting jury misconduct that worked to [my] advantage;... participating in ex parte contacts with a judge;... cross-examining a witness for the purposes of harassment;... advising witnesses not to talk to opposing counsel;... [or] using inadmissible closing arguments;...[228]

---

224. *See* Chapter 5, notes 79–81 and accompanying text.

225. *See* Chapter 3, notes 159–71 and accompanying text.

226. Sammons, '*Cheater*'!, op. cit., at 282; Sammons, *Play*, op. cit., at 543.

227. Sammons, '*Cheater*'!, op. cit., at 278 (lusory goal of being declared the winner), 281 (true players), 282 (prelusory goal, lusory means, constitutive rules, and lusory attitude "within the game of representative adversarial advocacy"). *See also* Sammons, *Play*, op. cit., at 542–43 (summarizing this part of the account in '*Cheater*!').

228. Sammons, '*Cheater*'!, op. cit., at 273. Sammons lists several additional examples of "cheating" in the game of "representative adversarial advocacy," such as "billing two clients for the same work" or "advertising deceptively." *Id.* While some of these additional examples may or may not involve violation of "constitutive rules," they certainly violate "constitutive

And again, observance of the constitutive rules clearly also helps to con-stitute the virtues, including those distinctive virtues that are specific to the practice of lawyering — think, for example, about such distinctive profes-sional virtues as fidelity to the law and legal institutions, or civility[229] — and to sustain the relationships of giving and receiving within the practice, whereas cheating by violating such rules will erode these virtues and relationships.

d) Broader Concerns and Interdependencies. Even if we are commit-ted to achieving and sustaining the powers of an independent practical reasoner in the relationships of giving and receiving within our own law craft practice and to discovering, attaining, and continuing to learn about its common goods, and are therefore also committed to developing and exhibiting the necessary virtues and observing the necessary rules, are we also committed to realizing these same things for all other legal profes-sionals, and indeed for *every* able and potentially able inhabitant of *Jurop-olis* in their various practices? Do we understand the extensive and per-vasive direct and indirect mutual interdependencies that exist among the inhabitants of *Juropolis* and how our own flourishing depends upon the flourishing of others, and that we should therefore want them to attain the common goods of practices as well as adequate goods of effectiveness too?

Specifically, if I am a practicing lawyer, do I understand that my own excellence and flourishing — my own success — in the law craft practice of lawyering depends directly on other practicing lawyers who value and attain the goods of excellence to stimulate healthy competition in striving for excellence, to correct my mistakes, and to perform well so that defi-ciencies in their performance do not impede my own performance?[230] And do I understand how my success in this practice also depends di-rectly on other legal professionals — judges, for example — valuing and attaining the goods of excellence in their own law craft practices?[231] If

---

norms." *See id* at 284 (discussing different types of constitutive norms and a broad under-standing of "cheating").

229. *See supra* note 146 and accompanying text (identifying these "distinctive virtues of the professional lawyer").

230. For the crew member Drew analog of this point, see Chapter 4, notes 51–52 and accompanying text. Of course, in any given case I may benefit in the short-term from the deficiencies of other lawyers. But even if this is not technically "cheating," as discussed in subsection 2 c) above, is it necessarily a "good" win when I do so?

231. For the crew member Drew analog of this point, see Chapter 4, notes 87–88 and accompanying text

I am a practitioner in one of these other law craft practices — if I am a judge, a lawyer assisting the legislature, or an academic lawyer — do I understand that something similar is true regarding others engaged in the same practice as my own, and regarding legal professionals engaged in the other law craft practices? And if I am a law student, do I understand how something analogous applies — even regarding my fellow law students (although this may require major reforms in the methods of assessment in legal education)?[232]

Do I understand, too, that I should seek to attain the common goods not only of my law craft practice but of all the practices in which I participate because each one is constitutive of my flourishing and because my success in one may contribute directly or indirectly to my success in another? Moreover, do I understand that I should promote the excellence and flourishing of those engaged in practices and activities in which I do not participate or upon which my success in practices is not directly dependent (as my success in the practice of lawyering, for example, is directly dependent upon judges), because my success in practices depends *indirectly* upon so many others to do their jobs well and to do them well also for all those upon whom I depend directly or indirectly? And do I understand that I should want the other inhabitants of *Juropolis* to acquire adequate goods of effectiveness, especially money, as well as to attain goods of excellence because I may be less successful in the practice of lawyering, for example, if others cannot sustain their own practices and activities or afford my legal services? Do I have a sense of the vast interconnectedness among things in "the world of law," and perhaps also beyond?[233]

D. Attitude Toward Goods of Effectiveness, and Role of the Virtues[234]

Although we understandably and inevitably pursue goods of effectiveness as well as goods of excellence, is our primary motivation for engaging in our particular law craft practice intrinsic, so that we are commit-

---

232. *See, e.g.,* Timothy W. Floyd, *Legal Education and the Vision Thing*, 31 Ga. L. Rev. 853 (1997) (discussing several reforms that would promote a more cooperative *ethos* for law students).

233. For the crew member Drew analog of these several points, see Chapter 4, notes 92–98 and accompanying text. *See also supra* note 58 and accompanying text (world of law).

234. For discussion of this topic in *Piscopolis*, see Part II, Section D of Chapter 5.

336 Professions and Politics in Crisis

ted to systematically subordinating goods and qualities of effectiveness to goods and qualities of excellence in this practice? Or is our primary motivation extrinsic, so that we systematically subordinate excellence to effectiveness instead? Do we primarily aspire to inward growth or are we primarily ambitious for external validation?[235] In other words, are we more like fishing crew member Drew, or are we more like crew member Cash? Are we guarding against the moral risks that, as a result of undue concern with economic or other extrinsic considerations, we might succumb to the individual or collective temptation to "cheat" or otherwise contribute to corrupting the common goods of our particular law craft practice (and the common practice of maintaining the rule of law), or might too readily

---

235. *See* Judge Lee H. Rosenthal, *Hallows Lecture: Ambition and Aspiration: Living Greatly in the Law,* MARQUETTE LAWYER 19–37 (Fall 2019) (discussing the relative place of "ambition" and "aspiration" in the law craft practices of adjudication, lawyering, and legal education (including among law students), with several responses from various commentators interspersed throughout her article). Although Judge Rosenthal does not use the terminology of effectiveness versus excellence, her contrast between ambition and aspiration is more or less equivalent. Thus, ambition "is the desire for external validations that you already know you want ... [and] ... tries to acquire what we already value — whether money, praise, publication, tenure, or promotion," whereas aspiration "is a distinctive form of purposeful action directed at acquiring new values, and these values are not abstract, but deeply practical and active." *Id.* at 20, 23. Drawing on the work of philosopher Agnes Callard, Judge Rosenthal elaborates on the distinction as follows:

> Ambition helps propel us down a path we already want to travel. It does not help us explore a new path or go to a new place.... Callard describes aspiration as a "form of agency in which one acts upon oneself to create a self with substantively new values by allowing oneself to be guided by the very self one is bringing into being." It can be an aspiration to expand understanding or knowledge into a new area. It can be an aspiration to become a more effective counselor, a gifted teacher, a wise judge. This is not because it will bring material reward or external praise but, rather, because it will change oneself.... As aspirants we try to see the world through another person's eyes, especially through the eyes of the person who has the value we aspire to acquire. In aspiration, it is this created self, the self with the desired values, that can make intelligible the path this person wants his or her life to take.... Aspiration is not merely a vague hope or wish, although it often begins that way. It is, as Callard puts it, "rational, purposive value-acquisition." In order to value something, we must engage with it in a way that takes time, effort, and practice.

Id. at 23 [citing and quoting AGNES CALLARD, ASPIRATION: THE AGENCY OF BECOMING (2018)]. At least one commentator is more skeptical of ambition as a "laudable goal" than Judge Rosenthal appears to be. *See* Darren Bush, *Doing the Right Thing, id.* at 22.

abandon our particular practice situation or even the common goods of the practice altogether?

Specifically, if I am a lawyer in private practice, am I able to resist the economic and other pressures to be a narrow "lawyer-technician" who just does my client's bidding, no questions asked, and thereby avoid betraying the art of lawyering?[236] Am I able, more generally, to resist the economic pressures resulting from the growing commercialization of law practice in which it becomes a business rather than a profession in "frenzied times of excess commercialism," marked by an "exponential increase in the number of lawyers in the last forty years and the rampant commercialism that seems to permeate society generally"?[237] Or am I unable to resist these pressures because of my ambition "to win the approval of more-senior associates, partners, and clients — those with power to promote and reward" — and my ambition "to make money, to accumulate wealth, not just to attain financial security"?[238] But is it very difficult for me, and even unreasonable to expect me, to eschew such ambition and resist such pressures if I face an enormous debt in the form of student loans equivalent to a mortgage (or even greater), especially in times of economic downturn and a declining market for lawyering services?[239] And if I am a lawyer in public service or practice public interest lawyering, am I able to resist other

---

236. *See supra* notes 149–65 and accompanying text (discussing the rise of a "narrow view" of lawyering).

237. *Supra* notes 213, 220 and accompanying text. *See* Longan, *Professionalism*, op. cit., at 674 (discussing how economic considerations pose challenges for the professional virtues of fidelity to the client, public service (specifically pro bono work), fidelity to the court, and civility in lawyering in general), 676–77 (discussing how such considerations can further "competence as technical capacity" but challenge "competence as practical wisdom" as well as the other four virtues in large firm practice), 677 (discussing how in house lawyers' economic dependence upon one client can challenge fidelity to the law), 677–78 (discussing how a public service lawyer's long term economic interest in possible employment by a regulated entity can challenge fidelity to the client), 678 (discussing how high volume, low cost lawyering can challenge competence and fidelity to the client). In this early article Longan included practical wisdom under competence and therefore identified only five of the six distinctive professional virtues discussed *supra* note 146 and accompanying text.

238. Rosenthal, *Ambition and Aspiration*, op. cit., at 20. Judge Rosenthal contrasts such ambition with, for example, the aspirational "value of developing the skills of a fine craftsman in the practice of law." *Id.* at 34.

239. *See supra* note 163 (for sources discussing these economic matters and giving relevant statistics).

types of extrinsic pressures and temptations resulting, for example, from my overly zealous devotion to a worthy goal or "cause"?[240]

If I am a legal academic at a certain type of law school, am I complicit, if only through silence, in efforts by my law school and university administrations, engaged in the secondary practice of making and sustaining the institution, to lure prospective students with little or no chance of success in order to obtain their tuition dollars or achieve a higher law school ranking, or both?[241] Even if this is not a concern at my particular law school, do I support, encourage, and participate in serious deliberation about needed curricular reform to properly prepare students for a life in the law, or do I instead just seek to protect my own selfish interests in the undue pursuit of extrinsic goods such as a more leisurely life or my personal ambition "to win the approval of those hiring, making decisions to publish, to promote, to grant tenure, and perhaps to confer that oh-so-coveted named chair" and thereby to move up in the law school world and the hierarchy of law schools?[242] Is my scholarship unduly driven by such ambition, moreover, or by my commitment to a cause or to a totalizing theory (for example, certain versions of law and economics), so that I do not adequately serve the needs of an appropriate audience, or betray the art of law teaching, or am tempted to compromise my scholarly integrity in various ways, or all

---

240. *See* Longan, *Professionalism*, op. cit., at 678 (discussing how a "fervent prosecutor['s]" desire to win and "protect the public… at all costs" may challenge fidelity to the court, and how cause lawyering can challenge fidelity to the client). *See also* Sammons, *'Cheater'!*, op. cit., at 291–92, 303 (discussing the "well-meaning prosecutor" who overlooks planted evidence or false police testimony in the name of "justice"). *See also id.* at 273 (listing failure to reveal exculpatory prosecution evidence as an additional example of cheating).

241. *See supra* notes 192–93 and accompanying text (discussing charges leveled at law schools and scandals involving law school misconduct in this regard).

242. *See supra* notes 174–90 and accompanying text (discussing migration of the apprenticeships of practice and professional formation from the law craft practice of lawyering to the law craft practice of legal education and the resulting impact on, and implications for, the content of a law school's curriculum and the qualifications needed by its teaching staff). For the quote on ambition, see Rosenthal, *Ambition and Aspiration*, op. cit., at 20. For a good discussion of the issues involved in hiring "scholars" at lower-ranked law schools, see Philip L. Merkel, *Scholar or Practitioner? Rethinking Qualifications for Entry-Level Tenure-Track Professors at Fourth-Tier Law Schools*, 44 CAP. U. L. REV. 507 (2016).

of these?[243] Am I able in general to resist the temptation to unduly pursue extrinsic material and psychic rewards that might prevent me, not only in these but in other respects, from discharging my ethical and professional responsibilities in teaching, scholarship, and institutional deliberation as specified, for example, in the Association of American Law Schools (AALS) Statement of Good Practices?[244] And if I am a law student, am I unduly driven by my ambition for "wealth, [my] parents' or teachers' approval, and professional or social status" and my ambition "to get good grades; a coveted position on a journal, on moot court, as a research assistant or judicial intern; a judicial clerkship; a desired summer job; a permanent offer"?[245]

---

243. *See supra* notes 195–98, 204–09 and accompanying text (discussing potential audiences, including law students, the development of anti-prudentialist and advocacy tendencies in legal scholarship, and the negative impact of these tendencies on the art of law teaching). Regarding the advocacy role of legal academics, on the one hand, section V of the AALS Statement discussed immediately below (on Responsibilities to the Bar and General Public) states that "engaging in law reform activities or advocating for improvements in law and the legal system is a valued role of legal academics," and on the other hand, section II (on Responsibilities As Scholars) states that "[t]he scholar's commitment to truth requires intellectual honesty and open-mindedness." Judge Rosenthal "worr[ies] that ambition, not aspiration, accounts for some of the esoteric, hyper-specialized subjects of [scholarly] publications" and she also "worr[ies] about the broad, sometimes seemingly reflexive, academic hostility to justices and lower-court judges appointed by a president of a certain political party, about an incentive to take this position because it is popular in the academy and perceived as enhancing the likelihood of publication." Pursuing such ambition divides "natural allies [who] are united in having the luxury of the ultimate aspiration: of having the duty only to be right, fair, and just, free of any duty of advocating for a client's interest." Moreover, "with both the academy and judiciary under what can feel like a siege," she urges "that both aspire to understand one another and to speak to, and if possible for, each other's concerns and fears." Rosenthal, *Ambition and Aspiration*, op. cit., at 34. For a rousing critique of the scholarship "game," see Lawprofblawg and Darren Bush, *Law Reviews, Citation Counts and Twitter(Oh my!): Behind the Curtains of the Law Professor's Search for Meaning,* 50 Loy. U. Chi. L.J. 327 (2018) (discussing the institutional and personal corruptions involved in seeking "external validation" by "measuring scholarship success using metrics such as law review ranking, citation counts, downloads, and other indicia of scholarship 'quality'").

244. Ass'n Am. Law Sch'ls, Handbook, Statement of Good Practices: Law Professors in the Discharge of Their Ethical and Professional Responsibilities (1989; am'd. 2017), https://www.aals.org/about/handbook/good-practices/ethics/.

245. Rosenthal, *Ambition and Aspiration*, op. cit., at 23, 33. Judge Rosenthal contrasts such ambition with the concerns of aspiration: "What do I aspire to in becoming a lawyer? What am I learning to value, through a rational and purposive process of working to learn

We can ask analogous questions regarding the practices of adjudication and assisting the legislature. Thus, if I am a judge, whether appointed or elected, do I let extrinsic political or ideological considerations compromise appropriate self-restraint or unduly influence my decision-making in other ways?[246] Do I let extrinsic "economic" pressures related to judicial efficiency and productivity otherwise unduly diminish the quality of my decision-making?[247] Do I betray the art of judging in these ways because of my ambition "for appointment or nomination; then, high rankings in bar polls; being cited and affirmed; and reelection, retention, and promotion," and to attain the associated material or psychic extrinsic rewards?[248] And if I am a lawyer engaged in the practice of assisting the legislature, am I able to uphold the art of statutory drafting by resisting "economic" pressures from lawmakers to "produce" in an extremely busy, even chaotic, law-making environment in which the quality of the resulting product may leave something to be desired?[249]

Even if I am personally able to resist the sorts of temptations and pressures discussed above, am I also committed more generally to the systematic subordination of goods of effectiveness by practitioners of all four law craft practices and of other practices in *Juropolis*, to help guard against the moral risks resulting from the undue pursuit of such goods? And am I committed to exhibiting, and to other members of the legal profession and other inhabitants of *Juropolis* exhibiting, the virtues necessary to exercise powers of independent reasoning in relationships of giving and receiving

---

and care about something new, something more than I came to law school already valuing." *Id.* at 33.

246. *See supra* notes 111–12 and accompanying text (discussing politicization of the judiciary).

247. *See supra* notes 113–21 and accompanying text (discussing managerial judging and bureaucratization of the judiciary).

248. *See supra* notes 122–25 (discussing the negative impact on the art of judging); Rosenthal, *Ambition and Aspiration*, op. cit., at 20 (for the quoted language). Judge Rosenthal cautions that "[a] judge who appears ambitious to the extent of excluding aspiration can lend credibility to the perception of judges as politicians in robes," especially "[i]f an ambitious judge is one willing to reach a particular result, or follow a particular approach, even if the record and law do not support it." *Id.* at 34. And she contrasts such ambition with the aspiration of being "independent and accountable," specifically of being "constrained — by precedent, by the facts and record, and by concerns for institutional integrity and independence." *Id.* at 37.

249. *See supra* notes 172–73 and accompanying text (discussing the negative impact of these features of the legislative process on the art of statutory drafting).

within practices — virtues of independence such as justice, courage, honesty, temperateness, humility, and practical wisdom — in order to resist any pressures or temptations to weaken or even reverse a shared commitment to the systematic subordination of goods and qualities of effectiveness to goods and qualities of excellence?[250] Indeed, am I committed to exhibiting these virtues — perhaps courage, above all — even when I am told to simply accept certain "realities" or else suffer negative consequences for challenging them? Or would such a commitment and willingness to suffer negative consequences, depending on my individual and family circumstances, be impossibly "heroic"?

E. Just Allocation of Goods of Effectiveness and Other Community Resources, and Role of the Virtues[251]

Do we have shared commitments to certain norms of justice and related matters regarding the allocation of goods of effectiveness and other resources, including time and talent as well as treasure, among the inhabitants of *Juropolis*, so that allocation decisions are not simply the subject of competing and conflicting interests? Do the relevant commitments and resulting arrangements subordinate "economic considerations...to social and moral considerations"?[252]

With respect to those norms of justice that are the analog to the norms of justice in *Piscopolis* governing the allocation of resources among independent practical reasoners based on desert — norms based on contribution to the common good — and focusing on members of the legal profession who are independent practical reasoners in their respective law craft practices, are we committed to norms of justice that allocate resources according to the contribution of each individual and group to achieving the overarching common goods of the relevant law craft practice(s) and of our common practice, so that they have what they need to make such contribution and are then rewarded accordingly? Specifically, if I am a law firm partner determining associate salaries, for example, do I appropriately recognize not only contribution to the "bottom line" in the form of numbers

---

250. *See* Chapter 5, notes 99–101 and accompanying text.
251. For discussion of this topic in *Piscopolis*, see Part II, Section E of Chapter 5.
252. *See* Chapter 5, notes 104–07 and accompanying text.

of billable hours logged, but also excellence of performance as a lawyer and extent of pro bono or low bono work undertaken?[253] If I am a law school dean or other university administrator determining faculty salaries, as well as teaching and research stipends, do I appropriately recognize not only contribution to the "bottom line" in the form of number of student "contact" credit hours generated by teaching (and hence tuition dollars earned) or number of publications, especially articles in prestigious law reviews, and number of citations by others (or even number of footnotes), but also excellence of performance as a teacher or scholar and service activities undertaken?[254] And if I am an associate in a law firm or a faculty member in a law school, what is my attitude toward such matters, and how does this attitude affect my own work and perception of such allocation decisions? If I am a judge, do I allocate my time and attention when dispensing legal justice to conscientiously give the lawyers' arguments (and thus the litigants' claims) the careful, unbiased consideration they deserve?[255]

More generally, do I consider that resources are appropriately allocated to the various types of practitioners within a particular law craft practice and among the four law craft practices? For example, are resources appropriately allocated to lawyers representing government entities and non-profit organizations, or are they misallocated resulting in significant disincentives to entering public service?[256] Similarly, are resources appro-

---

253. For discussion of the increasing importance of the quantitative criterion of billable hours relative to other, qualitative criteria as the basis for measuring lawyer performance and worth, see KRONMAN, LOST LAWYER, op. cit., at 301–02; NANCY LEVIT & DOUGLAS O. LINDER, THE HAPPY LAWYER: MAKING A GOOD LIFE IN THE LAW 55–56 (2010).

254. For a sense of some of the complex factors involved in making such decisions, see Merkel, *Scholar or Practitioner?*, op. cit. (for the perspective of a law school faculty member); Chemerinsky, *Why Write?*, op. cit. (for the perspective of a law school faculty member and Dean). *See also* Lawprofblawg and Darren Bush, *Behind the Curtains*, op. cit. (critically discussing the use of various externally focused "metrics" to measure "scholarship success").

255. Regarding this question, see, e.g., Peter S. Green & John Mazor, *Corrupt justice: what happens when judges' bias taints a case?*, THE GUARDIAN (October 18, 2015), https://www.theguardian.com/us-news/2015/oct/18/judge-bias-corrupts-court-cases (discussing, with respect to judges in local, state, and federal courts, "what experts say is one of the most troubling threats to our nation's system of justice: judges, who, through incompetence, bias or outright corruption, prevent the wronged from getting a fair hearing in our courts").

256. *See, e.g.,* KRONMAN, LOST LAWYER, op. cit., at 296–97 (suggesting that the widening gap between compensation at a large corporate law firm and in public service, together with the increased emphasis on moneymaking, discourages lawyers in such firms from following

priately allocated to lawyers representing the indigent — public defenders in criminal matters or legal aid service providers in civil matters — and to different types of courts and their personnel, or are they misallocated resulting in a denial of justice?[257] The same question can be asked regarding "Main Street lawyers" who provide legal services to low and middle income individuals who do not qualify for indigent legal assistance.[258] How do I respond to the stark assertion made by one scholar that "there is a huge gap between the need for legal services to people of limited means and the supply of such services,"[259] or to the 2011 study of the World Justice Project in which "the U.S. ranked among the lowest developed nations in providing access to justice to its citizens[,] … as 50th out of 66 nations in the ability of individuals to obtain legal counsel"?[260] And to the extent such resource misallocations exist, what is the appropriate mechanism for effectuating any needed reallocation or other reforms, and what is my role, if any, in helping to bring about such reforms?[261]

---

the traditional pattern of alternating periods of public service with private practice, especially in mid-career).

257. For discussion of the vast unmet legal services need in the United States and of the grossly inadequate number, and under-resourcing, of lawyers serving as public defenders or legal aid lawyers, see Herrera, *Main Street Lawyers*, op. cit., at 191–92. For sources discussing "problem solving courts," such as drug courts, mental health courts, veterans courts, homeless courts, truancy courts, community courts, and fathering courts, see, e.g., NATIONAL CENTER FOR STATE COURTS, PROBLEM SOLVING COURTS GUIDE, https://www.ncsc.org/Topics/Alternative-Dockets/Problem-Solving-Courts/Home.aspx.

258. For a description profiling "Main Street lawyers," who serve individuals, especially those of low and moderate income, or community business interests as opposed to corporate interests, see Herrera, *Main Street Lawyers*, op. cit., at 190. Herrera considers that high levels of educational debt may prevent main street lawyers from being able to charge lower fees. *Id.* at 207.

259. Longan, *Professionalism*, op. cit., at 681. For a withering critique of this "huge gap" and the multiple factors contributing to it, see Jed S. Rakoff, *Why You Won't Get Your Day in Court*, NYRB (November 24, 2016). For recent relevant statistics, see LONGAN ET. AL., PROFESSIONAL IDENTITY, op. cit., at 75.

260. Herrera, *Main Street Lawyers*, op. cit., at 193 (discussing the 2011 World Justice Project study).

261. For discussion and evaluation of strategies to help close the gap, see *id.* at 194–97 (measures to facilitate self-representation and the provision of legal services by non-lawyers, such as Limited License Legal Technicians, or legal information and documentation by technology-based entities such as LegalZoom), 207 (Main Street lawyers charging lower fees after reducing business overhead through the integration of technology into their practices and living expenses through a more frugal life-style), 208–10 (legal education reform to support and

Let us now consider the analogs in *Juropolis* to the four corollary commitments in *Piscopolis*. What answer do I give to the questions asked with respect to each one? First, to what extent are there inequalities of income or wealth among practitioners of my particular law craft practice and among the four law craft practices?[262] Are these inequalities likely to generate conflicts of competing interests in relationships among members of the legal profession inimical to realizing the common goods of my particular law craft practice and our common practice? If so, am I committed to reducing these inequalities to a more appropriate level? Second, one analog to avoiding another type of inequality by taking one's turn to perform jobs that are "tedious or dangerous" would be undertaking pro bono work and other types of public and professional service for which clients cannot be billed. We already noted above one scholar's observation regarding the "huge gap" between the need for legal services to people of limited means and the supply of such services.[263] The same scholar goes on to note, however, that "[d]espite the professional expectation that lawyers will do pro bono work, the statistics indicate that few actually do so."[264] The apparent unwillingness or inability of so many lawyers to do pro bono work is ironic given the data showing that doing such work contributes significantly to lawyer satisfaction.[265] How should I respond, then, to the insufficiency of pro bono representation, and how does this

---

better prepare prospective Main Street lawyers); Longan, *Professionalism*, op. cit., at 681–82 (possible institution of mandatory pro bono service requirements, in addition to loosening restrictions on the provision of legal services by non-lawyers or by lawyers hired by entities such as Wal-Mart); Rakoff, *Day in Court*, op cit. (state-sponsored legal insurance, constitutionally guaranteed right to counsel in civil not just criminal matters, lawyer-subsidized legal services).

262. For some suggestive comparative salary data, see, for example:

http://www.abajournal.com/magazine/article/what-lawyers-earn (lawyers); https://www.glassdoor.com/Salaries/law-professor-salary-SRCH_KO0,13.htm (law professors); https://www.payscale.com/research/US/Job=Attorney%2C_Legislative_Counsel%2C_Public_Affairs/Salary (legislative counsel);

https://www.uscourts.gov/judges-judgeships/judicial-compensation (federal judges); https://ballotpedia.org/State_court_budgets_and_judicial_salaries (state judges); https://www.thestreet.com/personal-finance/how-much-do-judges-make-15046259 (federal and state judges).

263. *See supra* note 259 and accompanying text.

264. Longan, *Professionalism*, op. cit., at 681.

265. *See, e.g.*, LEVIT &LINDER, HAPPY LAWYER, op. cit., at 90, 107, 196–97 (2010) (discussing survey data on lawyers providing pro bono services).

response relate to my previous answer regarding mechanisms for effectu-ating needed resource allocations or other reforms?[266] Third, at first sight it may seem there is no analog to adopting self-imposed limits on the movement of labor to help ensure the continuity and stability of families and other institutions. But upon further reflection, should I ask myself, for example, how I view the breakdown of traditional loyalties between lawyers and their law firms, especially large corporate law firms,[267] and the impact of long working hours, often undertaken to improve career mobility, on family life?[268] Fourth, at first sight it may seem, similarly, that there is no analog to investing in children's education based on consider-ations other than economic productivity, in order to promote full human flourishing. But here again, upon further reflection, should I ask myself how I view those components of a legal education, such as so-called "per-spectives" courses, that cannot be reduced to an easily quantifiable payoff in terms of specific career preparation or a specific salary figure and the way in which the current culture of law student consumerism places these components under stress and perhaps even threatens their continued ex-istence altogether?[269]

We turn now to those norms of justice that are the analog to the norms of justice in *Piscopolis* governing the allocation of resources among those who are not independent practical reasoners and are based on need — norms applicable "[b]etween those capable of giving and those who are most dependent and in most need of receiving."[270] Continuing

---

266. *See supra* note 261 and accompanying text.

267. *See, e.g.,* KRONMAN, LOST LAWYER, op. cit., at 277–81 (discussing the weakening of solidarity and mutual loyalty within law firms, especially large corporate law firms, the related emergence of competitive markets for lawyers, and the resulting fluidity and mo-bility of attachments); LEVIT &LINDER, HAPPY LAWYER, op. cit., at 56–58 (discussing how economic forces and a law firm "business" mindset have reduced job security and loyalty within law firms).

268. For discussion of the impact of long working hours, driven by the system of bill-able hours and technology, including the negative impact on family life, see, e.g., KRO-NMAN, LOST LAWYER, op. cit., at 281–82, 300–07; LEVIT &LINDER, HAPPY LAWYER, op. cit., at 53–56, 209–10. For the disparate impact on women, especially women with children, see *id.* at 11–13, 210–11.

269. For a detailed discussion of the value of "perspectives" courses in the curriculum, see generally Jones, *"Perspectives,"* op. cit.

270. ALASDAIR MACINTYRE, DEPENDENT RATIONAL ANIMALS: WHY HUMAN BEINGS NEED THE VIRTUES 130 (1999).

our focus on the legal profession, are we committed to norms of justice that allocate resources for the education and nurturing of those who have not yet become independent practical reasoners in a particular law craft practice, and thus who are not yet able to make a direct contribution to achieving the overarching common goods of that practice and of our common practice? Specifically, if I am an academic lawyer, do I consider that money for student scholarships should be allocated based on merit, financial or other type of need, or some combination of these? Am I prepared to assume, and prepared for my law school to assume, more of the responsibility for the "apprenticeship of practice" and the "apprenticeship of professional formation" to the extent the practicing bar is no longer able or willing to provide these apprenticeships?[271] If I am a practicing lawyer or a judge, am I prepared to share my time and talent to participate in an Inn of Court association or in various types of law school curricular initiatives intended to help provide the apprenticeships of practice and professional formation? As a practicing lawyer, am I prepared to volunteer to serve as a mentor in my state bar mentoring program?[272]

Are we committed to allocating resources for the care and rehabilitation of members of the legal profession who have become unable to exercise their powers of independent practical reasoning in their particular law craft practice? Specifically, whatever my position in the legal profession, am I prepared to give my care, concern, and attention to promote well-being within the profession and to help alleviate the disabling distress and dysfunction due to substance use disorders or mental illness afflicting so many? Am I prepared, then, to be counted among my "brothers' and sisters' keepers" in this way?[273]

Looking beyond the legal profession to the other inhabitants of *Juropolis*, who may be independent practical reasoners in their own practices and activities but who lack powers of independent practical reasoning in the law craft practices, are we committed to allocating resources to those in dire need of legal services for which they cannot afford to pay? To recur to our fishing metaphor, are we committed to feeding them justice too? Spe-

---

271. *See supra* notes 177–78, 211–13 and accompanying text.

272. *See supra* notes 214–15 and accompanying text.

273. *See The Path to Lawyer Well-Being: Practical Recommendations for Positive Change*, The Report of the National Task Force on Lawyer Well-Being 47 (ABA, August 2017)(for the quotation); Chapter 1, notes 20–33 and accompanying text (for discussion of distress, dysfunction, and well-being in the legal profession).

cifically, do I understand that although those of low or moderate income in such dire need may theoretically be inhabitants of *Juropolis*, their rights and duties under the law are *functionally meaningless* if they cannot afford to pay for legal services, including perhaps mine? And that, as long as this remains the case, *Juropolis* does not exist for them in practice so that such inhabitants may be more like those in dire need outside the community of *Piscopolis* than like those in dire need within this community?[274] Whether regarded as within the community or as de facto outside it, how do I respond to the existence of such dire need? For I cannot believe, surely, that the noble ideal to which I have pledged myself — "Justice for all" — should mean "Justice for those who can afford to pay?"[275] This returns us, of course, to questions we have already asked above.[276] And now we can see also how norms of justice allocating resources among independent practical reasoners, who contribute directly to achieving the overarching common good of the practice, intersect and overlap with norms of justice allocating resources among those in dire need, who contribute in other ways by teaching me about the common good and my individual good and by calling forth mutually reinforcing exercises of the virtue of just generosity, as discussed further below. Now, too, other questions suggest themselves. For example, those who cannot afford to pay for legal services in effect experience a type of discrimination or disadvantage based on wealth. How should I respond, then, to other types of related discrimination or disadvantage in the legal system based on factors such as race, gender, or alienage?[277] And does discrimination or disadvantage based on this last factor suggest an analogy to relationships of hospitality to passing strangers who arrive in *Piscopolis*?

---

274. *See* Chapter 5, notes 147–51 (discussing this distinction).

275. As the Pledge of Allegiance has it, "I pledge allegiance to the Flag of the United States of America, and to the Republic for which it stands, one Nation under God, indivisible, with liberty and justice for all."

276. *See supra* notes 256–61 and accompanying text.

277. *See, e.g.,* NATIONAL CENTER FOR STATE COURTS: GENDER AND RACIAL FAIRNESS RESOURCE GUIDE, https://www.ncsc.org/Topics/Access-and-Fairness/Gender-and-Racial-Fairness/Resource-Guide.aspx (providing resources on several different types of discrimination across multiple aspects of the U.S. legal system); IMPLICIT RACIAL BIAS ACROSS THE LAW (Justin D. Levinson & Robert J. Smith, eds., 2012) (focusing specifically on race-based discrimination and disadvantage across the U.S. legal system); THE SENTENCING PROJECT: REPORT TO THE UNITED NATIONS ON RACIAL DISPARITIES IN THE U.S. CRIMINAL JUSTICE SYSTEM (April 19, 2018) (focusing on race-based discrimination and disadvantage in the U.S. criminal justice system in particular).

Are we committed to exhibiting the virtues necessary to implement the preceding shared commitments (and corollary commitments) to norms for the just allocation of resources in *Juropolis*? Specifically, am I committed to "becom[ing] ... the kind of human being — through acquisition and exercise of the virtues — who makes the good of others her or his good,"[278] and in particular who exhibits "the central virtue" of just generosity not only within the networks of relationships of giving and receiving in *Juropolis* within which apprentice lawyers are nurtured, as already discussed above, but more generally?[279] Am I disposed to give disproportionately to what I have received, to give to those from whom I have not received or will not receive, and to give unconditionally in that the measure of giving is largely based on needs?

Do I understand, moreover, that members of the legal profession are encouraged, indeed called, to engage truthfully with the world, to live truthfully in contingency but with responsibility, not only because we are disposed, for example, to see arguments on both sides and to be concerned about how others will respond,[280] but because, existentially, lawyers, perhaps more than any other professionals, are so often given an opportunity to see life in its great variety and fullness, and to see and minister to both human brokenness and the potential for healing?[281] But do I also understand that if I accept this and see myself in this way, then I must do my part to alleviate the distress of the many inhabitants of *Juropolis* who need legal services but cannot afford to pay for them, as well as the distress of the many members of the legal profession afflicted by substance use disorders and mental illness? Do I recognize that each inhabitant of *Juropolis* has something to teach me about our common good and my own good and that the other in distress "could have been [me]"?[282] And that failing to exercise the particular virtue of *misericordia*

---

278. MacIntyre, Rational Animals, op. cit., at 108.

279. For discussion of the exercise of virtues, including just generosity, in nurturing apprentice lawyers, see *supra* notes 218–20 and accompanying text.

280. *See supra* note 147 and accompanying text (discussing Jack Sammons' identification of various specific, distinctive virtues of the lawyer as rhetorician).

281. Sammons Email Exchange (March 23–24, 2012) [on file with author].

282. *See* Chapter 5, note 151 and accompanying text (discussing this latter point in the context of *Piscopolis* and citing MacIntyre, Rational Animals, op. cit., at 100, 125, 128 for expression of the quoted notion).

within just generosity to help alleviate such distress would be a form of self-deception, a sin of omission if you will, because I then allow such brokenness to continue and refuse to help heal it to the extent I could make a difference?

F. Character, Structuring, and Conduct of the Legal Conversation, and Role of the Virtues[283]

As we have already noted, the legal conversation in *Juropolis*, in which the community of legal professionals as a whole is jointly engaged as they carry on their common practice of maintaining the rule of law in the liberal democratic state, is the analogue to the political conversation in *Piscopolis*, in which those inhabitants who are independent practical reasoners are jointly engaged as they carry on their common practice of politics in the fishing village.[284] We noted, too, that the community of legal professionals displays the "deliberative" characteristics that MacIntyre considers essential for the existence of a *polis*. These characteristics include possessing a shared language (the specialized language of the law) and shared formal and informal modes of deliberation (legal institutions such as courts and legal procedures), and being "always, potentially or actually, a society of rational enquiry, of self-scrutiny" ("a rhetorical community" characterized by "a culture of argument") so that "individuals are always able to put in question through communal deliberation what has hitherto by custom and tradition been taken for granted both about their own good and the good of the community."[285]

Of course, despite the significant stressing of the common goods of the four law craft practices and the challenges involved in living up to our traditional politico-ethical commitments, it is reasonable to conclude that just like Drew and the other inhabitants of *Piscopolis*, we also "share ... a large degree of common understanding of practices and institutions," including an "understanding of the relationships between goods, rules, and virtues" entailed in the proper ordering of these practices, and thus display another deliberative characteristic essential for the existence of a

---

283. For discussion of this topic in *Piscopolis*, see Part II, Section F of Chapter 5.
284. *See supra* note 7 and accompanying text.
285. *See supra* notes 14–16 and accompanying text.

polis.[286] Consequently, just as political conversation in *Piscopolis* will usually focus on how best to implement the traditional commitments that reflect and sustain such understanding and proper ordering in the fishing village, the same is true for much of the legal conversation in *Juropolis*. Thus, the legal conversation involved in transactional lawyering, for example, typically involves the application of "black letter" law established by settled precedent or precise and unambiguous statutory provision. But even here "individuals are always able to put in question through communal deliberation what has hitherto by custom and tradition been taken for granted," as countless law reform initiatives demonstrate. Moreover, it is not only where the law is unsettled that "hard cases" arise. Indeed, even where case law precedent seems very settled, a bold litigation strategy may challenge the status quo and transform a case that appears to be an easy case in the black letter core into a "hard case" at the margins of creative legal development.[287]

But just how far does our commitment to putting matters in question extend? Just how far do we share a commitment that the "institutionalized forms of deliberation" — forms which exhibit the practical, non-fragmented rationality common to the four law craft practices and captured in the phrase "thinking like a lawyer" — are indeed accessible to all, excluding "no-one from whom something might be learned," including "individuals and groups who hold… radically dissenting views on fundamental issues"? What can we infer in this respect from how "the legal establishment" and some other inhabitants of *Juropolis* react to the representation of "unpopular" clients or causes, the advancing of unconventional claims and defenses, or movements of radical critique such as critical legal stud-

---

286. *See* Chapter 5, notes 8–9, 153 and accompanying text.

287. For earlier discussion of the distinction between apparently easy cases and hard cases, see *supra* note 36 and accompanying text. The transformation of the former into the latter is perhaps seen most visibly and dramatically in constitutional jurisprudence in the area of civil rights. A noteworthy recent example concerns the constitutional recognition and protection of same-sex marriage. *See United States v. Windsor*, 570 U.S. 744 (holding in 2013 that Section 3 of the Defense of Marriage Act (DOMA), which denied federal recognition of same-sex marriages, was a violation of the Due Process Clause of the Fifth Amendment); *Obergefell v. Hodges*, 576 U.S. 644 (holding in 2015 that the fundamental right to marry is guaranteed to same-sex couples by both the Due Process Clause and the Equal Protection Clause of the Fourteenth Amendment).

ies, feminist legal theory, and critical race theory?[288] Do we need to recall here MacIntyre's observation that "[t]he lawyers, not the philosophers, are the clergy of liberalism."[289] Which way does that observation cut in the present context? And which way does it cut with respect to the apparent lack of commitment to ideological diversity on law school faculties,[290] bearing in mind also MacIntyre's equally scathing criticism of liberalism and contemporary conservatism?[291]

However we answer these questions, it is reasonable to consider that our procedures for decision-making are "generally acceptable" to the community of legal professionals; that the participatory and procedural norms in *Juropolis* enable legal professionals to "come through shared rational deliberation to a common mind" that reflects and constitutes "the rule of law"; and that our deliberations about what the norms of justice discussed in the previous section require must include not just legal professionals as independent practical reasoners in the practice, but also those speaking as a proxy on behalf of those other inhabitants of *Juropolis* "whose exercise of [such] reasoning is limited or nonexistent." Regarding this last point, MacIntyre explains that "a key role" in "communities of giving and receiving" is the role of "someone who acts as a proxy for the radically disabled, for those who will only have a voice in the deliberations of the community, if someone else speaks for them."[292] In the present context the analogue to the "radically disabled," whose reasoning is nonexistent, is not all those in *Juropolis* who lack powers of independent practical reasoning in the law craft practices and who therefore have an attorney with such powers to represent them. As clients they can exercise reasoning powers to have a voice in their own representation and thus in the relevant community deliberations.[293] Rather, the analogue is those inhabitants who cannot ob-

---

288. For discussion and evaluation of critical legal studies, feminist legal theory, critical race theory, and related movements of radical critique such as LatCrit theory and queer theory, see BIX, JURISPRUDENCE, op. cit., at 243–64.

289. MACINTYRE, WHOSE JUSTICE?, op. cit., at 344 [quoted *supra* note 72 and accompanying text].

290. *See supra* notes 199–203 and accompanying text.

291. *See* Chapter 6, notes 103–05 and accompanying text.

292. MACINTYRE, RATIONAL ANIMALS, op. cit., at 147. For elaboration of this point, see *id.* at 139–40.

293. How far they will have such a voice varies under different models of lawyering. Their voice will be greater under the models of client autonomy and client goodness but

tain legal representation and who are therefore effectively disabled from accessing the machinery of justice and from exercising any such reasoning powers and having any such voice at all.[294] With regard to those whose reasoning powers are limited as opposed to nonexistent, the analogue is those whose voice is muted or distorted because they are otherwise dis- criminated against or disadvantaged in the operation of this machinery, even when they do have legal representation. To continue the theme begun in the previous section, then, it is vital that members of the legal profession exhibit the virtue of just generosity to speak for such inhabitants to ensure that they receive needed legal representation and also in other ways are able to receive appropriate legal justice.

And to continue this focus on virtues, what then are the analogues in *Juropolis* to the particular political virtues in *Piscopolis*? As "a rhetorical community" characterized by "a culture of argument," aren't we necessar- ily committed to developing and exhibiting the general dialogical virtues identified by MacIntyre and Roche,[295] as well as the fifteen specific dialog- ical virtues of "the lawyer as rhetorician" identified by Sammons, which overlap but also supplement these more general dialogical virtues?[296] In- deed, don't these dialogical virtues occupy a central place among the qual- ities of excellence of all four law craft practices? Of course, in *Piscopolis* each of the dialogical virtues is in some way concerned with the search for empirical and moral truth, whereas in *Juropolis* we are concerned with the search for legal truth — the truth about law and justice.[297] And be-

---

much less under the models of client victory or client rectitude. *See supra* notes 126–27 and accompanying text (discussing these four models of lawyering), notes 128, 131, 149–52 and accompanying text (discussing Kronman's comparison of the models of client autonomy and client goodness, although he uses different terminology to describe them).

294. It might be thought that those inhabitants of *Juropolis* who act *pro se*, without legal representation, are also able to have a voice in the relevant legal process. Lacking the benefit of lawyer involvement, however, those so acting are frequently at such a radical dis- advantage, especially in litigation, that their situation is functionally tantamount to having no voice at all. *See* Herrera, *Main Street Lawyers*, op. cit., at 194–95; Longan et.al., Profes- sional Identity, op. cit., at 75 (discussing pro se representation and the obstacles faced by pro se litigants).

295. *See* Chapter 5, notes 167–72 and accompanying text.

296. *See supra* note 147 and accompanying text.

297. *See supra* Section B.1 and accompanying text (discussing the search by our com- munity of legal professionals for a proper understanding of the realizing justice component of the ultimate excellence of our common practice), note 95 and accompanying text (dis-

cause each of the law craft practices performs its own particular role in this search, they vary in how the dialogical virtues are generally and characteristically exhibited as qualities of excellence of the practice. However these virtues are exhibited, though, they operate interdependently with other professional virtues among the qualities of excellence such that the dialogical virtues and the other virtues help to constitute and reflect one another.

To illuminate how the dialogical virtues are exhibited variously in the different law craft practices, we will focus on the general dialogical virtues identified by MacIntyre and Roche. The closest analogue in *Juropolis* to how these virtues are exhibited in *Piscopolis* would seem to exist in the practice of legal education, the next closest in the practice of adjudication and possibly in legislative drafting, and the least close in the practice of lawyering. This point is focused and illustrated by Peter Henning's observation that "[f]inding the truth is the object of the judicial system, but it is not the governing principle for the lawyer."[298] Indeed, a moment's reflection on the lawyer's professional virtue of fidelity to the client, central to which are the obligations of zealous representation and confidentiality, makes it clear that "finding the truth" cannot possibly be the governing principle for the lawyer.[299] And this reflects a societal judgment that other

cussing White's identification of the primary goal of the "art of law" as being to achieve justice rather than scientific truth).

298. Peter J. Henning, *Lawyers, Truth, and Honesty in Representing Clients*, 20 Notre Dame J.L. Ethics & Pub. Pol'y 209, 214 (2006). Henning's article explains the many ways in which finding the truth is not, and cannot be, "the governing principle for the lawyer."

299. For discussion of the lawyer's professional virtue of fidelity to the client, *see id.* at 210 (observing that "[t]he rules governing the legal profession recognize that a lawyer must be a zealous advocate for the client, putting that person's interests ahead of all others" and citing CANONS OF PROFESSIONAL ETHICS Canon 15 (1908) stating that "The lawyer owes 'entire devotion to the interest of the client, warm zeal in the maintenance and defense of his rights and the exertion of his utmost learning and ability.'" (quoting GEORGE SHARSWOOD, AN ESSAY ON PROFESSIONAL ETHICS 78–79 (photo. reprint 1993) (5th ed. 1896))); LONGAN et.al., PROFESSIONAL IDENTITY, op. cit., at 43–47 (addressing the concept of "[l]awyers as fiduciaries of clients," entailing "duties of loyalty, honesty, and candor" as well as "duties of competence and diligence," and those rules in the American Bar Association (ABA) Model Rules of Professional Conduct "based upon the duty of fidelity to the client," including rules relating to "confidentiality[,] ... avoiding conflicts of interest[,] ... [r]egular and candid communication with the client[,] ... wise counsel and good advice[,] [and] ... [f]ees and client property"). *See also id.* at 25–28 (addressing the lawyer's professional virtue of competence, excellence, or craftsmanship, and the components of "knowledge, skill, and diligence" included within this virtue under the Model Rules, as well as a variety of other skills beyond

values — the trust and participation of the client that confidentiality helps to promote, for example — are more important than "finding the truth." On the other hand, lawyers are one of the few professional groups that have an ethical obligation to "tell the truth," or are expected otherwise to act against immediate interest, in certain circumstances.[300] Consequently, the virtue of fidelity to the client is in tension with other professional virtues, such as the virtue of fidelity to the law (central to which is the lawyer's obligation of candor toward the tribunal as an "officer of the court" and the lawyer's obligation of candor toward opposing counsel in discovery and information disclosure),[301] or the virtue of civility (central to which are expectations of cooperation with opposing counsel and of fair play in eschewing "hardball" or "Rambo" tactics to harass or delay).[302] It is the function of the rules of lawyer professional responsibility and relevant judicially articulated standards to help resolve such tensions among the professional virtues.[303] And it is the function of the "master virtue" of practical wisdom to help the lawyer resolve these tensions among the professional

---

those identified in the Model Rules, including "good judgment, emotional intelligence, and cultural competence and inclusive thinking").

300. I am indebted to Jack Sammons for bringing these points to my attention. Sammons Email (September 23, 2020) [on file with author].

301. For discussion of the lawyer's professional virtue of fidelity to the law and the duties it entails, see LONGAN et.al., PROFESSIONAL IDENTITY, op. cit., at 59–65 (addressing "duties of candor to the courts" and duties "to assert only meritorious claims and contentions[,] ... to expedite litigation[,] . . not to counsel or assist a witness to testify falsely[,] ... not to assist with crimes or frauds[,] [and] ... not to unlawfully impede access to evidence," as well as "[s]pecific duties relating to fruits, instrumentalities, and evidence of client crime" and "[t]he criminal law generally"). See also Henning, Representing Clients, op. cit., at 223–30 (duties regarding discovery to opposing counsel), 239–43 (duty of candor toward the tribunal). Henning observes that the courts have approached a lawyer's duty in discovery "as an adjunct to the duty of candor to the tribunal." Id. at 223–24.

302. For discussion of the lawyer's professional virtue of civility and the duties it entails, see LONGAN et.al., PROFESSIONAL IDENTITY, op. cit., at 87–92 (addressing "[c]ourtesy[,] ... cooperation[,] ... [h]onesty[,] [and] [f]air play"). See also Henning, Representing Clients, op. cit., at 230–39 (inadvertent disclosure of confidential information by opposing counsel), 244–51 (unwarranted attacks on members of the judiciary).

303. Henning observes that "[d]espite their detail, the Model Rules provide little specific guidance to attorneys for dealing with the obligation to the truth[,]... which leaves it to the courts and the disciplinary authorities to work out the details." Henning, Representing Clients, op. cit., at 219–20. Much of Henning's article is devoted to explicating how courts and disciplinary authorities have attempted to articulate these details.

virtues when no rule or other relevant standard addresses the situation or when the rules and standards provide no clearly right answer for the situation.[304]

Perhaps one way to describe the resulting resolution, at least in many situations, is to say that the lawyer must exhibit what Sammons identifies, among his fifteen specific dialogical virtues, as "a very particular form of honesty."[305] Similarly, after observing that "[f]inding the truth is the object of the judicial system, but it is not the governing principle for the lawyer," Henning explains that "[i]nstead, the focus for the lawyer should be *honesty*." Although a lawyer's honesty will, of course, assist in "finding the truth," the difference is that "[w]hile truth is focused more on determining the existence of an historical fact, honesty focuses on the accuracy and authenticity of the lawyer's current assertions on behalf of the client," whether those assertions are of fact, legal argument, or negotiating position.[306] Such

---

304. For discussion of the "master virtue" of practical wisdom and of how it is needed to resolve such tensions among the professional virtues appropriately or to determine how best to exhibit a particular professional virtue — for example, how best to exhibit fidelity to the client — in the particular circumstances of a given situation under conditions of inherent uncertainty, see LONGAN et.al., PROFESSIONAL IDENTITY, op. cit., at 103–08 (addressing the general nature of practical wisdom and illustrating its operation, and explaining that "[p]ractical wisdom is often called the 'master virtue'[,] ... requires constant movement between the general and the particular[,] ... is dependent upon the lawyer's having acquired other needed virtues and skills[,] [and] ... as applied in professional life is what many people think of as expert judgment, or expertise").

305. For discussion of Sammons' fifteen specific virtues of the lawyer as rhetorician, see *supra* note 147 and accompanying text.

306. Henning, *Representing Clients*, op. cit., at 214–15. Honesty is related to trust. Thus, "[a]n honest lawyer is one who can be trusted. For the purposes of analyzing the rules that govern a lawyer's conduct, I define honesty to mean that an attorney's expressions and conduct are both *accurate* and *authentic*." *Id.* at 221. Henning then explains what he means by accuracy and authenticity. Regarding accuracy:

An accurate statement is one that is truthful and does not intentionally deceive or mislead another person. Accuracy deals with the problem of the technically true but misleading statement or failure to disclose information that the listener would consider important. A deceptive statement would be inaccurate and therefore dishonest. At the same time, a lawyer's statements will be accurate even if they do not fully disclose the truth about a situation. The attorney-client privilege, for example, may restrict what a lawyer can state to third parties, and accuracy requires that the lawyer not mislead while he also is maintaining the confidences protected by the rules of confidentiality.

Id. at 221–22. Regarding authenticity:

356 Professions and Politics in Crisis

honesty does require being "truthful," even if it does not require a commitment to "finding the truth."[307] A well-known and well-worn example given by Henning suffices to highlight this difference between truth and honesty. Thus, although a criminal defense lawyer-advocate may not offer evidence the lawyer knows is false,

> It is universally accepted that the defense lawyer can put the government to its proof — a process that could well result in a not-guilty verdict if a crucial witness fails to appear or testifies poorly or if important physical evidence is unavailable. While the truth-seeking function of the trial is undermined by a factually incorrect verdict, the lawyer has not been dishonest through any inaccurate or inauthentic communication. The lawyer's knowledge of — or even strong suspicion about — the client's guilt does not change the obligation to represent the client zealously, nor does it affect the requirement of honesty.[308]

An authentic expression is one that comprehends fairly the lawyer's (and in certain circumstances the client's) intentions. Even if the lawyer can argue that statements were accurate in the terms described above, the lawyer has a further obligation to ensure that the representation of the client is fair both to the client and to others, including courts and opponents. Not all expressions are factual, or at least their accuracy cannot be easily measured, so that a requirement of authenticity in the lawyer's representation covers a broader array of conduct than just assertions that can be checked for their accuracy. For example, bombastic comments in a legal brief attacking the integrity of the judge may be correct statements of the lawyer's opinion, and hence accurate, but they are not honest statements because their authenticity is open to question in the context in which the remarks are made. A lawyer's statements and positions can be authentic while favoring the position of the client — indeed, that is required by the fiduciary relationship of the lawyer to the client. Authenticity does not mean achieving a result that is less than what the client seeks, so long as the lawyer has not acted dishonestly.

Id. at 222–23.

307. This is clear from Henning's explanation of the requirement of "accuracy." Thus, "[a]n accurate statement is one that is truthful and does not intentionally deceive or mislead another person." *Id.* at 221.

308. *Id.* at 271. ABA Model Rule 3.3(a), "Candor Toward the Tribunal," states that "A lawyer shall not knowingly . . . (3) offer evidence that the lawyer *knows* to be false," although, in contrast to other evidence, a lawyer may not refuse to offer a criminal defendant's testi-

Exhibiting Sammons' "very particular form of honesty" in this context, then, is clearly quite different from exhibiting Roche's dialogical virtue of honesty and integrity by following the evidence even against interest, which seems more applicable to the role of the judge who presides in the case or the role of the academic lawyer who evaluates it.[309]

And so it goes, too, with other dialogical virtues. What honesty and other dialogical virtues mean for the criminal defense lawyer-advocate, the judge, and the academic lawyer in the above case, and what they mean for them generally, is determined by their differing goals, duties, and other needed virtues.[310] But all of them may have to resolve tensions among conflicting duties and virtues as they exhibit dialogical virtues, in light of any relevant rules of professional conduct and through the exercise of practical wisdom. To take a very prosaic everyday example, as I write this section of the chapter I have to be mindful of the tension between the virtue of fidelity to intellectual enquiry and the advancement of knowledge (which calls for me to continue writing in my role as a scholar) and the virtue of fidelity to students (which calls for me to prepare for my next class in my

---

mony "that the lawyer *reasonably believes* is false" (emphasis added). *See id.* at 239 (reproducing Model Rule 3.3(a)).

309. Thus, the criminal defense lawyer follows the evidence only up to a point. Indeed, the lawyer and the lawyer's client, the criminal defendant, have an interest in critical evidence *not* being presented to the court (the situation is clearly different for the lawyer as counselor when seeking to acquire all relevant information enabling the lawyer to evaluate the client's case and determine the most appropriate defense strategy). By contrast, the judge has no interest in limiting the evidence in this way. Indeed, ideally the judge is interested in presiding over a trial that is as complete as possible, with all relevant and admissible empirical evidence being considered by the fact finder and all relevant legal arguments being advanced by the lawyers. And the academic lawyer is interested in considering not only this, but *all* the issues relevant to the particular academic enquiry he or she is pursuing when studying the case. Regarding the affinity between judges and academic lawyers in this respect, recall Judge Rosenthal's observation, *supra* note 243, that the academy and the judiciary are "natural allies [who] are united in having the luxury of the ultimate aspiration: of having the duty only to be right, fair, and just, free of any duty of advocating for a client's interest."

310. For example, in the above case, the meaning of MacIntyre's "justice in respect of the opportunity that each participant receives to advance her or his arguments, and an openness to refutation" (similar to Roche's justice by entertaining the views of others), and of Roche's respect for others and for truth by engaging in the give and take of discussion or intellectual hospitality by actively drawing in others and their ideas, is clearly different for the criminal defense lawyer-advocate, the judge, and the academic lawyer.

role as a law teacher), and must find a wise balance in the time, energy, and effort spent on each activity.

As legal professionals, then, we should ask ourselves such questions as: Do I exhibit the dialogical virtues in the way appropriate to the particular role(s) I perform in my law craft practice? Am I, for example, being honest and "truthful" in the way appropriate to my role, or am I being inappropriately dishonest and "untruthful?" When exhibiting the dialogical virtues in the appropriate way, do I exhibit "not merely a passive tolerance, but an active and enquiring attitude towards radically dissenting views," including the required capacity for sympathetic detachment toward relevant others — by advancing an unpopular claim or defense on behalf of my client, as a lawyer, for example; or by attending and actively entertaining an address given by a speaker at my law school, as a faculty member with a very different political or ideological allegiance? And do I avoid the vices, such as arrogance or defensiveness, which correspond to a lack of virtue and impede successful performance of my role?

What about the *Juropolis* analogues to other particular political virtues in *Piscopolis*? We saw that in *Piscopolis* "the key virtue" of those holding political office is the virtue of integrity in the sense of exhibiting unified and authentic character in pursuing their own good and the common good across different spheres of activity. Do we exhibit the equivalent as members of the legal profession in *Juropolis*? Is it important, if I am a candidate for a judicial appointment or for election as an officer of the ABA, for example, that those considering my candidacy are able to say that I am basically the same person, exhibiting the same moral character, in my role as a senior partner of my law firm or as a senior faculty member or Dean of my law school as I am in my role on a state bar committee or as a CLE presenter? And that those who then later on evaluate my performance as such a judge or officer are able to say, subject to any necessary differences in professional character within the different law craft practices, that I have remained the same person in all these different roles? More broadly, can I say of myself that I am the same person in my non-legal roles, at home or as a participant in other practices and activities in the local community — in my religious worship community, for example, or in the local concert association — as I am in my legal roles? Do I consistently try to exhibit the same values and general virtues in these various spheres, or am I instead fragmented into separate and compartmentalized roles? Research shows that such fragmentation is psychologically unhealthy, resulting in distress and anxiety.[311] Moreover, just as the "master virtue" of practical wisdom may be needed to help resolve tensions among professional virtues, so also it may be needed to resolve tensions between professional virtues and personal values deriving from non-legal roles and to achieve the integrity that prevents such fragmentation and compartmentalization.[312] We will revisit the virtue of integrity at the beginning of Chapter 8 when we consider engagement of members the legal profession with the liberal democratic state beyond *Juropolis*.

How do matters stand with regard to the foundational bedrock virtue of "political friendship" in *Juropolis* — in liberal democratic society viewed through a legal lens, as opposed to a political lens? As we noted toward the beginning of this section, it is reasonable to conclude that just like Drew and the other inhabitants of *Piscopolis*, members of the practice community of legal professionals as a whole "share ... a large degree of common understanding of practices and institutions," including an "understanding of the relationships between goods, rules, and virtues" entailed in the proper ordering of these practices. Similarly, we also noted above that the participatory and procedural norms in *Juropolis* enable us to "come through shared rational deliberation to a common mind" that reflects and

---

311. Pat Longan, Daisy Floyd, and Tim Floyd explain why it is important for members of the legal profession to exhibit the virtue of integrity across this broader range of roles. *See* LONGAN et.al., PROFESSIONAL IDENTITY, op. cit., at 4:

> Your development of a professional identity as a lawyer does not mean the disappearance of your other identities.... [W]e all live our lives every day with multiple senses or ourselves in our different roles. As you navigate the various roles you have or acquire in life, you may act simultaneously as a lawyer *and* a spouse, as a lawyer *and* a person of faith, or as a lawyer *and* a parent, and so on. You will never be *just* a lawyer. Although you are not *replacing* your existing identities, you will need to find a way to *integrate* them. For your own psychological health, your senses of yourself in your different roles should not conflict with each other in fundamental ways — they should cohere in integrated, mutually enforcing ways. It is unhealthy to be "one person at home" and "another person at the office." Psychological research makes it clear that such a lack of integrity (in the sense of "wholeness") among your various roles is a formula for distress and anxiety.

Id.

312. *See id.* at 103–05 (discussing and illustrating this function of the "master virtue" of practical wisdom).

constitutes "the rule of law." In *Juropolis* our "large degree of common understanding" of relevant matters, then, centers on the proper ordering of our common practice of maintaining the rule of law — and on the proper ordering of the four law craft practices that co-constitute this common practice — to the ultimate excellence and overarching common good of the common practice, which is "social peace in the liberal democratic state through the realization of justice for its inhabitants." And as in *Piscopolis*, the virtue that both reflects and constitutes our common understanding is the virtue of political friendship exhibited by our practice community of legal professionals as a whole.

More broadly, *all* the inhabitants of *Juropolis* exhibit the virtue of political friendship, reflecting and constituting their understanding of the larger common practice of maintaining *and living by* the rule of law in the liberal democratic state, when they seek resolution of their disputes through the legal conversation rather than through force or violence. Crucially, they do so because, as Jack Sammons observes, lawyers keep clients within the community by speaking for them to the community, and the "justice" of the judgments made by judges and jurors is acknowledged as authoritative by others, in particular "the political other."[313] A critical factor in securing this acknowledgment is exercise of the judicial statesmanship that, in Anthony Kronman's words, helps "to preserve the bonds of political fraternity, to strengthen the willingness of opposing groups to continue as members of a common enterprise" when conflicting claims are incommensurable.[314] We have already identified various developments — increased politicization of the judiciary, judicial bureaucratization, and managerial judging — that threaten the exercise of important judicial virtues, including judicial statesmanship.[315] But now we also need to raise a related question of even greater concern: How confident can we be, especially in these fractious, divisive, and hyper-partisan times, that "the political other" will continue to acknowledge the "justice" of judgments made by judges and jurors as author-

313. *Supra* notes 80–82 and accompanying text.

314. *Supra* note 119 and accompanying text. *See also supra* note 103 and accompanying text (noting Kronman's explanation that the judge's overall concern with "the good of the community represented by the laws" also includes a specific concern for "the bonds of fellowship that legal conflict strains but that must be preserved to avoid other, more destructive conflicts").

315. *See supra* notes 111–25 and accompanying text.

itative? Starkly put, how confident can we be that the rule of law will hold, and that the virtue of political friendship in *Juropolis* will not be replaced by the vice of political enmity? In this regard, political rhetoric emanating from the President of the United States and attacking the judiciary is troubling to say the least.[316] In the sobering words of one recent State Bar report:

> Elected officials in both the legislative and executive branches have a right, if not a responsibility, to criticize the courts when they perceive a judicial decision to be flawed or misguided. But comments by the President of the United States that question not the reasoning behind a particular judicial decision but the very legitimacy of the decision-making process itself; or a judicial appointment process that focuses on how a judge will rule in cases about which the appointing authority has a particular interest; or efforts to remove a judge from office based on an unpopular, though legally justified, decision, warrant our resistance and response. Such attacks go far beyond caustic criticism and take dead aim at the rule of law itself.[317]

G. "External Relations" with the Modern Liberal Democratic State, and Role of the Virtues[318]

And so, as in *Piscopolis*, we turn to questions regarding a final set of "protective" commitments.

1. Protecting *Juropolis*

Are we committed to protecting *Juropolis*, as far as possible, from influences originating in the dominant politics, economics, and morality of the liberal democratic state and its capitalist, large-scale market economy that are incompatible with, and destructive of, our shared way of life, common goods, politico-ethical commitments, and communitarian *ethos*, and to exhibiting the virtues necessary to ensure such protection? In answering

---

316. For several examples of attacks on the judiciary by President Donald Trump, see *In His Own Words: The President's Attacks on the Courts*, BRENNAN CENTER FOR JUSTICE, https://www.brennancenter.org/our-work/research-reports/his-own-words-presidents-attacks-courts.

317. *Judicial Independence*, BOSTON BAR ASSOCIATION, op. cit., at 11.

318. For discussion of this topic in *Piscopolis*, see Part II, Section G of Chapter 5.

this question we also need to address another question, raising a three-fold concern: Given the particular character of *Juropolis* as the *polis of the law*, aren't its inhabitants so directly and unavoidably implicated in the dominant politics, economics, and morality of the liberal democratic state — certainly to a far greater extent than are the inhabitants of other professional *poleis*, such as the medical *polis* — that ultimately any such protection is chimerical? Despite the call to arms in the State Bar report quoted above, shouldn't we honestly acknowledge that the legal system, the legal profession that operates its machinery, and the law and justice that it delivers are necessarily, inevitably, and inextricably *part of* the governmental apparatus which is so tied up with the politics of the state? Isn't much of our work as members of the legal profession necessarily, inevitably, and inextricably concerned with facilitating transactions occurring within, and governed by the forces of, the large-scale market economy? And in the case of many clients and litigants, aren't we necessarily, inevitably, and inextricably involved with furthering the goals and projects of those whose morality is that of constrained preference maximization? How can we members of the legal profession — how can we who are, according to MacIntyre, "the clergy of liberalism"[319] — possibly respond effectively to these concerns?

With regard to the concern about implication in the dominant politics of the liberal democratic state, we must readily concede that the statutory and regulatory norms which govern the inhabitants of *Juropolis* as mediated through the activities of the legal profession do indeed originate in the political branches of government. And as the legal realists and their descendants have taught us, we must also concede that judicial interpretation of these statutory and regulatory norms, judicial articulation of constitutional and other legal norms which govern us, and judicial outcomes in the courts, are all in fact significantly determined by "extra-legal" factors (including political, ideological, economic, social, and psychological factors), and not solely by "legal" considerations as the now largely discredited legal formalists would have it.[320] Indeed, shouldn't we perhaps also concede the

319. *See supra* note 72 and accompanying text.

320. For short, concise introductions to legal formalism and American legal realism, see EDWARDS, LEGAL WRITING, op. cit., at 237–40 (formalism), 240–42 (realism); KUKLIN & STEMPEL, FOUNDATIONS OF THE LAW, op. cit., at 143–45, 147–50 (formalism), 150–51, 153–

claim of even more radical critics — in particular, those associated with critical legal studies, certain types of feminist jurisprudence, and critical race theory — that the entire legal enterprise is essentially political and ideological, reflecting the influence of social power and resulting in systemic hierarchies of domination and oppression that hide behind the mask of an asserted, but fictitious, objective and neutral rule of law?[321]

But even if all this is conceded, we must not overlook a critical and fundamental point. To be sure, all of the politico-ethical commitments examined in Part II of this Chapter, including those under consideration in the present section, are not only reflected in and sustained by the standards, goods, and qualities of excellence — the common goods — of the four law craft practices which co-constitute our common practice of maintaining the rule of law in the liberal democratic state. They also represent the standards, goods, and qualities of excellence — the common goods — of a coterminous common *political* practice as well. As we noted early on in this Chapter, this is because we are unavoidably engaged in a political enterprise due to the public good we provide — the common good of "social peace in the liberal democratic state through the realization of justice for its inhabitants." And as we have just seen, pursuit of this public good is guided by more than "purely legal" considerations and may even be implicated in the perpetuation of hierarchies of domination and oppression. But we must also remember that this public good operates as an alternative to the use of force both by individuals and by the state.

And so, can't we respond to those critical voices which, justifiably, reject the claims of legal formalism or challenge the asserted objectivity and neutrality of the rule of law, by pointing out that there is a fundamentally important distinction — a distinction we ignore at our peril — between

---

58 (realism). For a longer treatment, see BIX, JURISPRUDENCE, op. cit., at 197–209 (addressing formalism within a discussion of realism). *See also Judicial Independence*, BOSTON BAR ASSOCIATION, op. cit., at 18 (conceding that "[b]ecause each judge has biases — conscious and/or unconscious — the ideal of an unbiased judiciary that provides impartial ruling regardless of the identities of those involved in a dispute remains aspirational," but arguing that "[n]evertheless, a diverse bench, including, but not limited to, one that is diverse in terms of race, ethnicity, gender, sexual orientation, gender identity, ability, religion, socioeconomic background and political view, will bring us closer to that ideal").

321. For short, concise introductions to these critical perspectives, see EDWARDS, LEGAL WRITING, op. cit., at 248–49; KUKLIN & STEMPEL, FOUNDATIONS OF THE LAW, op. cit., at 174–76, 178–82. For a longer treatment, see BIX, JURISPRUDENCE, op. cit., at 243–64.

social and political power exercised indirectly through, and constrained by, the forms of law, on the one hand, and the direct and unconstrained exercise of raw social and political power, which disrespects and disregards such legal forms, on the other? Aside from those instances when it may be necessary to protest injustice and seek change through peaceful civil disobedience,[322] the forms of law in liberal democracy can generally be *re*formed in an orderly manner, including through the law-governed processes of legislative enactment, constitutional amendment, and judicial development of the common law — often indeed in response to critical voices of dissent from the status quo. By contrast, a routine exercise of raw social and political power that disrespects and disregards these forms risks either a descent into societal turmoil characterized by a Hobbesian "war of all against all,"[323] or transformation into an authoritarian regime, perhaps even characterized by a "war between rulers and subjects" or a "war among rulers" or both,[324] and thereby unleashing the sorts of diabolical forces Robert Bolt's Thomas More so aptly warns against.[325] It is in this sense, then, that we should understand the character and value of Aristotle's "government of law, not of men"[326] and Jack Sammons' "alterity" of the

---

322. For a helpful discussion and evaluation of the arguments for and against civil disobedience, see, e.g., J.G. RIDDALL, JURISPRUDENCE 322–35 (2nd ed., 1999).

323. For Hobbes' use of this famous phrase or its equivalent, see THOMAS HOBBES, DE CIVE (1642, rev. ed. 1647) (Preface, Chapter 1, Sections 12, 13); THOMAS HOBBES, LEVIATHAN (1651) (Chapter XIII).

324. Regarding the risk of authoritarianism, see, e.g., *Judicial Independence*, BOSTON BAR ASSOCIATION, op. cit., at 12:

> ... [I]n the end, judicial independence is one of a democracy's critical guardrails. As we look around the world at recent events in Turkey, Poland, Nigeria, Venezuela, Argentina, Hungary, and elsewhere, it is therefore no surprise that those who seek to transform a liberal democratic system into an authoritarian regime begin by undermining their independent judiciaries. The swiftness with which some of those judicial systems have been transformed from checks on authoritarian overreach to enabling bureaucracies is in some cases stunning. In all cases, it is a testament to the fragility of judicial independence and the need for lawyers, in particular, to be vigilant and vocal in its defense.

Id. Regarding conflict, including the risk of violent conflict, between authoritarian elites and the masses and among authoritarian elites in authoritarian regimes, see, e.g., MILAN W. SVOLIK, THE POLITICS OF AUTHORITARIAN RULE (2012).

325. *See supra* note 83 and accompanying text.

326. For Aristotle's forceful articulation of this concept, see ARISTOTLE, THE POLITICS 126–29 (Ernest Barker trans., rev. R.F. Stalley, 1995).

legal conversation (although Sammons urges us also to view matters more positively and hopefully).[327] And it is in this sense, and for this reason, that we must remain committed to protecting *Juropolis* against destructive incursions and influences emanating from the "dominant" politics of the liberal democratic state.

As the practice community of legal professionals responsible for maintaining the rule of law in *Juropolis*, clearly we must counter dangerous political rhetoric attacking the judiciary by speaking out forcefully to defend judicial independence.[328] But we must also ask ourselves what else we can and should do to protect such judicial independence, and the rule of law that depends upon it, against threats originating in such politics.[329] And this may require us to answer some uncomfortable questions such as: Have some judges in fact become too "politicized" by failing to exercise due self-restraint under the influence of the "romantic ideal" of judging, or

---

327. For Sammons' discussion of the legal conversation's "alterity," see Sammons, *Play*, op. cit., at 541–50. Sammons raises and explores the question, with respect to legal rhetoric in ancient Greece and today, why "those who wield power within the polity" accept the resulting judgments as "justice" and "[do] not instead see the alterity of legal rhetoric, implying … a separate and sovereign polity, as a threat … to be kept subordinate to the political." *Id.* at 544–45. In our own case, his account described in Section B above seeks to provide the answer.

328. For an example of a judge forcefully speaking out to defend judicial independence, see Katie Shepherd, *Trump 'violates all recognized democratic norms,' federal judge says in biting speech on judicial independence*, THE WASHINGTON POST (November 8, 2019) (discussing U.S. District Judge Paul L. Friedman's speech at the annual Judge Thomas A. Flannery Lecture), https://www.washingtonpost.com/nation/2019/11/08/judge-says-trump-violates-democratic-norms-judiciary-speech/. For an example of members of the practicing bar doing so, see Kevin Judd and Keith Watters, *Trump's Attacks on Courts Undermine Judicial Independence*, ABA JOURNAL (June 28, 2018), www.abajournal.com/news/article/trumps_attacks_on_courts_undermines_judicial_independence.

329. *See generally Judicial Independence*, BOSTON BAR ASSOCIATION, op. cit. The Boston Bar Association report discusses the meaning, history, and importance of judicial independence, ways in which it has been under attack in recent decades and currently, the consequences of such attacks, strategies and mechanisms to provide structural support for judicial independence as well as judicial accountability, and recommendations for protecting judicial independence, including by members of the legal profession speaking out in appropriate ways to promote and defend judicial independence and respond to unwarranted attacks on the judiciary. *See also id.* at 34–40 (listing and linking several types of very useful additional resources on the topic of judicial independence).

are they at least perceived as being too politicized in this sense?[330] Has this type of politicization or perception helped to fuel the other type of politicization that seeks to exert undue external pressure on judges to conform judicial outcomes to satisfy the wishes, or forestall the criticism, of political actors who appoint, elect, or promote them?[331] Has the politicization of the judiciary in these ways eroded public trust in the judicial branch, and even provided a colorable justification for the kinds of dangerous political rhetoric mentioned above?[332] Has it indeed weakened the commitment of inhabitants of *Juropolis* not only to maintain but to *live by* the rule of law?[333] If the answers to these questions are in the affirmative, how can and should we respond? In seeking to answer this question, is it relevant also to ask whether such politicization helps to dismantle hierarchies of domination and oppression, reinforces such hierarchies, or perhaps both, dismantling some while reinforcing others?

And if the issues seem too complex or intractable and satisfactory solutions not readily apparent, does Justice Gorsuch provide a way out, or at least a way forward, when he urges all judges to exhibit appropriate judicial humility and exercise due self-restraint by respecting the proper separation of powers, and to adopt originalism when applying the Constitution and textualism when interpreting statutes?[334] Or is this approach also unrealistic in the deepest, most profound sense because, as Jack Sammons argues, the law cannot be "captured in texts" or "reduced to concepts," so

---

330. *See supra* notes 106–10, 125 and accompanying text.

331. *See supra* note 112 and accompanying text.

332. *See Judicial Independence*, Boston Bar Association, op. cit., at 10–15 (discussing how such influences and forces risk eroding public trust in the judiciary).

333. *See supra* note 313 and accompanying text.

334. Neil Gorsuch, A Republic, If You Can Keep It 10, 22, 25, 47–58, 60, 105–75 (2019); Sherif Girgis, *Neil Gorsuch's Judicial Humility*, National Review (December 5, 2019), https://www.nationalreview.com/magazine/2019/12/22/neil-gorsuchs-judicial-humility/?utm_source=recirc-desktop&utm_medium=blog-post&utm_campaign=river&utm_content=more-in&utm_term=fourth. But even an approach purporting to exercise judicial humility by focusing on text can sometimes lead to socially progressive outcomes. *See, e.g.,* Bostock v. Clayton County Georgia (June 15, 2020) (U.S. Supreme Court Opinion, authored by Justice Gorsuch, ruling that discrimination against gays, lesbians, and transgender individuals, is discrimination "because of ... sex" proscribed by Title VII of the 1964 Civil Rights Act). In his dissent, Justice Alito excoriated the Court as anything but humble ("If today's decision is humble, it is sobering to imagine what the Court might do if it decided to be bold"). *Id.*

that the way out, or at least the way forward, is instead for judges to exhibit appropriate judicial humility and exercise due self-restraint by submitting themselves to the "mystery" that is involved when they "listen truly" to all voices and seek to uncover the law and justice that "flows from our true identity" — or, as James Boyd White puts it, when they properly uphold the art of judging within the general "art of law"?[335]

Moreover, what about the practicing bar and the legal academy? Are there analogous concerns, and could similar questions also be asked, regarding the "politicization" of the ABA, for example, when rating judicial candidates for the federal bench or taking other positions,[336] or regarding the "politicization" of law professors when producing scholarship and undertaking faculty hiring?[337]

---

335. *See supra* notes 47–62 and accompanying text (Sammons), notes 62, 93–100, 122–24 and accompanying text (White).

336. For claims of ABA liberal bias in evaluating judicial nominees for the federal bench, see, e.g., Richard L. Vining Jr., Amy Steigerwalt & Susan Navarro Smelcer, *Bias and the Bar: Evaluating the ABA Ratings of Federal Judicial Nominees*, 65 POLITICAL. RES. Q. 827 (2012), https://www.researchgate.net/publication/228263130_Bias_and_the_Bar_Evaluating_the_ABA_Ratings_of_Federal_Judicial_Nominees; Adam Liptak, *Legal Group's Neutrality is Challenged*, The New York Times (March 30, 2009), https://www.nytimes.com/2009/03/31/us/31bar.html; Tim Ryan, *Senate Scours American Bar Association for Liberal Bias*, Courthouse News Service (November 15, 2017), https://www.courthousenews.com/senate-scours-american-bar-association-liberal-bias/; Carrie Campbell Severino, *Yes, the ABA Is Still a Left-Wing Advocacy Group*, NATIONAL REVIEW (September 27, 2019), https://www.nationalreview.com/bench-memos/yes-the-aba-is-still-a-left-wing-advocacy-group/. For a strong denial of ABA liberal bias in evaluating judicial nominees, see, e.g., Debra Cassens Weiss, *ABA president defends ratings of judicial nominees after GOP senators claim liberal bias*, ABA JOURNAL (November 15, 2017) (noting then ABA president Hilaire Bass's defense that "[For] 64 years — through both Republican and Democratic administrations — the ABA's Standing Committee on the Federal Judiciary has thoroughly vetted thousands of nominees using a fair and nonpartisan process that no other organization can match"), https://www.abajournal.com/news/article/aba_president_defends_ratings_of_judicial_nominees_after_gop_senators_claim.

337. For a study evaluating claims of political bias in legal scholarship, see, e.g., Adam S. Chilton & Eric Posner, *An Empirical Study of Political Bias in Legal Scholarship*, Coase-Sandor Institute for Law & Economics Working Paper No. 696, 2014, https://chicagounbound.uchicago.edu/law_and_economics/707/. Regarding the ideological balance in the legal academy more generally and possible political discrimination in law faculty hiring, see, e.g., Adam Bonica, Adam Chilton, Kyle Rozema & Maya Sen, *The Legal Academy's Ideological Uniformity*, 47 J. LEGAL STUD. (January 2018), https://scholar.harvard.edu/files/msen/files/law-prof-ideology.pdf; James C. Phillips, *Political Discrimination and Law Professor*

368 Professions and Politics in Crisis

We can address the concerns about our implication in the dominant economics and morality of the liberal democratic state more briefly, although this does not mean the task of protecting *Juropolis* against threats originating in the dominant economics and morality is any easier than is protecting against threats originating in the dominant politics. Indeed, in some ways this task may be even more challenging because the threats are even more seductive and insidious in their allure. To be sure, judges, practicing lawyers, and legal academics may sometimes find it difficult to resist the temptation to seek psychic goods of effectiveness, such as power, status, and fame, by unduly engaging in different types of "social engineering" through their various activities, and they thereby risk corrupting the common goods of the practice. But when they are attacked, justifiably or unjustifiably, by a President or other political actor for being too "politicized," they can always defend against an easily identifiable and recognizable threat originating in the dominant politics from behind the barricades of principle — invoking principles such as the rule of law, the independence of the judiciary, zealous representation, and academic freedom.

In the case of the dominant economics and morality, however, it seems not unreasonable to suggest that the threats are not as easily identifiable and recognizable. In theory, of course, it is always possible to continue "thinking and acting in Aristotelian and Thomistic terms," but MacIntyre alerts us to the practical challenges involved in actually being able to do so.[338] On the one hand, then, just because many clients or litigants may be individualistic and acquisitive, albeit constrained, rational preference maximizers rather than Thomistic Aristotelians — or, at least, just because they may be such rational preference maximizers regarding the types of claims they generate within *Juropolis*, however they may be in the context of their particular practices — doesn't mean we also have to act in a similar manner, either in our dealings with those clients and litigants or in our dealings with each other. And the American Bar Association Model Rules of Professional Conduct certainly permit practicing lawyers to engage their clients in moral conversation regarding their dealings with

Hiring, 11 N.Y.U.J.L. & LIBERTY 915 (2019), https://papers.ssrn.com/sol3/papers.cfm?abstract_id=3224508.

338. *See* Chapter 6, note 141 and accompanying text [quoting MACINTYRE, CONFLICTS OF MODERNITY, op. cit., at 166–67].

others.[339] On the other hand, just how easy is it in practice for members of the legal profession to resist the allure and potential corruptions presented by goods of effectiveness, especially material goods of effectiveness, when so much of our very "business" — by no means all, of course — not only occurs within the liberal democratic state's large-scale market economy, as do the activities of clients and litigants, but also is concerned with actively, even aggressively, facilitating (or should one rather say, championing) attainment of such goods of effectiveness by others in this market? Are we not arguably at even greater risk of resolving the tension between the practical rationalities of constrained preference maximization and Neo-Aristotelianism in favor of the former in our law craft practices in *Juropolis* than are clients and litigants in their own practices? Are we not at even greater risk, in other words, of becoming more like Cash than Drew? To answer this question, we need to ask and answer the sorts of questions we have asked in previous sections, especially Section D. But if the answer is in the affirmative, don't we need to redouble our efforts to protect against this even greater risk?

---

339. *See* AMERICAN BAR ASSOCIATION MODEL RULES OF PROFESSIONAL CONDUCT Rule 2.1: "In representing a client, a lawyer shall exercise independent professional judgment and render candid advice. In rendering advice, a lawyer may refer not only to law but to other considerations such as moral, economic, social and political factors, that may be relevant to the client's situation." *See also* Comment [2]:

> [2] Advice couched in narrow legal terms may be of little value to a client, especially where practical considerations, such as cost or effects on other people, are predominant. Purely technical legal advice, therefore, can sometimes be inadequate. It is proper for a lawyer to refer to relevant moral and ethical considerations in giving advice. Although a lawyer is not a moral advisor as such, moral and ethical considerations impinge upon most legal questions and may decisively influence how the law will be applied.

Id. See also supra notes 126–28, 131 and accompanying text (discussing the lawyering model of "client goodness"). In addition, Comment [1] to Rule 1.16 (a) of the Model Rules states that "[a] lawyer should not accept representation in a matter unless it can be performed competently," which may not be possible where the lawyer has a fundamental moral disagreement with the client. And subject to certain procedural conditions Rule 1.16 (b)(4) explicitly permits a lawyer to withdraw from representing a client if "the client insists upon taking action that the lawyer considers repugnant or with which the lawyer has a fundamental disagreement."

For the text of the ABA Model Rules of Professional Conduct, see https://www.americanbar.org/groups/professional_responsibility/publications/model_rules_of_professional_conduct/model_rules_of_professional_conduct_table_of_contents/.

In sum, when performing our professional roles in *Juropolis* and ful-filling our public responsibility to do good work under the social contract allowing us the privilege of self-regulation, don't we need to deal with the liberal democratic state — and with its dominant politics, economics, and morality — as do the inhabitants of *Piscopolis*, which is to say, defensively, as far as possible only on our own terms? Indeed, doesn't our professional integrity require us to do so? Otherwise, aren't the noble and inspiring sentiments about justice and the rule of law, and service to clients and the public good, that are the staple of law school Commencement addresses just an exercise in self-indulgence calculated to make us feel good at best, or cynically empty rhetoric at worst?

2. Protecting the Republic

But perhaps the stakes are even higher than we realize and the above discussion suggests. Perhaps what is at stake is not only protecting *Ju-ropolis* (and the Republic) against overt threats to the rule of law and the independence of the judiciary from the political branches, and resisting the insidious allure and potential corruptions presented by goods of effec-tiveness. Perhaps what is at stake, even more fundamentally, is protecting the integrity of *Juropolis* in preserving the art that animates the law — the "art of law" that is the practical wisdom of the legal profession, viewed as a rhetorical community — and with it, the integrity of the Republic itself.

James Boyd White considers that law and democracy are inextricably intertwined, at least in the United States, and that *both* are under threat. Law and democracy are inextricably intertwined because, on the one hand, unlike other countries such as France, "[a]ll of our law has its roots in democratic institutions which derive their authority, directly or indi-rectly, from what we call 'the people,'" and on the other hand, "democracy works through the law, again directly or indirectly." Consequently, the law "both depends on and maintains" democracy. Moreover, "[i]t is... this combination of law and democracy that gives us our national character and identity."[340] As a result,

---

340. WHITE, KEEP LAW ALIVE, op. cit., at xviii–xix, 107. In elaborating on how law and democracy are inextricably intertwined, White explains how powers are not concentrated "into a single force" but distributed among separate institutional actors that must each "ac-knowledge and respect judgments made by others" (for example, the legislature respecting

At the simplest level, what the law teaches is that we live in a world in which different people can have different, decent, and reasonable views; that we need a way to respect these views and judge among them fairly, that is, openly and honestly; that the world constructed by the law is one that distributes the power to decide such questions differentially to various public and private agents — so that even if we lose this case, or this issue, we have a residue of autonomy and freedom and a real reason to remain faithful to the law as such ... [341]

This being the case, White continues, "we cannot fairly and rightly decide disputes by reference to theory, or our own estimate of costs and benefits, or to the sorts of clichés and buzzwords and slogans that characterize much political talk" because doing so severs law from the "structure of authority" in our democratic institutions and culture.[342] And White considers that due to the types of stresses on our common goods and other developments examined in this Chapter, this is precisely what is happening and that law is increasingly "becoming an instrument of empire and power, and in the process losing its essential character."[343] Consequently, law and democracy are *both* under threat from an empire of power and control that is "committed to rule by force and propaganda," that is external as well as internal, and in which "all are subject to the same imperial and dictatorial

---

the Constitution, courts respecting the legislature, lower courts respecting higher courts, etc.), how lawyers and judges respect or defer to authoritative texts that "all rest in some way upon the authority of democratic institutions" (for example, "statutes passed by elected legislatures, or opinions issued by judges appointed by elected governors, or contracts written by the parties themselves"), and how law is also "deeply democratic" in being open to and committed to learning from other systems of knowledge (for example, engineering, sociology, psychology, history, and medicine), and in having to make sense in some contexts to "ordinary people" in their "ordinary language, the language of the citizen as such" (for example, in jury instructions and closing arguments). *Id.* at 121 & n15.

341. *Id.* at 121–22.

342. *Id.* Thus, "in the world of theory," whether a result is right or not depends on whether it is consistent with a philosophical, political, or economic theory "without any basis in democratic authority but resting solely upon the commitments of those who are persuaded by it: the community of believers," and "[i]n the world of pure power, the only thing that matters is what the powerful want." *Id.* at 121.

343. *Id.* at 122. White is especially troubled by the developments in the courts and the legal academy. For White's discussion of these developments see *id.* at 115–20; *supra* notes 125, 207 and accompanying text.

regime" and "[o]ur nation is on its way to becoming a third-world country politically as well as economically."[344]

In addition to lamenting what is happening to law, then, White also laments the "official dehumanization" of those not belonging to the "white" race as manifested, for example, in the practice of torture guided by irrational cost-benefit thinking and in the governmental cruelty toward asylum applicants and their children at the southern border,[345] But what White seems to lament most of all is how we have accepted as a society the indefensible level of economic inequality that has occurred in our lifetimes, and the related "astonishing transfer of national wealth" to an unelected oligarchic elite of superrich private individuals and corporations who seek wealth and power, operate in an increasingly unregulated market economy driven by the demands of efficiency rather than justice, and lack democratic legitimacy yet wield inordinate economic and political power over our lives.[346] Their "main object seems to be to extract as much economic value as possible from the earth and the oceans and the air, and from the labor — and unemployment — of billions of people."[347]

White identifies several related factors explaining why we acquiesce in our subjection to this empire of power and control. To begin with, our minds have been colonized by "economic" thinking focused on wealth, ownership and consumption, or "simple gratification of desire," getting whatever we want, coopting even potential critics who benefit from the same policies enriching the super-rich (and he suggests that this might include you and me too).[348] And our minds are manipulated by deceptive consumer and political advertising and propaganda using slogans, clichés, images, sound bites, buzzwords, and falsehoods inimical to independent and critical thought and memory.[349] Consequently, we suffer from a "learned helplessness" in which our culture's "consumer dream ... teaches us that we have no responsibility for public action, no right to

344. WHITE, KEEP LAW ALIVE, op. cit., at 103, 114, 130–31.

345. Id. at 122–28 & notes 16, 19, and 22, 134. White considers that "enemy combatants" and "people at the border, including children" are "the juridical equivalent of slaves," treated effectively as "not persons under the law." Id. at 128 n24,

346. Id. at 107, 109, 111–12, 113–14, 134.

347. Id. at 114.

348. Id. at 109–10, 114.

349. Id. at 112–13, 123–24, 131.

demand meaning in our work and lives, and no obligation for the welfare of others."[350]

Much of White's critique is, of course, already familiar from Part I of Chapter 6, and indeed in many ways White and MacIntyre speak in the same voice. But what White shows, as MacIntyre does not because his focus is elsewhere, is how the dominant political, economic, and moral environment of the liberal democratic state poses a threat not only to *Juropolis* but to democracy itself. How, then, should we respond as legal professionals to the threat to law and democracy White describes? Do we agree that, in addition to the types of protective commitments already discussed, we should also commit to preserving the "art of law" in the ways White describes in the following passage?

> We can continue to insist that law is not rules, not policy, not theory, but an art of confronting and using certain essential and structural tensions ... We can see it as a way of respecting the authority of legal institutions, and public and private actors within them — a form of respect that can do much to ensure that we also respect the dignity of those to whom law speaks. We can see it as a mode of collective and individual learning....Every class, every case, in which we insist upon doing real law can be its own act of resistance to the corruption I have described. No one class or case will reverse the course of institutional decay, but if in what we do we can find a way to insist upon our own integrity and the integrity of law, we shall at the very least not be contributing to the destruction I see, and may be contributing to its reversal, ... [T]here are few things that would be better for the world in its present state than to have lots of law teachers teaching law as the art it is, an art that has justice as its constant topic. What is most valu-

---

350. *Id.* at 110, 112. For example:

> [T]hough some people still argue for these things, it seems that we are not really to expect equality, or fairness, or compassion, from our society or its government; we are not to expect decent social and medical services, or clean air, or a mature response to the immense problems of global warming; we are not to expect lawyers and judges to talk in an earnest and serious way about what justice requires. These things are not going to happen, so don't waste your energy complaining.

Id. at 110. In *Conflicts of Modernity* MacIntyre discusses factors resonant with the first two factors discussed in the paragraph in the text. *See* Chapter 5, note 32 and accompanying text.

able about our country is not its gross national product, but its constitutional and legal tradition, based as it is upon the idea, never of course fully achieved, of the fundamental equality of human beings — an equality of which we are now losing even the pretense.[351]

Perhaps some of us may consider that White overstates his case, and may question his "glum conclusion" that as a society "we do not believe that we really have democracy at all any more, at least in the sense in which we once thought we did" — a conclusion, however, that is resonant with Jeffrey Stout's assessment of the current state of our democracy referenced in Chapter 1.[352] But if we accept White's claim that in the United States law and democracy have traditionally been inextricably intertwined (or have been for at least the last seventy years or so),[353] then when we defend *Juropolis* against the various destructive influences emanating from the dominant environment of the liberal democratic state — from the empire of power and control — by being Thomistic Aristotelian lawyer-statesmen and women practicing the art of law, we can understand ourselves as also defending the Republic. As White says:

> [W]e must know who we are in reading ... and in writing [law], and what it calls upon us to do and to be. We need to know what is distinctive about our history, for good and ill: the nature of the experiment of government of the people, by the people, and for the people, and of the forces that threaten it[354]

In the next Chapter we address the question whether we should do more than just defend *Juropolis* and the Republic in this way.

---

351. White, Keep Law Alive, op. cit., at 156–57.

352. *Id.* at 113–14; Chapter 1, note 50 and accompanying text. White's overall attitude toward the ultimate fate of law and democracy also seems to echo Stout's apparent attitude of hope combined with Stoicism, combatting something close to despair, although White recommends not Stoicism but the *Confessions* of Saint Augustine to help educate our sensibilities and responses as members of the legal profession and as citizens, so that we can at least "keep law alive" among ourselves and like-minded others if, and as, it proves impossible to "keep law alive" institutionally "in an increasingly corrupted world" in the way White urges. *See* White, Keep Law Alive, op. cit., Chapter 6 (on "Difficulty and Responsibility in the Face of Evil").

353. *Id.* at 135–36.

354. *Id.* at 42.

EIGHT

BEYOND *JUROPOLIS*

Toward the Liberal Democratic State as a
Republic of Virtue

In Chapter 7 we saw that members of the legal profession can "live *against* the cultural grain" and "learn to act as economic, political, and moral antagonists of the dominant order"[1] by doing three things: First, by embracing a set of politico-ethical commitments that are analogous to the commitments instantiated by Drew and the other inhabitants in the ideal fishing village of *Piscopolis*; second, by meeting the many challenges involved in instantiating these commitments in our lives and relationships in *Juropolis*, the fishing village of the law; and third, among these challenges, by dealing with the liberal democratic state — and with its dominant politics, economics, and morality — as far as possible, defensively and only on our own terms. Being intentional about doing these three things will be of great benefit to the legal profession. It will enhance our prospects for living a meaningful, purposeful, and fulfilling life — a flourishing life — through the work to which we have been called, and in this way enhance our prospects for achieving professional well-being and for avoiding and alleviating the distress and dysfunction that currently ails the profession and rightly receives so much attention nowadays. Moreover, improving the well-being and performance of the legal profession will it-

---

1. For the quoted language, see Chapter 6, note 112 and accompanying text [quoting ALASDAIR MACINTYRE, ETHICS IN THE CONFLICTS OF MODERNITY: AN ESSAY ON DESIRE, PRACTICAL REASONING, AND NARRATIVE 237–38 (2016).].

self also benefit those we serve in the Republic. And defending *Juropolis* will also help defend the Republic itself.

But are we — or are some of us at least — called to do more in living against the cultural grain and acting as antagonists of the dominant order? Is it enough that in our professional roles in *Juropolis* we defensively seek protection *from* the cultural grain and dominant order, or should we, in our roles as citizens concerned about the well-being of the Republic and our fellow inhabitants, also actively seek to *transform* the culture and dominant order? Is *this* arguably a matter of integrity too: Wouldn't it be hypocritical to have one type of character and set of values in *Juropolis* and another type of character and set of values in the broader liberal democratic state beyond it? Moreover, isn't offense often the best defense anyway? Specifically, should we seek — through example, invitation, and rational argument — to transform the dominant political, economic, and moral environment of the modern liberal democratic state with its individualist *ethos* into a political, economic, and moral environment with a more communitarian *ethos* like *Piscopolis*? Wouldn't doing so not only further strengthen our defense of *Juropolis* (and the Republic) against threats originating in the dominant order, but also enhance the prospects for all inhabitants of our Republic to lead a meaningful, purposeful, and fulfilling life — a flourishing life — and thus enhance our collective prospects for achieving political well-being and for avoiding and alleviating the political distress and dysfunction that currently ails the Republic and also rightly receives so much attention nowadays? Certainly, doing so would respond to White's lament about the "learned helplessness" in which our culture's "consumer dream ... teaches us that we have no responsibility for public action, no right to demand meaning in our work and lives, and no obligation for the welfare of others," and is also consistent with White's claim that "[t]he premises of democracy" require "an equal access to the essentials of human thriving."[2]

But perhaps this proposal sounds Utopian, even quixotic. Indeed, MacIntyre himself might be skeptical about it. However, we can recall MacIntyre's own response when discussing characteristics reflecting the subordination of "economic considerations... to social and moral con-

---

2. JAMES BOYD WHITE, KEEP LAW ALIVE 110, 112, 134 (2019). *See also* Chapter 7, note 350 and accompanying text (regarding the lament).

siderations" in ideal, more or less complete local communities: "These are of course Utopian standards, not too often realized outside Utopia, and only then... in flawed ways. But trying to live by Utopian standards is not Utopian, although it does involve a rejection of the economic goals of advanced capitalism."[3] Moreover, arguably the suggestion becomes less Utopian as the flaws and crises of the liberal democratic state and advanced capitalism come under increasing scrutiny.[4]

I. A Three-Step Strategy

How might we prosecute such a project for social and cultural transformation? It is always possible, of course, to seek the adoption, through regular political processes in the Republic, of legislation aimed at creating the conditions needed to achieve human flourishing through the promotion of excellence and the cultivation of virtue. For reasons given in Chapter 1 and Chapter 6, however, such a direct approach seems unlikely to succeed until the political, economic, and moral environment has been sufficiently prepared to become receptive to such a direct approach.[5] To effect the pre-requisite preparation requires an indirect approach that envisages and measures progress over a longer time frame, although unavoidable imperatives to address existential threats such as climate change or other problems resulting from the crises of the liberal democratic state and advanced capitalism may perhaps accelerate the process. Although we cannot predict how much time will be required for this preparatory phase, we can identify at least three different steps in the process. The first step is a pre-requisite for the second and third steps, but these latter steps can occur simultaneously.

And when we engage in relevant conversation under each of these steps, we will need to exercise our best judgment — our practical wisdom — both to determine the specific point(s) we should address in a particular con-

---

3. ALASDAIR MACINTYRE, DEPENDENT RATIONAL ANIMALS: WHY HUMAN BEINGS NEED THE VIRTUES 145 (1999).

4. In addition to the current political dysfunction, there is related economic dysfunction. *See, e.g., The Future of Capitalism*, 99 FOREIGN AFFAIRS 8–49 (January/February 2020) (containing five articles examining the merits and flaws of advanced capitalism and evaluating possible alternative models).

5. *See* Chapter 1, notes 37–39, 43–44, 50–52 and accompanying text; Part I of Chapter 6.

378 Professions and Politics in Crisis

versation and, as in the case of any conversation, to choose the words that are most appropriate and effective in communicating the position we are seeking to convey. And here again, as suggested in Chapter 2 (Part III, Section C), sometimes we may need to pause to make sure that our reasoning has not become unduly untethered from the pre-existing world of Being, if necessary engaging in a dialectical back and forth between our reasoning and the givenness of Being until we reach a point of "reflective equilibrium" regarding the point(s) in question. (As we will see in Part II of this Chapter, Jack Sammons proposes a procedure that explicitly builds such a pause into the third step.) Everything said below, then, is subject to these general qualifications.

The first step focuses on those of us who are already, at least to some significant extent, pursuing a *Piscopolis*-like way of life. Specifically, following MacIntyre's lead, members of the legal profession inhabiting *Juropolis*, members of other self-regulated professions inhabiting their own professional *poleis*, and those living their lives in various local communities and particular practices must become aware of the extent to which we are all already pursuing a *Piscopolis*-like way of life, informed by the premises and exhibiting the virtues of Thomistic Aristotelianism and focused on the achievement of human flourishing through attaining the common goods of practices.[6] Related, we must resolve to continue pursuing such a way of life despite the many challenges and temptations we face from the dominant political, economic, and moral environment of the liberal democratic state. Our resolve will be greatly aided if, through dialectical moral argument, we are persuaded of the rational superiority of Thomistic Aristotelianism over the dominant morality,[7] and of Neo-Aristotelian practical rationality over the dominant practical rationality of constrained preference maximization,[8] and if we are able to confirm this superiority

---

6. For MacIntyre's lead on this, see Chapter 6, notes 132–34 and accompanying text.

7. *See* Chapter 5, notes 27–30, 33–34 and accompanying text (discussing how the inhabitants of *Piscopolis* regard Thomistic Aristotelianism as rationally superior to all rival "traditions of [moral] enquiry" and "the best theory so far" emerging from the "dialectic" among competing moral traditions, including liberalism); Chapter 6, notes 89–91, 100–11 and accompanying text (discussing the dominant, secular "Morality" in advanced modernity).

8. *See* Chapter 6, notes 18, 71, 92–100 and accompanying text (describing the dominant rationality of constrained preference maximization), notes 132–39 and accompanying text (comparing Neo-Aristotelian practical rationality with this dominant practical rationality).

in our narratively lived individual and collective experience — in other words, in the stories of our lives in community.⁹ Clearly, through appropriate conversation we can help each another acquire and maintain the necessary self-awareness, rational understanding, and mutual resolve. Moreover, we may be able to find an additional source of resolve in our sense of vocation, as we consciously seek to respond to what the deepest truths of our lives are calling us to become — something that for many of us may be rooted in our respective religious faith traditions.¹⁰ With our self-identification as Thomistic Aristotelians thus in place, we can further self-identify as collectively already forming a broader, inchoate "republic of virtue" within the larger Republic, and make common cause with one other as we move from defense to offense in undertaking the second and third steps, through which we seek to further expand and strengthen this "republic of virtue."

For the second step we remain in the context of our respective practices but look for opportunities to engage in appropriate moral conversation with those we serve (clients, patients, customers, etc.), when they conceive of themselves, expressly or by implication, as rational preference maximizers and do not yet self-identify as resolute Thomistic Aristotelians. In such conversation we can explain that we find Thomistic Aristotelianism and its practical rationality attractive and persuasive due to their

---

See also Chapter 3, Part II, Section B.1 and 3 (discussing the "master virtue" of practical wisdom exhibited by the expert practitioner in a practice), notes 116–18, 127–31 and accompanying text (comparing practical rationality in the perspective of the goods of excellence of a practice, exhibited in the practical wisdom of the practice, with practical rationality in the perspective of goods of effectiveness).

9. See Chapter 5, note 31 and accompanying text. All this may be facilitated if initiatives such as those of the University of Birmingham's Jubilee Center for Character and Virtues in the United Kingdom and the University of Chicago's Center for Practical Wisdom in the United States come to exert an increasingly significant influence, especially in the educational continuum. See, e.g., the Jubilee Center's *Statement on Virtue, Character, and Practical Wisdom in Professional Practice* (2016), https://www.jubileecentre.ac.uk/userfiles/jubileecentre/pdf/Statement_Character_Virtue_Practical_Wisdom_Professional_Practice.pdf; the Jubilee Center's *Character Education in Universities: A Framework for Flourishing* (2020), https://www.jubileecentre.ac.uk/userfiles/jubileecentre/pdf/character-education/Character_Education_in_Universities_Final_Edit.pdf; and the University of Chicago Center's dissemination of the latter document, https://wisdomcenter.uchicago.edu/news/wisdom-news/character-education-universities-framework-flourishing.

10. See Chapter 2, notes 120–22 and accompanying text.

rational superiority over the dominant morality and practical rationality of constrained preference maximization, that we are able to confirm this superiority in the stories of our lives, and that we invite those we serve to consider instantiating it in their own lives by following courses of action that exhibit its virtues and seek to achieve human flourishing through the attainment of common goods of practices. When appropriate and necessary, we can begin, as in our own case, by asking them to consider the extent to which they may in fact already be pursuing a *Piscopolis*-like way of life, at least to some extent, focused on attaining the common goods of various practices in which they themselves participate, such as the "practices of families, workplaces, schools, clinics, theatres, [and] sports."[11] In *Juropolis*, for example, there are numerous opportunities for members of the legal profession to engage in moral conversation of this sort with those we serve. Thus, practicing lawyers can engage in such conversation when counseling clients (in estate planning, for example), judges can engage in such conversation when sentencing and supervising criminal defendants (in accountability courts, for example), and law professors can engage in such conversation when advising law students (on career options, for example).[12] Although we should always respect appropriate ethical limits so that we seek only to encourage considered reflection, not to impose our own views on others, we should also recognize that, at least to some extent, those we serve are always inevitably shaped by us anyway.[13]

---

11. *See* Chapter 6, notes 130–31 and accompanying text [quoting MacIntyre, Conflicts of Modernity, op. cit., at 110, 175–76].

12. Judge Verda Colvin, a Superior Court judge in the Macon Judicial Circuit in Georgia from 2014 until her elevation to the Georgia Court of Appeals in 2020, is a striking example of how a judge can engage in such conversation addressing matters and using language appropriate to the audience. *See, e.g.,* https://www.youtube.com/watch?v=-7MIuqqWIvQ&app=desktop (one of Judge Colvin's powerfully moving talks to troubled teenagers in 2016 in the monthly "Consider the Consequences" program of the Bibb County Sheriff's Office); https://www.youtube.com/watch?v=Tf2DKZpJy6s&app=desktop (at 19:00 minutes: Judge Colvin describing her work in accountability courts in Pat Longan's Legal Profession course at Mercer University School of Law in 2016). I do not know whether Judge Colvin thinks of herself as a Thomistic Aristotelian but although she does not use words like "flourishing," "virtue," or "vocation" and "calling" when talking to troubled teenagers or defendants in accountability court, it seems very clear that she is effectively invoking those notions. Certainly, what she says is quite consistent with Thomistic Aristotelian premises and tenets.

13. In the case of practicing lawyers, for example, we saw in Chapter 7 that under ABA Model Rule 2.1 and Comment [2] to that Rule, "[i]n representing a client, a lawyer shall ex-

In the third step we move beyond the context of our own practices to engage in explicitly political conversation with our fellow citizens in the larger Republic. This third step, although crucial, is perhaps the most challenging of all and requires the longest treatment because our political conversation has become so degraded. The symptoms of the crisis of well-being, distress, and dysfunction in the Republic mentioned in Chapter 1 — hyper-partisanship, political gridlock, deepening economic, cultural, and racial divisions, an identity politics of fear, suspicion, and outrage, social media tribalism, poisonous incivility and dishonesty, and so on — manifest in the political relationships with our fellow citizens, not just in relationships among our elected political leaders.[14] If modern politics was "civil war carried on by other means" when MacIntyre originally wrote those words in *After Virtue* in 1981,[15] it is now "civil war... by other means on steroids." How do we, the ordinary citizens of the Republic, "take our country back" from the political, social, and technological forces that have divided us into social and political tribes — frequently, it seems, even invading and poisoning relationships among family members and erstwhile friends? How do we overcome our mutual alienation and find our way back to one another, re-enabling meaningful political conversation to occur? These questions are likely to remain urgent even if the 2020 general election produces a change of Administration.

---

ercise independent professional judgment and render candid advice" and such advice may "refer to relevant moral and ethical considerations" because such considerations "impinge upon most legal questions and may decisively influence how the law will be applied." *See* Chapter 7, note 339 and accompanying text. However, "[i]ndependent professional judgment is for the purpose of helping the client make decisions. It is emphatically not for the purpose of telling the client what to do. The client gets to decide what the client wants, and the client determines what is in his or her best interest." PATRICK EMERY LONGAN, DAISY HURST FLOYD, AND TIMOTHY W. FLOYD, THE FORMATION OF PROFESSIONAL IDENTITY: THE PATH FROM STUDENT TO LAWYER 46 (2020). But this said, as Jack Sammons observes, "practitioners tend to create their clients....[T]hose who think their clients are only interested in money, for but one example, treat their clients as if this were true and by doing so create clients only interested in money. The clients learn what they are to be from them." Sammons Email (September 23, 2020) [on file with author].

14. *See* Chapter 1, notes 36–37 and accompanying text.

15. *See* Chapter 6, note 62 and accompanying text [quoting ALASDAIR MACINTYRE, AFTER VIRTUE: A STUDY IN MORAL THEORY 253 (3d. ed., 2007) (1981).

II. The Third Step – Grassroots Political Conversations

We have already mentioned the views of Justice Gorsuch and Jack Sammons regarding the issue of appropriate judicial humility and due self-restraint.[16] Both of them also address the issue of appropriate political conversation among citizens of the Republic and how to achieve it. In Justice Gorsuch's vision of constitutional design the framers created a governmental structure aimed at ensuring the right of self-government for which the revolution had been fought — a structure, in other words, ensuring that the people would not be "ruled by a monarch or any other unelected elite, judges included" but would "rule themselves."[17] However, self-government not only requires "citizens who know how their government works — and who are capable of, and interested in, participating in its administration." It also requires that those citizens are "able to listen as well as speak, to learn as well as teach, and to tolerate as well as expect tolerance."[18] Justice Gorsuch is very concerned about "[w]hat happens to our experiment in self-government when we have such difficulty talking with and learning from one another in civil discussion" and lack the necessary knowledge and tolerance.[19] And so, in addition to emphasizing civic education and civic engagement, Justice Gorsuch emphasizes the critical importance of restoring civility to political conversation:

> Without civility, the bonds of friendship in our communities dissolve, tolerance dissipates, and the pressure to impose order and uniformity through public and private coercion mounts. In a very real way, self-governance turns on our treating each other as equals — as persons, with the courtesy and respect each person deserves — even when we vigorously disagree. Our capacity for civility is, in this way, no less than a sign of our commitment to human equality and, in turn, democratic self-government.[20]

Like Justice Gorsuch, Jack Sammons also proposes reinvigorating and restoring civility to our democratic political conversation in the Republic,

---

16. *See* Chapter 7, notes 334–35 and accompanying text.
17. Neil Gorsuch, A Republic, If You Can Keep It 7, 9–10 (2019).
18. *Id.* at 7–8.
19. *Id.* at 11, 19–20.
20. *Id.* at 26–31.

and he offers a very specific suggestion for how to do so — a suggestion that in many ways parallels his account of how to realize justice in Part II, Section B.1 of Chapter 7.[21] Sammons considers that our political conversation "is no longer a rhetorical one," meaning that "speakers in it no longer seek means of persuasion."[22] Because our politics has forgotten to ask honestly who "we" are, what we have instead is "the dead language of an exchange of concepts understood as prejudices and interests" that reflect and constitute our current false and inauthentic identities — identities that are very difficult to resist because they provide "a certain security and stability."[23] More specifically,

If we do ask the identity question at all, who we seem to be in this, the default identity I suppose you might call it, are a people trapped in the inauthenticity of trying to identify ourselves through associations with one or more of the competing cultural groups doing battle over control of the control we think we have. Anyone who identifies himself or herself, or any important aspect of his or her identity, as a liberal, conservative, independent, or none of the above, or as on one side of some social issue or another — taxation, abortion, gay rights, racial equality, fiscal policy, energy policy, environmental policy, economic fairness, Wall Street, Palestine, and so on — has this sense

---

21. Jack L. Sammons, *Some Concluding Reflections - Recovering the Political: The Problem with Our Political Conversations*, 63 MERCER L. REV. 899 (2012). Much of the discussion of Sammons' account here is taken from Mark L. Jones, *Beyond Punks in Empty Chairs: An Imaginary Conversation with Clint Eastwood's Dirty Harry — Toward Peace Through Spiritual Justice*, 11 U. MASS. L. REV. 312, 359–61 (2016). Both Sammons' account of "realizing justice" and his account here center on the question of our true identity.

22. Sammons, *Concluding Reflections*, op. cit., at 906.

23. *Id.* at 901–02, 904, 912. Sammons provides an illuminating comparison of the legal, religious, and political conversations, observing that:

[They] are in their essence about this question: who are we? Each one… focuses on different aspects of our identity, and each imagines the "we" of its particular conversation differently, but, in their essence, all three are about the same thing. They are about us. In addition, each offers its own resources for addressing the hubris that has led us astray.

The political conversation…, however, has forgotten that this is the case.

Id. at 900–01 and n8 (also observing that of the three the law is the most dependent upon a "mythical 'we'" constituting a "polity" that is "imagined," which is not to deny that it is "real").

of being trapped, even when his or her side is in control. This is because the associations, which provide this identity, can offer no personal satisfaction as an identity. They are not the "we" we seek.

Yet such identities are extremely hard to resist, providing as they do a certain security and stability, however false and incomplete these might be.

The problem, then, is that

Rather than the comfort of a truer identity, these identities produce only constant apprehension, defined as they are against others we do not understand and over whom we have no real possibility of control. A people so defined feel the constant, unrelenting tug of the impossible demands of needing to master the wills of difficult others. They feel the fear that if this tug is not acted upon, the others, who feel the same need, will master them.[24]

Consider how these false and inauthentic identities are typically reflected in "labels" or "slogans" used to describe various groups. The intent behind such descriptions may be positive or negative, depending on whether they are in-group self-descriptions or other-directed descriptions of an opposing out-group. Examples come readily to mind. Thus, those who see themselves as protecting the lives of babies in the womb through restricting access to abortions use sympathetic language such as "pro-life" for in-group self-description and pejorative language such as "pro-abortion" or "baby killer" for out-group other-directed description, but those who see themselves as protecting reproductive freedom through preserving a woman's access to legal abortion use radically different language such as the sympathetic term "pro-choice" (not "pro-abortion") for in-group self-description and the pejorative slogan "war on women" (not "pro-life") for out-group other-directed description. Another example would be the use by Trump supporters of the sympathetic term "freedom-loving nationalist" for in-group self-description and the pejorative term "freedom-hating socialist" for out-group other-directed description, in contrast to their opponents' use of the sympathetic term "seeking economic justice" for in-

_____

24. *Id.* at 901–02.

group self-description and "deplorable white supremacist" for out-group
other-directed description. The very same person then, may be described
as "pro-life" *and* engaged in a "war on women" or as "pro-choice" *and*
"pro-abortion" and "baby killer," or as a "freedom-loving nationalist" *and*
a "deplorable white supremacist" or as "seeking economic justice" *and* a
"freedom-hating socialist," depending on who is doing the describing.

Political conversation conducted in such superficial and trivial terms
just will not do. We must get beyond language that paints cartoonish car-
icatures more suited to the school playground than mature political conversation, and instead use language that articulates and engages with the
deeper justifications for our political beliefs and positions. Although the
superficial and trivial language by which, and in which, we are currently
trapped gestures toward these deeper justifications, it is woefully incomplete or misleading or both, so that we see through a glass darkly. In the
case of other-directed pejorative language used to describe out-groups,
we see very darkly indeed because such language tends to demonize "the
other," and this, when sufficiently pervasive, naturally tends toward universal mutual demonization. It is terribly injurious to the body politic,
representing as it does the deployment of language as a weapon in our
"civil war... by other means on steroids." And, of course, it is intended
to be irrationally manipulative, relying predominantly on the triggering
of emotional responses. It is symptomatic of the "deeper contagion" that
Sammons seeks to cure through his ideal of democratic conversation.[25]

What we need to do, then, is to "go beyond [our current dead language]
to the point of judgment."[26] However, such judgment can only be attained
if we prepare for and engage in "repeated, long, face-to-face talks with
opposing others about matters that [are truly] serious" because they are
about "who we are."[27] Here Sammons seems to be proposing that we need
to listen to and try to understand one another as we simultaneously seek
to persuade.[28] Thus:

---

25. *Id.* at 902.

26. *Id.* at 912.

27. *Id.* at 911–12.

28. For discussion of what, more precisely, is and is not involved in such "understanding" of one another, see *infra* notes 42–43 and accompanying text.

[We need to] talk more. We need to talk, face-to-face, with those we oppose; talk about political matters far more serious than what level of taxation is optimal, or how to deliver health care, or more serious than abortions, gay rights, immigration, race, or what to do about various other social inequalities. Pick the issue you care most about right now, ask why anyone, you included, should care about it at all aside from self-interest; take your most thoughtful answer to that question and ask why anyone, you included again, should care about the value(s) upon which it rests; take your most thoughtful answer to that question and ask what the words you just used to describe these value(s) mean, where they come from, and why and how they prompt your caring. Now offer this thought in as persuasive and as personal a manner as you can in a face-to-face political conversation with someone with whom you typically disagree, someone about whom you might now say you do not understand how he could hold the views he does.[29]

Sammons stresses that "the last question, the one requiring you to examine the language you are using" is of critical importance because "the idea is to get to the openings that language, and only language, can provide."[30] We need to get to these openings because "for language… to have the potential of uncovering truthful aspects of our identity in political conversation, we have to reach the point at which language itself opens and even threatens to unravel."[31] Although these truthful aspects of our identity can be uncovered by language, they cannot be "articulate[d]" or "conceptually mediated."[32] In this way, such "serious" conversations will take us to the place where the conversation will point beyond itself to the "ordinary mystery and silence that surrounds us," to the "mysteriousness of our being" which is "not us, but defines us," to the "imagined communit[y]" or "polity" that constitutes our truer, more authentic identity and that informs our judgments.[33] By

---

29. Sammons, *Concluding Reflections*, op. cit., at 905–06.

30. *Id.* at 906 n25 (noting that "[t]his is an easy thing to do with law … and with text-based religions").

31. *Id.* at 911.

32. *Id.* at 907 n29.

33. *Id.* at 903, 908, 912 (mystery), 904 (not us but defines us), 900–01 and n8 (imagined community or polity), 901, 902, 912 (inauthentic identities, truer identity), 904 and n18, 908–09, 912 (informing judgments). Regarding the meaning of "mystery" as used here, see

engaging in such conversations with humility before this mystery and with faith in, and hope for, what it might reveal to us,[34] we will discover more of the truth about ourselves, recover the art of rhetoric, and find our way to an honest and genuine civility.[35] And we will know what to do:

> In the back-and-forth of seeking assent in democratic political conversation, we are persuaded by those who uncover — *show* us in the conversation — somewhere within an understanding of our own experiences, broadly considered, some truth or some aspect of a truth about our identity. In other words, those who show us something about ourselves persuade us.[36]

Such democratic political conversation can have this effect because

> We are always saying to others in these conversations, *even if we are not aware of it*, that perhaps your experiences match my offered claims about who we are. We are always saying that perhaps my of-

---

id. at 903 n15 (explaining "mystery," not as "something that is a mystery *to us*" but as "something that *is* mystery; something that could not be approached in the way of explanation at all without utterly destroying it").

34. *Id.* at 905 (humility), 903–04, 910 (faith), 906 (hope).

35. *Id.* at. 908–09 (truth about ourselves), 906–07, 910–12 (art of rhetoric), 902, 911 (civility). Sammons also considers that this will also "bind us to one another despite our differences," including by "providing the motivation to listen to speech that seeks (only!) to persuade us." *Id.* at 910 and n35.

Just as the "justice" realized through the practice of representative adversarial advocacy is not an "external" justice but a justice internal to the practice, so also the justification for engaging in such "serious" face to face conversations is not an external moral justification but a moral justification internal to the conversation. As Sammons explains in a comment on a draft of the account of his position given here:

> My argument begins with the one speaking. It is he who must take those steps you quoted and he does so to open himself in a way in which listening to others, among other things, does not require some external moral motivation for justification. It is an attempted practical turn to an appreciation of our grounding in mystery which makes any true conversation possible ... The key to it ... is the turn to language itself. ... The "imagined community" to which I refer is the one opened through this process of self-questioning through language. It is the same, one might say, as the imagined community of music.

Sammons Email (December 18, 2013) [on file with author].

36. Sammons, *Concluding Reflections*, op. cit., at 908.

fered claim uncovers an aspect of the truth of our identity (which is also, in great measure, your own) and, in this, that the political is our means towards recognition of a truth about ourselves. What is more, we are always saying that this truth of our identity is a matter of your experience of it within this particular conversation.[37]

The relevant experiences are "always beyond us" and "mysterious to us" because "[they] are always more than they appear to be, always more than we can articulate, always more than we can hold in our minds, and, in these ways, always more than we can know, and yet, these experiences are a living out of some possibility of our identity."[38] Consequently, although what is uncovered may seem "inevitable" after the uncovering, it is not knowable beforehand.[39] Notice, then, that Sammons is not arguing against all sense of identity, but rather in favor of a truer, more authentic identity in place of our false and inauthentic identities. The question we must consider, of course, is where our self-identity as Thomistic Aristotelians fits in all this.

In taking our face-to-face political conversation with one another to the more serious level Sammons urges upon us, in which we use language that articulates and engages with the deeper justifications for our political beliefs and positions, we have an opportunity to engage in the same sort of moral conversation described in the second step. Specifically, we have an opportunity to demonstrate — "in as persuasive and as personal a manner as [we] can" by drawing upon our own and others' life stories — "why and how" we care about human flourishing, common goods, and virtue, including the "master virtue" of practical wisdom, and how this is relevant

---

37. *Id.* at 909.

38. *Id.* at 908–09. Sammons provides a very illuminating footnote to prove the point:
   For proof of this I offer: "I can't find the words"; "words fail me"; "more than words can say"; or the very interesting, "words get the best of me." What more proof — "I wish I had the words;" "there aren't words enough"; "what could I possibly say," and so on — could you possibly want?
   Id. at 909 n32.

39. *See id.*at 910–11 (analogizing political conversation as "the art of rhetoric" to how "an artist might approach the materials of any art[,] ... permitting the art itself to speak [and] permit[ting] the artist to be surprised by what is uncovered in her art[,] ... something that ... can suddenly appear to the artist as having been inevitable and yet not capable of being determined prior to its revelation").

for the particular issue(s) under discussion.[40] The other participant(s) in
the face-to-face conversation, too, may discover that the deeper justifications for their own political beliefs and positions regarding the same
issue(s) can also be rooted in a more profound moral identity — such
as utilitarian, Kantian, or adherent of a particular religious faith tradition — even though they may have previously been unaware of it, and they
may then offer a similar demonstration from their own particular perspective. Moreover, when we articulate these deeper justifications and reveal
these more profound moral identities to one another in the thoughtful,
linguistically sensitive, and personal manner Sammons recommends, and
when we discover, by doing so, our foundational identity as a people that
transcends our particular moral identities, we will also have succeeded in
humanizing, or re-humanizing, one another, especially when we expose
our fears and vulnerabilities to one another.[41]

What is the role of the dialogical virtues in this kind of personal political conversation? We can best answer this question by considering Sammons' explanation of what this conversation does *not* involve:

It is important to note that I am not intending to describe a dialectic.
Nor do I mean to be saying that participation in the political conversation requires openness to opposing positions, or that all beliefs are
to be held tentatively, or that expressed beliefs be capable of a pub-
licity of reason or, if religious, equally motivated by secular reasons
before being offered in political conversation. What I am intending
to describe is not a conversation in which each speaker honestly

---

40. *See supra* note 29 and accompanying text.

41. *Cf.* Eric Liu, *Americans Don't Need Reconciliation — They Need to Get Better at Arguing*, THE ATLANTIC (November 1, 2016) (proposing a three-step program involving more
listening, serving, and arguing). Regarding the first step, Liu envisages "talking circles"
across the country in which people with different world views are "presen[t]" to each other,
practice "radically compassionate listening: without judgment, without response" as they
address "a simple universal question," and "try to see and hear each other [and] feel the pain
and pride and hope and fear of [their] putative antagonists." Regarding the second step, Liu
envisages national service projects that "bring[] people together across lines of race, class,
and politics" not to work on each other but on something else. Liu considers that both steps
will re-humanize the participants, even erstwhile enemies, and considers that they are a
necessary preparation for the third step. *Id.* Regarding this third step, Liu's article was the
genesis of the Better Arguments Project discussed *infra* note 51 and accompanying text.

seeks to correct the other with the other wishing for the correction because both agree that such is the way towards the truth.[42]

However, Sammons concedes that the conversation does require "openness," albeit "not the openness that dialectic requires." Instead, the openness envisaged seems to require listening to the other participant(s) in the conversation and understanding their position, not necessarily with a view to possibly accepting that position or modifying one's own, but rather to "being open to what might be uncovered in the saying."[43] Such a conversation will require that the participants exhibit the general dialogical virtues identified by MacIntyre and Roche[44] but, as we saw with the distinctive role of the different law craft practices in the search for "legal truth," many of these virtues may be exhibited very differently — with a very different scope and focus — from the way they are exhibited in *Piscopolis*.[45] This is because, unlike the inhabitants engaged in political conversation in *Piscopolis*, the participants in Sammons' personal democratic conversation are not engaged in an open-minded dialectical search for objective moral truth, but in a search for a very different kind of truth about their foundational identity. Consequently, the types of arguments that are relevant and that the participants must entertain as a matter of conversational justice, for example, or the types of matters about which they must be open to refutation, are clearly quite different in the two contexts. And Sammons certainly does not expect the participants in his personal democratic con-

---

42. Sammons, *Concluding Reflections*, op. cit., at 907 n29. As indicated above, *supra* notes 32–39 and accompanying text,

> It is, instead, a conversation in which speakers know that some aspect of that which persuades the other is something that neither speaker can articulate although it can be uncovered by language — something in fact that cannot be conceptually mediated and yet is central to the sharing of identity that the speaker seeks with the other as an act of persuasion.

Id. Analogizing how we should think of the language of rhetoric to how composers think of the language of music, Sammons explains that it is like "composers debating how to approach a musical problem, each for deep reasons committed to a musical approach that each sees as a manifestation of who they are. In this heated conversation, there is a 'who are you' answered by music that is beyond either composer." *Id.*

43. *Id.* at 908 n31, 910 n35.

44. *See* Chapter 5, notes 167–72 and accompanying text.

45. *See* Chapter 7, notes 295–310 and accompanying text.

versation to exhibit the capacity for "sympathetic detachment" — in other words, "to place [themselves] imaginatively in the position of others and to entertain their concerns in the same affirmative spirit they do, while remaining uncommitted to the values and beliefs that give these concerns their force" yet also being open to revising their preliminary views and making a more informed choice among the alternatives.[46]

As with our discussion of Sammons' phenomenological account of "realizing justice" in Part II, Section B.1 of Chapter 7, once again we have scarcely done justice here to the lovely ideal of personal democratic conversation he proposes, and the reader is therefore encouraged to read Sammons' original article in its entirety for full effect. Similarly, once again, there is something in this ideal of the call to come out of the Cave into the light of the Good, and something too of the Quest for the Grail. Adapting the Allegory of the Cave to the present context, we Cave dwellers in the liberal democratic state should seek to overcome the limitations of "the dead language of an exchange of concepts understood as prejudices and interests" and our current false and inauthentic identities, reflected in the labels and slogans of superficial and trivial conversation, by engaging in a rhetorical conversation that is an existential-theological quest to discover (or, perhaps better said, uncover) the experiential truth about "who we are" and thus about the meaning and purpose of our lives as inhabitants of the Republic. And once again, then, this echoes the distinction between the "rationalists" and the "hybridists" in the practice of natural theology noted at the end of Part II of Chapter II (although the superficial and trivial conversation only gestures toward a deeper rationality). But here again too, the reader may wonder why we have focused so much on Sammons' particular conversational ideal. The reason is that, like the claim that we have concealed from ourselves the reality of how we in fact experience the law and thus potentially threaten to do injustice, the claim that our politics has forgotten to ask honestly who "we" are — that it has forgotten that it is "about us" — is also a serious and disturbing one, which we should therefore take seriously and which should indeed disturb us.[47] Not only

---

46. *See* Chapter 5, note 175 and accompanying text (citing and quoting from ANTHONY T. KRONMAN, THE LOST LAWYER: FAILING IDEALS OF THE LEGAL PROFESSION 93–101 (1993).

47. As discussed above, *supra* note 23 and accompanying text, the legal conversation is also about our identity — about the question "who are we?" However, unlike the political

does Sammons propose a way for us to remember, but arguably, too, in the notion of uncovering our truer, more authentic identity as a people he is proposing a particular phenomenological understanding of the ultimate excellence of the practice of politics to serve as our overarching common good and is, once again, inviting us, his fellow inhabitants, to join in the existential-theological quest for meaning and purpose involved in seeking to achieve it.

Whether or not we should understand Sammons as seeking to transform our current politics into a genuine practice, with an overarching common good, we can certainly combine his account with other approaches in a manner that moves us toward this goal. Thus, in addition to the types of face-to-face political conversations Sammons proposes, we can also engage in other types of face-to-face political conversations that *do* involve a dialectical search for objective truth. Indeed, Sammons himself makes it clear he is not claiming that "political conversations must always address annoying questions with annoying people[,] ... any more than all musical compositions must be Beethoven's Ninth," but rather that "we need some such conversations to serve as models for the recovery of the political."[48] Moreover, although Sammons does not address the point explicitly, conceivably what the participants in his ideal of personal democratic conversation may sometimes end up assenting to, is precisely to undertake a dialectical search for the truth together. And any such additional or further political conversations will presumably require the dialogical virtues and the capacity for sympathetic detachment to be exhibited as they are in *Piscopolis*.[49] In these conversations, too, we can again seek to demonstrate the superior merits of Thomistic Aristotelianism and pursuing a way of life exhibiting virtue, including the "master virtue" of practical wisdom, focused on the achievement of human flourishing through attaining the

---

conversation, it has not forgotten that this is the question even though, as discussed in Part II, Section B.1 of Chapter 7, it may have difficulty answering it.

48. Sammons, *Concluding Reflections*, op. cit., at 912.

49. *See* JEFFREY STOUT, DEMOCRACY AND TRADITION 10–11, 14 (2004) (democratic conversation on morally controversial matters involves "full-fledged truth-claims" and "an exchange of views in which the respective parties express their premises in as much detail as they see fit and in whatever idiom they wish, try to make sense of each other's perspectives, and expose their own commitments to the possibility of criticism"). For Stout's discussion of the process involved "in deciding which ethical claims to accept as true," see *id.* at 276–82.

common goods of practices, and how this is relevant for the particular issue(s) under discussion.

There are many initiatives currently underway across the country aimed at healing our ailing body politic through face-to-face political conversations among citizens at the grassroots level and offering various models for structuring such conversations. Examples include the Living Room Conversations initiative,[50] the Better Arguments Project,[51] and the America in One Room experiment.[52] Of these three examples, the first

---

50. *See What Is a Living Room Conversation?*, LIVING ROOM CONVERSATIONS, https://www.livingroomconversations.org/. A "living room conversation" is "a conversational model developed by dialogue experts" aimed at bridging divisions between people and identifying areas of common ground and shared understanding. The numerous conversation guides can be used to structure conversations within small groups in any setting, and the ground rules are intended to enable members of the group to listen to and be heard by one another, and to share and learn from, rather than to debate or convince, one another. *Id.*

51. *See What Is a Better Argument?: The Better Arguments Project Report on Key Operating Principles*, THE ASPEN INSTITUTE CITIZENSHIP & AMERICAN IDENTITY PROGRAM (March 19, 2018), https://www.aspeninstitute.org/publications/better-arguments-project-report-key-operating-principles/. The goal of the Better Arguments Project is to ensure that the citizen-led efforts occurring across the country and aimed at bridging the divisions created or revealed by the 2016 election are productive and constructive rather than making the problems worse. The Project Report identifies three dimensions of arguing, five principles of a better argument, and seven core action steps. *Id.* Eric Liu's article in The Atlantic, cited and quoted *supra* note 41, was the genesis for the Better Arguments Project. *Id.* at 4. In his Atlantic article Liu asserts that "America doesn't just have arguments; America *is* an argument — between Federalist and Anti-Federalist world views, strong national government and local control, liberty and equality, individual rights and collective responsibility, color-blindness and color-consciousness, *Pluribus* and *Unum*," and that "[t]he point of civic life in this country … is for us all to wrestle perpetually with these differences, to fashion hybrid solutions that work for the times until they don't, and then to start again." Therefore, he urges that we

> [Teach] ourselves how to argue better, how to identify and name our foundational fights over principle, how to argue all sides and not just one's own, how to change one's own mind as well as another's, and how to put together solutions that draw from each pole of principle — as if we had responsibility for solutions, not just posturing.

Liu, *Americans Don't Need Reconciliation*, op. cit.

52. *See America in One Room*, STANFORD UNIVERSITY CENTER FOR DELIBERATIVE DEMOCRACY, https://cdd.stanford.edu/2019/america-in-one-room-results/. This experiment brought 523 registered voters to Dallas from across the country for a long weekend in September 2019 to deliberate in moderated small groups, and in plenary session with experts and politicians, on policy proposals in five areas — the economy, healthcare, the

conversational model seems closest to the ideal proposed by Sammons, the third closest to a dialectical search for the truth, and the second somewhere in-between.[53] As former President of the Association of American Law Schools (AALS), Wendy Collins Perdue, explained in her 2018 Presidential Address, members of the legal profession inhabiting *Juropolis* may also have an important role to play in the efforts to heal our body politic through such conversations, due to our unique training and skill set. Her address is well worth quoting at length:

> Lawyers are healers of a sort — the doctors of our social lives. As our society struggles with th[e] problem of deep polarization, lawyers and law schools have an important role to play. Resolving conflict is central to what [lawyers] do. And today, perhaps more than ever before, the skills that we as lawyers have, and we as law professors teach, are of critical importance.
>
> Lawyers understand how to structure decision-making and dispute resolution processes. We understand the importance of the opportunity to be heard and other aspects of fundamental fairness, of considering both sides and crediting the merits of opposing views, of facts — the ones we can prove, not merely the ones we wish to be true — and of getting opposite sides of an issue to the table, to get them talking to each other in the first place. Lawyers approach disagreements with a methodology that is built on recognizing the strength of the opposing views. Legal pedagogy, like good lawyering, emphasizes the importance of developing a deep, even empathetic understanding of the arguments on the other side. We constantly push our students away from the psychological comfort of certainty to that uneasy place where opposing views loom large. Good lawyers and good judges also understand fallibility. This lawyerly approach to conflict and disagreement is reflected in legal scholarship as well.

---

environment, immigration, and foreign policy — using a briefing booklet that gave balanced arguments for and against policy proposals in each area. The experience resulted in some dramatic changes of opinion among the participant voters. *Id.*

53. Also noteworthy are related projects such as Benjamin Watson's documentary *Divided Hearts of America*, which features interviews with those on both sides of the abortion debate and which Watson hopes will "bring[] empathy and understanding to all sides of the abortion debate," https://thewatsonseven.com/theirs/divided-hearts-of-america.

The best scholarship engages with opposing views. It seeks to per-suade on the strength of the ideas presented, never by simply belit-tling or dehumanizing those who hold opposing views.

The point is not that arguments should be drained of emotion. Where the stakes are high, emotions will run high. But lawyers un-derstand that disputes, even on matters upon which convictions are deeply held, need not be personal, that it is possible to separate the substance of an argument from the person making that argument [and] to disagree without being disagreeable — indeed, we are ad-monished to do just that in our principles of professionalism. Law-yers are not social workers, but they are architects of social structure. And in that role, they can be — we can be — enormously helpful in reconnecting a fractured world. That is to say, in building bridges.

Society needs us to model civility [and] listening skills, so that we can openly and honestly build dialogue with respect for one anoth-er's views. And society needs us to lead the way in dispute resolution, which requires civility, listening, open mindedness, and a host of other skills that are part of the lawyerly repertoire. Let us put our traditions of professionalism, civility, and reasoned disagreement on display for all to see, and let us inspire the next generation to "think like a lawyer" about society's problems — to listen, consider, reason, collaborate, resolve, and even heal.[54]

There is good reason, then, to remain hopeful about the future of po-litical conversation among motivated citizens at the grassroots level in the near term, and among politicians at the institutional level in the longer term.[55] Our further hope as Thomistic Aristotelians is that, as we par-

---

54. Wendy Collins Perdue, *2018 Presidential Address: Building Bridges*, AALS News, The Association of American Law Schools, https://www.aals.org/about/publications/newsletters/aals-news-winter-2018/2018-presidential-address/ (observing that law schools are already "[offering] programs explicitly designed to model our ideals of informed, re-spectful debate; training law students in the skills of dialogue across difference; serving as the facilitators of deliberative decision making on important policy issues; and reaching out to local schools to train students and administrators in the skills of conflict resolution"). The pertinent passages from the Presidential Address have been edited to avoid the need for excessive, distracting ellipses.

55. For discussion of some ways in which citizens may be motivated to participate in such grassroots political conversations in the first place, see Sammons, *Concluding Reflec-*

ticipate in the healing process of "reconnecting a fractured world" and "building bridges " in political conversations, we will — through example, invitation, and rational argument — make a unique contribution to the process of "re-envisioning what it means to live the life of a [citizen]" and to "caring for the well-being of one another, as well as ourselves,"[56] and thereby to the process of transforming the liberal democratic state into a "republic of virtue" more like *Piscopolis* and its citizens into flourishing human beings more like Drew than Cash.

Silent Words: A Postscript on the Covid-19 Pandemic

And in the naked light I saw
Ten thousand people, maybe more
People talking without speaking
People hearing without listening
People writing songs that voices never share
And no one dared
Disturb the sound of silence[57]

To recur to a notion articulated at several points in the book, and although they might express matters differently themselves, Alasdair MacIntyre, Jack Sammons, and James Boyd White show us that citizens of liberal democracies must move beyond their false selves, manufactured in the compelled silence imposed by noisy, meaningless chatter, toward their true selves, rooted in the mysterious silence respected by quiet, meaning-

----

tions, op. cit., at 909–10 and n35; Jones, *Imaginary Conversation*, op. cit., at 363–70. These hopes may have received a significant boost with the release in June 2020 of *Our Common Purpose: Reinventing American Democracy for the 21ˢᵗ Century*, the comprehensive final and bipartisan report of the American Academy of Arts and Sciences Commission on the Practice of Democratic Citizenship, https://www.amacad.org/ourcommonpurpose/report (identifying six strategies and making thirty-one tactical recommendations, including recommendations for fostering improved political conversation).

56. *See* Chapter 1, notes 39, 46 and accompanying text.

57. *See The Sound of Silence* (Simon and Garfunkel, Columbia 1965), as performed by the band Disturbed (Reprise, 2015), https://www.youtube.com/watch?v=u9Dg-g7t2l4.

ful conversation.[58] Each seeks to disturb us; and we need to be disturbed. Being disturbed in this way enhances our prospects of emerging out of the Cave of illusion into the light of our true individual and common good and attaining our individual and collective Grail in the form of our proper flourishing. Although no-one would have chosen such an occasion, the Covid-19 pandemic represents an additional disturbance — a dreadful one in which, this time, Being *shouts* its truth at us — providing us with an opportunity to move further along the path of enlightenment. It has often been observed that a breakthrough enabling encounter with the true self is especially likely in times of great loss or other adversity, when the defenses of the ego — both individual and collective — are typically at their weakest.[59] Thus, the pandemic has paused the frenetic activities of

---

58. Of the three, White may come closest to intimating the movement toward the "true self" discussed in Part II. Section B of Chapter 2. As observed in note 352 at the end of Chapter 7, in Chapter 6 of his book KEEP LAW ALIVE White recommends the *Confessions* of Saint Augustine to help educate our sensibilities and responses as members of the legal profession and as citizens "in an increasingly corrupted world." Specifically, he invites us to undergo, as Augustine did, "a kind of dismantling of the self" in which we

> [A]ttain … an awareness of the evanescence of all things; of the unreliability of memory and intellect; of the essential emptiness of most goals of ambition or competition; of the springs of life and strength within oneself, upon which one may rely; of the hope of speaking always to another as that person is, in that situation at that moment, *out of the center of oneself and of one's mind*; of the openness of our texts and practices of authority to multiple readings and uses; and ultimately of the power each of us might hope to have of speaking in ways that are true and alive — for only though such speech is justice possible.

WHITE, KEEP LAW ALIVE, op. cit., at 141, 147 (emphasis added). Moreover, the "dismantling of the self" produces "a fundamental humility" in which another person's different interpretation of a text is "worthy of respect" if they have undergone a similar dismantling and if they approach the text in the same spirit of humility and integrity. *Id.* at 146. Although White seems to be addressing members of the legal profession specifically in the above passage, he also intends to address citizens more generally in the Chapter, and the passage also seems applicable, therefore, *mutatis mutandis*, to everyone. *See id.* at 137. It is also reasonable to conclude that the "dismantling of the self" is a dismantling of a certain type of "false self." And although White offers the example of Augustine's experience as an analogy that, as such, is also available to nonbelievers, it is telling that after the dismantling of Augustine's "false self," the only thing of which he could be certain was "the presence of God within him." *Id.* at 137, 143–44.

59. For expression of this notion within the Judeo-Christian religious tradition, see RICHARD ROHR, FALLING UPWARD: A SPIRITUALITY FOR THE TWO HALVES OF LIFE xix–xxii

advanced capitalism and rampant consumerism; it has resulted in far too many deaths as well as economic devastation; and it has starkly revealed our shared vulnerabilities, ultimate lack of control, and dependence upon one another.

But the pandemic has revealed more. The coronavirus does not just attack the individual physical body. In the words of one observer, George Packer, it has "exploited … ruthlessly" a collective body politic "with serious underlying conditions," including "a corrupt political class, a sclerotic bureaucracy, a heartless economy, [and] a divided and distracted public."[60] It has starkly revealed, then, the nature of "the American landscape that lay open to the virus":

> [I]n prosperous cities, a class of globally connected desk workers dependent on a class of precarious and invisible service workers; in the countryside, decaying communities in revolt against the modern world; on social media, mutual hatred and endless vituperation among different camps; in the economy, even with full employment, a large and growing gap between triumphant capital and beleaguered labor; in Washington, an empty government led by a con man and his intellectually bankrupt party; around the country, a mood of cynical exhaustion, with no vision of a shared identity or future.[61]

Of course, this landscape was already familiar. But perhaps it was too familiar. Perhaps it was familiar to the point of complacency — a complacency fueled by labels, slogans, and dead conceptual language that served to mask ugly realities and dull our sensibilities. But now that the circum-

(2011); RICHARD ROHR, IMMORTAL DIAMOND: THE SEARCH FOR OUR TRUE SELF 62–66, 139–43 (2013); DAVID BROOKS, THE SECOND MOUNTAIN: THE QUEST FOR A MORAL LIFE xi–xiv, 26–29, 36–38, 42–51 (2019). For expression of the notion within a broader spiritual tradition, see ECKHART TOLLE, THE POWER OF NOW: A GUIDE TO SPIRITUAL ENLIGHTENMENT 43–48, 218–20 (1999); ECKHART TOLLE, A NEW EARTH: AWAKENING TO YOUR LIFE'S PURPOSE 25–28, 101–03, 125–27 (2005).

60. George Packer, *We Are Living in A Failed State*, THE ATLANTIC (June 2020 Issue), https://www.theatlantic.com/magazine/archive/2020/06/underlying-conditions/610261/.

61. *Id.* Arguably, this should also prompt us to ask ourselves about our collective "shadow self." *See* Chapter 2, note 131.

stances of the pandemic have unmasked and exposed the landscape in all its nakedness, perhaps we can be touched at a more visceral level.

In a post-Covid-19 world, then, we will have an opportunity for sober reflection upon the above features of our American landscape and upon our collective experiences during the pandemic. Perhaps most prominently, these experiences include our shared vulnerability and mutual interdependence, as well as innumerable examples of commitment to excellence and extraordinary, heroic virtue exhibited by those on the front lines battling the virus to save lives in the professional *polis* of medicine, and by many other "frontline workers" in "essential industries" who have also exposed themselves to significant risk of illness and even death while the rest of us sheltered in place.[62] As we engage in such reflection, it is not unreasonable to hope that we may undergo a radical shift of perspective and a fundamental reordering of priorities making the re-envisioning and transformation referred to in the concluding paragraph before this Postscript even more attractive and attainable. And as a result, the process of necessary change may be accelerated.[63] To quote Packer again:

---

62. For a good sense of the number and demographics of "frontline workers," see Adie Tomer & Joseph W. Kane, *Report: To protect frontline workers during and after COVID-19, we must define who they are* (Brookings Institution, June 10, 2020). The Report defines "essential industries" as "businesses, organizations, and government agencies whose functions are critical to public health, safety, and economic and national security" and therefore "that should stay in operation during national emergencies, especially public health crises," and it defines "frontline workers" as those "employees within essential industries who must physically show up to their jobs" and "who face a variety of health risks in their workplaces." It finds, among 808 occupations for which data is available, "380 frontline occupations that employ nearly 50 million workers nationally, or around a third (34.5%) of all U.S. workers," and that "[f]rom personal care aides to delivery service drivers to retail salespersons, frontline workers make up a majority of the 90 million essential workers," with 75% of them earning below-average wages. *Id.* (emphasis removed).

63. There are encouraging signs that societal shifts in the right direction may be possible. *See, e.g.,* Gene Sperling, *Economic Dignity,* DEMOCRACY: A JOURNAL OF IDEAS (Spring 2019), https://democracyjournal.org/magazine/52/economic-dignity/ (arguing that economic policy should focus on the end goal of promoting human happiness, well-being, and fulfilment through "economic dignity" before focusing on the means, economic dignity being defined by "three essential, interlocking pillars," specifically "[t]he capacity to care for family and experience its greatest joys[,] … [p]ursuit of potential and purpose[,] [and] … [e]conomic participation without domination and humiliation," and exploring the policy implications of pursuing such a goal). Sperling wrote this article before the pandemic but has now elaborated it at length in a book published in May 2020, several months into the

We're faced with a choice that the crisis makes inescapably clear. We can stay hunkered down in self-isolation, fearing and shunning one another, letting our common bond wear away to nothing. Or we can use this pause in our normal lives to pay attention to the hospital workers holding up cellphones so their patients can say goodbye to loved ones; the planeload of medical workers flying from Atlanta to help in New York; the aerospace workers in Massachusetts demanding that their factory be converted to ventilator production; the Floridians standing in long lines because they couldn't get through by phone to the skeletal unemployment office; the residents of Milwaukee braving endless waits, hail, and contagion to vote in an election forced on them by partisan justices. We can learn from these dreadful days that stupidity and injustice are lethal; that, in a democracy, being a citizen is essential work; that the alternative to solidarity is death. After we've come out of hiding and taken off our masks, we should not forget what it was like to be alone.[64]

On the other hand, although the pandemic has already led to greater social solidarity and political cooperation as we face a common enemy, many tensions remain. We can expect to see — indeed, we are already seeing in the heated arguments about when and how to "reopen the economy" — the moral confusion that characterizes the dominant environment of the liberal democratic state with its individualist *ethos*, as it tries to meet the political and economic challenges created by the recession, possibly even depression, induced by the pandemic. Moreover, even within those social contexts in which it has still been possible to pursue a *Piscopolis*-like way of life within this dominant environment, it would not be surpris-

---

pandemic. GENE SPERLING, ECONOMIC DIGNITY (2020). The widespread and broad-based protests against racial injustice sparked by the death of George Floyd at the hands of the police in Minneapolis may signify that we are indeed at a unique historical crossroads. *See, e.g.*, Michelle Alexander, *America, This Is Your Chance*, NEW YORK TIMES (June 8, 2020), https://www.nytimes com/2020/06/08/opinion/george-floyd-protests-race.html (calling for us to face our racial past and present and to achieve racial justice in a reimagined criminal justice system and transformed economic system, and observing that "[o]ur only hope for our collective liberation is a politics of deep solidarity rooted in love" and that the broad-based protests offer "a reflection of the best of who we are and what we can become").

64. Packer, *Failed State*, op. cit.

ing — understandable even, given the massive unemployment caused by
the pandemic — if a greater emphasis were placed upon the pursuit and
attainment of individualistic goods of effectiveness, even at the expense
of common goods of excellence. In sum, it is quite conceivable that the
learning Packer describes in the above passage will not occur, most of us
will retreat behind the masks of our false selves and continue to hide from
one another, and we will see a return to business as usual — more or less, at
least — with a continuation of dysfunctional politics and frenetic capitalist
and consumerist activity.

But even if this happens, the pandemic experience will surely confirm
Thomistic Aristotelians in their convictions and their resolve to share
these convictions with others. In this sharing they may speculate about
what might have happened with the pandemic if the liberal democratic state had already become a MacIntyrean "republic of virtue" — in the
United States, in other Western countries, and in countries elsewhere in
the world subject to the influences of Western modernity. Emphasizing
that, in such a MacIntyrean republic of virtue, both political leaders and
the general populace exhibit honesty, courage, justice, temperance, and
practical wisdom, as well as just generosity, especially its component virtue of *misericordia*, they may speculate that the general exercise of such
virtues would have helped minimize the toll exacted by the pandemic.
Related, they may also speculate that the pandemic would not have become as widespread as it did. They may even speculate that it would not
have occurred at all. Such speculations would not be without empirical
support. For example, one need only contrast the situation of the United
States with that of New Zealand. Even allowing for important contextual
differences, the latter country has shown what is possible. New Zealand
has not just "flattened the curve" but has eradicated the virus altogether
as a result of decisive, wise leadership and a virtuous, communitarian
response from a cooperative, trusting, and disciplined populace prepared
to make the necessary sacrifices.[65] By contrast, according to one observer
of the American scene, in light of its bungling response to the crisis the

---

65. For discussion of New Zealand's distinctive and successful approach and of determining contextual factors, see Anna Fifield, *New Zealand isn't just flattening the curve. It's
squashing it*, WASHINGTON POST (April 7, 2020), https://www.washingtonpost.com/world/
asia_pacific/new-zealand-isnt-just-flattening-the-curve-its-squashing-it/2020/04/07/
6cab3a4a-7822-11ea-a311-adb1344719a9_story.html; Amy Gunia, *Why New Zealand's*

United States evokes little more than pity in the eyes of others (although many expect less bungling if the 2020 general election produces a change of Administration).[66] But all this is the subject for another book, one of many the pandemic will doubtless generate in the coming months and years.

Coronavirus Elimination Strategy Is Unlikely to Work in Most Other Places, TIME (April 24, 2020), https://time.com/5824042/new-zealand-coronavirus-elimination/.

66. *See* Fintan O'Toole, *Donald Trump has destroyed the country he promised to make great again*, THE IRISH TIMES (April 25, 2020), https://www.irishtimes.com/opinion/fintan-o-toole-donald-trump-has-destroyed-the-country-he-promised-to-make-great-again-1.4235928?, reproduced at https://johnmenadue.com/?s=fintan+o%27toole. *See also* David Leonhardt, *The Unique U.S. Failure to Control the Virus*, NEW YORK TIMES (August 6, 2020) (detailing multiple missteps of the Trump Administration, and identifying these missteps and America's libertarian tradition "prioritizing individualism over government restrictions" as the two central themes explaining "the unique failure of the United States" in trying to contain the coronavirus).

INDEX

C